Research Methods in Sign Language Studies

Guides to Research Methods in Language and Linguistics

Series Editor: Li Wei, Birkbeck College, University of London

The science of language encompasses a truly interdisciplinary field of research, with a wide range of focuses, approaches, and objectives. While linguistics has its own traditional approaches, a variety of other intellectual disciplines have contributed methodological perspectives that enrich the field as a whole. As a result, linguistics now draws on state-of-the-art work from such fields as psychology, computer science, biology, neuroscience and cognitive science, sociology, music, philosophy, and anthropology.

The interdisciplinary nature of the field presents both challenges and opportunities to students who must understand a variety of evolving research skills and methods. The *Guides to Research Methods in Language and Linguistics* addresses these skills in a systematic way for advanced students and beginning researchers in language science. The books in this series focus especially on the relationships between theory, methods and data- the understanding of which is fundamental to the successful completion of research projects and the advancement of knowledge.

Published

1. *The Blackwell Guide to Research Methods in Bilingualism and Multilingualism*
   Edited by Li Wei and Melissa G. Moyer

2. *Research Methods in Child Language: A Practical Guide*
   Edited by Erika Hoff

3. *Research Methods in Second Language Acquisition: A Practical Guide*
   Edited by Susan M. Gass and Alison Mackey

4. *Research Methods in Clinical Linguistics and Phonetics: A Practical Guide*
   Edited by Nicole Müller and Martin J. Ball

5. *Research Methods in Sociolinguistics: A Practical Guide*
   Edited by Janet Holmes and Kirk Hazen

6. *Research Methods in Sign Language Studies: A Practical Guide*
   Edited by Eleni Orfanidou, Bencie Woll, and Gary Morgan

Research Methods in Sign Language Studies

A Practical Guide

Edited by Eleni Orfanidou, Bencie Woll, and Gary Morgan

WILEY Blackwell

Contents

Notes on Contributors

Robert Adam is a Research Associate at the Deafness Cognition and Language Research Centre, University College London. His areas of research include the sociolinguistics and psycholinguistics of sign language contact, sign language attrition and bilingualism. He is a Deaf native signer who has worked as a sign language researcher, lecturer, and Deaf interpreter in Australia, the UK, and USA.

Thomas E. Allen is the founding director and current co-PI of the National Science Foundation Science of Learning Center on Visual Language and Visual Learning at Gallaudet University. He formerly was the director of the Gallaudet Research Institute, where he oversaw the Annual Survey of Deaf and Hard of Hearing Children and Youth.

Joanna Atkinson is a clinical psychologist with additional qualifications in clinical neuropsychology and holds an academic research post at the Deafness, Cognition and Language Research Centre at University College London.

Cheryl M. Capek earned her PhD from the University of Oregon. She is currently a lecturer at the School of Psychological Sciences, University of Manchester, where she is director of the MSc in neuroimaging for clinical and cognitive neuroscience. Her research has been published in a number of journals, including *Trends in Cognitive Science*, *Journal of Cognitive Neuroscience*, *Proceedings of the National Academy of Sciences of the United States of America*, and *Nature Communications*.

Rachel Channon is a researcher in sign language phonology. She is currently working on the second SignTyp grant from the National Science Foundation, which will provide online dictionaries and transcribed and coded information for signs in 15 different sign languages around the world.

Kearsy Cormier is a senior researcher at the Deafness, Cognition and Language Research Centre at University College London. Her research interests include grammaticalization, lexicalization, and nativization processes in signed and spoken languages, the relationship between language and gesture, sign language documentation and corpora, morphosyntax, and language acquisition.

Onno A. Crasborn is a senior researcher at the Centre for Language Studies of Radboud University Nijmegen in the Netherlands. His research interests include the phonetic and phonological analysis of signed languages, corpus construction and related standardization and tools, and language attitudes in the deaf community.

Tanya Denmark is a postdoctoral researcher at the Deafness, Cognition and Language, University College London (UK). Tanya is a hearing native signer from a deaf family of over six generations.

Jordan Fenlon is a postdoctoral research associate at the Deafness, Cognition and Language Research Centre, University College London (UK). His research experience within sign languages includes corpus linguistics, sociolinguistic variation, phonology, morphology, prosody, and lexicography.

Peter C. Hauser is a Deaf clinical neuropsychologist and a professor at the National Technical Institute for the Deaf at Rochester Institute of Technology in Rochester. His laboratory studies the effect of language experience on cognition, develops sign language assessment instruments, and consults other countries on how to develop similar tests.

Joseph C. Hill is an assistant professor in the Specialized Educational Services department at the University of North Carolina at Greensboro. He is an author of *Language Attitudes in the American Deaf Community* (2012) and one of the co-authors of *The Hidden Treasure of Black ASL: Its History and Structure* (2011).

Trevor Johnston is professor of sign language linguistics in the Department of Linguistics, Macquarie University (Sydney, Australia). He has researched and published on Auslan since the 1980s concentrating on lexicography, grammatical description, bilingual deaf education, and corpus linguistics both for research into sociolinguistic variation and for empirical language description.

L. Viola Kozak is a PhD candidate in linguistics. She has been a member of Gallaudet University's Bimodal Bilingual Binational lab since 2009, and her research focuses primarily on sign language phonology. She has co-authored research papers on bimodal bilingual acquisition, bimodal bilingual phonology, sociolinguistics, and weak-hand drop in signing.

Fiona E. Kyle PhD, is a lecturer in the Division of Language and Communication Science at City University London. She holds a PhD in Psychology from Royal Holloway, University of London (UK). Her research focuses on identifying predictors of literacy development in deaf children and investigates the relationship between phonology, speech-reading and reading in deaf and hearing children.

Amy M. Lieberman is a research scientist at the Center for Research on Language at the University of California, San Diego. She investigates the development of joint attention in deaf children and how early experiences shape language-processing abilities in deaf individuals. She received her PhD from the University of California, Berkeley. She previously worked as a teacher-researcher at Gallaudet University's Clerc Center.

Diane Lillo-Martin is Board of Trustees Distinguished Professor in Linguistics and director of the Cognitive Science Program at the University of Connecticut, and senior research scientist at Haskins Laboratories. Her research focus is on the structure and acquisition of sign languages and the development of bimodal bilingualism.

Amber J. Martin was a postdoctoral researcher at Barnard College and is currently at Hunter College in New York City. Her research explores how age of first language acquisition in Deaf children impacts developing cognition, how Deaf children without a language model develop gestures, and how grammatical and semantic differences between languages can impact cognitive abilities.

Rachel I. Mayberry is professor of linguistics at the University of California, San Diego, where she is also affiliated with the Cognitive Science Program, the Center for Research on Language, the Anthropogeny Program, and the Joint Doctoral Program in Language & Communicative Disorders. She investigates critical period effects on language and neural development, as well as the psycholinguistic processes underlying word recognition in signed and written language. She is co-editor of the influential book *Language Acquisition by Eye* and serves on the editorial board of the *Journal of Child Language*.

Jill P. Morford is professor of linguistics at the University of New Mexico and affiliated researcher at the NSF Science of Learning Center on Visual Language and Visual Learning (VL2). She investigates language acquisition and processing in the visual modality, including signed languages and augmentative and alternative communication systems.

Gary Morgan is professor of psychology at City University London. He has published widely on sign language acquisition, theory of mind development, and psycholinguistic studies of sign languages. He is co-author of several books, including *Directions in Sign Language Acquisition* (2002) and *The Signs of a Savant* (2010).

Ronice Müller de Quadros is a full professor in linguistics at the Universidade Federal de Santa Catarina. Her research is in sign language studies. She has written papers and some books on sign language acquisition, bimodal bilingual development, sign language grammar, deaf education, and sign language translation and interpretation.

Helen J. Neville has a PhD from Cornell University. She is professor of psychology and neuroscience, director of the Brain Development Lab, and director of the Center for Cognitive Neuroscience at the University of Oregon. Her work experience includes neuropsychology at the Salk Institute. She has received many honors, including the Mind, Brain and Education Society Award for Transforming Education through Neuroscience, American Academy of Arts and Sciences, the William James Award, the Cognitive Neuroscience Society, the Academic Panel of Birth to Three, and is active in many educational outreach programs.

Brenda Nicodemus is associate professor in the Department of Interpretation at Gallaudet University and director of the Interpretation and Translation Research Center. Her publications include *Prosodic Markers and Utterance Boundaries in American Sign Language Interpreting* (2009) and (with co-editor Laurie Swabey) *Advances in Interpreting Research* (2011).

Victoria Nyst is a research fellow and lecturer at Leiden University. She has done various documentary and descriptive studies of urban and microcommunity sign languages in Africa. Her main research interests include the impact of sociolinguistic settings on sign language structures, language contact and emergence, and African sign languages.

Eleni Orfanidou is lecturer in the Department of Psychology, University of Crete.

Carol A. Padden is professor of communication and a member of the Center for Research in Language at the University of California, San Diego. Her research interests include new sign languages, lexical structure in sign languages, and gesture in sign language. She has published widely on comparative sign language grammars, language emergence, deaf children's reading development, and deaf communities and deaf culture in the United States.

Nick Palfreyman is a research fellow at the International Institute for Sign Languages and Deaf Studies based at the University of Central Lancashire (UCLan), UK. Nick has worked with the Indonesian deaf community since 2007, and for his PhD degree he is investigating lexical and morphosyntactic variation in the urban sign language varieties of Indonesia.

Jeffrey Levi Palmer is a native bimodal bilingual. Currently he is investigating bilingual word order acquisition in hearing children of deaf parents and pursuing a doctoral degree at Gallaudet University.

Pamela Perniss is lecturer in linguistics at the School of Humanities, University of Brighton, UK; previously she was a research associate at the Deafness, Cognition and Language Research Centre at University College London, London, UK. She is a sign language linguist and psycholinguist. Her research takes a multichannel approach to language, spoken and signed, and investigates the role of the visual modality and iconicity in shaping language structure and processing.

Deborah Chen Pichler is associate professor of linguistics at Gallaudet University. Her research areas are the acquisition of ASL by L1, L2, and bimodal bilingual learners. Her publications on sign linguistics include an upcoming video textbook on sign language development, presented entirely in ASL.

Aline Lemos Pizzio is a full professor at the Universidade Federal de Santa Catarina. Her current research interests are focused on the areas of sign language acquisition and sign language morphology.

David Quinto-Pozos is a linguist and an assistant professor in the Department of Linguistics at the University of Texas. In addition to his theoretical linguistics scholarship, his laboratory focuses on identifying and describing the characteristics of signed language disorders.

Carina Rebello Cruz is speech/sign and language therapist since 1996. She is a doctoral student in linguistics at Universidade Federal do Rio Grande do Sul. Her research activities and publications are mainly on acquisition language by deaf and hearing children (monolinguals or bimodal bilinguals) and on awareness phonology in sign language.

Wanette Reynolds is a PhD candidate at Gallaudet University, in the Linguistics Department. Her research focuses on ASL narrative development of bimodal bilinguals.

Keiko Sagara is a project researcher at Minpaku, the National Museum of Ethnology in Osaka, Japan. Prior to this she coordinated the Sign Language Typology Project at the International Institute for Sign Languages and Deaf Studies. For her MPhil research, Keiko produced a cross-linguistic comparison of number systems in sign language, with particular attention to Japanese Sign Language.

Adam Schembri is associate professor in linguistics at La Trobe University and has worked on the lexicon, grammar, and sociolinguistics of Australian Sign Language and British Sign Language. Adam is co-author (with Trevor Johnston) of the book *Australian Sign Language: An Introduction to Sign Language Linguistics* (2007).

Jenny L. Singleton is professor of psychology at Georgia Institute of Technology in Atlanta, Georgia, USA. She investigates how early childhood social and linguistic experiences can shape developing biological systems such as visual attention. Singleton is also affiliated with the NSF Center on Visual Language and Visual Learning at Gallaudet University.

Martha E. Tyrone is assistant professor in the Department of Communication Sciences and Disorders at Long Island University, Brooklyn, and senior research scientist at Haskins Laboratories. Her research interests include the phonetics of signed language, kinematic analyses of sign production, and comparisons of typical and atypical signing.

Erin Wilkinson is assistant professor of linguistics at the University of Manitoba and a member of the executive team of the NSF Science of Learning Center on Visual Language and Visual Learning (VL2). Her research interests include cross-language processing in bimodal bilinguals and typological patterns across signed languages.

Bencie Woll is professor of sign language and deaf studies at University College London and the director of the Deafness Cognition and Language Research Centre, the largest research centre in this field in Europe. Before moving to London she was at Bristol, where she was co-founder of the Centre for Deaf Studies, pioneering research on the linguistics of BSL and on deaf studies. Her research and teaching interests embrace a wide range of topics related to sign language: the linguistics of British Sign Language (BSL), the history and sociolinguistics of BSL and the Deaf community, the development of BSL in young children, and sign language and the brain, including developmental and acquired sign language impairments, and cognitive processes in relation to sign language, such as bilingualism and sign language interpreting. She was elected Fellow of the British Academy in 2012.

Ulrike Zeshan is director of the International Institute for Sign Languages and Deaf Studies, at the University of Central Lancashire. She is one of the leading proponents for the development of sign language typology and, more recently, cross-modal typology. Ulrike has considerable experience of linguistic research in many different sign languages and is currently leading a major project on sign multilingualism, funded by the European Research Council.

Introduction

Eleni Orfanidou, Bencie Woll, and Gary Morgan

There has been considerable research since the 1970s on sign languages from linguistic, psycholinguistic, and – more recently – neurolinguistic perspectives. Alongside the substantial literature on sign language in specialist journals and books, there is also a growing embedding of sign language research in mainstream conferences in these fields, as well as in linguistic and psychology books and journals. Increasingly sign language is seen as a "natural experiment" for testing how particular theories respond in the light of studies on language in the visual–gestural modality (e.g., Vigliocco, Perniss & Vinson, 2014. http://rstb.royalsocietypublishing.org/content/369/1651. toc). The UK government's *Cognitive Systems Report* (2003, p. 9) stated: "A more dramatic type of cross-linguistic contrast that may be uniquely valuable in elucidating the underlying properties of speech and language, comes through the comparison between spoken languages and native sign languages, such as BSL (British Sign Language)."[1] The report went on to identify the investigation of features common to how the brain processes spoken language and sign language as one of the six key questions facing language researchers.

Even with this flourishing of interest in sign language and despite the recognition of the importance of this field, no general text on fieldwork or research methods for researchers has yet been published. The aim of the current volume is to summarize all the relevant methodologies in sign language research and to provide a detailed synopsis of how to conduct social, linguistic, psycholinguistic, and neurolinguistic research. Each chapter is written by a specialist in the field and explains the "how" to other sign language researchers, as well as to mainstream language scientists who may consider incorporating sign language research into their research and teaching

Research Methods in Sign Language Studies: A Practical Guide, First Edition.
Edited by Eleni Orfanidou, Bencie Woll, and Gary Morgan.
© 2015 John Wiley & Sons, Inc. Published 2015 by John Wiley & Sons, Inc.

programs. Importantly, the authorship of the chapters also represents collaboration between Deaf and hearing authors.

To the researcher entering the field of sign language as well as to the experienced sign language researcher, the volume provides a thorough review of research methods in key areas of study (sociolinguistics, psycholinguistics, and so on). In particular, new researchers will become familiar with how to appropriately approach the study of a minority language and community that has its own cultural features and how to work with Deaf colleagues and with the Deaf community. They will learn how to deal with practical issues and with the challenges of data collection and analysis of a visual–manual language. Lastly, they will be informed as to what types of data-bases, tools, and methodologies are available to the sign language researcher and how these can be used to address important research questions.

The book is divided into five sections. Part I, "Collecting Data WITH the Deaf Community," sets the scene for research in this field by addressing the ethical and political issues that arise in working with a community that can be considered both a minority linguistic group and a group with a disability. Chapter 1, by Jenny Singleton, Amber Martin, and Gary Morgan, addresses ethical issues involved in studying sign languages – including the consideration of "deaf-friendly" research. In Chapter 2 Thomas Allen discusses the need and benefit of approaching research from a diversity rather than disability perspective. In Chapter 3 Robert Adam considers how to achieve knowledge exchange between communities of researchers and Deaf communities.

Part II, "Different Ways of Collecting Sign Language Data," covers the methodologies required to capture sign language data. It starts with Pamela Perniss describing the requirements for video annotation software that permits time-locked video and coding. In the following chapter Onno Crasborn describes the range of transcription and notation methods appropriate for use with sign language data captured on video. The final chapter in Part II is Martha Tyrone's description of instrumented measures of sign production and perception: motion capture, movement analysis, eye tracking, and reaction times.

Part III, "Collecting Linguistic Data on Sign Languages," comprises six chapters that cover the main methods used in the various fields of sign linguistics research. Victoria Nyst describes methods of sign language fieldwork. Rachel Channon discusses methods for phonological research, while Carol Padden describes methods for grammatical studies. In the next two chapters of Part III, Jordan Fenlon, Adam Schembri, Trevor Johnston and Kearsy Cormier present documentary and corpus-based approaches, while Nick Palfreyman, Keiko Sagara and Ulrike Zeshan describe typological research methods. Finally, Joseph Hill describes the range of methods used in sociolinguistic research with Deaf communities (Chapter 12).

Part IV, "Collecting Cognitive Data on Sign Languages," covers methods used in developmental, psycholinguistic, and educational research. Chapter 13, by Jill Morford, Brenda Nicodemus, and Erin Wilkinson, reviews the range of research methods in psycholinguistic investigations of signed language-processing. Ronice Müller de Quadros, Deborah Chen Pichler, Diane Lillo-Martin, Carina Rebello Cruz, L. Viola Kozak, Jeffrey Levi Palmer, Aline Lemos Pizzio and Wanette Reynolds discuss research methods in bimodal bilingualism (Chapter 14). This is followed by a chapter on methods in sign language acquisition research, by Amy Lieberman and Rachel Mayberry. The section is completed by Fiona Kyle's discussion of research methods in studying reading and literacy development in deaf children who sign (Chapter 16).

The final section of the book, Part V, "Collecting Brain Data on Sign Languages," considers methodology used in neuroscience and neuropsychological studies of sign languages. The section begins with a discussion of methods in functional imaging research – fMRI, ERP, MEG, and TMS – by Cheryl Capek and Helen Neville. Peter Hauser, David Quinto-Pozos, and Jenny Singleton's Chapter 18, next, reviews atypical sign language users and neuropsychological approaches to data collection. The final chapter by Tanya Denmark and Jo Atkinson describes methods used in linguistic and cognitive assessment of typical and atypical sign language users.

The editors would like to thank all the authors for their willingness to contribute to this volume, and also to the reviewers for their careful reading and critical advice, both to the authors and to the editors. Thanks are also due to Professor Li Wei of Birkbeck College, for inviting us to create this volume, and to Julia Kirk at Blackwells, for her support throughout the process of bringing it to publication.

Note

1 This document was published by UK government's Foresight Project; visit www.foresight.gov.uk/ Cognitive%20Systems/FS_CogA4_SpeechLang.pdf

Part I Collecting Data WITH the Deaf Community

1 Ethics, Deaf-Friendly Research, and Good Practice When Studying Sign Languages

Jenny L. Singleton, Amber J. Martin, and Gary Morgan

Chapter Overview

This chapter addresses a range of issues that become important during sign language research, where hearing and Deaf researchers work together. The aim of the chapter is to highlight ethical and practical factors that sometimes can get sidelined during the research process but are crucial for its sustainability. The three sections cover working with Deaf people, issues with fieldwork in other countries than your own, and working with organizations where Deaf people are participants.

Research Methods in Sign Language Studies: A Practical Guide, First Edition.
Edited by Eleni Orfanidou, Bencie Woll, and Gary Morgan.
© 2015 John Wiley & Sons, Inc. Published 2015 by John Wiley & Sons, Inc.

Introduction

The three authors are interested in how researchers can work best with Deaf people, Deaf schools, Deaf children and families, and other professionals who work in the area of deafness. In this chapter we weave these interests together to inform the future researcher of important considerations when embarking on studies that involve Deaf people and their sign languages. This is not just a philosophical question anymore; increasingly research funding agencies are expecting ethical compliance, good quality dissemination, and knowledge exchange, as well as evidence of how research is actually making an impact on the everyday lives of the participants and on wider society. We argue that sign language research that is *with* rather than *on* Deaf people will both be superior in scientific terms and will achieve more societal impact.

Historically, the study of Deaf[1] people has been influenced by the cultures of different disciplines (e.g. linguistics, medicine, or politics). Researchers thus bring to their investigations a set of practices that likely reflect discipline-specific goals such as the promotion of hearing and speech remediation, assistive technologies, Deaf education reform, the genetics of Deafness, sign language linguistics, psycholinguistics, and the study of Deaf cultures and communities. Regardless of their viewpoint, researchers who include Deaf participants in their research are nevertheless expected to conduct their investigations in an ethical manner, protecting the integrity of their research and the individual rights of the participants regardless of age, ethnicity, cultural and linguistic background and respecting and protecting the Deaf community by understanding the broader concerns of community-engaged research (CEnR) (Ross et al., 2010a, 2010b). CEnR is much more sustainable, as it is enables researchers to build up long-term relations with the Deaf community on the basis of mutual respect and benefit, and these are relations where Deaf people are seen not only as informants but also as collaborators.

A number of scholars have raised important ethical issues in deafness-related research (Baker-Shenk and Kyle, 1990; Harris, Holmes, and Mertens, 2009; Pollard, 1992, 2002; Singleton, Jones, and Hanumantha, 2012, 2014). Of central importance is the risk that hearing researchers take on when conducting studies on a community to which they are considered "outsiders." Harris et al. (2009) and Singleton et al. (2012, 2014) suggest that hearing researchers may be controlling the topics of study (thereby validating to the scientific community what issues are deemed important) and interpreting their findings from only their narrow disciplinary perspective (often to the exclusion of a theoretical framework that draws on sociocultural understandings of deafness: see Ladd, 2003; Padden and Humphries, 1988). Baker-Shenk and Kyle (1990) also express concern over whether hearing researchers are able to represent Deaf people's views accurately if they work in isolation. Together, these authors argue that the scientific community will only attain some measure of ethical conduct if it adopts tenets held by the CEnR paradigm (Israel et al., 2008; Ross et al., 2010a; 2010b), namely by involving Deaf people in the research process and by encouraging hearing researchers to be more reflective about their role and to consider the possible detrimental perceptions or impact of their research findings on the Deaf community (Singleton et al., 2012; 2014).

When hearing researchers work closely with Deaf researchers, the resulting collaboration can bring positive rewards; but it does not come without preparation and conscientious effort (Benedict and Sass-Lehrer, 2007; Jones and Pullen, 1992). In the following three sections we outline some areas for reflection concerning the ethics of this collaborative research,with special attention to (1) Deaf-friendly research methods; (2) international work with Deaf communities in developing countries; and (3) the notion of agreements for good practice. We hope that serious reflection on these issues before embarking on a research study into deafness or sign language will mean that researchers (both Deaf and hearing ones) are able to ensure that their research is both scientifically valid and in harmony with the cultural and practical experiences of the people who are involved as participants or facilitators.

Deaf-Friendly Research Methods

The question of how Deaf people are involved in the research process is very important; some scholars argue that the authority for the construction of "admissible evidence" rests only with sign language community members themselves (Harris et al. 2009, p. 115; Ladd, 2003, p. 176). Harris et al. (2009) maintain that the Deaf community should be considered as *hosts* or *gatekeepers* and the researchers as *visitors*, and that the former should be collaboratively involved in the design, decision making, and monitoring of research projects from beginning to end. The CEnR framework provides helpful guidance for working with "host communities." The action research paradigm, common in education research studies, also provides guidance for research oriented toward obtaining organizational change(s) in a community of practice (see Napier, Leigh, and Nann, 2007).

A number of papers have suggested practical ways to address methodological procedures in Deaf comunity-based research that would be more inclusive and culturally appropriate – in other words, more Deaf-friendly (Harris et al., 2009; National Institute on Deafness and other Communication Disorders (NIDCD), 1999; Pollard, 1992). For example, Singleton et al. (2012; 2014) discuss the importance of offering informed consent documents translated into the Deaf individual's native signed language – such as American Sign Language (ASL) or British Sign Language (BSL) – in order to ensure comprehension for Deaf participants with limited spoken language proficiency. These authors also address confidentiality concerns with respect to using video-recorded data to collect Deaf participants' responses in sign language.

There are very few empirical data on the actual experiences of Deaf individuals as they engage in the research process, or on how best to make research more Deaf-friendly. To this end, Singleton et al. (2012, 2014) carried out a focus group study that directly engaged various people involved in the research enterprise. The focus groups were all conducted in ASL, which allowed interviewees to "own" the interview more (Balch and Mertens, 1999). The discussion reported in the focus groups covered experiences both as a research participant – "When you got to the research location, whom did you meet, what was it like being there, and was it what you expected?" – and as a researcher – "How should a researcher gain confidence that a Deaf research participant has truly given their informed consent?" The focus group participants' responses were organized around three domains: the research process; the deaf researcher; and negotiating paradigms.

Singleton and her team discovered that a number of Deaf former research participants described rather troubling encounters with researchers. The participants expressed the feeling that they lacked the power to change uncomfortable situations with researchers (including communication inadequacy and cultural insensitivity). They further conveyed the impression of being unsure how to handle researcher conduct that could be construed as unethical (e.g., when the researcher asked Deaf participants to read and sign complex written consent documents without offering translation into signed language). Participants sometimes reported that they took part in research in order to be better informed; but, without adequate explanations of the purpose of the research, they also developed potentially incorrect ideas about how the data would be used (e.g., they shared fears that their blood sample might be used to find a "deaf gene" and lead to eradicating the deaf population). This example highlights the need for researchers to understand the implications of their research protocol from the Deaf community's perspective and to be aware that they are ethically accountable for fully debriefing the Deaf participants and for sharing with the Deaf community the findings of their research.

The participants in the focus group study by Singleton et al. who were researchers themselves talked about the importance not only of having Deaf researchers in the research team, but that these people be appropriately trained to *lead* research activities. This is starting to happen in the USA and in the United Kingdom and is generally more expected these days than it was 20 years ago; but the availability of such people crucially depends on appropriate training and support for both Deaf and hearing researchers. Another topic emphasized was that most outlets for deafness-related research were in written academic English rather than in ASL (a notable counterexample is the *Deaf Studies Digital Journal*, which publishes online in ASL).

On the basis of prior literature and of the results of their focus group study, Singleton and colleagues offered several important recommendations for ethical practice in research involving Deaf individuals. Researchers coming to sign language research might from the outset consider the following points:

1 *Accessibility of informed consent* While funding agencies have developed some guidelines for scientists on obtaining informed consent from individuals who are deaf or hard of hearing (see NIDCD, 1999), this information does not appear to be widely disseminated in the research community, especially among professionals who review human subjects research and should be holding researchers accountable for providing evidence of their linguistic and cultural competence to work with the Deaf population and for creating consent procedures in the language most accessible to the Deaf participant. The NSF Science of Learning Center on Visual Language and Visual Learning (VL2) now provides on its web site (http://vl2.gallaudet.edu) some guidelines for ethical conduct in research involving Deaf participants, as well as informed consent sample videos in ASL.

2 *Awareness of "overtesting," confidentiality risks, and avoiding a "sample of convenience" mindset* As the Deaf community in any country is likely to be small and close-knit, researchers run the risk of overtesting Deaf children and adults (which possibly affects their reliability, if the same child is being retested on the same instrument). With such a low incidence, researchers must also be very careful about revealing background characteristics of individual subjects in their presentations and publications, as the individual may be identifiable to a reader or audience

member on the basis of this information. Morgan, Simpson, and Swanwick (2008) have proposed some guidelines on "good practice" in working with schools and professionals. These will be summarized later in this chapter.

3   *Give back to the Deaf community, disseminate research findings in ASL* It is also good practice for researchers to make the results of their study available to any participant who expresses an interest; brief research reports could be created in a sign language of the community and shared through video clips offered on websites that are considered Deaf-friendly. For example, Singleton and her team have published their research findings in two languages: English (2014) and ASL (2012). Because this kind of work centers on a topic of such great interest to the Deaf community, it is essential to ensure that its findings are disseminated in a manner accessible to this audience. On the basis of their focus group findings as well as from the extant research literature, Singleton and colleagues argue that it is critical for researchers to *give back* to the Deaf community by disseminating the findings through newsletters, research debriefing, websites, and conference presentations (both research and community-based ones). Other teams, such as Quadros, Lillo-Martin, Koulidobrova, and Chen Pichler (2012), have developed a bilingual approach, where research is simultaneously delivered in ASL and English. Before such outreach activities are carried out, researchers should consult with the target audience as to their areas of interest and appropriate level and mode of delivery. There may be little value in delivering a theoretical linguistics talk to teachers of Deaf children or to sign language instructors. However, with preparation, most sign language or Deaf studies research can be adapted to the needs of its target audience. Again, the benefits of this community-based knowledge transfer are mutual. Researchers gain the sustained support of the research facilitators, and these same professionals are able to incorporate relevant and useful research findings into their practice.

4   *Research team dynamics: The role of interpreters and communication accessibility* When a research team consists of signing Deaf people and hearing people who are either new signers or not fluent in a sign language, efforts are usually made to bring in an interpreter to mediate between the two languages. However, the communication dynamic of the team's research meeting often creates a situation where the science – with debate and argument – is conducted in the prevailing spoken language, whereas the Deaf researchers must follow the sign language interpreter in order to gain access to it. This dynamic significantly disadvantages the Deaf team members, as the sign language interpreter is likely less familiar with research terms and with the research project itself. Also, the time lag between spoken information and the signed translation prevents Deaf team members' equal participation in the debate (Harris et al., 2009). Depending on the interpreter's bidirectional ability to voice and convey the academic–professional discourse, Deaf researchers often struggle to establish and maintain their professional identity when relying on interpreters for adequate information sharing. It is important to discuss *ground rules* for research team meetings, so that every participant, Deaf or hearing, signing or non-signing, may feel to be an equal and productive member of the enterprise. It is often the case that a hearing lead researcher who can deliver information (or can chair a research or a lab meeting) in fluent sign language will engage the Deaf collaborators more than if this information were conveyed by an interpreter. A hearing principal investigator

who uses fluent sign in science meetings can greatly increase Deaf researchers' feeling that they "own" the research. Of course, this demands a significant time investment in learning to sign; but researchers starting in the field of sign language studies will benefit greatly from insights into the community as well as from the trust of their Deaf colleagues when they become able to discuss sign language research in sign language. Many Deaf scholars lose confidence when sign language researchers convey their scientific findings at a level of sign language proficiency that ranks far below that of their spoken language.

In 2014 leaders in the international sign language research community have adopted an ethics statement endorsed by the Sign Language Linguistics Society. Bringing these issues to a global stage encourages us to consider some of the very important issues that sign language researchers face when conducting their investigations in developing countries – especially in those where both hearing and Deaf members of society hold views about Deaf people and their signed language that are strikingly different from what these researchers have likely experienced in their own sign language and Deaf community.

Ethical Considerations for Research in Developing Countries

In the past decade there has been a growth of sign language research projects studying emerging sign languages and village sign languages around the world (e.g., Nonaka, 2011; Senghas and Coppola, 2001). The nature of this work often involves undertaking fieldwork to conduct the research, and this in turn requires researchers to travel outside of their laboratories and home institutions, and very often outside their home countries. Many of these research programs take place in developing countries whose cultural, ethnic, economic, and political contexts differ greatly from those of the researchers' home countries and institutions. The community of researchers involved in this kind of work is quite small by comparison to research communities in other areas of sign language and Deaf studies, although numbers are growing. Moreover, the nature of the fieldwork itself raises unique ethical considerations, which are rarely addressed in standard research ethics training and in courses on the protection of human subjects. Hence there is a dearth of resources and guidance tailored to these particular research contexts. The present section is not intended as a comprehensive overview of the ethical issues involved here, but only as a starting point in considering some of the unique ethical aspects of this kind of fieldwork (for a fuller picture, see also Cassell and Wax, 1980 and Pettifor and Ferraro, 2012).

The basic guiding ethical principles – such as *respect for persons* (to respect and uphold a person's right to autonomously make decisions about research participation) and *beneficence* (the researcher's obligation to maximize benefits and minimize harms to research participants) (Belmont Report, 1979; American Psychological Association, 2010) – do not change in the case of fieldwork in a foreign country. Deciding how to appropriately apply ethical principles in fieldwork, however, is a dynamic process that should be sensitive to an array of specific conditions, both within the academic area of the researcher (e.g., choosing research topics of current scientific value) and on the ground, in the host country (e.g., considering the social context of Deaf participants, or that the goals of the community may change over time). As with all research, we must carefully assess how to ensure participants' rights in the research process. But many of the day-to-day applications of these principles differ from the processes we use at home. In this section we focus on four ethical considerations that are unique to research fieldwork carried out in developing countries: informed consent regarding the nature of the research; appropriate compensation; maintaining personal and professional relationships; and preparing the research team for fieldwork.

Informed consent and the nature of the research

Informed consent is the cornerstone of the application of the principle of respect for persons (Belmont Report, 1979). It stipulates that the information needed to make an informed decision about research participation should be rendered understandable and accessible. We discuss elsewhere in this chapter the necessity of providing information and obtaining consent in the preferred language of the participant; but let us say here that the same practice applies when working in the field. However, in some communities additional considerations are warranted in order to ensure that participants receive all of the information they need to make a voluntary and informed decision.

The nature and purpose of the research may not be intuitive to people outside the research team. Researchers must be clear about what functions the work does and does not serve. Participants or their parents may believe, or hope, that the work is rehabilitative, or that it provides a service for themselves or for a Deaf family member. The research team must be clear that participation in the research will not likely benefit the participant or their family directly. Rather the participant and anyone designated to make decisions on his/her behalf should understand that they are the ones with the expertise in the language and community under study and that the researcher is learning from them. If it is the case that the findings of the research would benefit the community immediately or in the future, the participant should be aware of this. However, potential benefits should not be overstated. In many cases we do not know how or when the results of the work will be applied. In basic research it is often not before several years after the data are collected that any application is possible. Thus, when working in the field with a population that is not familiar with the research process, it is the responsibility of the researcher to anticipate potential sources of misunderstanding about the nature of the research and to resolve them.

Appropriate compensation for research participation

How does the researcher decide what is an appropriate compensation for research participants? Compensation must balance our respect for our participants' time without introducing undue influence or coercion (Grant and Sugarman, 2004). Many institutions have specific guidelines for compensating participants in the laboratory. The form and amount of participant compensation depends on various factors, including the length of time needed for participation, the intensity of the task, and the amount of potential risk. But, for participants who live in developing countries, researchers need to consider additional factors, such as potential loss of regular daily wages, the difficulty or expense involved in travel, and meals. Similarly, if we use "western guidelines" for compensation, participants could receive the equivalent to a week's salary, which most institutional review boards would consider to be coercive: research participants should participate on a voluntary basis, with reasonable compensation, and not be unduly enticed by large sums of money.

If participants stand to lose working wages on account of participating, then, even if the session lasts only part of the day, researchers should consider compensating them fully for time lost; otherwise they should take care to schedule participation on non-working days, if possible. In some cultures it may be inappropriate for participants to accept cash remuneration for work that could benefit the community as a whole; in such cases alternative ways to compensate can be arranged. Determining appropriate compensation requires a dialogue with participants and their community before the research starts.

In addition to compensating individual participants and in accordance with the principles of CEnR (Ross et al., 2010a; 2010b), researchers should actively seek ways to *give back* to the larger *host* communities; and there are multiple ways to do this. As in our work in our home communities, one of the most important ways is to disseminate research findings back to the local community. Publications, posters, or summaries of the work can be translated into the local written and sign language, or findings can be more formally introduced to members of the community in a conference-style presentation. Researchers can also give back by making a monetary donation to the local Deaf association or Deaf organizations. Dialogue with the community will reveal other meaningful ways to give back.

Maintaining professional relationships between researchers and informants

The very nature of most fieldwork and the conditions that make these studies scientifically valuable are the very same factors that pose some potentially difficult ethical problems concerning the relationships between the researcher and the community. There is considerable theoretical value in studying sign languages that emerge within communities of varying sizes – from just a few speakers to a few dozen, or to much larger language communities. Fieldwork often requires the research team to work in a small or close-knit community for a prolonged time and to be in closer contact with participants than would happen in a typical laboratory setting. For these reasons, field researchers face the unusual task of striking a delicate balance between creating a personal rapport with participants and maintaining a professional distance, as observers in a community that is not their own. The dynamics of these relationships may vary depending on the researcher's age and gender, on whether the researcher is Deaf or hearing, and on values held within the host community. Establishing a rapport with participants shows respect for them individually and ensures that they are comfortable and answer questions truthfully. But scientific and professional good practice stipulates that researchers be as unobtrusive as possible. Determining how to maintain this balance requires thoughtful consideration of the particular circumstances of both the researcher's work and the community.

Researchers who frequently return to the same community must also consider how to maintain contact with it between visits. E-mail and social media are convenient ways to maintain contact; but, because of their very personal nature, they also pose risks to the maintenance of professional boundaries with participants. Social media are widespread, and many participants are likely to use various platforms frequently and casually. A laboratory might consider establishing a lab e-mail account or a social media profile as a means of staying connected. A further challenge is how to stay in touch with remote communities on the other side of the digital divide. One possibility is to establish a relationship with a nearby non-governmental organization (NGO) or with a voluntary citizens' support group that could facilitate regular messages or contacts with informants or with Deaf community members in-between research visits.

Lastly, field researchers must be aware of how their position as researchers impacts their relationship with, or their influence in, the host community. Community members may regard a researcher as an authority in areas outside of his/her academic expertise and may seek out his/her opinions. Researchers must be considerate in addressing requests for advice or recommendations. This does not mean researchers cannot provide insight when asked, but they must carefully evaluate their potential influence. One important aspect of the principles of CEnR is the notion of a "social advocacy" role and of when such a role is appropriate. A sign language researcher from a developed country may also hold strong convictions about supporting and partnering with host community members who seek to strengthen the status of their Deaf community. Two examples of researcher-initiated social advocacy are Manos Unidas – an organization established to support equal access to educational and vocational opportunities for Deaf individuals in Nicaragua (visit http://www.manosunidas.org) – and Nicaraguan Sign Language Projects (whose site can be found at http://nicaraguansignlanguageprojects.org/Home_Page.php). The projects of both these organizations include offering sign language classes in rural communities that lack Deaf education and offering Deaf children scholarships to attend signing educational programs.

Preparing the research team for work in the field

Principal investigators should choose and train their research team carefully. At a minimum, research team members should have basic fluency in a world sign language and knowledge of core issues in Deaf cultures and communities (while acknowledging that not all Deaf communities share the same values). Prior experience in traveling abroad is helpful. Team members should have knowledge of the current local political context and be familiar with local cultures and customs (their attire, for instance, should be acceptable in the local community).

Preparing the research team to collect data with Deaf participants also requires establishing a Deaf-friendly research protocol. The entire protocol should be designed to be accessible to Deaf participants and researchers. For instance, if stimulus item numbers will be declared to a recording camera in order for coders to identify them, they should be declared visually, so as to be codable by Deaf researchers, but also in order for the Deaf participant to be able to see the process. The participant can list or number the items, or a visual cue can be signed to the camera by the researcher or presented on a small white board while the camera records. Hearing researchers should avoid speaking to the camera without a visual aid that is accessible to the Deaf participant. Throughout the research session researchers should converse with one another as much as possible, and in the language of the participant. Even simple instructions intended only for other research team members – such as when to begin or end a recording, or when to advance to a new stimulus item – can be signed in the participant's preferred language. Information that should not be revealed to the participant, such as which condition of an experimental task will be presented, should be discussed among the researchers before the participant's arrival. Minor adaptations to a research protocol may be all that is required to make the session fully accessible to a Deaf participant and to Deaf research team members.

Establishing Good Practices in Field Research

There are many ways to apply standard ethical principles in fieldwork on the ground, and researchers must adapt these applications to the communities in which they work. While the basic ethical tenets do not change from community to community, the ways they are applied in the field should be flexible and open to change – both in the circumstances of the research community and in those of the communities of our informants. We must remain receptive to changes from all sides: in the research community, in the informants' community, and in the interactions between them.

Good practice agreements

This section outlines the development of formalized agreements between researchers and schools where Deaf children are educated in the United Kingdom (Morgan et al., 2008). The process described here focuses on schools, but it could be applied to other organizations from which researchers might want to gain access in order to collect sign language data. The motivation behind setting up an agreement framework was to ensure that research was carried out in a positive and mutually beneficial way. In constructing this agreement, the developers focused their attention on the gap that sometimes exists between research teams and the people who facilitate the research, namely the parents and the teachers of Deaf children. The description of the development process might be illuminating for researchers who are embarking on other areas of sign language studies. The agreement is similar to other research–practitioner partnerships – for instance in research on hearing people with mental health problems, or in research on hearing people with acquired language impairments. The good practice agreement (GPA) and the agreement form itself are described in detail on the web site of the British Association of Teachers of the Deaf (BATOD; visit especially http://www.batod.org.uk/index.php?id=/articles/research/good-practice.htm).

The GPA came out of interventions from practitioners who asked how research and education can link up and support each other more. Deaf children are the most assessed (some would say overassessed) pediatric group in clinical and language sciences. This is especially true for children who use sign language. There is a range of research topics carried out with this group that vary in how quickly the results could be applied to the real-world lives of the participants. Some researchers test Deaf children with the aim of assessing how signing affects cognition, for example working memory, while other researchers aim to establish how Deaf children learn to read. Both these questions are valid, but they differ in their closeness to practical application. When embarking on research with Deaf people only, the researchers might want to ask themselves: How will my research benefit the population I am studying? The answers might not be obvious, but the challenge is to work with those organizations where the researchers recruit participants for the purpose of coming up with mutually beneficial results. A research question that is more distant from application could still lead to interesting interactions between researchers and research facilitators: researchers could do some work with facilitators on how to set up a systematic database and do simple statistics. Even so, this exchange of skills needs to come out of dialogue rather than just from the researcher side. While researchers might not be able to answer directly all the questions posed by facilitators, being aware of what is a priority in the work of facilitators can be beneficial for both groups. As research facilitators may be less aware of motivations for research, taking the time to explain the research objectives in a way that is accessible to this group is mutually beneficial for building sustainable relationships. A community-engaged approach, and one with clear practical linkages, need not compromise the scientific merit of the research. In fact, in the current research-funding climate, research proposals with clearly articulated and achievable impact plans (that is, links with the users of the funded research) have greater chance of success.

The GPA happened because schools felt that they were faced with an increasing demand from researchers, which needed to be balanced against the schools' capacity to deliver the project and manage the interruption to their pupils' education. For example, getting parents to sign informed consent documents takes a great deal of the school personnel's time and attention. Schools conveyed some negative experiences of researchers who set up their research without considering the practical demands they were making on the schools they visited. The GPA document now includes sets of responsibilities for both sides to endorse before any research starts. On the side of facilitators, this would involve working on recruitment, providing space for testing, and helping with informed consent. On the researchers' side, it would include arranging the tests at the best time for the school's timetable, explaining fully the research objectives, and exploring the possibility of including extra studies or workshops, warranted more by the needs of the school than by those of the researcher. The agreement also allows for clear planning of researcher follow-up and for dissemination strategies that are appropriate for both the participants and the schools.

The process of co-signing an agreement can guide schools and researchers on how to lead effective and relevant research projects and can provide schools with information toward improving children's progress and future learning objectives and toward supporting curriculum-planning efforts. It also gives criteria against which schools can assess the relevance of a particular research project for their own priorities. Moreover, it ensures that researchers work with the schools on the basis of mutually agreed feedback mechanisms, so that the goals and outcomes are shared with staff in an accessible way and thus can be more easily implemented by the schools.

Conclusion

We are very much aware that researchers undertake research primarily for theoretical reasons. However, when carrying out sign language work in the Deaf community, we should always bear in mind that the social impact of doing so is great. One conclusion is that doing Deaf-friendly CEnR will lead not only to better science, but also more sustainable research programs. It sometimes happens that new researchers into sign language would say: The Deaf community is a difficult population to work with. As is clear from what we write in this chapter, Deaf people are for the most part very motivated to take part in research, when this research is presented in a way that promotes a two-way process. Care in planning how the Deaf community is to be involved in the research will lead to much more satisfactory outcomes for all stakeholders.

Note

1 We adopt the common convention in this literature of capitalizing the term *Deaf* to refer to the community of individuals who identify with Deaf culture and consider themselves a part of a linguistic and cultural minority group.

Keywords

community-engaged research; deaf children; ethics; field-based studies; good practice; knowledge exchange; partnerships

See Also

Chapter 3; Chapter 7; Chapter 11

Suggested Readings

Czaykowska-Higgins, E. (2009). Research models, community engagement, and linguistic fieldwork: Reflections on working within Canadian indigenous communities. *Language Documentation and Conservation* 3, 15–50.

Frankham, J. (2009). Partnership research: A review of approaches and challenges in conducting research in partnership with service users. ESRC, National Centre for Research Methods. Accessed September 2, 2014. http://eprints.ncrm.ac.uk/778

National Science Foundation (1999). Social science and the common rule. In *Frequently asked questions and vignettes: Interpreting the common rule for the protection of human subjects for behavioral and social science research*. Accessed February 16, 2014. http://www.nsf.gov/bfa/dias/policy/hsfaqs.jsp

Watkins, M. (n.d.). Ethical guidelines for community/ecological fieldwork and research. Accessed February 20, 2014. http://www.pacifica.edu/gems/EthicalGuidelinesCommunity.pdf

References

American Psychological Association (2010). *American Psychological Association: Ethical principles and code of conduct*. Accessed November 7, 2013. http://www.apa.org/ethics/code/index.aspx.

Baker-Shenk, C., and Kyle, J. G. (1990). Research with Deaf people: Issues and conflicts. *Disability, Handicap & Society* 5(1), 65–75.

Balch, G., and Mertens, D. (1999). Focus group design and group dynamics: Lessons from Deaf and hard of hearing participants. *American Journal of Evaluation* 20(2), 265–278.

Belmont Report (1979). *The Belmont Report: Ethical principles and guidelines for the protection of human subjects.* Accessed October 20, 2014. http://www.hhs.gov/ohrp/humansubjects/guidance/belmont.html

Benedict, B., and Sass-Lehrer, M. (2007). Deaf and hearing partnerships: Ethical and communication considerations. *American Annals of the Deaf* 152(3), 275–282.

Cassell, J., and Wax, M. L. (1980). Ethical problems of fieldwork. *Social Problems* 27, 259–378.

Grant, R., and Sugarman, J. (2004). Ethics in human subjects research: Do incentives matter? *Journal of Medicine and Philosophy* 29(6), 717–738.

Harris, R., Holmes, H., and Mertens, D. (2009). Research ethics in sign language communities. *Sign Language Studies* 9(2), 104–131.

Israel, B. A., Schulz, A. J., Parker, E. A., Becker, A. B., Allen, A. J., and Guzman, J. R. (2008). Critical issues in developing and following community based participatory research principles. In M. Minkler and N. Wallerstein (Eds.), *Community-based participatory research for health: From process to outcomes.* San Francisco, CA: Jossey-Bass, pp. 53–76.

Jones, L., and Pullen, G. (1992). Cultural differences: Deaf and hearing researchers working together. *Disability, Handicap & Society* 7(2), 189–196.

Ladd, P. (2003). *Understanding Deaf culture: In Search of deafhood.* Tonawanda, NY: Multilingual Matters.

Morgan, G., Simpson, K., and Swanwick, R. (2008). Deaf children and research: Developing a model of good practice and participation. Accessed February 16, 2014. http://www.staff.city.ac.uk/g.morgan/BATOD_article_on_GPA_081008.pdf

Napier, J., Leigh, G., and Nann, S. (2007). Teaching sign language to hearing parents of deaf children: An action research process. *Deafness Education International* 9, 83–100.

National Institute on Deafness and other Communication Disorders (NIDCD) (1999). Working group on communicating informed consent to the deaf or hard of hearing. Accessed February 16, 2014. http://www.nidcd.nih.gov/news/releases/99/inform/pages/toc.aspx

Nonaka, A. (2011). Interrogatives in Ban Khor Sign Language: A preliminary description. In G. Mathur and D. J. Napoli (Eds.), *Deaf around the world: the impact of sign language.* New York: Oxford University Press, pp. 194–220.

Padden, C., and Humphries, T. (1988). *Deaf in America: Voices from a culture.* Cambridge, MA: Harvard University Press.

Pettifor, J., and Ferraro, A. (2012). Ethical dilemmas, cultural differences, and the globalization of psychology. In M. Leach, M. Stevens, G. Lindsay, A. Ferraro, and Y. Korkut (Eds.), *The Oxford handbook of international psychological ethics.* New York: Oxford University Press, pp. 28–41.

Pollard, R. Q. (1992). Cross-cultural ethics in the conduct of deafness research. *Rehabilitation Psychology* 37(2), 87–101.

Pollard, R. Q. (2002, July). Ethical conduct in research involving Deaf people. In V. Gutman (Ed.), *Ethics in mental health and deafness.* Washington, DC: Gallaudet University Press, pp.162–178.

Quadros, R., Lillo-Martin, D., Koulidobrova, H., and Chen Pichler, D. (2012). Noun phrases in Koda bimodal bilingual acquisition. Paper presented at the conference *Theoretical issues in sign language research,* London, UK.

Ross, L. F., Loup, A., Nelson, R. M., Botkin, J. R., Kost, R., Smith, G. R., and Gehlert, S. (2010a). Nine key functions for a human subjects protection program for community-engaged research: Points to consider. *Journal of Empirical Research on Human Research Ethics* 5(1), 33–47.

Ross, L. F., Loup, A., Nelson, R. M., Botkin, J. R., Kost, R., Smith, G. R., and Gehlert, S. (2010b). The challenges of collaboration for academic and community partners in a research partnership: Points to consider. *Journal of Empirical Research on Human Research Ethics* 5(1), 19–31.

Senghas, A., and Coppola, M. (2001). Creating language: How Nicaraguan sign language acquired a spatial grammar. *Psychological Science* 12(4), 323–328.

Singleton, J. L., Jones, G., and Hanumantha, S. (2012). Deaf friendly research? Toward ethical practice in research involving deaf participants. *Deaf Studies Digital Journal* 3. Accessed September 7, 2014. http://dsdj.gallaudet.edu/index.php?issue=4&section_id=2&entry_id=123

Singleton, J. L., Jones, G., and Hanumantha, S. (2014). Toward ethical research practice with Deaf participants. *Journal of Empirical Research on Human Research Ethics* 9, 59–66. doi: 10.1177/1556264614540589.

2 The Deaf Community as a "Special Linguistic Demographic": Diversity Rather Than Disability as a Framework for Conducting Research with Individuals Who Are Deaf

Thomas E. Allen

Chapter Overview

This chapter points to the fact that the much of the published research on individuals who are deaf[1] derives from population models that embrace medical, rehabilitation, and normative educational descriptions of the population sub-groups of interest. Nowhere is this more evident than in the literature specifically oriented toward demographic analyses of the population of individuals who are deaf and hard of hearing. As a result, our current understanding of the population

Research Methods in Sign Language Studies: A Practical Guide, First Edition.
Edited by Eleni Orfanidou, Bencie Woll, and Gary Morgan.
© 2015 John Wiley & Sons, Inc. Published 2015 by John Wiley & Sons, Inc.

is based on models in which deviation from normality guides the design of research and the interpretation of results. This chapter argues that an alternative strategy for enumeration, one based on linguistic diversity, will lead to a valuable (and very different) knowledge base, which may contribute to the improvement of society and of the lives of deaf individuals. Focusing on "difference" rather than "disability" may help us design studies that honor and document differences among individuals in the rich tapestry of human experience.

Introduction

Researchers intending to do population-level studies, as well as other researchers who intend to include background questions for their participants in order better understand the characteristics of their samples, should be aware that there are complex issues surrounding how questions are phrased and how response categories are defined. For over 100 years in the United States, population studies of individuals who are deaf and hard of hearing have sought to characterize deaf people according to medical, rehabilitation, or normative-based educational (M/R/NE) models. These models, in turn, have driven research design efforts and have contributed heavily to determining relevant categories for enumeration in demographic studies and for understanding the background characteristics of deaf participants in experimental studies. During this time, a considerable amount has been amassed of data that contribute to our understanding of the "demographics of deafness." From one perspective, this has been a good thing: both the demonstration and the documentation of prevalence and incidence rates using categories of interest based on M/R/NE modes have certainly contributed to policies that have directed considerable resources to M/R/NE improvements. For example, when "degree of hearing loss" has equated to "degree of deviation from wellness," access to federal health dollars has been in direct proportion to the magnitude of the deviation. Equally, the "achievement lag" in literacy for deaf children (documented through studies of academic achievement that rely on normative comparisons between deaf and hearing test takers), has contributed to the direction of resources (at federal and state levels) toward attempting to remediate this lag.

From another perspective, the focus on M/R/NE categories for enumeration has created a frame of mind for determining progress that derives from the same normative conceptions of wellness and achievement that have driven the research agendas – a focus on reducing the gaps and on bringing deaf individuals "closer" to hearing individuals on indicators of societal attainment. This is a narrow view of attainment, and also one that is very difficult to achieve.

Of course, there are many situations in which we do wish to improve the lives of persons who are deaf by increasing their levels of academic attainment, by reducing the incidence of mental health problems, by improving their prospects for successful employment, and so on. In pursuing these societal ends, comparisons to individuals who are hearing are unavoidable as indicators of success. Yet an a priori presumption that what constitutes normalcy for hearing individuals is the sole lens through which we should judge the attainments of deaf individuals can lead society down errant pathways.

It can also prompt researchers to ask inappropriate questions, develop hypotheses that derive from inappropriate assumptions and theories about language development, and employ measures that have very limited validity for this unique population.

Consider the acquisition of reading skills, for example. We certainly want to reduce gaps in reading skills between deaf and hearing individuals; but, if we believe that deaf children have difficulty reading *because they cannot hear the words they are reading and therefore have no auditory phonological basis for reading the letters on the page*, we will be tempted to focus our research – and the guiding schema that determines how we see the population – on categories of hearing loss and speech perception rather than on visual language experience and the visual nature of print literacy.

An alternative framework for working with deaf participants – whether the researchers are population scientists, neuroscientists, or linguists – is to adopt a linguistic or sociocultural model for defining the population under study, formulating research questions, and developing appropriate empirical measures. This approach derives from an interest in understanding human differences (as opposed to understanding their disabilities) and recognizes that considerable variation exists within the range of "normal" language behavior and that attainment in society is a diverse concept. In this way it furthers not only the articulation of the myriad of outcomes that contribute to a complex human world, but also the idea that individual outcomes (reading English, for example), may be achieved through developmental pathways that M/R/NE approaches fail to notice.

This chapter makes a case for this alternative strategy and will, throughout, suggest specific examples of how questions should be asked under this model. Our primary focus will be on population studies. Such studies are critical to all research with deaf participants, as these provide a demographic and social context from which generalizations can be made from individual studies to the broader population of deaf people. Given the importance of these studies, the nature of the data collected and reported from them must be reviewed, in order for us to ensure that the manner in which categories of enumeration are defined, the procedures by which individuals are selected for inclusion, and the analytical strategies used to summarize population characteristics will accurately reflect the population for which emerging research studies have relevance. In many ways, the decisions demographers make about how to categorize people set the stage for all the research that is carried out on individuals within a society, as they prescribe how society is defined. To date, there has been a mismatch between the voluminous amount of demographic data on the "deaf and hard of hearing" population and the growing interest that researchers have in understanding the social and linguistic characteristics of deaf people.

We will discuss the predominant medical frameworks that have determined the course of demographic studies to date, describe their shortcomings and limitations, summarize some of the issues that are pervasive in existing demographic analyses of this population (as well as some of the challenges for conducting any kind of population study of this population), and make some specific suggestions about how questions might be posed to participants.

Embracing this diversity perspective is important not only for demographers, but for all researchers interested in conducting sign language studies. Understanding the extant literature requires sensitivity to how deaf individuals have been viewed and portrayed in society, expressed by researchers and authors throughout history. Thus, when quoting population statistics, one must take care to contextualize individual studies when generalizing specific results. Going forward, researchers must always be aware of their own biases in formulating their research questions and hypotheses, in designing their studies, in conducting their statistical analyses, and in interpreting their results.

How might the methods selected by researchers interested in studying language use in the classroom, for example, differ between those who espouse a medical/normative model of social context and those who are more embracing of a diversity perspective? In the case of the former, there will be an emphasis on the language of the majority (a spoken language), and little attention will be given to understanding sign language. The focus of studies will be on teaching deaf children to master this language, and assessments will focus on measures of English (or other spoken languages). The ultimate goal will be that all children in the classroom achieve equality in the acquisition of the majority language.

Researchers who view classrooms as places where diversity should flourish will have a different set of questions and will employ a different array of methods. They will be interested in understanding the structure of a visual language and in identifying its variations; they will be interested in evaluating the strategies for maximizing the cognitive benefits of bilingual instruction; they will be interested in looking at social interactions among deaf and hearing children; they will be interested in understanding the early language experiences of children in classrooms, in the impacts that these early experiences have on cognitive development, and in how teachers can facilitate this development by employing the child's existing language skills; they will be interested in how higher order literacy skills are developed through a visual language – for example, how narrative abilities can be developed through the use of sign language and gesture. And the list goes on. In sum, embracing the diversity perspective opens the realm of questions that are of critical importance to directing research toward discoveries that honor and account for individual differences evident among individuals in society. Statistical methods will focus on characterizing smaller segments of the population, with known social, cultural, and linguistic backgrounds.

Suggestion for Researchers

Ask questions of your participants that probe their history of sign language use, especially during their early childhood. For example:

To the best of your memory, or from what your parents have told you, which of the following best describes your use of sign language in your home during your early childhood?

    ☐ We only signed and used no spoken language.
    ☐ We mostly signed, but we used some spoken language as well.
    ☐ We signed and spoke in roughly equal amounts.
    ☐ We mostly spoke, but used some sign language too.
    ☐ We only spoke and used no sign language.
    ☐ We rarely spoke or signed, but relied on gestures to communicate.

This question (or one similar to it) does not attach a higher value to spoken or signed languages and will give you a sense of the modalities of communication (spoken and signed) that contributed to your participants' language development.

Predominant Medical/Rehabilitation/Normative–Educational Frameworks in the Demographic Studies of Individuals Who Are Deaf and Hard of Hearing

While the US Census Bureau began asking national samples of citizens about the prevalence of hearing loss in its first National Health Interview Survey in 1957 (National Center for Health Statistics, 1963), the real impetus for the scientific study of the demography of deafness in the United States, especially with a focus on education, originated in 1964, with the appointment of an Advisory Committee on the Education of the Deaf by then US Secretary of Health, Education, and Welfare Anthony Celebrezze. The report of this committee, now famously called "The Babbidge Report," after the chair of the committee (US Department of Health, Education, and Welfare, 1964), was published a year later and lamented the poor state of education for deaf children as well as the lack of federal data pertinent to understanding the nature of the population of deaf children in schools and their needs. The decade following the publication of the Babbidge Report witnessed a burgeoning of interest, federal support, and general activity in response to this lack of information, which was needed so desperately to inform educational policy. The Bureau of Education of the Handicapped (BEH) awarded a grant to Gallaudet College to establish the Annual Survey of Hearing Impaired Children and Youth in 1968 (Rawlings and Gentile, 1970). The National Association of the Deaf was awarded a grant from the Social and Rehabilitation Services Administration to conduct a National Census of the Deaf Population (NCDP) in 1971 (Schein and Delk, 1974). Other initiatives, such as the National Health and Nutrition Examination Survey, conducted by the National Center for Health Statistics, and the Survey of Income and Program Participation, conducted by the US Bureau of Labor Statistics, have also included questions about hearing loss, which were designed to inform medical and employment policy respectively.

Researchers who are carrying out studies of the deaf community as a linguistic demographic group should realize that we are aiming at a scientific approach to population studies that is radically different from those that grew out of the work of demographers in the 1960s and 1970s. Mitchell frames the issue clearly:

> In the process of identification and enumeration of deaf persons, or any other particular group within the population, at least four constraints are encountered: *the context of the inquiry* [emphasis added], the indicators used to establish group membership, the methods employed to collect indicator data, and the resources available to execute the project. (Mitchell, 2005, p. 113)

Critically, any enumeration or study of a population must articulate the context of the inquiry, and those studies that are based on medical or normative–educational contexts will yield quite different information from those based on a linguistic context. The indicators to establish group membership will be radically different, as will the methods used to collect indicator data. Researchers should put this contextual information clearly up front in the research process.

A research project about American Sign Language (ASL) use that employs survey questions, whether administered only to deaf participants or to a broader population, has to take several factors into consideration. Consider the initiatives described previously. The National Health Interview Survey and the National Health and Nutrition Examination Survey are designed to report on the health status of Americans. The context of these surveys is medical, and the indicators used to establish a respondent's membership as a deaf person derive from answers to a survey question that asks: "Do you have no trouble hearing, a little trouble hearing, a lot of trouble hearing, or are you deaf?" (Ironically, the self-report of being "deaf" may be an effective indicator of membership in the deaf community, although clearly this was not the intent of the survey writers, who simply view "deaf" as the most severe level of pathology.) The critical words in these questions are: "trouble hearing," clearly identifying deafness as a medical burden to be overcome. In the NCDP, Schein and Delk (1974) define their population as "those persons *who could not hear and understand speech and who had lost (or never had) that ability prior to 19 years of age*" (p. 2). This definition is more oriented to a perceived requisite for success in schools, namely the ability to hear and understand speech. In the Annual Survey, data records are gathered from schools across the United States for those "deaf and hard of hearing children and youth who have been identified as requiring an individualized education program (IEP) or an individualized family service plan (IFSP)" (Mitchell, 2004, p. 337). As Spencer and Marschark (2010) point out, "this is a bit of a circular definition, but it is a practical solution" (p. 10). Interestingly, the definition focuses more on the practices of individual schools and on the manner in which they categorize and serve a group of students than on the characteristics of the students themselves. Thus it is important to point out that a given child attending a school in one location may be counted as a "deaf or hard of hearing child," while she might not be so counted if she attended a different school, with different IEP criteria.

Suggestions for Researchers

Avoid using the term "deafness." It implies a unidimensional condition in which more deafness is bad and less deafness is good. It also confounds cultural definitions with medical or audiological definitions pertaining to the level of hearing. Use phrases such as "individuals who are deaf," or, preferably, "individuals who are deaf and come from families where sign language was regularly used." The more the definitions are oriented toward language use, the greater their ability to shed light on the characteristics of linguistic and culturally defined subgroups.

Schein and Delk, in their introduction to the report on the NCDP, state:

Impairment of hearing is the single most prevalent chronic disability in the United States. More persons suffer a hearing defect than have visual impairments, heart disease, or other chronic disabilities ... Because deaf people constitute such a small minority within the general population, they must accommodate to the larger group, rather than vice versa. The extent of the accommodation can be seen in the communication patterns adopted by deaf people. Most use speech, expressively, and lipreading, receptively, at least some of the time in their daily intercourse. But they also use fingerspelling, signing, and writing in their interpersonal contacts. (Schein and Delk, 1974, p. 8)

This quotation set the stage for the contexts that have guided demographic studies of individuals who are deaf over the past 40 years. Words like "suffer," "defect," and "disability" clearly place population studies into a medical context. The notion of "single most prevalent" is highly misleading, in that it refers to all degrees of hearing loss, in individuals of all ages. If cited incorrectly, this phrase might lead one to grossly overestimate the prevalence of signing deaf individuals in the United States. The implication in a population statistic that individuals with different language and cultural backgrounds (ASL and English, for example) can be grouped together is that these backgrounds hold little relevance for enumeration studies. Unfortunately these studies are used in order to determine policy in areas such as education, which should be paying closer attention to the language and cultural backgrounds of students with particular needs.

Mitchell, Young, Bachleda, and Karchmer (2006) have thoroughly discussed issues associated with trying to estimate the number of people who use ASL by relying on highly divergent estimates of prevalence of deafness. (Their paper will be discussed in a little more detail in the following sections.) Holt, Hotto, and Cole (1994) report that 8.6 percent responded to the National Health Interview Survey that they had some "trouble hearing." However, when prevalence rates are reported by age, the numbers range from 1.8 percent for children between the ages of 3 and 17, to 29.1 percent for individuals aged 65 and older. Clearly individuals who lose their hearing later in life (the overwhelming majority) are native speakers of English (or of other spoken languages) and would not be considered among the population of ASL users. Further, when the definition shifts to "deaf in both ears," the national rate (for individuals of all ages) is only 0.18 percent (which represents fewer than two people in a thousand). While Holt et al. (1994) do not report the rates for children aged 3–17 in the "deaf in both ears" category, they do report prevalence rates for this age group in a broader category, defined as "at best can hear words shouted in their better ear"; and this is 0.1 percent (one person in a thousand). Thus the overwhelming majority of individuals typically referenced in national statistics are older hard-of-hearing Americans who are English speakers, and the overgeneralization of this fact to the full population is patently incorrect.

Suggestions for Researchers

Do not overgeneralize your results to individuals who do not share relevant background characteristics. Define what constitutes meaningful subgroups within the population and relevant to your research questions, for instance older individuals who lose their hearing late in life; individuals of all ages who are hard of hearing versus those who are deaf; or deaf individuals using specific language systems in their homes, at school, and at work (including sign languages). This last suggestion is very important; the recognition of sign language as a language and the reporting of demographic data about the prevalence of its use would greatly enhance our understanding of the use and importance of sign language in society.

One can easily see how this disability normative framework has influenced population studies of deaf individuals over the years. In turn, these studies have propagated the idea that deaf persons are "impaired." But many have questioned the ethics of a strict adherence to norm-referenced notions of "wellness." For example, Kawa and Giordano (2012) point to controversies surrounding the medicalization of cognition, emotion, and behavior (and we might emphasize the inclusion of language as a medical issue in the case of deaf individuals), which in turn fosters presuppositions about what constitutes "normal" or "abnormal" in the context of society and culture. The application of this medical view, in the context of "oppression," to persons who are deaf has been well discussed in the literature (see Friedner, 2010; Ladd, 2003; Lane, 1993). Population studies must embrace (and indeed celebrate) behavioral diversity and sociocultural differences, with a view toward providing research findings that shed light on population patterns of language diversity and on their implications for the improvement of a multilingual and multicultural society.

A Linguistic Basis for Demographic Studies

Research with deaf participants or research on sign language use in the general population could consider an alternative approach to categorizing participants. In 1960, three years after the National Health Interview Survey began to pose questions to American survey respondents about the status of their hearing, William Stokoe published a monograph in which he began outlining a taxonomy for the phonological (which he called "cherological" to differentiate it from the sound-based sublexical units of spoken languages) and morphological analysis of ASL. In his introduction he states:

> The primary purpose of this paper is to bring within the purview of linguistics a virtually unknown language, the sign language of the American deaf. Rigorous linguistic methodology applied to this language system of visual symbols has led to conclusions about its structure, which add to the sum of linguistic knowledge. (Stokoe, 1960, p. 1)

There is, perhaps, some historical irony in the fact that these two events occurred so close in time. Just as the National Center for Health Statistics began charting a path that would be followed for the next fifty years by documenting the hearing status of a population for medical reasons and needs, the linguistics community began taking note of, and describing, the natural language of those who are deaf. These trajectories derive from different, if not opposing scientific worldviews. In one view, the focus is on disability; in the other, the focus is on the development and use of a natural, visual language. To understand ASL users as a linguistic minority, we must, as Mitchell (2005) suggests, re-specify the *context* in which population enumeration takes place so as to focus on the diversity of languages and on the implications of this diversity for social and educational programming.

Issues and Challenges

In conducting or evaluating research on ASL usage among individuals we would want to consider as members of a particular linguistic subgroup – in this case, the "Deaf community" – there are a number of critical issues that need to be examined by researchers in the future. These include considerations of the role of parental hearing status and parents' use of ASL in the home in establishing the social context for language use, confusions about language and modality, controversies over the benefits and risks of bilingualism, and misunderstandings about how prevalence rates are determined and interpreted.

Taking one of these examples (parental hearing status and use of ASL in the home), it should be evident how a medical perspective that relies on hearing norms to define what it means to be "healthy" would differ dramatically from a linguistic or cultural perspective. A medically oriented researcher would point both to the deafness of the parent as a pathology and to the use of ASL early in life as potentially damaging to a deaf individual's subsequent ability to learn speech; this researcher might use the argument that ASL activates or "recruits" areas of the auditory cortex normally recruited by spoken language in hearing individuals. The common claim of those who adopt this perspective is that "the brain is naturally wired for learning language through hearing … Auditory–Verbal professionals agree that sign language and lip reading at an early age inhibit the child's dependence on LISTENING to acquire language" (Auditory–Verbal Communication Center, 2013). This perspective would have a huge impact on the types of research that may be undertaken, leading to an emphasis on speech perception and the listening abilities of the participants.

However, other researchers (for example, Petitto, 2000), looking *at the same data about the brain* and noting that regions of the auditory cortex are activated by ASL in deaf native signers but not in hearing non-signers, draw very different conclusions: these researchers claim that this area of the brain is responding to the phonologically structured and segmented language input regardless of its modality – spoken or signed. They interpret these data as providing evidence that there is a visually based phonology of sign language, which performs the same role in language processing by deaf individuals as the sound-based phonology of spoken language performs for hearing individuals. To be sure, research studies that emanate from this perspective focus on such topics as models of bilingual ASL–English learning, the importance of early exposure and access to a visual language, and the cognitive benefits of having an early visual language experience.

In the following sections we elaborate on a few of the more prominent issues that have emerged from previous studies, in hope that what we say here will inform future researchers. Importantly, almost all of these issues derive from definitions and perspectives that are imprecise and proceed from erroneous assumptions. For example, there is no legal definition of "deaf," nor is there a universal definition of ASL. Therefore, as research develops, attempts must be made to improve the level of precision in the definitions used and to clearly specify the assumptions that underlie the interpretation of findings. The collection of issues we present here is by no means exhaustive, and the short treatment given to each one comes nowhere near to a complete treatment.

Prevalence of deaf individuals and prevalence of ASL usage

This issue combines three important questions: (1) How many deaf people are there? (2) How many ASL users are there? (3) What is the relationship between 1 and 2? We have already presented the problem related to question 1, noting that national prevalence rates typically do not acknowledge either the huge differences in the rates of deafness of individuals with different levels of hearing or the relationships of these differences to the individuals' age. Questions 2 and 3 are largely unanswered. In spite of the growing recognition of ASL as a full language (e.g., Armstrong, Karchmer, and Van Cleve, 2002; Chamberlain, Morford, and Mayberry, 2000; Emmorey and Lane, 2000; Liddell, 2003; Stokoe, 1960; Valli and Lucas, 2001), there are no national census questions pertaining to its use. The recent paper by Mitchell et al. (2006) presents this issue in great detail. They tackle the common belief that "ASL is the fourth most prevalent language in the United States"; they disentangle concepts of native languages versus languages used in the home; and they describe the imprecisions of definitions and the repeated use of secondary and tertiary sources as primary ones. Interestingly, in their review, Mitchell and colleagues trace citations regarding the prevalence of ASL usage back to a single source: the National Census of Deaf Persons in the United States (Schein and Delk, 1974). That census, as we have noted, viewed deafness as a medical "condition." Its queries into sign usage avoid the term ASL, focusing on a more generic "sign," which, as we have noted, Schein and Delk view as only useful for deaf people in informal communication.

Regarding the question of whether the prevalence of deaf people yields information about the prevalence of ASL, Mitchell et al. (2006, p. 312 observe: "American Sign Language is a social and linguistic phenomenon, for which deafness is a necessary human condition motivating its sustained use (Johnston, 2004), but an individual's deafness is neither a necessary nor a sufficient condition for becoming an ASL signer." Even if prevalence rates for deaf individuals were precise and known, we would still not be able to infer the prevalence rates for ASL usage.

Language and modality

Demographic studies of deaf individuals have often failed to separate the very different constructs of language and modality. For example, the 2007–2008 Annual Survey (Gallaudet Research Institute, 2008) asked schools to report on the communication mode used in the classroom for each of the 36,710 children and youth reported to the survey in that school year. The response categories (and the resulting percentages from the survey) were: speech only (52 percent); sign with speech (35 percent); sign only (11 percent); cued speech (0.2 percent); and other (1.5 percent). Clearly this question is oriented toward language modality and not toward language per se, and therefore the language implications are quite ambiguous. First, the majority of children are reported to fall in the "speech only" category; however, inspection of the hearing levels of the sample reveals that only 41 percent of the children had hearing losses in the severe to profound categories. Clearly these percentages have to be interpreted very carefully. Educational policy often flows from demographic data, and there is a danger that, when demographic findings are overgeneralized, policies can be easily misdirected. Using the above figures, only 11 percent use "sign only" in the classroom, but this does not mean that 11 percent of the children with severe to profound levels of deafness use sign only in the classroom. Further, the "sign and speech" category is totally ambiguous with respect to whether classroom communication is bilingual (children receive some instruction in English and other instruction in ASL) or whether teachers are using a communication method that incorporates the simultaneous use of signs and speech. Finally, can we infer that children in the "sign only" category are receiving instruction in ASL? Probably not. There are different sign systems that bear different approximations to English and ASL (Stedt and Moores, 1990; Woodward and Allen, 1986).

Suggestions for Researchers

Differentiate language questions from modality questions and allow for multiple responses for each question, as in the following example from a recent survey at http://signupvl2.gallaudet.edu:

What languages and/or language systems do you use on a regular basis? (Check all that apply.)

Languages:
☐ English
☐ ASL
☐ A sign language other than ASL, such as BSL or LSQ
☐ Spanish
☐ French
☐ Chinese
☐ Japanese
☐ German
☐ Other

Language Systems:
☐ Spoken English
☐ Signed English
☐ Cued language/Cued speech
☐ Fingerspelling
☐ Gestures
☐ Other

These questions permit participants to respond separately for language and modality (here broadened to incorporate different systems of language use), and also allow for the use of multiple languages and multiple modalities for each participant. This strategy will more accurately reflect the diversity in your samples and will help specify the populations to which you wish to generalize.

Another confusion arises over the imprecise definition of ASL and the possibility that participants in a study will employ quite different understandings of what is meant by "ASL." Woodward, Allen, and Schildroth (1985, p. 481) amusingly quote a teacher's verbatim response to a survey question about the communication policy of her school district:

> Our policy follows the view that sign language is speech or specifically manual speech and American Sign Language is English. We use only ASL signs and put them in straight English Syntax. Some words are only fingerspelled in Sign Language. We use the formal ASL usage and not the colloquial form used in everyday life of the deaf. The students will develop that naturally when they start to sign fast.

While this quotation is taken from a study that is 25 years old – and it is (hopefully) unlikely that such a quotation would be found today if a similar study were undertaken – it is no doubt true that the term "ASL," from the vantage point of classroom teachers, still covers a wide range of language usage, with varying approximations to English grammar. Effective population studies that include a category for ASL usage (whether in classrooms or in the general public) will need to make clear what is meant.

Suggestions for Researchers

Devise linguistically based behavioral questions that will differentiate ASL use from other manually coded language systems. Woodward and Allen (1986) employed a scaling technique that assumed a continuum between ASL and English. They posed a small number of behavioral questions that asked participants to look at two short English sentences, such as "I am looking for him" and "She is looking at me." Respondents were then asked to report whether they would sign "looking" the same or differently in the two sentences; whether they would sign "I" and "me" the same or differently in the two sentences; and so on. For each choice, there was one option that represented use of ASL and one that represented use of signing in English. Using this simple scaling strategy rather than asking participants to self-classify as to whether they were using ASL gives a behavioral indication of the kind of signing being used and avoids possible ambiguities associated with the term "ASL."

Bilingual and bimodal

Bilingualism has been a very controversial topic in research and in social policy. Research debates have centered on the impact of bilingualism on the developing brain and on the acquisition of language and literacy. Traditional views posited that being presented with two languages would have a harmful impact on children's development. However, current research has challenged this view, pointing to the benefits of bilingualism on a range of developmental characteristics – such as reading and cognitive control. These are discussed more fully in Chapter 14. Social debate centers on the potential harm that bilingualism might have by preventing the

> ## Suggestions for Researchers
>
> In the research literature on deaf individuals the terms "bilingual" and "bimodal" are frequently used, though not always consistently. Bilingual refers to having knowledge of two languages (ASL and English), and, most often (though, confusingly, not always), "bimodal" refers to speaking and signing. The importance of these constructs cannot be overemphasized, and the recognition that most deaf users of ASL are bilingual is central to what distinguishes population studies that derive from the M/R/NE models described above from those that derive from the perspective of language diversity.

"assimilation" of bilinguals into a monolingual society. This view is thankfully fading away, as society becomes increasingly tolerant and embracing of different languages and cultures.

Turning to modality, ASL is a language that is almost universally rendered in the visual–gestural modality. On the other hand, English (and other spoken languages) are rendered primarily in the auditory–spoken modality. However, in the case of written languages, spoken words are given visual form through a writing system. Some writing systems employ an alphabet to convey the sound-based phonological information encoded in the written words (as in the case of English), while others are logographic (for instance, Chinese characters) – that is, they convey the semantics or the ideas of the words through their symbols. There are ongoing efforts to develop writing systems for conveying ASL; this is a seemingly logical progression in the evolution of a language, especially given the visual nature of the sign and the possibility for logographic representation of is phonology, morphology, and syntax on the written page (see Arnold, 2012 and Sutton, 2002 for examples).

Confusions arise in understanding and describing the nature of ASL/English bilingualism, particularly with respect to issues surrounding modality. What is the written word? To be sure, written words are encountered in the visual modality, yet their close association with the sound-based phonology of the spoken words they represent has led many to believe that successful reading requires knowledge of these sound–grapheme associations.

Not all researchers believe this to be true. Citing a wealth of correlational research that demonstrates a strong relationship between ASL skill and reading ability, many have postulated that a sound-based phonological knowledge is neither necessary nor sufficient for the development of the reading skill (e.g., Allen et al., 2009; Morere and Allen, 2012; Prinz and Strong, 1998). Additionally, Mayberry, del Guidice, and Lieberman (2011) conducted a meta-analysis of over 60 studies on the relationship of sound-based phonology to reading skill among samples of deaf individuals and found a remarkably low effect size for phonological knowledge on the prediction of reading skill. Given these findings, a considerable amount of research and thinking has been directed toward understanding why and how ASL fluency can lead to reading ability in the absence of sound-based phonological knowledge.

One subgroup of individuals is truly bilingual *and* bimodal: children who are learning both ASL and speech. While most research on this mixed bilingual and bimodal group is carried on hearing children born to deaf parents, deaf children who come from signing families and receive cochlear implants make up an important sub-population for study. This group is increasing in prevalence, as more and more signing families are electing to implant young deaf children (and, conversely, more and more children with cochlear implants are coming from families who sign). Allen and Anderson (2010) report 11 percent of the 8,325 students with profound deafness reported to the 2008 Annual Survey as *both having a cochlear implant and coming from a signing family*. In a recent research brief that summarizes the research evidence on the advantages of a bilingual and bimodal approach, Mitchiner, Nussbaum, and Scott (2012) conclude that educational programs that foster the development of both speech and ASL for children with cochlear implants have the potential for providing considerable bilingual advantages for the children enrolled in these programs. Future enumeration studies examining ASL as a linguistic subgroup should devote some attention to this "subgroup of the subgroup" and should consider the broad range of implications of being both bilingual and bimodal for language development in children.

Age at onset of deafness, age at identification, and age of exposure to a visual language

The ages at which deaf individuals become deaf, are identified as being deaf, and are exposed to a visual language are extremely critical characteristics and they need attention in any attempt at population enumeration within a language diversity model, as both perceptual and language experiences in childhood will greatly influence these individuals' later language choices and abilities. A baby who is born deaf, is known to be deaf at birth, and has access to a visual language from birth will, as an individual, develop quite differently from one who is born hearing and becomes deaf later, is born deaf but not identified as being deaf until later, or is not exposed to a visual language until later, in spite of being born deaf and identified early. Clearly the timing of these events is critical in determining the language development of young deaf children. There is near-universal agreement that early identification is important, and there is common support for universal newborn hearing screening (see, e.g., Yoshinaga-Itano, Sedey, Coulter, and Mehl, 1998). However, the support for early visual language is not universal: promoters of approaches such as auditory–verbal therapy actively discourage the use of any visual language (or really any visual support up to and including lip-reading), believing that developing listening skills, even among deaf children with profound hearing loss who use assistive technologies, is the only way to optimize chances for developing speech and language skills (A. G. Bell Academy for Listening and Spoken Language, 2012). This prescription is highly controversial, and there is little published research to support the claim on which it is based. In fact there is mounting evidence to support the idea that early visual language exposure ensures the development of areas of the brain responsible for language processing and ultimately benefits the development of both spoken and signed language skills, as well as the development of literacy (Mayberry, Chen, Witcher, and Klein, 2011; Petitto, 2000; Yoshinaga-Itano, 2006).

> ## Suggestions for Researchers
>
> Given the importance of these three questions (age when a participant became deaf, age when a participant was identified as being deaf, and age of exposure to visual and spoken languages) to a full understanding of any deaf individual's use of language at any age, you should consider asking your participants to report on these factors. As noted above, language experiences during a child's first few years of life will have a profound impact on their language usage throughout their lives.

Parental hearing status and language use in the home

Another critical characteristic of deaf individuals is whether they were born to deaf parents and, as a related issue, what language (or languages) are used in the home. From a cultural perspective, being born into a deaf family clearly has implications for the course one's life will take (Padden and Humphries, 1988; 2006). Not only does having a deaf parent usually imply an early access to visual language; it also appears to be true that deaf parents are more adept at managing the visual gaze of their children during critical activities like book sharing (Lieberman, Hatrak, and Mayberry, 2011; Singleton and Crume, 2010) and during critical periods in language and cognitive development. While one might be tempted to focus studies of the demographics of deaf ASL users as a linguistic subgroup solely on the group of deaf individuals from deaf families, it should be noted that this focus might lead to some erroneous oversimplifications. The prevalence of deaf children with deaf parents is very low (Mitchell and Karchmer, 2004). One often hears "one in ten" as representing the percentage of deaf children born to deaf parents; however, a close scrutiny of the research fails to validate this contention. Early studies in the 1970s (both in the Annual Survey and in the NCDP) are plagued with missing and unknown responses to questions about the hearing or deaf status of parents, especially the father. Mitchell and Karchmer (2004) performed an analysis of 1999–2000 data from the Annual Survey. They take note of the pattern of missing and unknown data, the differential response rates for mother's and father's hearing status, and conclude that previously reported rates of 10 percent are significantly overstated (the true rates are most likely in the 5–6 percent range). Thus, limiting study of linguistic diversity to deaf individuals from deaf families will result in the study of a very small number of individuals indeed. While it is critically important to study this population to fully understand the nature of being culturally deaf and born into a social environment where the language in the home is a fully accessible visual language, a field of inquiry that seeks to describe and understand ASL use in a broader context will lead to a greater understanding of how ASL is used throughout society. Important questions about ASL use extend beyond comparisons of native and non-native users. For example, how do teachers use ASL in classrooms for deaf individuals? What are the most effective means of teaching ASL? Given that hearing parents will often be learning ASL at the same time their children are, what constitutes "enough" ASL to effectively prepare deaf children for school? What variations in sign are in evidence among different societal subgroups?

Sociocultural studies of sign use and linguistic diversity among deaf signers is a fascinating area of study that contributes to our understanding of cultural diversity in our society.

The lives of deaf children in hearing families are not well studied or understood (other than from the M/R/NE perspectives). Allen and Anderson (2010) analyzed data from 8,325 students with a profound level of hearing loss (90dB average hearing threshold in their better ear). In 88 percent of the 7,358 students for whom parental hearing status was reported, *both* parents were hearing (see the previous cautions about missing data and its potentially biasing influence on prevalence rates), and 53 percent of these 7,358 students came from homes where signing was regularly used. Thus it is clear that signing is regularly used in many homes of deaf children whose parents are both hearing.

We do not know the nature or the quality of the sign communication that is going on in the homes of deaf children with hearing parents, even when they report that they are signing with their children. Young (1997), in an interesting qualitative study that employed semi-structured interviews of hearing parents, their deaf child's hearing teachers in a bilingual early intervention program, and deaf home visitors (consultants) who served as role models and provided some sign instruction in the homes, queried the informants about how they conceptualized parents' early sign language use. She found quite different frameworks employed by her three types of informants. Teachers were likely to focus on the parents' lack of ability to employ formal aspects of British Sign Language (BSL) grammar and vocabulary. For teachers, parents were not using BSL at all, and parents' communication was different from the language that was used in the classroom. Quite differently, the Deaf consultants saw little relevance in whether parents were signing in formal BSL or not. They were concerned with the more practical and functional relevance of the parents' signing, and they expressed more concern over visual quality and the child's appropriate use of individual signs in specific situations. Finally, parents were split between those who were striving to master formal BSL and those who were focused on achieving effective communication with their children. This research points to the pursuit of linguistic rigor versus effective pragmatic communication as a useful distinction that will inform studies on ASL use.

Conclusion

In all research with human participants, researchers must define a population of interest on a clearly defined set of research questions, develop a means for sampling from this population, create indicators for determining membership in subgroups of the population that have relevance for the stated research questions, and employ strategies for collecting data that will provide information on how answers to the research questions are informed by a knowledge of the characteristics of the sample. It is evident that there is considerable diversity *within* the overall population of sign language users. Thus any piece of research must identify its place within the broader population and be clear about the extent and limitations of its generalizations. Hopefully, future demographic studies will provide a means for better positioning individual research projects within the population at large and will provide a framework that takes language use and family experiences into consideration in defining the nature of the inquiry.

In the case of studies based on the M/R/NE models described earlier, establishing the categories of interest is straightforward. Nonetheless, as we have seen, in spite of the fact that the categories of interest may be easily defined (an audiogram, a grade equivalent, an income), the means for collecting and interpreting data are by no means simple, and we have seen how methodological issues (missing data on one or both parents' hearing status, for example) can cause misleading and incorrect conclusions.

Moving from an M/R/NE model to one that has language diversity as the underlying framework certainly makes the research endeavor more complex, as we do not have a clear, unambiguous understanding of ASL. We have noted earlier how simple questions to participants about whether or not they use ASL may result in identical responses that represent quite different actual communication practices. This compounds the lack of a legal or accepted definition of who is either audiologically deaf or culturally deaf (often spelled "Deaf"). If the latter is a matter of individual choice, we would still be at a loss as to how best to calculate or enumerate any reliable prevalence rates. Who can be defined as Deaf? Only people with abnormal audiograms? Hearing individuals who are fluent users of ASL, given that children of deaf adults often identify with the Deaf community? Much of the critical work in ASL also pertains to its role in the learning experiences of young deaf children (including infants). Certainly young children do not themselves choose to identify with a particular culture. In the situation of deaf children *born* into Deaf signing families, we might make assumptions that allow us to accurately describe a Deaf, ASL-using subgroup. Indeed this would be an excellent approach for studying the linguistics of ASL. However, many questions about deaf people and their use of ASL are much broader, extending into domains of cognitive psychology, child development, sociology, education, and neuroscience. Answering these questions requires a more inclusive view of the population of interest. Throughout this chapter we have argued that it is precisely this inclusive point of view that will embed the findings of our research in a cultural, social, and linguistic context that will enhance the relevance of our work as researchers.

As we have seen, this work is complex, but sorting out this complexity is worth the effort for all researchers working in sign language research, as well as for population scientists who seek more appropriate ways to describe a unique population of individuals. Returning to Mitchell's four constraints for population enumeration (context, indicators for group membership, methods of data collection, and resources available), the first constraint (specifying the context) drives the others. Cultural contexts in which our goal is to understand the interactions among Deaf individuals within the Deaf community may indeed benefit from a narrowly defined population. But often our interests are broader, especially given the higher prevalence of deaf children born to hearing parents and the profound impact that early language experience has on the wellbeing of deaf individuals as they grow. Critical studies of this population, more broadly defined to include hearing families who may be emerging as bilingual, will contribute to a deeper understanding of the role of linguistic diversity in society and education and of the benefits that accrue with a greater understanding and appreciation of human differences.

Note

1   Throughout this chapter we will use a lowercase *d* when referring to deaf individuals. While the uppercase *D* is often used to refer to members of the Deaf community, our point here is to encourage the adoption of a diversity perspective when evaluating language use in a population, across a wide span of linguistic and cultural contexts, which include individuals who may or may not identify with the Deaf community but may use sign language regularly in their lives.

Keywords

ASL prevalence; deaf culture; demographics of deafness; linguistic diversity

See Also

Chapter 12; Chapter 14; Chapter 15; Chapter 17

Suggested Readings

Alderson, P., and Morrow, V. (2004). *Ethics, social research and consulting with children and young people.* Ilford, United Kingdom: Barnado's.
Andrews, J. F., Leigh, I. W., and Weiner, M. T. (2004). *Deaf people: Evolving perspectives from psychology, education, and sociology.* New York: Allyn & Bacon.
Burch, S. (2000). In a different voice: Sign language preservation and America's Deaf Community. *Bilingual Research Journal: The Journal of the National Association for Bilingual Education* 24(4), 443–464.
Harmon, K., and Nelson, J. L. (2012). *Deaf American prose, 1980–2010* (Gallaudet Deaf Literature Series 1). Washington, DC: Gallaudet University Press.

References

A. G. Bell Academy for Listening and Spoken Language (2012, August 31). Auditory verbal therapy. Accessed September 20, 2014. http://listeningandspokenlanguage.org/AcademyDocument.aspx?id=802
Allen, T., and Anderson, M. (2010). Deaf students and their classroom communication: An evaluation of higher order categorical interactions among school and background characteristics. *Journal of Deaf Studies and Deaf Education* 15(4), 334–347.
Allen, T., Clark, D., del Giudice, A., Koo, D., Lieberman, A., Mayberry, R., and Miller, P. (2009). Phonology and reading: A response to Wang, Trezek, Luckner, and Paul. *American Annals of the Deaf* 154(4), 338–345.
Armstrong, D. F., Karchmer, M. A., and Van Cleve, J. V. (Eds.) (2002). *The study of signed languages: Essays in honor of William C. Stokoe.* Washington, DC: Gallaudet University Press.
Arnold, R. (2012, August 31). Introduction to si5s (Video). Accessed August 29, 2014. http://www.si5s.org/videos
Auditory–Verbal Communication Center (2013, August 7). *Auditory verbal therapy.* Accessed August 30, 2014. http://www.avcclisten.com/avt.html
Chamberlain, C., Morford, J. P., and Mayberry, R. I. (Eds.) (2000). *Language acquisition by eye.* Mahwah, NJ: Laurence Erlbaum.

Emmorey, K., and Lane, H. L. (Eds.) (2000). *The signs of language revisited: An anthology to honor Ursula Belluigi and Edward Klima*. Mahwah, NJ: Laurence Erlbaum.

Friedner, M. (2010). Biopower, biosociality, and community formation: How biopower is constitutive of the deaf community. *Sign Language Studies* 10(3), 336–347.

Gallaudet Research Institute (2008). *Regional and national summary report of data from the 2007–2008 Annual survey of deaf and hard of hearing children and youth*. Washington, DC: GRI, Gallaudet University.

Holt, J., Hotto, S., and Cole, K. (1994). *Demographic aspects of hearing impairment: Questions and answers*. Washington, DC: Gallaudet Research Institute.

Johnston, T. (2004). W(h)ither the deaf community? Population, genetics, and the future of Australian sign language. *American Annals of the Deaf* 148(5), 358–375.

Kawa, S., and Giordano, J. (2012). A brief historicity of the *Diagnostic and statistical manual of mental disorders*: Issues and implications for the future of psychiatric canon and practice. *Philosophy, Ethics, and Humanities in Medicine* 7(2). doi: 10.1186/1747-5341-7.

Ladd, P. (2003). *Understanding Deaf culture: In search of deafhood*. Tonowanda, NY: Multilingual Matters.

Lane, H. (1993). *The mask of benevolence: Disabling the deaf community*. New York: Vintage Books.

Lieberman, A., Hatrak, M., and Mayberry, R. (2011). The development of eye gaze control for linguistic input in deaf children. In N. Danis, K. Mesh, and H. Sung (Eds.), *Proceedings of the 35th Boston University conference on language development*. Somerville, MA: Cascadilla Press, pp. 391–403.

Liddell, S. K. (2003). *Grammar, gesture, and meaning in American Sign Language*. New York: Cambrisdge University Press.

Mayberry, R., del Guidice, A., and Lieberman, A. (2011). Reading achievement in relation to phonological coding and awareness in deaf readers: A meta-analysis. *Journal of Deaf Studies and Deaf Education* 16(2), 164–188.

Mayberry, R., Chen, J. Witcher, P., and Klein, D. (2011). Age of acquisition effects on the functional organization of language in the adult brain. *Brain and Language* 10(1), 16–29.

Mitchiner, J., Nussbaum, D., and Scott, S. (2012, June). *The Implications of Bimodal Bilingual Approaches for Children with Cochlear Implants* (Research brief No. 6). Washington, DC: Gallaudet University Visual Language and Visual Learning Science of Learning Center.

Mitchell, R. E. (2004). National profile of deaf and hard of hearing students in special education from weighted survey results. *American Annals of the Deaf* 149(4), 336–349.

Mitchell, R. E. (2005). How many deaf people are there in the United States? Estimates from the Survey of Income and Program Participation. *Journal of Deaf Studies and Deaf Education* 11(1), 112–119.

Mitchell, R. E., and Karchmer, M. A. (2004). Chasing the mythical ten percent: Parental hearing status of deaf and hard of hearing students in the United States. *Sign Language Studies* 4(2), 138–162.

Mitchell, R. E., Young, T., Bachleda, B., and Karchmer, M. (2006). How many people use ASL in the United States? Why estimates need updating. *Sign Language Studies* 6(3), 306–335.

Morere, D., and Allen, T. (2012). *Assessing literacy in deaf individuals: Neurocognitive measurement and predictors*. New York: Springer.

National Center for Health Statistics (1963, August). Origin, program, and operation of the US National Health Survey (National Center for Health Statistics, PHS Publication No. 1000, Series 1, No. 1; reprinted April 1965). Vital and Health Statistics, Series 1(1).

Padden, C., and Humphries, T. (1988). *Deaf in America: Voices from a culture*. Cambridge, MA: Harvard University Press.

Padden, C., and Humphries, T. (2006). *Inside Deaf Culture*. Cambridge, MA: Harvard University Press.

Petitto, L. (2000). On the biological foundations of human language. In K. Emmorey and H. Lane (Eds.), *The signs of language revisited: An anthology in honor of Ursula Bellugi and Edward Klima*. Mahway, NJ: Lawrence Erlbaum, pp. 447–471.

Prinz, P., and Strong, M. (1998). ASL proficiency and English literacy within a bilingual deaf education model of instruction. *Topics in Language Disorders* 18(4), 47–60.

Rawlings, B., and Gentile, A. (1970). Additional handicapping conditions, age at onset of hearing loss, and other characteristics of hearing impaired students, United States, 1968–1969: Data from the Annual Survey of Hearing Impaired Children and Youth (Series D, No. 3). Washington, DC: Gallaudet College, Office of Demographic Studies.

Schein, J. D., and Delk, M. T., Jr. (1974). *The deaf population of the United States*. Silver Spring. MD: National Association of the Deaf.

Singleton, J., and Crume, P. (2010, July). Socializing visual engagement in early childhood deaf education. Poster presented at the 21st International Congress on the Education of the Deaf, Vancouver, British Columbia, Canada.

Spencer, P., and Marschark, M. (2010). *Evidence-based practice in educating deaf and hard-of-hearing srudents*. New York: Oxford University Press.

Stedt, J. D., and Moores, D. F. (1990). Manual codes on English and American Sign Language: Historical perspectives and current realities. In H. Bornstein (Ed.), *Manual communication: Implications for education*. Washington, DC: Gallaudet University Press.

Stokoe, W. C. (1960). Sign language structure: An outline of the visual communication systems of the American deaf. *Studies in Linguistics* (Occasional Paper No. 8). Buffalo, NY: University of Buffalo.

Sutton, V. (2002). *Lessons in sign writing* (3rd ed.). La Jolla, CA: The Deaf Action Committee for Sign Writing.

US Department of Health, Education, and Welfare (1964). Education of the deaf: A report to the secretary of Health, Education, and Welfare by his Advisory Committee on the Education of the Deaf. Washington, DC: Author.

Valli, C., and Lucas, C. (2001). *Linguistics of American Sign Language: An introduction* (3rd ed.). Washington, DC: Gallaudet University Press.

Woodward, J., and Allen, T. (1986). Two analyses of the ASL to English Continuum. In S. DeLancey and R. Tomlin (Eds.), *Proceedings of the second annual meeting of the Pacific linguistics conference*. Eugene, OR: University of Oregon, Department of Linguistics, pp. 481–488.

Woodward, J., Allen, T., and Schildroth, A. (1985). Teachers and deaf students: An ethnography of classroom communication. In S. DeLancey and R. Tomlin (Eds.), *Proceedings of the first annual meeting of the Pacific linguistics conference*. Eugene, OR: University of Oregon, Department of Linguistics, pp. 479–491.

Yoshinaga-Itano, C. (2006). Early identification, communication modality, and the development of speech and spoken language skills: Patterns and considerations. In P. E. Spencer and M. Marschark (Eds.), *Advances in the spoken language development of deaf and hard-of-hearing children*. New York: Oxford University Press, pp. 298–327.

Yoshinaga-Itano, C., Sedey, A., Coulter, D., and Mehl, A. (1998). Language of early- and later-identified children with hearing loss. *Pediatrics* 102(5), 1161–1171.

Young, A. M. (1997). Conceptualizing parents' sign language use in bilingual early intervention. *Journal of Deaf Studies and Deaf Education* 2(4), 264–276.

3   Dissemination and Transfer of Knowledge to the Deaf Community

Robert Adam

Chapter Overview

There is currently a great emphasis on knowledge transfer during the research process. While in the past this has been an additional element for researchers to consider, presently it is a central component of any successful research team's work. In the context of carrying out research into sign language, this transfer involves disseminating the findings of the research in a timely, accessible, and appropriate way to the Deaf[1] community. The ultimate aim of knowledge transfer is to appropriately inform and in the long term empower the Deaf community. This chapter discusses the origins of linguistic and cultural research into the Deaf community as a research population (over the years, this has been the subject of research undertaken by hearing and Deaf researchers who have

Research Methods in Sign Language Studies: A Practical Guide, First Edition.
Edited by Eleni Orfanidou, Bencie Woll, and Gary Morgan.
© 2015 John Wiley & Sons, Inc. Published 2015 by John Wiley & Sons, Inc.

examined the history, culture, anthropology, linguistics, sociolinguistics, and neuroscience of being Deaf). Then it focuses on the examination of the public engagement process as undertaken in British universities, with specific reference to the Deafness Cognition and Language Research Centre (DCAL). Finally this work will be used to make some recommendations concerning information dissemination and the transfer of knowledge to the Deaf community.

Introduction: The Sign Language Community as a Research Population

The genesis of modern sign language research can be traced back to the early investigations in the Netherlands during the 1950s by Bernard Tervoort at the University of Amsterdam, who was looking at how Deaf school children had their own esoteric communication system (Tervoort, 1953). Tervoort concluded with this advice for teachers: "if you want deaf children to learn your language, you first have to learn theirs" (quoted in Knoors, 2007, p. 242). While he tantalizingly refers to "their" language, he was not the first to describe this communication system as sign language; the first to do this was William Stokoe, then a professor of English at Gallaudet College, a liberal arts college for Deaf people in Washington, DC. Stokoe, who is considered a pioneer of sign language research, suggested that Deaf people did not use a poor form of English in their signing; in his view signing was in fact a proper language (Stokoe, 1960). Stokoe's pioneering study was followed by a dictionary compiled by him and colleagues (Stokoe, Casterline, and Croneberg, 1965), which included a form of sociolinguistic description of the Deaf community of the United States. This was the impetus for early research into American Sign Language (ASL), which thus led to the early neuroscientific analyses of sign language by Klima and Bellugi (1979) and the first sociolinguistic discussions of the sign languages of Deaf people in the USA by James Woodward (1973).

Sign language research commenced in the United Kingdom in the early 1970s, and the name "British Sign Language" (BSL) made its first appearance during this period (Brennan, 1975); it was followed by early publications by researchers at the University of Bristol (Woll, Kyle, and Deuchar, 1981) and by the first book on BSL (Deuchar, 1984). The first sociolinguistic discussion of the Deaf community in the UK appeared in 1981 (Woll et al., 1981). The first dictionary of BSL was published in 1992 (Brien, 1992), although this research was not replicated all around the world.

It is important to recognize that research on Deaf people as a cultural minority only began in earnest once it was established that they were actually a language community. In terms of knowledge transfer, most of these early insights were useful for the academic community; but the questions raised by this research, while being scientific, inevitably had social implications for the lives of Deaf people. For example, once it was established that ASL was a real language, it became important that interpreters for Deaf people be appropriately trained – just like any other language interpreters. Lou Fant, a well-known American actor and interpreter, did not realize that ASL was a true language until he first met two American academics, Edward Klima and Ursula Bellugi, who referred to Stokoe's early work and assured him that ASL was a full-blown language (Fant, 2000). However, this was some time before research findings on sign language were translated into sign language, for the Deaf community to use them in their own political and professional lives.

While research on aspects of Deaf culture has appeared in various articles, book chapters, and dictionary introductions, the first book devoted to Deaf culture in the USA was published by Carol Padden and Tom Humphries (1988) and in the UK by Paddy Ladd (2003), all of whom are Deaf people. These books have been followed by knowledge transfer activities at community, college, and university level through courses and workshops in Deaf culture. Further investigation of Deaf culture has not been highly prioritized over the years, and research into the linguistics of sign language has always been better resourced than the research into cultural aspects of being a member of this language community. Hence research methodology relating to Deaf people has tended to focus on sign language data, as opposed to social and cultural data. Yet cultural research yields an important part of our understanding of sign language and of the people who use this form of communication.

It can be said that this body of research into the language and culture of Deaf people has led to a better understanding of them as a linguistic minority, and this in turn has caused an improvement in the quality of their life. The recognition of BSL by the British government in 2003, for example, stimulated increased funding for specific sign language initiatives, although full legal recognition has not yet been achieved and there is more work still to be done in this area. In Australia, the publication of the first Auslan dictionary (Johnston, 1987) was followed by the mentioning of Auslan in the National Policy on Languages (Dawkins, 1991). Other organizations, such as the World Federation of the Deaf, have over the years relied on this academic body of research to substantiate their policies and position papers (visit its web site at www.wfdeaf.org).

It is important to recognize that research on Deaf culture and sign language would not have been possible without the participation of Deaf people as a linguistic group. This is why knowledge transfer activities as part of the research process become very important. Sign language research depends on collaboration with Deaf people and Deaf organizations around the world. If researchers want the Deaf community to engage positively with their research, Deaf people need to understand what the research is about and what its benefits for their community are. Yet public engagement and research dissemination are not always factored into research projects, and this is so for a number of reasons. In the past, sign language researchers have often been hearing people who are for most part from outside the Deaf community. Consequently data have been collected by various means, conclusions drawn by hearing and Deaf researchers, and findings published in books and journals or presented at academic conferences. These published books, book chapters, and journal articles are all in a written language and the presentations and lectures are mostly in a spoken language – and not in the first language of Deaf people.

The situation relating to the accessibility of academic publications for Deaf people is changing. One of the earlier books on the linguistics of BSL included a CD-ROM with a BSL version of the book signed by Deaf people (Sutton-Spence and Woll, 1999), and a more recently published dissertation by a Deaf PhD student on the citizenship of Deaf people included a translation on a DVD (Emery, 2011). These are more the exception than the rule. Other canonical publications on sign language and Deaf culture still do not have an equivalent translation or a version in sign language, either in print or on the Internet. Sign language researchers, both Deaf and hearing, have from time to time been invited to local, national, and international conferences of Deaf people to present their research, and this has been a form of public engagement; however these invitations have usually been the initiative of the conference organizers as opposed to being an objective of the research project. Consequently, as a research population, Deaf people have largely not had access to research and research findings in their own language.

Another important consideration is that Deaf people do not know as much about their sign language as hearing people know about their spoken language: sign language is not studied as a language in schools, and there are very few places in the UK where it can be studied as part of a university degree. Deaf people do not always understand the nature of their language and how being Deaf can influence their experience. They do not have equal access to society, because not everyone can sign and interpreters are not readily available. To repeat: in the past, research on Deaf people and sign language has often not been made accessible for Deaf people. Here is where knowledge transfer comes in.

The Public Engagement Process

Public engagement has become more relevant in recent years as research funders became more aware and more concerned about how researchers and the public interact with each other. Brown (2011) quotes Alan Leshner, the chief executive officer (CEO) of the American Association for the Advancement of Science, as saying:

> simply trying to educate the public about specific science-based issues is not working. We need to move beyond what too often has been seen as a paternalistic stance. We need to engage the public in a more open and honest bidirectional dialogue about science and technology.

Hence, in the UK and USA, there have been moves to enhance the public engagement process between research and science on the one hand and the wider community on the other.

The Research Councils UK (2011) defines public engagement as "any activity that engages the public with research, from science communication in science festivals, to consultation, to public dialogue." Rowe and Frewer (2005) discuss some of the terminology used in the "public participation" process by listing three key concepts which can be seen in Figure 3.1: public communication, public consultation, and public participation; these are distinguished by differences in how information flows between the "exercise sponsors" and the "participants." Rowe and Frewer's typology

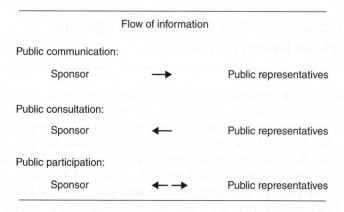

Flow of information

Public communication:

Sponsor →
Public representatives

Public consultation:

Sponsor ←
Public representatives

Public participation:

Sponsor ← →
Public representatives

Figure 3.1 The three types of public engagement. Source: Rowe and Frewer, 2005, p. 255.

has four communication, six consultation, and four participation mechanism classes. The authors discuss the great vagueness in defining the terminology related to public involvement and public engagement, as well as the mechanisms of this participation process. Because of differences in how information flows between the "sponsors" of the process and the "public representatives," public participation is generally defined as having three concepts of "engagement."

"Public communication" is characterized by an information flow from the sponsors to the public; "public consultation" is characterized by a flow from public representatives to the sponsor; and in "public participation" information is exchanged as part of a dialogue, usually in groups of participants.

Public engagement, on the other hand, can take a variety of forms – Rowe and Frewer refer to almost a hundred different forms (including question-and-answer sessions, task forces, workshops, and action planning) and discuss the possible vagueness of and overlaps between the different terms used. Within the typology, the different forms of communication engagement include cable TV, drop-in centers, hotlines, information broadcasts, the Internet, public hearings, and public meetings with question-and-answer sessions. Consultation engagement includes citizens' panels, consultation documents, electronic consultation, focus groups, open spaces, opinion polls, referenda, study circles, surveys, and telepolling. Participation engagement includes action-planning workshops, citizens' juries, consensus conferences, deliberative opinion polls, negotiated rulemaking, planning cells, task forces, and town meetings with voting.

Each of these mechanisms differs from the others in terms of whether the selection of participants is controlled or uncontrolled, whether facilitation includes elicitation of responses, whether responses are open or closed, whether the information input is set or flexible, whether the process is face to face or not, and whether the whole process is structured or unstructured. Rowe and Frewer conclude that public engagement takes different forms and is enacted through different mechanisms and that this proposed typology should enable further development and elaboration and more extensive discussion.

Researchers working with the Deaf community could therefore engage with their research population – Deaf people – by using various means; and there are many opportunities for them to do this.

Public Engagement at the Deafness Cognition and Language Research Centre

A number of research institutions around the world undertake research into various aspects of Deaf people's lives. Such are the Visual Language and Visual Learning (VL2)—a science of learning center (SLC) on visual language and visual learning funded by the National Science Foundation and hosted by Gallaudet University—and the International Institute for Sign Languages and Deaf Studies (iSLanDS) based at the University of Central Lancashire, UK. Other universities – such as the University of Hamburg, the Chinese University of Hong Kong, the Centre for Deaf Studies at Bristol, and the University of the Witwatersrand in South Africa – have centers that undertake academic teaching and research in this field. Here I will use the Deafness Cognition and Language Research Centre (DCAL) as a model of good practice for knowledge transfer: this is a multidisciplinary research centre based at University College, London and is funded by the Economic and Social Research Council, the British government's research funding organization (Adam, 2009). DCAL opened in 2006 with a first tranche of funding for five years and was awarded its second five-year funding in 2011; this will take it to the end of 2015. According to its web site, DCAL brings together researchers from different areas, including sign linguistics, psychology, and neuroscience (visit www.ucl.ac.uk/dcal). This is the largest research centre of its type in Europe, and its researchers are both hearing and Deaf.

The DCAL web site explains what distinguishes its work: the vast majority of research studies on language and thought are based on languages that are spoken and heard, whereas DCAL's research provides a unique perspective on language and thought on the basis of Deaf people's communication; hence also its great need to engage with the Deaf community. DCAL places sign languages and Deaf people at the center of the general understanding of how language and communication work within linguistics, psychology, and child development. Deafness offers an important model for exploring questions in linguistics, cognitive sciences, and neuroscience. This is now much more widely recognized, thanks in large part to DCAL's research efforts over the past five years.

Three years of research and publication were followed by the decision to initiate a public engagement program and to disseminate information to the Deaf community. After publishing research updates in the *British Deaf News* (Adam, Orfanidou, McQueen, and Morgan, 2007; Stone, Adam, and Carty, 2008) and in the *World Federation of the Deaf News* (Adam, 2009), DCAL decided to host workshops to be attended by members of the Deaf community and other interested people. A Deaf Open Day was thus held at UCL on March 20, 2010, with presentations in BSL from Deaf and hearing researchers and with hands-on interactive sessions and posters in the foyer outside the lecture theater. Researchers reported back to members of the Deaf community on research undertaken at DCAL; and this was done for the first time in BSL, the language of the Deaf community. The Deaf Open Day was also supported by Beacons for Public Engagement program, an initiative funded by the UK funding councils, Research Councils UK, the Wellcome Trust, and the Economic and Social Research Council (ESRC) Festival of Social Sciences.

The presentations, the hands-on interactive sessions, and the posters illustrated a range of disciplines at DCAL, particularly neuroscience, psycholinguistics, sociolinguistics, and sign language interpreting. The presentations were well received, and the hands-on activities were a great success; people queued up for an opportunity to have a try. The posters were modified so as to be accessible to the general Deaf audience. The interactive activities included a fingerspelling game where Deaf people were challenged to a high-speed set of fingerspelled words – which was most popular.

Presentations highlighted a number findings that, until then, had not been formally disseminated to the Deaf community in BSL:

- In a study of the Deaf brain, it was found that the same classical language processing regions in the brain were activated in sign language as in spoken language, particularly the Broca's and Wernicke's regions. This is neuroscientific evidence that sign languages are processed in a similar way to spoken languages (MacSweeney, Waters, Brammer, Woll, and Goswami, 2008).
- Deaf people are unique in that the visual processing areas of the brain are also activated when watching sign language and the mouthing of words that occurs with sign language (MacSweeney, Capek, Campbell, and Woll, 2008).
- The same area of the brain that is used for reading is also used when watching fingerspelling. This has significant implications for teaching Deaf children reading through fingerspelling (Waters et al., 2007).
- In Deaf people the auditory cortex is still activated when sign language is used (Capek et al., 2008).
- A study of how Deaf people segment signs while watching a constant stream that contains both real signs and nonsense signs found that they made, in their sign language, phonological errors similar to those made by hearing people when listening to real words and nonsense words (Orfanidou, Adam, McQueen, and Morgan, 2009).
- Another study found that Deaf children do have a specific language impairment; this is a significant finding in that it highlights the need for parents and teachers to understand the needs of these children. This impairment may manifest itself in sign production (the ability to produce sign language) or in sign comprehension (Mason et al., 2010).
- Deaf people act as translators or language brokers within the community (Adam, Carty, and Stone, 2011).
- An update on the British Sign Language Corpus project, a three-year corpus project funded by the ESRC (www.bslcorpusproject.org), included information about dialect change in the British deaf community (Stamp et al., 2014).

The Deaf Open Day ended with a cultural event where two Deaf poets performed and three short films made by emerging Deaf directors were screened: a relaxed ending to a very detailed and informative workshop. With such events, researchers could ensure that public engagement activities are not only informative in terms of the research being disseminated but also educationally fun and culturally appropriate.

There was also a video booth where it was possible to give evaluations in BSL. The feedback was overwhelmingly positive, with minor comments relating to the lack of afternoon tea. Many participants also asked when it would be possible to have another such day. A total of 175 individual enquiries were logged, although just over

100 people attended; it can be said that, through this activity, the DCAL was able to reach a wider cross-section of the community for the first time. This public engagement activity can be said to have been conducted face to face, in a structured form, although it had open participation (as opposed to controlled participation), with a question-and-answer session at the end. However, this public engagement process was not restricted to one single research project; it was conducted separately from the funding objectives of the various projects that featured in the DCAL Deaf Day.

After the Open Day in London, it was decided to take this event out of the capital, to Deaf people in other areas of the UK. Funds were then obtained from the UCL Beacons for Public Engagement to organize a roadshow and visit six other cities in Britain and to add pages to the DCAL web site where Deaf people would be able to find out more, in BSL, about research at DCAL. The following cities were visited as a part of this initiative: Birmingham (March 19, 2011), Glasgow (April 9, 2011), Newcastle (May 7, 2011), Manchester (May 28, 2011) and Belfast (September 3, 2011). A deliberate decision was made to hold each of these events in the local Deaf club, to encourage as many Deaf people to attend as possible. People are less likely to attend a workshop in an unfamiliar location. The fact that these events were held outside London is in itself an acknowledgement that Deaf communities exist in both metropolitan and regional cities and that public engagement should not be confined to major cities.

At each roadshow, three to four DCAL researchers presented their work on topics such as language acquisition, the Deaf brain (MacSweeney, Capek, et al., 2008), Deaf interpreters (Adam et al., 2011), Deaf people and autism, Deaf people and dementia, the sign segmentation project (Orfanidou, Adam, Morgan, and McQueen, 2010), and the BSL Corpus project (Stamp et al., 2014). Deaf people have been very interested to come and learn about our research at DCAL.

Feedback was, again, positive. Participants were given feedback forms to complete that had the following questions:

1   What did you find the most useful about the day?
2   What did you find the least useful about the day?
3   Is there anything we could have done better?
4   Was the use of academic language easy to understand?
5   How did you hear about the DCAL Deaf Roadshow?
6   How would you like to hear about our research in future (newsletter, another open day, etc.)?

Quotations from the feedback include:

> *Having access to the research that is being carried out at DCAL firsthand!* (Belfast)
> *All the presentations were useful and interesting.* (Bristol)
> *Keep up the fantastic work!* (Glasgow)
> *Yes, very (much) looking forward to the next one!* (Glasgow)
> *The statistics and proof are very important, and it was very interesting.* (Birmingham)

The 10th-year anniversary of the recognition of BSL was seen as another opportunity for DCAL to pass on research findings to the Deaf community for political lobbying outcomes, with the aim of further enhancing the standard of life for Deaf people in general. Organized in partnership with the British Deaf Association, this event was called "BSL Recognition: The Way Ahead" (British Deaf Association, 2013). Speakers included Robert Adam, a doctoral researcher into bilingualism, Paddy Ladd, an anthropologist who proposed the Deafhood framework, Maartje De Meulder, a PhD student from the University of Jyväskylä, Finland, and two representatives of the British Deaf Association – David Buxton, the chief executive and Terry Riley, the chair. This event was attended by 99 people and was streamed live over the Internet and continually watched by 187 people (with 1,333 hits over the duration of the event).

The DCAL presentation by Robert Adam covered a range of research aimed at empowering Deaf people, which covered historical, linguistic, neuroscientific, psycholinguistic, and genetic aspects of being Deaf. Maartje De Meulder spoke on language policy and legislation in the UK and Europe, and Paddy Ladd spoke on the Deafhood concept and how it related to minority linguistic rights and cultural rights (as opposed to rights under national and international disability legislation). David Buxton and Terry Riley spoke at length about how the British Deaf Association planned to represent the linguistic human rights of Deaf people.

This public engagement session was unique in that it was not originally proposed or written into a research funding proposal but sought to collate currently available research relating to Deaf people and their linguistic and cultural rights and to present this information in BSL; so it could perhaps be said that this exercise was based on previous public engagement efforts and was aimed at engaging Deaf people not on a research project, but on a very specific aspect of their everyday lives: their linguistic human rights. It can also be said that this activity prepared this group of Deaf people by equipping them with current knowledge and making them ready for any future public engagement activity specifically related to a research project. As a consequence, the British Deaf Association established a Legal Status of British Sign Language working group, which will report back to another public engagement seminar to be held on March 18, 2014 – one year on from the 10th-year anniversary event. This illustrates the importance of the relationship between research and community lobbying; the seminar in 2013 led to the formation of this working group. Similarly, the publication of the *Dictionary of British Sign Language* (Brien, 1992) led to an enhanced status of BSL and its recognition by the British government in 2003. Without such research evidence to show that BSL exists as a full language, it would not have been possible to lobby for this recognition.

Another possible area of empowering Deaf people is work with Deaf children in schools. There is no reason why this information should not be available to school-age children, especially as other hearing children have access to new developments in their own language. This has a very positive, long-term empowering potential.

In summary, there are a number of ways in which a researcher (whether Deaf or hearing) can engage with the Deaf community. The engagement can be either formal or informal, but it is essential for researchers to become involved with the Deaf community at a social level, to get involved in its events, and to familiarize themselves with the local community. One can even start by subscribing to the local or national Deaf community newsletter. The researcher should also learn the language of this community. Public engagement can take many different forms, as long as it is a two-way process and is factored into research programmes. Only then will it be possible for researchers to engage effectively and ethically with the Deaf community and undertake research that will be of scientific interest and will at the same time benefit a disadvantaged group in society.

Conclusion

Research-funding councils are increasingly interested in the impact factor of research undertaken by sign language researchers and in funding research projects that outline public engagement with the research population. Not only should conference presentations be factored into funding applications; public engagement and information dissemination should be included as a matter of course into every project dedicated to the development of a research question, planning a research project, outlining data collection from Deaf people, and reporting back to the Deaf community. To not consider doing this is often seen by Deaf people as opportunistic and deeply unethical, and such practices should be discontinued where they existed in the past. This is also a challenge, as many sign language researchers who are hearing cannot sign and are not able to engage with Deaf people. Parallels can be drawn with cases of feminist research (Sanger, 2003) where the researcher benefits personally from undertaking research into a disadvantaged group whose members do not necessarily find their situation improved. It is hoped that, with an increased awareness of the need for scientists and researchers to take part in public engagement processes, the Deaf community and the general public will have, in the long term, greater involvement with scientific research. Given the bidirectional process of the public engagement process, the Deaf community will be able to have a greater stake in research, and researchers, Deaf or hearing ones alike, will have a greater awareness of what is high on the agenda for Deaf people, be that a social, cultural, political, or linguistic agenda.

Acknowledgments

The support of the Economic and Social Research Council (ESRC) is gratefully acknowledged: Robert Adam was supported by the ESRC Deafness Cognition and Language Research Centre (DCAL) Grant RES-620-28-0002.

Note

1   When capitalized, the word *Deaf* refers to the social and cultural aspects of membership of a language community. Simple *deaf* refers to the medical and pathological aspects of deafness.

Keywords

Deaf community; knowledge transfer; public engagement; public communication; public consultation; sign language

See Also

Chapter 1; Chapter 2

Suggested Readings

Maile, S., and Griffiths, D. (2014). *Public engagement and social science*. Bristol: Policy Press.
National Co-ordinating Centre for Public Engagement (2014). Web site. Accessed September 2, 2014. https://www.publicengagement.ac.uk

References

Adam, R. (2009). DCAL Research Centre. *WFD News* (July), 14–15.

Adam, R., Carty, B., and Stone, C. (2011). Ghost writing: Deaf translators within the Deaf community. *Babel* 57(3), 375–393. doi: 10.1075/babel.57.4.01ada

Adam, R., Orfanidou, E., McQueen, J. M., and Morgan, G. (2007). The sign segmentation project at city university. *Sign Matters* (November), 16–17.

Brennan, M. (1975). Can Deaf children acquire language? *American Annals of the Deaf* 120(5), 463–479.

Brien, D. (1992). *Dictionary of British sign language/English*. Boston: Faber & Faber.

British Deaf Association. (2013). BSL recognition: The way ahead. Accessed June 5, 2013. http://www.bda.org.uk/News/115

Brown, P. (2011). Public engagement with science: What it means. Accessed February 24, 2014. http://www.scilogs.com/from_the_lab_bench/public-engagement-with-science-what-it-means/

Capek, C. M., Waters, D., Woll, B., MacSweeney, M., Brammer, M. J., McGuire, P. K., David, A. S., and Campbell, R. (2008). Hand and mouth: Cortical correlates of lexical processing in British sign language and speechreading English. *Journal of Cognitive Neuroscience* 20(7), 1220–1234.

Dawkins, J. (1991). Australia's language: The Australian language and literacy policy. Canberra: Australian Government Publishing Service.

Deuchar, M. (1984). *British sign language*. London: Routledge & Kegan Paul.

Emery, S. (2011). *Citizenship and the Deaf community*. Nijmegen: Ishara Press.

Fant, L. (2000). Two memorable meals with Ursula and Ed. In K. Emmorey and H. Lane (Eds.), *The signs of language revisited: An anthology to honor Ursula Bellugi and Edward Klima*. Mahwah, NJ: Lawrence Erlbaum, pp. 3–4.

Johnston, T. (1987). *Auslan dictionary: A dictionary of the sign language of the Australian deaf community*. Sydney: Deafness Resources Australia.

Klima, E., and Bellugi, U. (1979). *The signs of language*. Cambridge, MA: Harvard University Press.

Knoors, H. (2007). Obituary: Bernard Theodoor Marie Tervoort. *Journal of Deaf Studies and Seaf Education* 12(2), 242.

Ladd, P. (2003). Understanding Deaf culture: In search of deafhood. Clevedon, UK: Multilingual Matters.

MacSweeney, M., Capek, C. M., Campbell, R., and Woll, B. (2008). The signing brain: The neurobiology of sign language. *Trends in Cognitive Sciences* 12(11), 432–440. doi: 10.1016/j.tics.2008.07.010

MacSweeney, M., Waters, D., Brammer, M. J., Woll, B., and Goswami, U. (2008). Phonological processing in deaf signers and the impact of age of first language acquisition. *NeuroImage* 40(3), 1369–1379. doi: 10.1016/j.neuroimage.2007.12.047

Mason, K., Rowley, K., Marshall, C., Atkinson, J., Herman, R., Woll, B., and Morgan, G. (2010). Identifying specific language impairment in deaf children acquiring British sign language: Implications for theory and practice. *British Journal of Developmental Psychology* 28(1), 33–49.

Orfanidou, E., Adam, R., McQueen, J. M., and Morgan, G. (2009). Making sense of nonsense in British sign language (BSL): The contribution of different phonological parameters to sign recognition. *Memory & Cognition* 37(3), 302–315. doi: 10.3758/MC.37.3.302

Orfanidou, E., Adam, R., Morgan, G., and McQueen, J. M. (2010). Recognition of signed and spoken language: Different sensory inputs, the same segmentation procedure. *Journal of Memory and Language* 62(3), 272–283. doi: 10.1016/j.jml.2009.12.001

Padden, C., and Humphries, T. (1988). *Deaf in America: Voices from a culture*. Cambridge, MA: Harvard University Press.

Rowe, G., and Frewer, L. J. (2005). A typology of public engagement mechanisms. *Science, Technology & Human Values* 30(2), 251–290. doi: 10.1177/0162243904271724

Sanger, P. C. (2003). Living and writing feminist ethnographies: Threads in a quilt stitched from the heart. In R. P. Clair (Ed.), *Expressions of ethnography: Novel approaches to qualitative methods*. Albany: State University of New York, pp. 29–44.

Stamp, R., Schembri, A., Fenlon, J., Rentelis, R., Woll, B., & Cormier, K. (2014). Lexical variation and change in British Sign Language. *PLoS ONE* 9(4), e94053. doi: 10.1371/journal.pone.0094053

Stokoe, W. (1960). Sign language structure: An outline of the visual communication systems of the American Deaf. *Studies in Linguistics Occasional Papers* 8, 1–78.

Stokoe, W. C., Casterline, D. C., and Croneberg, C. G. (1965). *A dictionary of American sign languages on linguistic principles*. Washington, DC: Gallaudet College Press.

Stone, C., Adam, R., and Carty, B. (2008). Deaf translators from within the Deaf community. *British Deaf News* (June), 16–17.

Sutton-Spence, R., and Woll, B. (1999). *The linguistics of British sign language: An introduction*. Cambridge: Cambridge University Press.

Tervoort, B. (1953). *Structurele analyse van visueel taalgebruik binnen een groep dove kinderen*. Amsterdam: University of Amsterdam.

Research Councils UK (2011). What is public engagement? Accessed June 5, 2013. http://www.rcuk.ac.uk/documents/scisoc/peupdate.pdf

Waters, D., Campbell, R., Capek, C. M., Woll, B., David, A. S., McGuire, P. K., Brammer, M. J., & MacSweeney, M. (2007). Fingerspelling, signed language, text and picture processing in deaf native signers: The role of the mid-fusiform gyrus. *NeuroImage* 35, 1287–1302.

Woll, B., Kyle, J., and Deuchar, M. (1981). *Perspectives on British sign language and deafness*. London: Croom Helm.

Woodward, J. (1973). Implicational lects on the deaf diglossic continuum. Unpublished PhD thesis, Georgetown University, Washington, DC.

Part II   Different Ways of Collecting Sign Language Data

4 Collecting and Analyzing Sign Language Data: Video Requirements and Use of Annotation Software

Pamela Perniss

Chapter Overview

This chapter provides researchers with a resource guide to making and managing video recordings of sign language data and to undertaking linguistic annotation with available software. Instead of focusing on technical details, the chapter focuses on how to obtain video data that are good and usable in terms of quality of the recording and appropriate in terms of answering specific research questions. With respect to annotation, the chapter provides guidelines on devising a coding scheme for specific research questions and on setting up a workflow in order to implement the coding scheme in the annotation software for successful and effective use. The chapter is aimed at researchers with a background in linguistics interested in working with sign language video data.

Research Methods in Sign Language Studies: A Practical Guide, First Edition.
Edited by Eleni Orfanidou, Bencie Woll, and Gary Morgan.
© 2015 John Wiley & Sons, Inc. Published 2015 by John Wiley & Sons, Inc.

Introduction

Any researcher interested in answering questions about the linguistic structure and usage patterns of a sign language must obtain and analyze primary language sources, that is, examples of actual sign language use and production. As sign language is produced visually, using the hands, face, and body as articulators, data collection necessarily relies on video recording. Subsequent analysis of the collected material requires transcription and coding of the video stream, a process that has been greatly facilitated in recent years by the development of sophisticated annotation software. This chapter provides the aspiring sign language linguist with a resource guide to making video recordings of sign language and to undertaking linguistic annotation of the data with available tools.

The next section focuses on how to obtain good and usable video data. "Good and usable" is meant here both in terms of the quality of the recording and in terms of getting the kind of data that are appropriate to answering specific research questions about the sign language under consideration. The section does not focus heavily on specific technical aspects of video recording like the specific kind of equipment to use, since the speed of technological development will soon render any details set out here obsolete.

The third section deals with how to develop and implement a workflow for the annotation and coding of video data. Software that allows annotations to be directly linked to and time-aligned with the video stream has been a great boon to working with sign language data. Primary examples are ELAN[1] and Anvil.[2] In addition, software that allows the creation of a lexical database in concert with time-aligned annotation, for example iLEX[3] and LEXUS,[4] is valuable to sign language linguists interested in lexicography and corpus analysis. The exposition in this section turns predominantly around the use of ELAN, the program most familiar to the author. Again, this section does not concentrate on technical details, nor does it go into the details of transcription methods. It offers the researcher guidelines on how to make decisions about what kind of annotation is needed for answering particular research questions and on how to best set up a workflow in order to carry out successful annotation. For ELAN, this will involve the elaboration of a number of key features, as well as some step-by-step instructions for specific things that personal experience has shown to be critical; these instructions will ultimately make annotating and coding sign language data more efficient and more enjoyable. Other annotation software is discussed at the end of this section, where differences between ELAN and other programs are highlighted.

The final section concludes the chapter by delineating its contribution from what has already been published on the topic of sign and spoken language video data collection and analysis. In addition, the conclusion stresses the overall importance of using video data to annotate and research language, in both the signed and spoken modalities, in order to understand the complex multimodal phenomenon of human communication and interaction.

Collecting Sign Language Data

Obtaining good video data of the sign language you wish to study is important for a number of reasons. These pertain, on the one hand, to the technical quality of the video and, on the other hand, to the content of the video and the type of data collected. In order to be able to work with video data as a record of language use, the conditions for filming need to be appropriate and the quality of the image needs to be good. Subsequent to filming, it must be ensured that the video is in a format that is suitable for further management and analysis. However, before actually obtaining the video data, there are important decisions to be made regarding the type of data to be collected. This is in the first instance a matter of deciding what kind of data – say, spontaneous narrative or stimulus-based elicitation – are best suited to answering a specific research question. We deal with this issue first, before moving on to the more technical aspects of data collection.

Type of data to collect

Two main types of language data are distinguished here: naturalistic data and elicited data. Both types are valuable and important in their own right, and both have advantages and disadvantages. Either way, it is important to make careful decisions about the what, the where, and the how of data collection. Data collection is rarely something that can be redone under the same circumstances. For example, if you are dependent on traveling to a specific – and possibly distant – field site, you may not have the time and resources to return to that site again and to interact with the same language users. Moreover, because time will have passed and circumstances changed, it will be impossible – and often scientifically unsound – to collect the same data from the same people for a second time. Particularly with language elicitation, repetition of a task may affect the data in ways that cannot be controlled for. This would not apply, however, to some types of longitudinal studies where the methodology may rely on obtaining data by using the same materials at different points in time. Finally, collecting sign language data of any kind requires good contact with the deaf[5] community and should always be done by and in close collaboration with deaf researchers and members of the deaf community.

Naturalistic data

Naturalistic language data consist in language produced spontaneously and naturally in typical interactional settings and environments. They reflect actual language use that is not influenced by the desires and demands – or even by the presence – of the researcher.

When would it be useful and advantageous to collect naturalistic data? Any research interest focused on understanding interaction and the dynamics of natural conversation must rely on naturalistic data. Examples are studying how turn-taking is managed in dyadic or multi-party conversations (see Coates and Sutton-Spence, 2001), or studying how interlocutors handle sequences of conversational repair – that is, the repair of communication problems that result from errors or misunderstandings (see Enfield et al., 2013). A researcher may also be interested in understanding how language is used in dyadic or multi-party interactions in a particular setting, for example over dinner, at a social event, or in meetings. The conversations occurring in these typical settings can only be captured through naturalistic data collection.

Other areas of research for which the collection of naturalistic data may be encouraged are sign language acquisition (see Baker, van den Bogaerde, and Woll, 2008) and the nature of child-caregiver interactions (see Smith and Sutton-Spence, 2008). Naturalistic data would be recommended, for example, in a longitudinal study of a deaf child acquiring sign language from deaf parents, as they would capture the natural interactions between the child and his/her parents and would track the development of increasingly complex linguistic productions by the child.

Finally, a growing number of sign language researchers is involved in the creation of sign language corpora. As sign languages have no written form, the existence of such corpora is particularly important for providing a store and record of sign language data that are accessible to sign language researchers and to the deaf community. In terms of research, corpora are hugely important for answering questions about the linguistic structure of a language and for understanding patterns of sociolinguistic variation or phenomena of language contact and language change (see Schembri, 2008). Obtaining naturalistic data is crucial to the creation of a sign language corpus. The corpus should include language use that is representative of a particular sign language as it is used by a wide range of signers – of different ages, from different regions, and of different genders.

A comprehensive corpus should also strive to include language use on a range of different topics and spanning different genres (e.g., personal narratives, interviews, descriptions). To achieve this, a researcher may want to introduce a measure of control into the type of data that are obtained. That is, the researcher may provide materials to elicit a certain type of language or may provide certain topics or formats for discussion. We are now getting into the realm of elicited data, the subject of the next section.

Elicited data

A major advantage of collecting elicited data is the control it offers over the type of language captured on video. If you are interested in analyzing a particular domain of language – say, possessive, reciprocal, or locative constructions – there is no guarantee that collecting naturalistic data will provide enough occurrences of the structures and constructions that you are interested in. Having enough occurrences is important for achieving a thorough understanding of the linguistic structure or domain at hand. Moreover, it is necessary for any substantive quantitative analysis.

Stimulus materials designed to elicit a certain kind of language can take different forms. For sign language elicitation, they should be in non-linguistic formats: pictures (e.g., a spatial scene), short video vignettes of single events (e.g., a motion or reciprocal action event), or selected episodes of a cartoon or movie (e.g., the Canary Row cartoon). The use of linguistic formats, like written words or sentences of the surrounding spoken language, runs the risk of structural influence from the spoken language on the sign language data. Elicited picture descriptions, event descriptions, and extended narratives can provide a wealth of valuable data on sign language structure in the targeted domains, for both adult and child language production. The use of a picture description task for eliciting complex verb constructions from children across different age groups in order to study the development of such constructions (Morgan, Herman, and Woll, 2002) is a good example of how an elicitation task may be fruitfully used in sign language acquisition studies.

In general, elicited descriptions and narratives should be produced for a (deaf) addressee, not for the camera or the researcher. This enhances the communicative, discursive nature of the situation and gives more assurance that the elicited material is representative of language use as it would occur in a naturalistic setting. Addressees may also be asked to perform a task, which may further improve the chances of getting the type of language targeted by the elicitation. For example, if the addressee must pick the correct picture out of a set, the signer may be more likely to give a full description of a spatial relationship. Similarly, if the addressee is asked to re-narrate a cartoon event, the signer may be more likely to provide details about the event and to make an effort to produce a coherent, cohesive story. Tasks involving stimulus materials may also be performed collaboratively between two participants. For example, participants can engage in a picture-matching task or in a picture-comparison task; such tasks have been used to elicit possessive and existential constructions across sign languages (Perniss and Zeshan, 2008).

Having comparable data from multiple signers – that is, data elicited using the same materials – is necessary for any serious quantitative and statistical analysis and for assessing whether the data obtained are representative of actual language usage. It addition, it facilitates cross-linguistic comparability, allowing controlled investigation of variation between sign languages in the expression of particular domains. Ideally, an empirical investigation of sign language structure, or the collection of a sign language corpus, should combine both types of data. In any case, as a researcher, you need to make sure that you get the type of data you need for the questions you want to answer. Care must also be taken that the method of data collection does not introduce artifacts into the data – that is, elements that are present as a result of the process of data collection itself. This means creating the best possible situations and settings for data collection. Making decisions about how and where to set up your recording equipment in order to create these optimal conditions is the topic of the next section.

Technical aspects of data collection

Technology is developing fast these days. Hence there is minimal focus here on specific technical details relating to equipment. What is stressed instead in this section is how to collect high-quality archivable data suited to your research purposes. This topic includes selecting the optimal settings and conditions for the filming itself, and ensuring that your data files are properly managed for further use and processing once you have finished filming.

Equipment

Increasingly, the video cameras available on the market are high-definition cam-corders that record directly onto an internal hard drive (HDD), SD memory card, or DVD.[6] These cameras have essentially replaced consumer devices that record onto tapes – that is, DV or HDV cameras; however, the use of tapes remains satisfactory, especially if you already possess such a device.

If and when you purchase equipment – camera(s) and tripod(s) – for collecting sign language data, inform yourself about what is out there and what best meets your demands. You can directly compare prices and specifications of different brands and models at any store that sells digital equipment, or you can do it online. If you work at a university or in a research institute, you may find it useful to consult with the IT staff. Once you have equipment at your disposal, especially if it is new, take time to familiarize yourself with using it and setting it up. Make sure you have enough storage space available for the amount of data you intend to collect. This means having enough space on the drive, disc, or memory card (or having a sufficient number of DV or HDV tapes). If possible, keep your camera plugged in to a power outlet while filming. If this is not possible, make sure you have enough battery power for the intended session of filming. Battery life is optimal with continuous recording, in which episodes of starting, stopping, and zooming are kept to a minimum.

When data have been collected, they must be transferred from the storage device to your computer. If you are recording to tape, the transfer of the digital video to a computer involves real-time capture from the camera and requires a program with which such capture is possible (e.g., Adobe Premiere, WinDV, iMovie, Final Cut Express, Final Cut Pro). The captured video will generally be in a format (MPEG, MOV, or AVI) that can be used in available annotation programs like ELAN or Anvil. Transfer from a drive or memory card is faster and easier by comparison: it requires an SD card slot if the data are stored on a card, or a connector cable (USB or Firewire) if they are stored on a camera-internal drive. However, the compressed format of these data (MTS, M2TS) requires conversion into one of the above for-mats (e.g., with TMPGEnc, ffmpeg, ffmpegX) before other editing and use with annotation programs is possible. For DVD discs, the underlying MPEG compression format can be used in available annotation programs, but the files need to be ripped from the disc to the computer using special software applications (which may be provided by the manufacturer). The use of DVD-RW discs allows the flexibility of re-recording on the same disc.

Settings, conditions, and techniques for filming

Filming may seem an easy thing – turn the camera on, aim, press record – but it is in fact important to be aware of – and follow – guidelines for the optimal settings, conditions, and techniques for filming in order to obtain good sign language data.

The first thing to bear in mind is that the camera should not be treated as a roving extension of your own gaze. Mount the camera on a tripod and keep the camera steady and static. Do not pan and do not zoom. Doing so creates shaky and blurry images that are difficult or impossible to analyze. It also increases the chances of missing valuable interaction – for naturalistic data in particular – and attracts

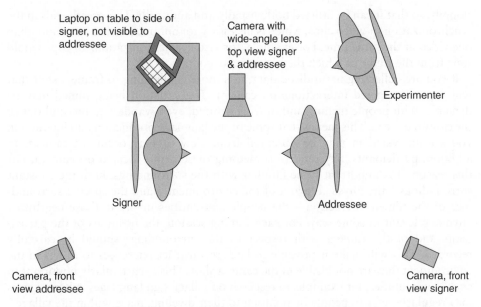

Figure 4.1 Example of camera and participant set up for the collection of elicited data.

unwanted attention to the presence of the camera. For both naturalistic and elicited data, however, getting a steady and static shot is more than simply a matter of setting the camera down.

If you are eliciting data in a controlled setting, you should prepare in advance a protocol that maps out where the video camera(s) will be positioned, where the participants will be seated, and where stimulus materials will be presented (see Figure 4.1). If you have a studio available, which you are using for multiple recording sessions, you may want to mark out the camera and participant positions on the floor, so that equipment and materials may always be placed in exactly the same locations.

Participants should be in good view, with enough space around the body, so that the signer's hands will not leave the frame during the stream of signing. A good rule of thumb is to frame the bottom of the shot at the knees to mid-thigh and to leave a head's worth of space above the head. Signers should be filmed at a slight side angle, not fully from the front, and slightly from above, with the camera angled slightly downward. This will lend better visual depth and distinguishability to the video. If you are using one video camera, frame both the signer and the addressee in the shot as sitting across from each other, turned halfway to the camera, halfway to each other. If you have more than one camera, you may want to focus one on the signer, another on the addressee. Alternatively, if you are interested in the use of non-manual features (e.g., information conveyed on the face), you may want one camera zoomed into the signer's face. If you are interested in the specific locations and movements of signs, getting a top view of the signer(s) is of extreme value. This can be done by placing the tripod and camera onto a table or by mounting the camera on a microphone stand with boom. If you use more than one camera, the use of a cue (e.g., clapping your hands together) that is captured by all cameras is highly recommended to signal the beginning of filming. The cue should be performed deliberately, not sloppily, so that it can be utilized both visually and auditorily. This greatly aids in the synchronization of video clips, which is necessary for annotation that uses more than one video at the same time. For example, for visual synchronization, all clips would start from the frame at which the hands make contact.

If you are collecting naturalistic data, it is more challenging to frame a shot that will capture targeted interactions on camera. The situation being filmed may be dynamic, with people turning and moving around, even wandering into and out of the captured scene. This means that some of the language production and interaction you are interested in may be obscured from view or may occur off camera. In addition, participants may refer to something or someone located off camera. For this reason, it is important to be familiar with the surroundings: both the constant surroundings – the physical layout of the environment – and the specific surroundings of the filmed interaction – the people and entities involved, those nearby, or anyone relevant in some way. For each filming session, the positions of the participants and of the camera with respect to the surroundings should be carefully recorded. This will make it possible to later reconstruct references to things in the environment that are not visible in the camera shot. This is particularly important in small communities, for example, in research on village sign languages, where signers may regularly refer to people by pointing to their dwelling place within the village.

In any data collection scenario, avoid filming against the light – against a window, if you are indoors, or against the sun, if you are outdoors. Filming against the light will result in a silhouetted signer, and details of the hands and face will be veiled in shadow. Always take care that the lighting is good. The face should be well lit and visible, but not overexposed. Finally, do not shy away from the camera's manual settings. In particular, auto-focus and auto-exposure may not be desirable, depending on the degree and nature of the movement and on the lighting conditions during a filming session.

Archiving and accessibility of video data

Another important aspect of dealing with video data is keeping files identifiable, manageable, and accessible over time. It is best to transfer the video to your computer as soon as possible after filming and to name the files immediately upon transfer. (If you are using tapes, you should label and lock the tapes immediately, such that the material cannot be recorded over accidentally.) It is generally useful to further edit the raw data by cutting them into smaller segments that correspond, for example, to the length of individual tasks or of stimuli, or by marking identifiable breaks in longer interactions or events. Shorter segments will alleviate potential problems related to memory and capacity load, making it easier to work with the files during transfer, viewing, and annotation.

It is also important to create metadata (that is, data about the data) for all video recordings as soon as possible. The metadata are crucial for archiving and for the structured accessibility of data; they should include information about the time, date, and place of recording, the content of the recording, and the participants (e.g., age, language background – paying heed to the ethics of data protection).[7] The metadata should be linked to the video they refer to via the label or file name assigned to the video. It is important to use consistent, systematic, and descriptive names that will be recognizable and informative to you later. Make sure that you have at least one back-up of all your data. It is necessary to keep in mind that the data format will need to be updated over time, in order to ensure that the data remain accessible as technological advances make older formats obsolete. Good labeling and metadata practices are crucial in this regard.

Annotating and coding the data is also a part of keeping them accessible and useful for scientific or community purposes (see Thieberger and Berez, 2012). Preserving language data – the recordings themselves, as well as the annotations and descriptions associated with them – is especially important for sign language, which lack records and descriptions of language use and structure (there is no written form of sign languages, and widespread documentation has only recently become possible, through advancements in video technology). The use of software to annotate sign language data is the subject of the next section.

Using Software to Annotate Sign Language Data

Data annotation refers to the process of labeling elements in the language data that you want to describe, analyze, quantify, and so on. These elements can be at any level – phonological, morphological, syntactic, semantic, pragmatic, prosodic, social, interactive, temporal, articulatory – and the annotations identifying and labeling them can be descriptive or analytical in nature. Modern software (e.g., ELAN, Anvil) allows you to time-align and link annotations directly to the corresponding segments of video. Using such software is highly recommended for the annotation of video data, particularly of sign language data. Non-time-aligned annotation, for instance using a spreadsheet or a table, is also possible, of course. However, the advantages of doing time-aligned annotation far outweigh the perceived difficulties of becoming a proficient user of the software. The reliability and functionality of programs is steadily increasing, as developers work in association with researchers to develop the features that will be most useful and functional.[8]

Before you start annotating data, however, you need to have a clear idea about what you want to annotate. The first subsection here focuses on devising an annotation or coding scheme suited to your research question. When you have done this, you can move on to implementing the scheme within the program you are using. As stated in the introduction, the exposition offered here focuses on sign language annotation using ELAN. The second subsection elaborates a workflow in ELAN that will help you work efficiently and effectively with sign language data. The third subsection discusses other annotation software, specifically Anvil and iLex, highlighting similarities with and differences from ELAN.

Devising a coding scheme: Deciding what to annotate

Decisions as to what elements of the data to analyze, and according to what criteria, need to be made in advance of the actual annotation. In effect, this means devising a coding scheme. The annotations you use to transcribe and code your data should allow you to extract all the information you are interested in when you get to the stage of analysis and quantification.

There is a vast multitude of possible research questions. You should approach your data – and indeed data collection itself – with an established idea of what you want to know and what your research aims are. For example, you may be interested in the properties of classifier predicates used to express location and motion; in co-articulation effects in the expression of a single sign in different environments; in the scope and temporal alignment of non-manual markers with the stream of manual signs (see Crasborn, van der Kooij, Waters, Woll, and Mesch, 2008); in how posses-sion is expressed in a particular sign language (see Zeshan and Perniss, 2008); or in the semantic and syntactic behavior of a sign that functions as a perfect marker (see Meir, 1999). Some discussion of how you would approach your data to devise a cod-ing scheme to answer such questions follows.[9]

For example, what would you need to extract from your data if you were inter-ested in the use of classifier predicates? You would want to know which (classifier) handshapes are used for which types of entities. You would want to know where the hands are placed in space in order to encode referent location and how the hands move in space in order to encode referent motion. You may want to know to what extent the use of space is topographic or iconic with respect to the scene or event being described. Your coding scheme should thus include ways to identify and label different handshapes (and the entities to which they refer) and different locations and areas in sign space. You may also want to know about the entire construction in which classifier predicates occur: for example, whether the predicates are preceded by nominal signs, whether they occur in final position in an utterance, or whether and when they occur in simultaneous constructions (see Vermeerbergen, Leeson, and Crasborn, 2007 on simultaneity in sign languages).

Similarly, if you are interested in studying co-articulation effects, you will need to identify all the occurrences of a particular sign or group of signs in your data and describe how articulation is affected in each case by the environment – that is, by the preceding and the following signs. Your coding scheme in this case would concentrate on phonetic and phonological aspects of the data. You would need to label the hand-shape, the place of articulation, and the movement characteristics of each sign occur-rence and compare it to the phonologically specified "target" form of the sign. Similar descriptions of the preceding and the following signs would allow you to analyze the effect of phonological environment on sign articulation and the phonetic variability of individual signs.

Finally, if you are interested in the scope and temporal alignment of non-manual markers with concurrent manual signing, you will need to label the occurrence of all non-manual markers of the kind you have decided to investigate (e.g., brow raise), marking the precise onset and offset (e.g., the moment at which the brows begin to move up and the moment at which they return to neutral position). These onsets and offsets would need to be temporally evaluated with respect to the lexicon and syntax of the manual signing stream. This kind of coding relies crucially on temporal align-ment and on being able to compare the timing of different articulatory channels that simultaneously contribute information to the language signal. Programs like ELAN or Anvil, which allow time-aligned annotation, are indispensable for this kind of coding.

Implementing the coding scheme: Learning how to annotate

After you have decided what elements of the data you want to code and according to what criteria, it is time to implement the coding scheme in the annotation program. This section aims at providing a workflow that will allow researchers interested in annotating sign language data to work effectively with ELAN. The section does not go into detail about the technicalities of the interface or into optimizing the use of functions, for instance the use of keyboard shortcuts. These things can best be learned by practice, by trial and error, and by consulting the user guides and manuals that are available for download.[10]

The defining feature of ELAN in terms of the annotation framework it provides is the simultaneous display of multiple tiers on a timeline that is linked to one or more language data video files (see Figure 4.2). All tiers are user-defined and reflect your specific annotation needs.[11]

Tiers are associated with various attributes – linguistic type, stereotype, controlled vocabulary, and parent – which define the constraints that apply to each tier and its annotations. For example, it is possible to create dependencies between tiers (that is, by assigning parent tiers and by defining dependency stereotypes). In addition, tiers can be assigned a fixed set of annotation values (that is, by creating controlled vocabularies associated with linguistic types). Understanding how tier attributes are related to each other and defining their values in an order that reflects their interrelationships is important to making ELAN work for you. Table 4.1 lists the tier attributes specified for each tier shown in the ELAN screen shot in Figure 4.2. Below, the tier

Figure 4.2 Screen shot of ELAN, showing multiple, simultaneously coded annotation tiers.

Table 4.1   Example of table listing tier names and tier attributes.

Tier name	Parent tier	Linguistic Type	Stereotype	Controlled Vocabulary
Stimulus	none	Stimulus	none	none
Gloss	Stimulus	Sign gloss	Include In	none
Localization type	Gloss	Loc type	Symb. Assoc.	Loc type
Referent	Gloss	Referent	Symb. Assoc.	none
Numeral	Stimulus	Numeral	Symb. Assoc.	Yes/no
Quantifier	Stimulus	Quantifier	Symb. Assoc.	Yes/no
Localization	Stimulus	Localization	Symb. Assoc.	Yes/no

attributes are defined and explained with reference to the example in Table 4.1, and this is followed by a description of how to create tiers and specify their attributes in ELAN. It is advisable to make a table of tier names and attributes (as the one in Table 4.1) before actually creating tiers in ELAN itself.

The tier name should identify the information being annotated. (A tier's linguistic type, which is specified together with the tier's name, can be similarly descriptive; we return to the linguistic type further below.) In our example the stimulus tier identifies the stimulus item (a picture of two boats) that has elicited the stretch of signing marked out by the annotation (i.e., the utterance comprising the description of the stimulus picture). We can see in Table 4.1 that the stimulus tier is the parent of a number of other tiers: the gloss, numeral, quantifier, and classifier tiers. The annotations on these dependent tiers are constrained by (or they refer to) the annotations on the parent tier in some way. For example, we can see in Figure 4.2 that the annotations on the numeral, quantifier, and classifier tiers are exactly the same length as the annotation on their parent stimulus tier. This type of dependency relationship – specified by the stereotype attribute – is called "symbolic association." Annotations on tiers with a stereotype of symbolic association are automatically the same length as annotations on their parent tier. Establishing this as an attribute of a tier can improve the time-efficiency of coding. For instance, on the numeral tier in our example, we want to know whether or not a numeral sign appears in the stimulus description. Annotations on the numeral tier (*yes* in this case) thus refer to the full length of the annotations on the parent stimulus tier, and the stereotype is specified accordingly as symbolic association.

Another type of dependency, or referring, relationship is reflected in the annotations on the gloss tier. On this tier the length of individual annotations is freely determined on the basis of the length of individual signs in the video data; but, overall, all glosses associated with a particular stimulus description are fully contained within the length of the annotation on the parent stimulus tier. The dependency stereotype for this type of relationship is called "included in." In Figure 4.2, for example, it would not be possible to create annotations on the gloss tier to the left or right of the *two boats* annotation on the parent stimulus tier (i.e., to the left or right of the selection marked in blue).

Defining a controlled vocabulary for use with a tier can greatly relieve manual annotation work. If you know that your annotations on a given tier will be from a

Table 4.2 Example of table listing names of controlled vocabularies and their entry values.

Controlled Vocabulary	Entry Values
Loc type	EC, HC, SASS, noun
Numeral	yes, no
Quantifier	yes, no
Localization	yes, no

fixed set (e.g., you will annotate only *yes* or *no*, as on the numeral tier), it is possible to predefine this set as a controlled vocabulary. Selecting annotations from a fixed set (that appears as a drop-down menu) is more time-efficient than typing each annotation in by hand, and is recommended when possible. In our example, four different tiers have a controlled vocabulary associated with them: the localization type, numeral, quantifier, and classifier tiers. It is useful to create a separate table listing the controlled vocabularies you would want to use, with all their entry values specified (see Table 4.2). Names for controlled vocabularies can be descriptive, like the tier name. For example, the "loc type" vocabulary associated with the localization type tier has four specified entry values that identify different types of signs that may be localized in space in the spatial description data from which our example is taken, namely EC (entity classifier), HC (handling classifier), SASS (size and shape specifier), and noun signs.

How do you get these attributes set up and defined in ELAN? For setting up tiers and working most successfully and effectively with them, it is important that steps are taken in an order that reflects the interrelationships between tiers, types, and their attributes. In ELAN, creating a tier requires defining three things: the tier name; the tier's linguistic type; and the tier's parent tier (i.e., dependency relationship), if applicable. Creating a linguistic type, in turn, also requires specifying three things: the type name; the stereotype (i.e., the type of dependency relationship); and the use of a controlled vocabulary, if applicable. Thus it is best to work backwards along these interrelationships in getting your tier structure set up.

With your tables of names and values at hand, first create all the controlled vocabularies that you want to work with. To do this, go to Edit in the menu bar and select Edit Controlled Vocabulary. In the window that appears, you can specify the names and entry values of each controlled vocabulary you wish to use. Once this is done, all linguistic types should be defined (Type > Add New Linguistic Type). Here the available stereotypes[12] and the controlled vocabularies you have created appear for selection from drop-down menus. The type name serves primarily to link a given tier to its type attributes (i.e., to the stereotype and controlled vocabulary values). This link can be made transparent by giving a tier and its associated linguistic type the same (or a very similar) name (see Table 4.1). Finally, the tiers themselves can be created (Tier > Add New Tier). The parent tier and the linguistic type are selected from the drop-down menus, which are populated on the basis of, and as a result of, your creation of tiers and types. The tier name, finally, is what you see in the ELAN annotation window itself. As the tiers are created, they appear on the left side of the timeline, vertically arranged.

It may be, of course, that you want to make changes to your tiers and tier attributes once you have started annotating. As you go along, it is possible to create new controlled vocabularies and to edit existing ones, and to associate an existing tier with a new or a modified controlled vocabulary. It is also possible to associate a tier with a different linguistic type after the tier has been created. It is difficult, however, to change the dependency relationships between tiers, in other words to specify the parent tier and the stereotype of a given tier after it has been created. When you have created all of your tiers – in effect, when you have implemented your coding scheme in ELAN – it is useful to save the file in order to use it as a coding template. Individual annotation files can be created and saved by linking the appropriate video files to the program file in each case (Edit > Linked Files). ELAN can display up to four video files simultaneously. The use of multiple videos allows you to display different views of the same signers at the same time, for example the front view and the top view displayed in the ELAN screen shot in Figure 4.2.

When you start annotating, your research question and the type of information you want to code will help you to fine-tune the use of program functions, tools, and modes that will be most suited and useful. You will become practiced at using the keyboard shortcuts (View > Shortcuts, for a list) and you will learn to navigate the active tiers and annotations; to copy, paste, or duplicate annotations between and along tiers; to modify the time alignments of existing annotations; and to modify the content of existing annotations as needed.

The annotation of sign language data requires careful attention to the video stream. You are likely to create many of your annotations in the default annotation mode (Options > Annotation Mode) by moving the red crosshair frame by frame along the timeline to find the beginning and end points of an individual sign. However, the more automated, coarse-grained method of creating annotations that the segmentation and transcription modes offer (Options > Segmentation Mode; Transcription Mode) may prove useful for an initial pass through the data. The segmentation mode allows the fast placement of annotations if you hit the Enter (or Return) key (↵) as the video plays at the set speed. For example, if your aim is to analyze the use of a particular sign as a perfect marker in a sign language (see de Vos, 2012), you may want to use the segmentation mode for an initial identification of all occurrences of this sign within a video file. The annotations created in the segmentation mode are empty. The transcription mode can prove useful for filling them with the intended label (e.g., the gloss identifying the perfect marker). This text-oriented mode allows you to efficiently enter the annotation text into each of the marked segments. Taking these grossly marked segments as a point of departure, you can return to the annotation mode and modify the annotations so as to fit the precise duration of the sign in each case and to create new annotations according to your aims.

When you have completed the annotation of your data, the next step is to use these annotations to analyze and quantify your data and to extract the relevant information about the sign language, according to your specific research questions. ELAN allows various functions within the program itself, including acquiring simple statistics (View > Annotation Statistics) and more sophisticated search functions within and between tiers, which can be implemented by using both temporal and structural constraints (Search > Find; Search Functions). In addition, ELAN allows the export of tiers and annotations as a tab-delimited text file, which can be opened and processed as an Excel spreadsheet. This is possible for single (Export As > Tab-Delimited Text) or multiple ELAN files (Export Multiple Files As > Tab-Delimited Text).

Other annotation software

This section offers an overview of other software that similarly allows time-aligned annotation of sign language data and highlights options for sign language lexicography and lemmatization (for a more comprehensive overview and discussion of such software, see Rohlfing et al., 2006).

Anvil is another popular annotation tool that provides the simultaneous display of multiple annotation tiers and time-locked video (for a detailed description of the program, see Kipp, 2014).[13] Anvil offers many of the same features as ELAN, albeit with different names. Anvil uses tracks instead of tiers, elements instead of annotations, and dependency relationships between tiers/tracks are reflected in the track type instead of the stereotype (for example the singleton track type corresponds to ELAN's symbolic association stereotype, creating automatic temporal overlap). Anvil also offers the option of creating and using controlled vocabularies, which it calls "value sets."

A significant difference between Anvil and ELAN lies in the file structure. Anvil keeps annotation files separate from the coding scheme files – that is, the specification files where the track structure is specified. All annotations point to, or are associated with, a particular specification file. This means that any changes made to your coding scheme along the way (like the addition of tracks, or the change of track attributes) will be automatically made within the annotation files. This is an advantage when dealing with large amounts of annotated data files, as existing coding schemes may develop and change over time. In ELAN, where this information is not stored separately, making changes to a coding scheme template file does not automatically implement these changes in the annotated files that have already been created using this template.[14]

A further feature of Anvil not offered by ELAN is that it supports motion capture viewing. Anvil can read the most commonly used motion capture data formats (BVH and ASF/AMC), allowing the viewing of the 3D image of the body and the time-aligned display of curve analyses (e.g., velocity and acceleration). Finally, Anvil is notable in that it allows users to code spatial information directly on the video frame. This is done by means of an attribute that stores screen locations associated with individual video frames. The Anvil GUI allows these screen locations to be defined by clicking directly on the video. ELAN files may be imported into Anvil, which offers the possibility of using these features of Anvil with data annotations (previously) created in ELAN. Finally, one drawback of Anvil compared to ELAN is its limited video format compatibility. Thus it may be difficult to get video to play in Anvil. In contrast, ELAN supports a wide range of video formats and codecs.

iLex is a tool that offers an annotation environment that is directly integrated with a lexical database. This is valuable for sign language lexicography and corpus analysis, particularly for the process of lemmatization (where different forms of a sign, such as inflected forms, must be associated to a single entry). In iLex, glosses in the annotation environment refer to token occurrences of signs and are linked automatically to type entries in the lexical database. This achieves consistent type/token matching that does not depend on the labeling consistency of the glosses themselves (Hanke and Storz, 2008). In addition, having an integrated lexical database means that the database is created simultaneously with the transcription and glossing of the sign language data.

This feature of lexical database incorporation is not offered by ELAN or Anvil. However, ELAN can be used in conjunction with the lexicon tool LEXUS, such that sign glosses (in ELAN) can be associated to lexical entries. Achieving consistent type/token matching with this combined functionality relies on consistent glossing across occurrences of different forms of a sign.

Conclusion

This chapter has aimed to provide researchers interested in working with sign language data with guidelines for recording video data and for annotating them with the help of dedicated software. It has focused on the decision-making and workflow required to translate research questions into obtaining suitable data, and on devising and implementing appropriate coding schemes. The technical details of using video equipment and annotation software have not been stressed.

This chapter fills a gap in the available literature on research methods. Research on sign language has been included in previous volumes that target research methods within a specific theoretical framework, for instance cognitive linguistics (see Wilcox and Morford, 2007), or within a specific area of research, such as sign language acquisition (see Baker et al., 2008). In addition, research method handbooks have included chapters dedicated to studying, coding, and recording co-speech gesture (see Mittelberg, 2007; Sweetser, 2007 within a cognitive linguistics framework; Seyfeddinipur, 2012 on linguistic fieldwork methods; and Müller et al., 2013 for a wide range of methods chapters) and chapters including general guidelines for using video to document language usage (e.g. Margetts and Margetts, 2012). A chapter dedicated to obtaining and annotating sign language data within a general volume on research methods for sign language research is an important addition to the literature. Moreover, by focusing on the effective development and implementation of a coding scheme, it is a valuable supplement to the technical and comprehensive detail of available user manuals and guides for ELAN, including user guides intended for use of ELAN with sign language data (Bickford, 2005; Crasborn and Sloetjes, 2008).

Finally, the use of video data and time-aligned, video-based annotation should not be reserved for language expressed in the visual modality. All of language and communication is a multimodal process. In order to understand it, we need to understand how it is constructed in usage – which includes patterns of eye gaze, gesture, speech, and sign. In general, the study of language should make use of video recording and visual annotation if it aims to understand the complex phenomenon of human communication and interaction.

Notes

1   ELAN is the Eudico Linguistic Annotation tool developed at the Max Planck Institute for Psycholinguistics, Nijmegen, Netherlands. The software is available for free download at http://tla. mpi.nl/tools/tla-tools/elan

2   Anvil is a video annotation tool developed by Michael Kipp from the University of Applied Sciences in Augsburg, Germany. The software is available for free download at www.anvil-software.org/download/index.html

3 iLEX is the integrated lexicon tool developed at the Institute of German Sign Language and Communication of the Deaf (Institut für Deutsche Gebärdensprache und Kommunikation Gehörloser, IDGS) at Hamburg University, Germany. See www.sign-lang.uni-hamburg.de/ilex

4 LEXUS is a web-based lexicon tool developed by the Language Archive at the Max Planck Institute for Psycholinguistics, Nijmegen, Netherlands. The software is available for free download at http://tla.mpi.nl/tools/tla-tools/lexus

5 In this chapter I use the lowercase form deaf throughout.

6 Devices allowing depth and motion sensing, e.g. Kinect devices and 3D cameras, are also on the market. These can be useful, for example, for purposes of automatic sign recognition and sign synthesis (and also for more sophisticated types of instrumented capture).

7 See, for example, www.mpi.nl/IMDI/ for information on the ISLE MetaData Initiative (IMDI) as a standard for structured metadata description.

8 The steady software improvements and general technological advancements have rendered largely irrelevant older concerns about platform and video format compatibility, as well as about processing capacity issues.

9 Independently of what your research question is, data annotation should include a transcription of the signing, which identifies and glosses all the signs in the utterances of interest. The use of consistent glosses to uniquely identify signs is crucial to creating a searchable and functional sign corpus and database (see Johnston, 2001 on ID-glosses for consistent type/token matching and Hanke and Storz, 2008 on integrated type/token matching in iLex).

10 The ELAN user guide and user manual are available for download from http://tla.mpi.nl/tools/tla-tools/elan; in addition, there is a forum for asking questions (http://tla.mpi.nl/forums/software/elan).

11 The use of a data category register (DCR) like ISOcat may aid in finding and defining tier and coding categories. ISOcat is the DCR utilized by CLARIN (Common Language Resources and Technology Infrastructure), which provides an integrated research infrastructure for language resources (see www.isocat.org and www.clarin.eu).

12 There are four predefined stereotypes. "Symbolic association" and "included in" have been mentioned; the other two are "symbolic subdivision" and "time subdivision." With these, the length of a parent tier annotation can be subdivided into multiple annotations on a dependent tier; but there can be no gaps between these individual annotations, and they are automatically assigned equal length.

13 In addition, there are good video tutorials available on the Anvil web site, as well as email support and access to a user forum (visit www.anvil-software.org).

14 To deal with this, ELAN offers options for merging and importing tiers between files, a slightly more cumbersome solution than that offered by Anvil. However, this is weighed against the ease, in ELAN, of creating tiers and implementing the coding scheme within the program: this is comparatively difficult in Anvil, where specification files are .xml files that must be created in an editor. Because creating these files from scratch may be daunting to users, the Anvil directory (to be downloaded and installed) includes a subdirectory called "spec," which contains examples of coding schemes that can be used and amended.

Keywords

annotation software; data annotation; data coding; data collection; data management; elicited data; naturalistic data; sign language; techniques for filming; video recording

See Also

Chapter 1; Chapter 5; Chapter 6; Chapter 7; Chapter 8; Chapter 10

Suggested Readings

Thieberger, N. (Ed.). (2012). *The Oxford handbook of linguistic fieldwork*. Oxford: Oxford University Press.

References

Baker, A., van den Bogaerde, B., and Woll, B. (2008). Methods and procedures in sign language acquisition studies. In A. Baker and B. Woll (Eds.), *Sign Language Acquisition*. Amsterdam: John Benjamins, pp. 1–50.

Bickford, A. (2005). Using ELAN: A getting-started guide for use with sign languages. No longer available. http://www.und.edu/dept/linguistics/textbooks/UsingElan.pdf

Coates, J., and Sutton-Spence, R. (2001). Turn-taking patterns in Deaf conversation. *Journal of Sociolinguistics* 5(4), 507–529.

Crasborn, O., and Sloetjes, H. (2008). Enhanced ELAN functionality for sign language corpora. In O. Crasborn, T. Hanke, E. Efthimiou, I. Zwitserlood, and E. D. Thoutenhoofd (Eds.), *Construction and exploitation of sign language corpora: Third workshop on the representation and processing of sign languages*. Paris: ELDA, pp. 39–43.

Crasborn, O., van der Kooij, E., Waters, D., Woll, B., and Mesch, J. (2008). Frequency distribution and spreading behavior of different types of mouth actions in three sign languages. *Sign Language & Linguistics* 11(1), 45–67.

Enfield, N. J., Dingemanse, M., Baranova, J., Blythe, J., Brown, P., Dirksmeyer, T., Drew, P., Floyd, S., Gipper, S., Gisladottir, R. S., Hoymann, G., Kendrick, K., Levinson, S. C., Magyari, L., Manrique, E., Rossi, G., San Roque, L., and Torreira, F. (2013). Huh? What? A first survey in 20 languages. In M. Hayashi, G. Raymond, and J. Sidnell (Eds.), *Conversational repair and human understanding*. New York: Cambridge University Press, pp. 343–380.

Hanke, T., and Storz, J. (2008). ilex: A database tool for integrating sign language corpus linguistics and sign language lexicography. In O. Crasborn, T. Hanke, E. Efthimiou, I. Zwitserlood, and E. D. Thoutenhoofd (Eds.), *Construction and exploitation of sign language corpora: Third workshop on the representation and processing of sign languages*. Paris: ELDA, pp. 64–67.

Johnston, T. (2001). The lexical database of Auslan (Australian Sign Language). *Sign Language & Linguistics* 4(1/2), 145–169.

Kipp, M. (2014). ANVIL: The video annotation research tool. In J. Durand, U. Gut, and G. Kristofferson (Eds.), *The Oxford Handbook of Corpus Phonology*. Oxford: Oxford University Press, pp. 420–436.

Margetts, A., and Margetts, A. (2012). Audio and video recording techniques for linguistic research. In N. Thieberger (Ed.), *The Oxford Handbook of Linguistic Fieldwork*. Oxford: Oxford University Press, pp. 13–53.

Meir, I. (1999). A perfect marker in Israeli Sign Language. *Sign Language & Linguistics* 2(1), 41–60.

Mittelberg, I. (2007). Methodology for multimodality: One way of working with speech and gesture data. In M. Gonzalez-Marquez, I. Mittelberg, S. Coulson, and M. J. Spivey (Eds.), *Methods in Cognitive Linguistics*. Amsterdam: John Benjamins, pp. 225–248.

Morgan, G., Herman, R., and Woll, B. (2002). The development of complex verb constructions in British Sign Language. *Journal of Child Language* 29, 655–675.

Müller, C., Cienki, A., Fricke, E., Ladewig, S., McNeill, D., and Teßendorf, S. (Eds.) (2013). *Body—Language—Communication: An international handbook on multimodality in human interaction* (vol. 1). Berlin: De Gruyter.

Perniss, P., and Zeshan, U. (2008). Possessive and existential constructions: Introduction and overview. In U. Zeshan and P. Perniss (Eds.), *Possessive and existential constructions in sign languages* (Sign Language Typology series 2). Nijmegen, Netherlands: Ishara Press, pp. 1–31.

Rohlfing, K., Loehr, D., Duncan, S., Brown, A., Franklin, A., Kimbara, I., Milde, J.-T., Parrill, F., Rose, T., Schmidt, T., Sloetjes, H., Thies, A., and Wellinghof, S. (2006). Comparison of multimodal annotation tools: Workshop report. *Gesprächsforschung* 7, 99–123. (Online journal on verbal interaction, also at www.gespraechsforschung-ozs.de)

Schembri, A. (2008). British Sign Language Corpus project: Open access archives and the observer's paradox. In O. Crasborn, T. Hanke, E. Efthimiou, I. Zwitserlood, and E. D. Thoutenhoofd (Eds.), *Construction and exploitation of sign language corpora: Third workshop on the representation and processing of sign languages.* Paris: ELDA, pp. 165–169.

Seyfeddinipur, M. (2012). Reasons for documenting gestures and suggestions for how to go about it. In N. Thieberger (Ed.), *The Oxford handbook of linguistic fieldwork.* Oxford: Oxford University Press, pp. 147–165.

Smith, S., and Sutton-Spence, R. (2008). Adult–child interaction in BSL nursery: Getting their attention. In A. Baker and B. Woll (Eds.), *Sign language acquisition.* Amsterdam: John Benjamins, pp. 119–140.

Sweetser, E. (2007). Looking at space to study mental spaces: Co-speech gesture as a crucial data source in cognitive linguistics. In M. Gonzalez-Marquez, I. Mittelberg, S. Coulson, and M. J. Spivey (Eds.), *Methods in cognitive linguistics.* Amsterdam: John Benjamins, pp. 201–224.

Thieberger, N., and Berez, A. L. (2012). Linguistic data management. In N. Thieberger (Ed.), *The Oxford handbook of linguistic fieldwork.* Oxford: Oxford University Press, pp. 90–118.

de Vos, C. (2012). The Kata Kolok perfective in child signing: Coordination of manual and non-manual components. In U. Zeshan and C. de Vos (Eds.), *Sign languages in village communitites: Anthropological and linguistic insights.* Berlin: Mouton de Gruyter, pp. 127–152.

Wilcox, S., and Morford, J. (2007). Empirical methods in signed language research. In M. Gonzalez-Marquez, I. Mittelberg, S. Coulson, and M. J. Spivey (Eds.), *Methods in cognitive linguistics.* Amsterdam: John Benjamins, pp. 171–200.

Vermeerbergen, M., Leeson, L., and Crasborn, O. (Eds.). (2007). *Simultaneity in signed language: Form and function.* Amsterdam: John Benjamins.

Zeshan, U., and Perniss, P. (Eds.). (2008). *Possessive and existential constructions in sign languages* (Sign Language Typology series 2). Nijmegen, Netherlands: Ishara Press.

5 Transcription and Notation Methods

Onno A. Crasborn

Chapter Overview

This chapter discusses various methods of notating sign forms, focusing on the manual aspect of signing, for which the largest number of different systems has been proposed. Rather than entering into great detail on the advantages and disadvantages of the various orthographic notation methods and phonetic transcription systems that have been proposed throughout the past forty years, the chapter discusses how notation and transcription can aid present-day researchers that make use of multimodal annotation tools to directly time-link text to videos. Sign language corpora that are currently being created include between 20 and 300 hours of video, which are impossible to fully notate or transcribe for most research groups, let alone individual researchers. For this

Research Methods in Sign Language Studies: A Practical Guide, First Edition.
Edited by Eleni Orfanidou, Bencie Woll, and Gary Morgan.
© 2015 John Wiley & Sons, Inc. Published 2015 by John Wiley & Sons, Inc.

reason, the chapter discusses various ways in which a basic annotation of a corpus in terms of glosses and sentence-level translations can be enriched with representations of aspects of the form of signs using notation methods that have been developed for other purposes.

Introduction

As Trevor Johnston emphasizes in recounting his experiences with the creation of a corpus for Auslan (the sign language used in Australia), a corpus is not a corpus unless it is machine-readable (Johnston, 2010). Despite rapid progress in computer vision technology in the past decade, we cannot directly search in video recordings of sign language. Some type of transcription is therefore required to allow for searching for aspects of the form of the language. It is this new context of the creation of annotated video resources that will be the focus of this chapter on notation and transcription. While modern technologies cannot replace manual transcription or annotation at this point in time, we are on the brink of letting computer vision techniques assist us in annotation. This chapter aims to describe present methodologies in (an)notating sign language data, while keeping an eye out on immanent changes in the way linguists work in the creation of sign resources.

Throughout the chapter I will use the term "notation" to refer to any type of text rendition, reserving "transcription" for phonetic transcription. "Annotation" will be used as a technical term to refer to a notation that is directly linked either to an audio or video source (as in the ELAN annotation tool) or to a text string. Thus a gloss annotation in ELAN is an annotation that refers to a certain time window in the video recording, while further properties of that gloss, such as meaning in context or precise phonetic form, can be added as child annotations pertaining to that gloss annotation itself. Phonetic transcription can thus be one type of annotation of a video source. Similarly, in text corpora, part-of-speech tags can be added to each word in the text, forming annotations that are not directly time-locked to audio or video. Where in the literature on text corpora "tag" and "annotation" are sometimes treated as equivalent, both being an attribute or a comment added to a piece of text, in the annotation of audio and video resources the initial layer of labeling an event in the source media file is also called annotation. "Orthographic notation" is used to refer to a notation system for everyday use, whether by language users or by linguists. (For further discussion of these different terms, see Johnston, 2010; Thompson, 2010; Baker, Hardie, and McEnerny, 2006.)

In the past decade there have been a considerable number of overviews of different notation systems for sign languages, from Miller (1994, 2001) to van der Hulst and Channon (2010) and to Frishberg, Hoiting, and Slobin (2012). Other publications have zoomed in on the transcription of child language data of sign languages (Morgan, 2005; Baker, van den Bogaerde, and Woll, 2005; Takkinen, 2005; Chen Pichler, Hochgesang, Lillo-Martin, and Quadros, 2010). Rather than trying to bundle all the details from these various overviews, this chapter aims to synthesize the issues involved in a broad outline, distinguishing orthographic and phonetic notation from other types of annotations and indicating in which situations each of these might be of use. It then tries to determine how phonetic transcription and other types of notation may be used in the present context of the availability of large sign language corpora to researchers and the general public, and it includes practical suggestions and references to studies that have followed certain methodologies. The chapter concludes by evaluating whether there is in fact a need for phonetic transcription in sign language corpora and by discussing the expected impact of computer vision technology on our research methodologies in the near future. Taken together, all the parts of this chapter aim to provide the reader with a solid understanding of different kinds and levels of sign notation and with suggestions for the use of sign notation in relation to developing sign language corpus methodologies, linking the latter both to more traditional approaches and to expected future technologies.

Sign Orthographies and Glossing

Sign languages can be characterized as unwritten languages, in the sense that there are no Deaf[1] communities that have a written tradition. Sign orthographies for daily use – not by researchers, but by ordinary language users – have been designed, however, and there are enthusiastic proponents for each of them. While these orthographies may be used by small subcommunities or in certain educational settings, it is fair to say that the role of the orthography of the surrounding spoken language(s) is more prominent in the lives of literate deaf people.

SignWriting is probably the best known sign orthography, and was designed in the 1970s on the basis of Sutton Movement Notation, originally developed for notating various types of movements, including dance (for a historical overview of the system, see Sutton, 1999; Bianchini and Borgia, 2012; for a discussion of various similar movement notation systems, Farnell, 1996). SignWriting aims to represent not only manual behavior but also non-manual information. Like the various phonetic transcription systems discussed in the next section, SignWriting is based on the phonological analyses of ASL by Stokoe and others in the 1960s and 1970s: the phonological parameters handshape, orientation, location, and movement are all represented by individual symbols (graphemes). In addition, several features of the face (states of the eyebrows and mouth, gaze direction) have their own representation. Rather than putting symbols in a string, like in most phonetic transcriptions, SignWriting puts graphs together to form an abstract frontal view of a signer. SignWriting is not restricted to the word level: it allows for the writing of sentences and texts by ordering symbols vertically.

Other similar efforts have been made in the past; so is the typographically much more elegant SignFont (Newkirk, 1989; for a discussion, see Frishberg et al., 2012). More recently, a new orthography has been proposed for American Sign Language (ASL) under the name of "si5s" (Clark, 2012). This system appears to be especially suited for handwriting, requiring very few lines to represent signs.

Perhaps because of the limited role that orthographic notation plays in the language communities themselves, researchers wanting to notate sign language have rarely used orthographic notation in collecting their research data or in presenting examples in publications (Miller, 2001; Frishberg et al., 2012). Rather, manual lexical items signs in sign language have been represented in text by means of glosses in a spoken language, be that the surrounding language used by signers of the sign language under investigation or the language of the international publication (often English). Thus, where the representation of examples of spoken Dutch in an English language publication would take the form of Dutch glosses using Dutch orthographic conventions with aligned English translations, the text representation of examples from Sign Language of the Netherlands would take the form of glosses in English. As the Latin script used for Dutch is based on phonetics (like many orthographies – but unlike the ideographic or semagraphic character orthography of Chinese, for instance), some information about the form of the Dutch example is also offered with a gloss. Sign language glosses, by contrast, do not contain information about the form of the sign and are necessarily based on a short translation to a spoken language. Use of glosses can therefore be deceptive, as it suggests that the semantics of the spoken language word or phrase chosen for the gloss overlaps with the semantics of the sign (Frishberg, 1983; Johnston, 2008; Frishberg et al., 2012). Such a full overlap might occur in some cases, but certainly not in all. Most signs therefore have multiple translation variants in a spoken language, but only one variant can be chosen as the gloss.

Johnston (2008) has introduced the term "ID-gloss" for a gloss that uniquely identifies a sign. This term emphasizes that a spoken language gloss for a sign should be interpreted as no more than a reference to a lexicon entry: it is not a full translation that captures all of its semantics, nor necessarily the best translation for a sign in a given context. ID-glosses could therefore just as well be numbers that refer to numbered items in a lexicon. Such a lexicon could be a traditional user's dictionary of a sign language, whether printed or electronic; but, in the context of sign language corpora, machine-readable lexicons are more likely to be scientific databases addressing the needs of the users of corpora. Spoken language words are chosen for various reasons and purposes, including to facilitate the quick reading of strings of glosses. Re-synthesis of lexical items on the basis of phonological or phonetic information in a lexicon by an avatar would help researchers to stay clear of spoken language words in glossing (Hanke, 2002). However, as with glosses for spoken languages, such a procedure would give easy access only to the form, but not to the meaning. The meaning of a sign in context has to be annotated separately, or the prototypical meaning from a lexicon needs to be made available together with the notation of the lexical item.

If one uses glosses in a publication to represent a series of signs, one typically chooses the translation of a sign that fits best, as a gloss, with that context. However, if the glosses in the example are intended as ID-glosses that refer to a lexicon or to a data collection that has been glossed in a systematic way by reference to that lexicon, the conventions of the lexicon must be followed.

The selection of glosses that function as ID-glosses in a lexicon will typically involve choosing the most frequent or the most neutral translation. This may not always be easy, as often multiple signs would all be translated by the same word if one chooses the most frequent meaning. For instance, regional sign variants referring to the same concept would ideally all be translated by the same word. In such a case, letter or number suffixes can be used to differentiate between signs, while one would still use the same word (Johnston, 2008; Crasborn and de Meijer, 2012). The compound created by the word and the suffix then functions as the ID-gloss.

To represent the semantics of a sign in a lexicon, researchers typically fall back on a spoken language as well, simply because it can be easily written and read by researchers and/or other users like language learners. For this purpose, English would be the best choice for sign language data collections that are accessible to an international audience of researchers. The gloss annotations in the initial open access release of the NGT corpus (Sign Language of the Netherlands; see Crasborn, Zwitserlood, and Ros, 2008) are in Dutch, and for most researchers they will therefore function as a mere number, providing little to no useful semantic information. In a local non-English context, other written languages can fulfill the same function: the Dutch glosses of the Corpus NGT may be useful to Dutch people, for example. Sign lexicons have thus always been bilingual to a certain extent, at least until now, but there is no principled reason why there could not be a fully monolingual sign lexicon. Ideally lexicons, and thus ID-glosses, would be multilingual. Currently ELAN is being modified such that it will allow for the display of multilingual annotations and metadata categories. Future releases of the Corpus NGT annotations will exploit that technology so as to become accessible to a broader international audience.

Creating an orthographic notation or using glosses can also be useful when presenting examples to readers in documents – from student assignments to scientific journals. Such aids are imperative when creating sign resources for one's own research or for publication and later use by others. Word-level annotations (together with sentence-level translations) typically form the backbone of corpus annotation; other annotations such as intonational non-manual activities are related to them and can be interpreted in relation to them.

Phonetic Transcription

Various systems have been proposed to describe the phonological and/or phonetic form of sign languages. The Stokoe Notation (Stokoe, 1960) was the first to create a graphic componential representation of signs; and it inspired many others. The ASL dictionary of Stokoe, Casterline, and Croneberg (1965) used this notation method to represent the forms of signs without presenting drawings or photographs to illustrate the signs themselves. There have also been systems that are not based on Stokoe's parameter analysis of lexical items. Miller (2001) and van der Hulst and Channon (2010) discuss these notation methods in relation to parameter-based systems, and Miller (2001, p. 16) gives a good overview of their relations. Systems differ in the extent to which they are intended to be language-specific or universal and in the level of granularity or detail that they allow, including more versus less detail of the form of signs. It will thus depend both on the language one needs to transcribe and on the level of detail whether or not one can use a given system.

A series of recent publications by Johnson and Liddell (2010, 2011a, 2011b, 2012) propose a very fine-grained transcription system of the manual component of signing, one that allows for the transcription of the position of each of the fingers in quite some detail and also explicitly includes the transcription of the transitional movements between signs – something that has not been addressed by any other notation system. Most systems make the explicit claim that such transitional movements are not linguistic units but rather phonetic epiphenomena (see Ormel and Crasborn, 2014 for a discussion). Yet, if these transitions are of interest for a specific phonetic study, the Johnson and Liddell system will prove useful. As Takkinen (2005) notes, working with an early version of the system, full transcriptions of every handshape alone can be very time-consuming and are very complex. This makes them good for searching – just as a database coding system like the ones proposed by van der Hulst and Channon (2010) or by Crasborn, van der Hulst, and van der Kooij (2001) – but impractical for reading and quickly reproducing a sign. While perhaps impractical for the transcription of longer strings, a very detailed system like Johnson and Liddell's could serve the purpose of providing standards for the coding of subaspects of manual sign forms for specific studies, where for instance only the position of the thumb is relevant. Two examples of such methodologies will be discussed later in this section.

There is a specific problem with the Stokoe Notation and its successors that, in order to represent handshapes, use letters also found in the hand alphabets; this makes them hard to use consistently for other sign languages. A letter such as "A" does not refer to the same handshape across sign languages. Iconic graphic symbols as in the HamNoSys transcription system (see Prillwitz and Zienert, 1990; and visit http://www.sign-lang.uni-hamburg.de/hamnosys) do not have that problem. Another problem that is shared among many transcription systems is that they have been developed in the context of lexicography, allowing for the sorting and searching of sign forms in dictionaries. When used for connected discourse, most transcription systems fail to accurately represent things like precise spatial locations and directions, holds of the non-dominant hand, and mouthings that may have their own time alignment.

For facial expression, some people have overcome the shortcomings of sign-specific systems by using the very detailed Facial Action Coding System (FACS), designed by psychologists to transcribe facial expressions showing emotions (Ekman and Friesen, 1969). Like any narrow phonetic transcription system, FACS has a steep learning curve and is not easily applied to long stretches of discourse simply because of the time needed for annotation. Ekman himself estimated that annotating the facial activities of signers may take as much as 2,400 times real time (Cohn and Ekman, 2005). Several researchers have productively used FACS in the analysis of intonational facial features in sign language (Baker-Shenk, 1983; Dachkovsky and Sandler, 2009; de Vos, van der Kooij, and Crasborn, 2009).

Until now, HamNoSys has been the only candidate for the sign language variant of the International Phonetic Alphabet (IPA) for the transcription of speech, especially if we focus on manual lexical items.

HamNoSys has been carefully designed for multilingual use over many years; like the IPA, it can be used for both broad (phonemic) and narrow (detailed) transcription, and it has a very elegant font for use on multiple computer platforms. Yet it is not so widely used as to be actually considered to have the status of a standard like the IPA. Many different factors may be involved in explaining why this is the case. First of all, there are some practical issues. HamNoSys takes quite some time to learn, given the large number of symbols needed for even a broad transcription of lexical forms. This problem is strengthened by the combination of a large number of frequently used symbols with the use of an ordinary keyboard, which requires the user either to memorize a lot of keyboard shortcuts or to use special input software. Also, the transcription of sign forms sometimes leads to very long strings of symbols (see the example sentence transcribed in various ways in Frishberg et al., 2012). The limited documentation available in English for HamNoSys and its tools may play a role as well in the restricted use of this system in the literature until now. In terms of linguistic considerations, it may be the case that use of ordinary citation forms without any type of (spatial, non-manual) modification is rare in any study of sign grammar, from morphosyntax to discourse. For detailed aspects of a broad range of non-manual behavior and simultaneous constructions, HamNoSys may not (yet) be well equipped.

However, it could also be the case that, in actual practice, despite the convincing arguments in favor of phonetic transcription put forward by Miller and others, the use of glossing and/or illustration by images is sufficient for many purposes. This holds especially for the presentation of sentences as illustrations in scientific publications. It is true, as Miller (2001) notes, that a transcription helps us to focus on certain properties of the signal and disregard the wide variety of other things going on; but one may wonder how big an issue this is if we can provide immediate access to the video source in combination with specific annotations on various tiers, in order to focus our attention both on categories of events and on the timing relations between events. In present-day electronic journal publications, links to video examples stored in archives can be added, and this provides direct access to the actual utterance with its annotations (Broeder, van Uytvanck, and Senft, 2012). Such "enriched publications" presenting source data can thus include examples; moreover, they allow readers to double-check that transcriptions or other annotations have been correctly produced.

Indeed the requirements that Miller (2001) listed for a universal transcription system appear to be largely fulfilled through the use of multi-tier annotation documents time-aligned to the source video, which include any type of systematic verbal description of what can be observed. Miller's requirements included the need to record properties such as multilinearity of signing (asynchronies and overlaps of different articulators, for instance the two hands or the hands and non-manual behavior), non-manual articulations such as mouthings, manual rhythm such as holdings of the hands in space, and spatial location and direction. Each of these can be annotated at separate levels in multimedia annotation tools like ELAN (http://tla.mpi.nl/tools/tla-tools/elan), iLex (http://www.sign-lang.uni-hamburg.de/ilex), SignStream (http://www.bu.edu/asllrp/signstream), or ANVIL (http://www.anvil-software.org), which makes them easily searchable. In the context of corpus construction (Crasborn et al., 2007; Johnston, 2010), full phonetic transcriptions are simply not realistic: even glossing in annotation software can take as much as 200 times real time to do consistently – assuming there is already a full lexicon with ID-glosses available for reference. If the lexicon has to be created or enriched with new entries as annotation takes place, the time needed for glossing will be even longer. Phonetic transcription of speech may also take as much as 150 times real time (Schultze-Berndt, 2006). Ideally, glosses refer to a lexicon that stores the phonological or phonetic properties of the citation form, whether in a transcription system like HamNoSys or in other alphanumeric codes, as in databases like SignPhon (Crasborn et al., 2001) or SignTyp (van der Hulst and Channon, 2010), so that some information on the form is available through the mediation of a gloss notation.

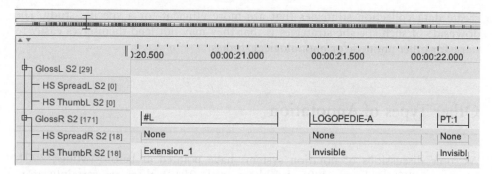

Figure 5.1 Phonetic coding appended to glosses in ELAN, for transcription of thumb position and finger spreading. "Extension_1" refers to full extension of the thumb. "Invisible" is used to indicate that the information cannot be seen on the available video because of the camera angle that was used.

Rather than creating full phonetic transcriptions for corpora, one can single out phonetic properties that are relevant for a particular study and annotate only those on specific tiers. This will speed up the process of data collection considerably in comparison to creating rich phonetic transcriptions of all data first and then extracting information from the transcriptions. Where possible, one can still follow the conventions for a transcription system like HamNoSys. As an example, take the methodology that was followed by Ormel et al. (2014). For a study of the co-articulation of handshape, they selected signs with flat handshapes from a published sign language corpus, adding a tier for the specific phonetic property of interest (precise position of the thumb) to the existing ELAN annotation documents of the corpus. In this way, rather than creating a full phonetic transcription, they transcribed only the phonetic property of interest; and this allowed for the collection of a large number of data points. Figure 5.1 illustrates how this phonetic information is appended to the gloss annotation by means of a dependent ("child") tier to the gloss tier in ELAN.

A slightly different yet related phonetic methodology, specific to the use of corpora, was followed by Russell, Wilkinson, and Janzen (2011), who investigated hand location in a corpus of ASL. This study aimed to find evidence for the phonetic undershoot of hand location. In a large corpus of conversational signing, specific signs were annotated with glosses. Within the time domain of that gloss, the frame was annotated where the active articulator was closest to the passive articulator (the place of articulation). This frame was then exported to an image file, and the location of the hand in terms of pixel coordinates was manually determined and further analyzed by using separate software. One could well imagine that, in the future, such functionality will be built into annotation tools, and that the resulting coordinate values will be stored as annotations, for further processing. Using this workflow, one is able to obtain quantitative information on the precise location of the hand that would be very hard to transcribe reliably with any transcription system.

As the two studies above show, there are ways of collecting corpus data that do not rely on full phonetic transcriptions of signs. Specific elements of signs are selected depending on the goal of the study, and specific coding schemes or measurement guidelines are developed that in some cases build on distinctions made in traditional phonetic transcription systems, yet in other cases (as the two studies illustrated) create data collection strategies that are more efficient for a specific study. The downside of such specific strategies is that they may not lend themselves easily to reuse for other phonetic or phonological studies.

Other Types of Annotation

As some discussions of notation systems have pointed at before (Miller, 2001; Morgan, 2005; Takkinen, 2005; Frishberg et al., 2012), there are certainly properties of signed languages that are not easy to capture with current notation systems, for instance the precise spatial localization of signs and simultaneous constructions of the two hands, but also more gestural and more variable productions – like manual pantomimic gestures or emotional facial expressions. However, there may also be properties of the form of signs that are only relevant for specific studies and that one would not necessarily include explicitly in a transcription system. The minute details of the location of the hand in the study of Russell et al. (2011) are a clear case in point. Another example concerns the exact points of dominance reversal in connected signing: where exactly do signers switch from a right-dominant production to a left-dominant production? This may be implicit in some notation systems (like SignWriting or HamNoSys), where the left and the right hand can be notated as such, but it is not something that can be expressed with the Stokoe Notation, for instance. For an ongoing study of dominance reversal in NGT, we have therefore created a separate set of tiers and categories to mark various properties of hand selection (Crasborn and Sáfár, forthcoming). Examples include cases where a production moves from left-dominant to right-dominant (and vice versa) and where a turn starts with the left or the right hand as dominant. These are properties of the form of signing, annotated on a separate tier in our ELAN annotation documents. In the same vein, one could spell out various aspects of the phonetics of signing that are specific to a given study without having need for a full phonetic transcription of that data set.

Slobin et al. (2001) and Hoiting and Slobin (2002) present the Berkeley Transcription System (BTS), which does not target phonetic form but rather morphological structure. While morphological properties are sometimes included in gloss notations, these glosses are rarely fully componential, so as to distinguish the various parts of polycomponential signs like classifier constructions, for instance. The BTS aims to do just that. In part, labels for morphological categories can also be copied from glossing conventions for spoken languages, as when using ".pl" after a noun gloss to indicate a plural morpheme (see, for example, the Leipzig Glossing Conventions, on which see Comrie, Haspelmath, and Bickel, 2008). For many other properties of signing, including ones where a morphemic analysis has not yet been made and more gesture-like components are involved, conventions have yet to be developed. If one wants to make a semantic or morphological analysis of signing, investigating for instance how plurality is expressed in nominal and verbal signs, then the extra time needed for BTS transcription as compared to ID-glossing may well pay off. How much time such transcriptions will actually take to create is not made explicit in the literature.

Both the glossing of whole signs and morpheme-by-morpheme annotation provide a basic layer of annotations in a sign language corpus that will serve as an entry point for researchers with a large variety of questions. In addition to this sign-level access to a corpus, sentence-level translations are often created that likewise serve as a basic layer of annotations that will facilitate the use of any corpus by any researcher. For researchers unfamiliar with the language, translations are of course needed to understand the signing. However, also for researches that are fluent or native users of the language, translations may serve various functions. Text views of sequences of sentences allow one to scan through the content of a conversation much more rapidly than would be achievable by skimming through the video source. If translations are made of rigidly identified syntactic domains, annotations containing a translation further provide the exact sentence boundaries. These can then be used for investigating the position of glossed signs within sentences, for example. Together with gloss annotations, translations therefore provide a first segmentation of a larger text, allowing researchers to locate the basic units (words and sentences); and, in the case of multiple discourse participants, sentence annotations may also inform the researcher about who is signing and about how turns in a conversation overlap (or not).

Standardization of Annotations

A standard transcription system is seen as desirable by many researchers. While direct access to the source video may reduce the need for standard phonetic transcriptions, the need for conventions on corpus annotations becomes larger – and for the very same reason: we need to be able to "read" each other's data (Schembri and Crasborn, 2010). While "reading" will less and less refer to humans reading phonetic transcriptions and more and more to computer-readability of larger data collections, some properties of and requirements for standards are shared. From a technical point of view, the chosen font (in the case of a notation system) or document (in the case of video annotations) needs to be readable to others. Ideally, the data should be available and accessible regardless of the computer platform one is using.

Second, the annotation conventions that are chosen should be properly documented and published (see Chen Pichler et al., 2010 and Johnston, 2014 for examples).

Creating annotation standards and publishing them is not sufficient for the creation of resources that can then be used by other researchers, however. We need to be sure that the standards have actually been interpreted correctly in every instance. In other words, what is the validity of the transcriptions that are generated? Inter- and intra-transcriber reliability can be calculated, but actual access to the source videos should be possible as well. There are fewer and fewer technological barriers to publishing videos, and researchers can use open source tools like ELAN to inspect others' annotations together with the source media. Aside from checking the validity of what is annotated, researchers can also check in the source media whether certain events are not left un-annotated. Decisions on what counts as an "event" to be transcribed are not self-evident, and, no matter how good and explicit the transcription guidelines or how standardized the categories, people will always differ somewhat in the interpretation of what is seen in the video.

With the publication of the annotation guidelines of the first published sign corpora (Johnston, 2014) and with the exchange of methodological knowledge at workshops (Crasborn, 2010), it would appear that the annotation of sign corpora is heading toward informal standardization on a number of issues, even if there is disagreement on whether and how to phonetically transcribe whole strings of signing. The current drive toward standardization in the spoken language resources world may contribute tools for this process, such as the ISOcat data category registry (Crasborn and Windhouwer, 2012). In this registry, linguistic categories of any kind can be defined, allowing annotators to be very explicit about what they mean for instance by "noun" or "handshape" by including references to these definitions in the controlled vocabularies that are related to tiers in ELAN. This explicitness and consistent referencing for specific annotation values through unique and persistent identifiers may promote standardization by avoiding ambiguity and by sharing categories and their definitions. As translations can be created in any (written) language, the same data categories can be easily reused for any sign language corpus, also if English is not the primary language of annotation.

An Outlook: Open Data and Computer-Assisted Annotation

While Miller (2001, p. 11), in his discussion of the "need for a common sign notation," acknowledges that at the time of writing (that is, around the year 2000) the use of video in the computer, and even on the Internet, was becoming more and more commonplace, he still assumed that we would always need a sign notation. Notation is useful because it provides focus, as opposed to raw video. One could debate whether this is still true, now that access to specific segments of the video on the basis of searchable annotations is possible (e.g. using ANNEX – for which visit http://tla.mpi.nl/tools/tla-tools/annex). As Miller also discusses, creating a phonetic transcription inevitably includes making theory-based decisions on what counts as an important and distinct category, both in designing a notation system and in actually transcribing video recordings. Even in the citation of examples in journal articles and e-books, perhaps we should no longer strive to use any type of phonetic transcription, but rather present the original text in its source format, which was available to the researcher: the video recording. This would allow readers to see not only an instantiation of the argument of the authors, but also the example that is brought forward in its context; thus it would also allow for an analysis of the form that is broader than just the elements highlighted by the authors. This is where the current movement toward "open data" could substantially contribute to our linguistic understanding of sign languages. The need for a common phonetic transcription method would become smaller.

Finally, developments in computer vision are proceeding rapidly, in line with the explosion of photo and video materials online, not to speak of the increase in CCTV recordings. Before long, the manual transcription of sign forms will be assisted by a first parse of computer vision algorithms for specific features, for instance in detecting marked movements of the eye brows or head (see Piater, Hoyoux, and Du, 2010 for a recent example of the state of the art). As in automatic speech recognition, such methods will not automatically lead to full and fully correct phonetic transcriptions of whole sentences, but at least they will be able to assist in the annotation of specific features. This will increase the amount of data that are available to linguistic studies and will have an impact on how we design our research. The need for a shared phonetic transcription system may well be much smaller than we thought until only a decade ago. Although we may not see a true sign language version of the IPA, we will also forego on the disadvantages of the IPA, which transcribes some events while neglecting others – from sentence prosody to facial expression.

Conclusion

In summary, nowadays there are more economic ways of transcribing data for research purposes than relying on full phonetic transcriptions. The size of the available data sets in larger sign language corpora calls for something more efficient than the transcription of connected discourse. Again, this is often made possible by the availability of ID-glosses as a basic entry point to the data collection. The corresponding entry in a machine-readable lexicon associated to the corpus contains phonological information on the citation form. Phonetic properties such as the precise location of the hand in space or the state of the thumb can be added as properties of a gloss annotation to a sign, depending on the methodology for answering specific research questions. The selection of relevant items for studies that call for phonetic annotations can be most efficiently made once sign-level annotations have been made before.

Acknowledgments

Writing of this chapter was supported by grants from the Netherlands Organisation for Scientific Research (NWO 276-70-012) and from the European Research Council (ERC 210373).

Note

1 In this chapter the capitalized form *Deaf* is used only when it refers to social entities, not to individuals.

Keywords

corpus annotation; corpus linguistics; ELAN; glossing; notation; orthography; phonetic transcription; transcription; writing systems

See Also

Chapter 5; Chapter 9; Chapter 10; Chapter 11

Suggested Readings

Fischer, R. (1994). The notation of sign languages: Bebian's Mimographie. In H. Bos and
T. Schermer (Eds.), *Sign Language Research 1994*. Hamburg: Signum Press, pp. 285–302.
Johnston, T. (2010). Adding value to, and extracting of value from, a signed language corpus
through secondary processing: Implications for annotation schemas and corpus creation.
In P. Dreuw, E. Efthimiou, T. Hanke, T. Johnston, G. Ruiz Martinéz, and A. Schembri
(Eds.), *Proceedings of the fourth workshop on the representation and processing of sign
languages: Corpora and sign language technologies*. Paris: ELRA, pp. 137–142.
Miller, C. (2006). Sign language: Transcription, notation, and writing. In K. Brown (Ed.),
Encyclopedia of language and linguistics, vol. 8. Oxford: Elsevier, pp. 353–354.
Millet, A., and Estève, I. (2010). Transcribing and annotating multimodality: How deaf chil-
drens' productions call into the question the analytical tools. *Gesture* 10(2/3), 297–320.
Ochs, E. (1979). Transcription as theory. In E. Ochs and B. B. Schieffelin (Eds.), *Developmental
pragmatics*. New York: Academic Press, pp. 43–72.
Thoutenhoofd, E. (1992). Trans-scribing and reading: What constitutes a writing system?
Signpost 4(2), 39–51.

References

Baker, A., van den Bogaerde, B., and Woll, B. (2005). Methods and procedures in sign lan-
guage acquisition studies. *Sign Language & Linguistics* 8, 7–59.
Baker, P., Hardie, A., and McEnerny, T. (2006). *A glossary of corpus linguistics*. Edinburgh:
Edinburg University Press.
Baker-Shenk, C. (1983). A microanalysis of the nonmanual components of questions in
American Sign Language. PhD Dissertation, University of California, Berkeley.
Bianchini, C. S., and Borgia, F. (2012). Writing sign languages: Analysis of the evolution of the
SignWriting system from 1995 to 2010, and proposals for future developments. Paper
presented at the International Jubilee Congress "Science and education for the future,"
Varna, Bulgaria.
Broeder, D., van Uytvanck, D., and Senft, G. (2012). Citing on-line language resources. In
Proceedings of language resources and evaluation 2012. Paris: European Language
Resources Association, pp. 1391–1394.
Chen Pichler, D., Hochgesang, J. A., Lillo-Martin, D., and Müller de Quadros, R. (2010).
Conventions for sign and speech transcription of child bimodal bilingual corpora in
ELAN. *Language, Interaction and Acquisition* 1(1), 11–40.
Clark, A. (2012). *How to write American Sign Language*. Burnsville, MN: ASLwrite.
Cohn, J. F., and Ekman, P. (2005). Measuring facial action. In J. A. Harrigan, R. Rosenthal,
and K. Scherer (Eds.), *The new handbook of methods in nonverbal behavior research*.
New York: Oxford University Press, pp. 9–64.
Comrie, B., Haspelmath, M., and Bickel, B. (2008). *The Leipzig glossing rules: Conventions
for interlinear morpheme-by-morpheme glosses*. Leipzig: Max Planck Institute for
Evolutionary Anthropology, Department of Linguistics.
Crasborn, O. (2010). *The sign linguistics corpora network: Towards standards for signed lan-
guage resources*. In *Proceedings of the seventh conference on international language*

resources and evaluation (LREC 2010). Paris: European Language Resources Association, pp. 457–460.

Crasborn, O., and & de Meijer, A. (2012). From corpus to lexicon: The creation of ID-glosses for the Corpus NGT. In O. Crasborn, E. Efthimiou, E. Fotinea, T. Hanke, J. Hedegaard Kristoffersen, and J. Mesch (Eds.), *Interactions between corpus and lexicon: Proceedings of the fifth workshop on the representation and processing of sign languages*. Paris: ELRA, pp. 13–17.

Crasborn, O., and Sáfár, A. (forthcoming). Annotation of hand dominance in the Corpus NGT. In M. Steinbach, R. Pfau, and A. Herrmann (Eds.), *Complex sentences and beyond*. Berlin: Mouton De Gruyter.

Crasborn, O., and Windhouwer, M. (2012). ISOcat data categories for signed language resources. In E. Efthimiou, G. Kouroupetroglou, and S.-E. Fotinea (Eds.), *Gesture and sign language in human–computer interaction and embodied communication*. Berlin: Springer, pp. 118–128.

Crasborn, O., van der Hulst, H., and van der Kooij, E. (2001). SignPhon: A phonological database for sign languages. *Sign Language & Linguistics* 4(1/2), 215–228.

Crasborn, O., Zwitserlood, I., and Ros, J. (2008). The corpus NGT: An open access digital corpus of movies with annotations of Sign Language of the Netherlands. Centre for Language Studies, Radboud University Nijmegen. Accessed September 6, 2014. http://www.ru.nl/corpusngtuk

Crasborn, O., Mesch, J., Waters, D., Nonhebel, A., van der Kooij, E., Woll, B., and Bergman, B. (2007). Sharing sign language data online: Experiences from the ECHO project. *International Journal of Corpus Linguistics* 12(4), 535–562.

Dachkovsky, S., and Sandler, W. (2009). Visual intonation in the prosody of a sign language. *Language and Speech* 52(2/3), 287–314.

Ekman, P., and Friesen, W. V. (1969). The repertoire of nonverbal behavior: Categories, origins, usage, and coding. *Semiotica* 1(1), 49–98.

Farnell, B. (1996). Movement notation systems. In P. Daniels and W. Bright (Eds.), *The world's writing systems*. New York: Oxford University Press, pp. 855–879.

Frishberg, N. (1983). Writing systems and problems for sign language notation. *Journal for the Anthropological Study of Human Movement* 2(4), 169–195.

Frishberg, N., Hoiting, N., and Slobin, D. I. (2012). Transcription. In R. Pfau, M. Steinbach, and B. Woll (Eds.), *Sign language: An international handbook*. Berlin: Mouton De Gruyter, pp. 1045–1075.

Hanke, T. (2002). HamNoSys in sign language generation context. In R. Schulmeister and H. Reinitzer (Eds.), *Progress in sign language research*. Hamburg: Signum Press, pp. 249–266.

Hoiting, N., and Slobin, D. I. (2002). Transcription as a tool for understanding: The Berkeley Transcription System for sign language research (BTS). In G. Morgan and B. Woll (Eds.), *Directions in sign language acquisition*. Amsterdam: John Benjamins, pp. 55–75.

van der Hulst, H., and Channon, R. (2010). Notation systems. In D. Brentari (Ed.), *Sign Languages*. Cambridge: Cambridge University Press, pp. 151–172.

Johnson, R. E., and Liddell, S. K. (2010). Toward a phonetic representation of signs: Sequentiality and contrast. *Sign Language Studies* 11(2), 241–274.

Johnson, R. E., and Liddell, S. K. (2011a). Toward a phonetic representation of hand configuration: The fingers. *Sign Language Studies* 12(1), 5–45.

Johnson, R. E., and Liddell, S. K. (2011b). A segmental framework for representing signs phonetically. *Sign Language Studies* 11(3), 408–463.

Johnson, R. E., and Liddell, S. K. (2012). Toward a phonetic representation of hand configuration: The thumb. *Sign Language Studies* 12(2), 316–333.

Johnston, T. (2008). Corpus linguistics and signed languages: No lemmata, no corpus. In O. Crasborn, E. Efthimiou, T. Hanke, E. Thoutenhoofd, D., and I. Zwitserlood (Eds.),

Fifth workshop on the representation and processing of signed languages: Construction and exploitation of sign language corpora. Paris: ELRA, pp. 82–87.

Johnston, T. (2010). From archive to corpus: Transcription and annotation in the creation of signed language corpora. *International Journal of Corpus Linguistics* 15(1), 104–129.

Johnston, T. (2014). Auslan corpus annotation guidelines. Manuscript, Macquarie University, Sydney. Accessed October 29, 2014. http://new.auslan.org.au/about/annotations/

Miller, C. (1994). A note on notation. *Signpost* 7(3), 191–202.

Miller, C. (2001). Some reflections on the need for a common sign notation. *Sign Language & Linguistics* 4(1/2), 11–28.

Morgan, G. (2005). Transcription of child sign language: A focus on narrative. *Sign Language & Linguistics* 8, 119–130.

Newkirk, D. (1989). *SignFont: Handbook*. Bellevue, WA: Edmark Corporation.

Ormel, E., and Crasborn, O. (2014). Kinematic properties of lexical and transitional movements in Sign Language of the Netherlands. Manuscript under review.

Ormel, E., Crasborn, O., and de Meijer, A. (2014). Coarticulation of handshape in Sign Language of the Netherlands: A corpus study. Manuscript under review.

Piater, J., Hoyoux, T., and Du, W. (2010). Video analysis for continuous sign language recognition. Paper presented at the fourth workshop on the representation and processing of sign languages "Corpora and sign language technologies," 22–23 May, Valletta, Malta.

Prillwitz, S., and Zienert, H. (1990). Hamburg notation system for sign language: Development of a sign writing with computer applications. In S. Prillwitz and T. Vollhaber (Eds.), *Current trends in European sign language research*, vol. 9. Hamburg: Signum Press, pp. 355–379.

Russell, K., Wilkinson, E., and Janzen, T. (2011). ASL sign lowering as undershoot: A corpus study. *Laboratory Phonology* 2(2), 403–422.

Schembri, A., and Crasborn, O. (2010). Issues in creating annotation standards for sign language description. In In P. Dreuw, E. Efthimiou, T. Hanke, T. Johnston, G. Ruiz Martinéz, and A. Schembri (Eds.), *Proceedings of the fourth workshop on the representation and processing of sign languages: Corpora and sign language technologies*. Paris: ELRA, pp. 212–216.

Schultze-Berndt, E. (2006). Linguistic annotation. In J. Gippert, N. Himmelmann, and U. Mosel (Eds.), *Essentials of language documentation*. Berlin: Mouton de Gruyter, pp. 213–251.

Slobin, D. I., Hoiting, N., Anthony, M., Biederman, Y., Kuntze, L., Lindert, R., and Weinberg, A. (2001). The Berkeley Transcription System (BTS) for sign language. *Sign Language & Linguistics* 4(1/2), 63–96.

Stokoe, W. C. (1960). *Sign language structure: An outline of the visual communication systems of the American Deaf*. Buffalo, NY: Department of Anthropology and Linguistics, University of Buffalo.

Stokoe, W. C., Casterline, D. C., and Croneberg, C. G. (1965). *A dictionary of American Sign Language on linguistic principles*. Washington, DC: Gallaudet College Press.

Sutton, V. (1999). SignWriting: On the occasion of its 25th anniversary, November 1999. *Sign Language & Linguistics* 2(2), 271–282.

Takkinen, R. (2005). Some observations on the use of HamNoSys (Hamburg Notation System for Sign Languages) in the context of the phonetic transcription of children's signing. *Sign Language & Linguistics* 8, 99–118.

Thompson, P. (2010). Building a specialised audio-visual corpus. In A. O'Keeffe and M. McCarthy (Eds.), *The Routledge handbook of corpus linguistics*. Abingdon: Routledge, pp. 93–103.

de Vos, C., van der Kooij, E., and Crasborn, O. (2009). Mixed signals: Combining linguistic and affective functions of eyebrows in questions in sign language of the Netherlands. *Language and Speech* 52(2/3), 315–339.

6 Instrumented Measures of Sign Production and Perception: Motion Capture, Movement Analysis, Eye-Tracking, and Reaction Times

Martha E. Tyrone

Chapter Overview

One of the central goals of linguistic research on sign language is to elucidate the mechanisms of language perception and production. Instrumented studies of sign language are designed to measure such mechanisms precisely and quantitatively. In many ways, instrumented research on sign language is analogous to acoustic phonetic research: those two subfields of linguistics take a physical, quantitative approach, which complements that of traditional descriptive phonetics. In addition to facilitating phonetic analyses of sign language, instrumented techniques are also useful for the development of systems for automated sign recognition and sign synthesis (which depend on perception and

Research Methods in Sign Language Studies: A Practical Guide, First Edition.
Edited by Eleni Orfanidou, Bencie Woll, and Gary Morgan.

production by machines rather than by human beings). Instrumented techniques and their associated measures can be applied to a broad range of research questions, but they are best suited to studies of adult sign language users. Particular techniques to be reviewed in this chapter include electronic motion capture, data glove systems, video-based motion analysis procedures, eye-tracking systems, and reaction-time paradigms.

Introduction

Linguistics as a field is concerned with discovering how human language (spoken or signed) is produced and perceived. While a variety of techniques are useful for examining theoretical issues in sign language research, experimental research on sign production and sign perception requires the use of instrumentation or automated data analysis. In speech research, instrumental techniques for capturing and analyzing production and perception are well established, but less is available for similar quantitative analyses of sign language.

Many of the techniques that linguists use for recording and transcribing speech cannot be easily applied to a language that uses no sound and has no widely used written form. In sign language research there are no universal conventions for phonetically transcribing sign productions, for representing the physical form of language, or for quantifying the physical correlates of sign structure. By contrast, spoken language research has a widely agreed upon transcription system (the International Phonetic Alphabet, IPA), conventions for representing the physics of speech (e.g., spectrograms and acoustic waveforms), and established physical correlates for the features of speech sounds (e.g., formant frequencies). Thus, describing sign production in precise terms is challenging, due to the comparative lack of specialized equipment, measurement techniques, and quantitative phonetic measurement units.

The limited availability of recording techniques and measurement schemata for sign language creates a challenge for sign language researchers. An additional challenge is the fact that the physical structure of sign language is fundamentally different from that of spoken language. Unlike speech, which uses an auditory–vocal production medium, sign language uses a visual–manual medium, the hands and arms being its primary articulators. Because the sign articulators are much larger than the speech articulators, sign language uses a large articulatory space than speech, which means that sign data must be captured from a broad region of space. In addition, because there are many sign articulators that can act independently of each other, data capture must allow for multiple streams of information to be recorded at once. This can be problematic, for example for automated sign recognition, in which a machine uses visual information to identify and translate signs during real-time production (see Vogler and Metaxas, 2004). Sign language uses a visual medium, which means that the capture system must be able to capture data that are four-dimensional, with dissociable x, y, and z spatial coordinates measured over time. (The one dimension along which sign may be easier to capture than speech is speed: because signs are produced more slowly than spoken words, it is possible to record signing at a much lower sampling rate; see Klima and Bellugi, 1979.)

These issues of data capture technology and sign structure are relevant to the study of sign perception as well as to that of sign production. The complex, multidimensional nature of sign language makes it difficult for researchers to record and present the type of naturalistic language stimuli that are used to assess language perception and processing. Language perception experiments typically involve presenting carefully controlled linguistic stimuli to language users and measuring these users' ability and aptitude for perceiving similarities and differences among the stimuli. For example, in speech research, listeners might be asked to identify the consonant that they hear in multiple recordings of CV syllables, in which acoustic aspects of the consonant vary only slightly (see Lisker and Abramson, 1964). In this way researchers can determine which factors the listeners use to categorize acoustically distinct speech sounds as a single phoneme. This type of study has been challenging for sign language researchers, because it is difficult to manipulate phonological parameters of signs with precision and without one parameter influencing another.

The purpose of instrumented research on sign language is to facilitate our understanding of the perception and production of language in the sign modality. In particular, instrumented techniques allow quantitative, objective measurements that can inform our understanding of sign language structure. For example, researchers have used instrumented techniques to examine co-articulation (Grosvald and Corina, 2012), emphatic stress (Wilbur, 1990), and verb agreement (Thompson, Emmorey, and Kluender, 2006) in the sign modality. The rest of this chapter will review specific techniques for recording and analyzing sign production and perception and will discuss some sign language studies that have used those techniques.

Motion Capture

One technique for collecting precise quantitative information about sign production is motion capture, which is distinct from standard video in that it collects three-dimensional information about movement at a fast sampling rate (~60–100Hz). It also differs from video in that it uses markers placed on the body in order to record the data. This has advantages and disadvantages, which will be outlined below. Motion capture is a technique that is primarily used in laboratory settings, although a few portable systems exist. Portable systems are useful for recording signers who are home-bound or have limited mobility, for example. In general lab-based systems are more reliable, because no measurement error is introduced by the reconfiguration of the cameras. Moreover, a lab-based setting allows for control over issues such as lighting. Motion capture recordings can be used to study a wide range of linguistic and paralinguistic phenomena, including the use of signing space, prosodic aspects of signing, differences in typical and atypical sign production, and the major phonological parameters of signs (handshape, movement, and location).

The markers that are attached to the body in a motion capture recording session send signals to some type of electronic device, which processes the information and relays the data to a personal computer. Various systems use different types of physical

Figure 6.1 Optotrak cameras.

signals (e.g., light, sound, magnetic fields) to track the positions of the markers. Optical systems use a set of cameras in conjunction with a set of light sources to track movement; for example, the Optotrak system (Northern Digital Inc.) uses a set of diodes that emit infrared light. The diodes are attached to participants' articulators (usually the hands), and a set of two or more cameras record pulses of light emitted by the diodes and compute the 3D coordinates of their locations over time (see Figure 6.1). Optical systems can be spatio-temporally very precise, with sampling rates of 100–750 Hz (depending on the software) and spatial resolutions of 0.1–0.15 mm. However, because they use an optical signal, they cannot record data when anything opaque comes between a diode and the cameras. Such situations include instances where the hand changes orientation, so that part of the hand itself comes between the diode and the cameras. This can be problematic for capturing sign production, because the hands change orientation often in the course of signing.

Other types of optical motion capture, such as the Vicon system, use passive markers placed on the body that reflect infrared light emitted by strobes on the camera units (see Figure 6.2 and Figure 6.3). The reflected light is received by the electronic cameras, and the locations of the markers are tracked over time. This type of system has comparable spatial resolution but lower temporal resolution (60–120 Hz), though this capture rate is sufficient for capturing limb and body movement during signing. Both types of optical motion capture systems have been used for research on speech (Ostry, Gribble, and Gracco, 1996), motor control (Lang and Bastian, 2002), and sign language (Brentari, Poizner, and Kegl, 1995; Poizner, Klima, and Bellugi, 1987; Mauk, 2003).

The motion capture systems that have been used most often for sign language research are optical. However, motion capture systems can instead be designed to

Figure 6.2 Vicon camera.

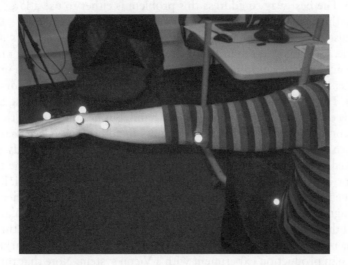

Figure 6.3 Reflective markers from a Vicon system.

detect changes in magnetic fields, ultrasonic sound waves, or rotational inertia and to use these signals to track motion (see Huenerfauth and Lu, 2010; Grosvald and Corina, 2012). These non-optical systems have an advantage over optical ones in that movement data are less likely to be occluded when the markers are oriented away from the device detecting the signal. Like the strobed optical systems, the non-optical systems are slightly less precise temporally (60–100 Hz), but they are nonetheless sufficient to capture most aspects of sign production. Only the most rapid fingerspelling is likely to pose a problem for motion capture recording.

Regarding the physics of the non-optical systems, magnetic motion capture systems employ a large magnet in combination with a group of small magnets: the small magnets are attached as markers on the body and, when they move through space, they disrupt the magnetic field generated by the large magnet, so that their positions can be tracked. Ultrasonic motion capture systems include a set of sound emitters that are placed on the body as markers; and a pressure-sensitive microphone tracks the ultrasonic waves emitted by the markers. Finally, inertial motion capture systems use electronic gyroscopes attached at different points on the body to detect movement rotation. This type of system is unable to track markers' absolute positions in space, but it is able to track markers' relative positions. So it is good for global, multi-articulator measures of signing – such as the timing and coordination of sequences of sign movements – but less well suited to measuring movements in relation to an external target.

As outlined above, with any of the motion capture systems, markers must be attached to a signer's articulators in order to record movements during signing. Strategic marker placement is one of the main challenges of experimentation with motion capture. Correct camera placement is important too, but this is simpler to implement, since cameras can remain in fixed positions from one experimental session to another, while markers are reapplied for each session. Light-emitting or -reflecting markers must be placed so that they are detectable by the capture system most (if not all) of the time. Marker occlusions are most problematic for hand and finger movements, since those movements are faster, smaller, and have many degrees of freedom. The best way to address this problem is either to use a large number of markers on those articulators or to use a data-glove system (see below). In addition, markers must be placed so that they do not interfere with the signer's movements. For example, for signs that require contact with the body, it is important not to place markers in a way that would block this contact. At the same time it is important to place markers so that they give information about where the articulators of interest are located. Thus, in order to measure where the hand is located during a particular sign, it is necessary to attach markers on the hand, but not on parts of the hand that will make contact with the body during signing. In addition, it is necessary to attach markers such that they will not change position in relation to the body part that is being tracked. So, for example, it is not feasible to use a marker on the forehead as an indicator of the chin's position, because the chin can move partially independently of the forehead. Finally, a single marker cannot indicate the orientation of a particular sign articulator. In order to determine orientation, the articulator must be defined as a three-dimensional rigid body, which requires placement of three markers that do not move relative to each other. Figure 6.4 illustrates the marker arrangement for a sign production experiment with a Vicon system. Note that three or more markers are used to represent individual sign articulators, such as the chin or the hand, and these markers remain fixed in relation to each other. (The color scheme in the figure has no special significance and is used simply to facilitate visualization for researchers during data-processing.) If markers are placed very precisely at specific joints or according to specific anatomical landmarks, then the movement data can be analyzed according to established biodynamic models for the movements of particular body parts. However, attaching markers directly on the finger joints can both impede movement and increase the likelihood of marker occlusion. Moreover, the more proximal joints of the arm are often not visible to the experimenter, which makes it impossible to place markers precisely in relation to those joints.

In this type of experiment the signer usually produces utterances from a script, which means that specific signs are produced in a specific order, as indicated by the

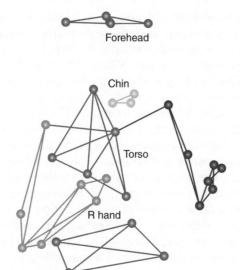

Figure 6.4 Marker schema for a Vicon experiment.

experimenter. There are two main reasons for this. First, motion capture systems collect many streams of data from multiple articulators, and the capture rate is high. As a result, it can be difficult to differentiate meaningful patterns in the data from random noise. On a related point, the other reason for the use of scripts is that motion capture lends itself well to comparisons of minute distinctions in sign production, such as the variation in a sign's position that results from the co-articulatory effects of other signs; hence it is useful to design one's experiments, in order to make sure that specific distinctions are elicited. In experiments that utilize spontaneous data, it is difficult to ensure that the relevant contrasts will emerge in the data set. In addition, it can take an enormous amount of time to identify and extract the data of interest from spontaneously generated productions. That said, studies that are more interested in automatic recognition or synthesis than in measurement are beginning to use motion capture to collect extended periods of signing (Jantunen, Burger, De Weerdt, Seilola, and Wainio, 2012).

Many of the earliest studies that used motion capture to analyze sign production investigated differences between typical signing and signing that was disrupted by neurological disorders such as stroke or Parkinson's disease. Poizner et al. (1987) were among the first sign language researchers to use motion capture. They carried out a series of studies that compared the productions of ASL signers who had aphasia, apraxia, or right hemisphere damage as a result of stroke. The goal of their research was to determine whether aphasia would take a different articulatory form from deficits in the production of meaningful gestures (apraxia) or from visuospatial deficits caused by right hemisphere damage. Poizner, Bellugi, and Klima (1990) extended this line of research to include signers with Parkinson's disease, a disorder that is primarily motoric rather than linguistic in nature. Similarly, Brentari et al. (1995) carried out an Optotrak study to compare an ASL signer with Parkinson's disease and an ASL signer with aphasia. Using motion capture data, they were able to show that the signer with Parkinson's disease preserved linguistic contrasts in production but showed a deficit in the coordination of handshape and movement. By contrast, the errors produced by the signer with aphasia were linguistic rather than motoric in nature.

Some early motion capture studies examined normal variation rather than comparing typical and atypical production. Wilbur (1990) used a WATSMART system to examine the realization of linguistic stress in the sign modality. WATSMART was one of the earliest motion capture system – its name is an acronym for Waterloo Spatial Motion Analysis and Recording Technique. Using this technique, she showed that native signers modified the duration of the movement transition prior to a stressed sign, whereas non-native signers increased the displacement of the sign itself. This distinction between native and non-native stress patterns would likely not be identifiable from descriptive analyses of video. In another study using WATSMART, Wilcox (1992) examined the production of ASL fingerspelling. His findings demonstrated that there was a large amount of co-articulation in fingerspelling and that features from an individual letter in a fingerspelling sequence would carry over into subsequent letters in the sequence. Moreover, he found that the transitions between letters were important for comprehension of fingerspelling in ASL.

More recent studies have applied motion capture methodologies to typical variation in sign production in order to study phenomena such as co-articulation, reduction, and articulatory undershoot and overshoot. Mauk (2003) used a Vicon system to examine articulatory undershoot of handshape and location in ASL (that is, situations when the articulators do not move far enough to achieve handshape or location targets). He found that undershoot occurred in both of these parameters as an effect of signing rate and phonetic environment. Similarly, Tyrone and Mauk (2012) collected a larger data sample using Optotrak in order to investigate phonetic reduction in the realization of location in ASL. Like the earlier study by Mauk (2003), theirs found that phonetic reduction in ASL occurred as an effect of factors that would be predicted from speech research. Their main result was that ASL signs with locations that are high in the signing space tended to be lowered at faster signing rates and when they were preceded or followed by a sign that was low in the signing space.

Grosvald and Corina (2012) used an ultrasonic motion capture system to examine linguistic and non-linguistic co-articulation in sign production, which they compared to co-articulation in acoustic speech data. They examined not only the effects of adjacent signs on the realization of location, but also the effects of signs that precede or follow the target sign at a distance of up to three intervening signs. They found that co-articulatory effects were weaker in the sign modality than in speech – in particular, distant speech segments had a stronger influence on vowel formants than distant signs had on sign location. In addition, they found that, in terms of co-articulation, linguistic co-articulation patterned more like non-linguistic co-articulation than like co-articulation in speech.

Data Glove Systems

A few studies have used electronic data glove systems to collect hand movement data during signing (Huenerfauth and Lu, 2010; Eccarius, Bour, and Scheidt, 2012). These systems have strain gauges (i.e., pressure-sensitive bendable strips), which are embedded in tight-fitting gloves that the signer wears during data collection. As the hand changes position, the strain gauges are bent and convert the mechanical energy from the hands' movements into an electrical signal transmitted to a computer. In this way researchers can measure degrees of flexion for the different joints in the hand.

In a recent study, Eccarius et al. (2012) measured the realization of ASL handshapes by using a set of cybergloves. The goal of their study was to define an articulatory joint space for ASL handshapes that would be analogous to the acoustic–articulatory vowel space from speech research. This was the first study to investigate the physiological limits of handshape structure and to try to determine the distribution of handshapes produced within those limits. Like the vowels in spoken language, the commonly occurring handshapes were maximally distinct from each other and were located near the outer limits of the articulatory space.

Huenerfauth and Lu (2010) used cybergloves in conjunction with an inertial motion capture system to develop a database of naturalistic ASL signing data. They put special emphasis on collecting productions of verbs that included spatial inflections, because it has been challenging for automated sign recognition and synthesis systems to deal with the variety of articulatory forms that occur with spatial verb inflection. Their database served as the basis for an automated sign synthesis program for ASL.

One of the limitations of data gloves is that the calibration process is lengthy and complicated. The gloves have to be calibrated separately for each participant. During this process, the signer is asked to hold a series of different hand configurations, so that the system can record the range of his/her movements and the approximate size and position of the hands' joints. In addition, probably the biggest limitation of data glove systems is that they are not only expensive but also relatively fragile, which means that the calibration has to be carried out slowly and carefully. If an experimental participant puts on or removes the gloves too quickly or too forcefully, the strain gauges can be irreparably damaged. In general it is difficult to collect instrumented data with children, but this is more true of data gloves than of any other type of instrumented movement recording.

In terms of phonological parameters, gloves can be used to measure handshape, while motion capture systems with separate markers are better suited to measuring location and movement. Either of these techniques can be used to examine phonetic correlates of phrase- or discourse-level phenomena such as emphatic stress or prosody. It should be noted that data glove systems vary in the number of motion sensors embedded in each glove, and only the systems with a large number of sensors are capable of distinguishing the full range of phonological handshape contrasts in a sign language.

Video-Based Movement Analysis

In addition to recording movement with a marker-based system, it is possible to record movement during signing by using ordinary video and applying a motion detection algorithm to the video data. The algorithm uses information about color and contrast in the video to detect edges and determine what is a moving figure versus a fixed background. In this way it is possible to track the articulators during sign production. Motion detection is advantageous, because standard video is widely available and video can be collected in a variety of settings, including Deaf[1] clubs or individuals' homes. By contrast, motion capture systems are less accessible and they most often have to be used in a laboratory setting, which is less naturalistic. Another important advantage of video motion detection is that it avoids the problem of markers that might constrain or otherwise affect movement.

Video-based motion detection is particularly useful for automatic sign recognition, in which a sign recognition algorithm searches for an approximate pattern of movement and compares it against a stored template of what a given sign should look like. However, motion detection is less useful for the type of precise measurements required for phonetic analysis. The temporal and spatial resolution of motion detection is only as good as the resolution of the video input itself. As a result, it is sufficient for differentiating signs from one another (i.e., for identifying phonological contrasts), but less good at capturing and quantifying phonetic variation that is non-contrastive but may reveal information about extralinguistic factors such as accent or language experience.

Vogler and Metaxas (2004) used video-based motion detection to develop an automatic recognition system for ASL. They used a movement-hold model to parse the data in a way that it could be processed by their recognition system. In a similar study, Karppa, Jantunen, Koskela, Laaksonen, and Viitaniemi (2011) collected videotaped signing data in Finnish Sign Language and used automated motion detection to analyze head and hand movement during signing. They demonstrated that information from these articulators could be extracted from video data, and resulting visual displays could be integrated into existing sign language annotation programs, such as ELAN. Both of these studies suggest that video data can successfully be used for automatic sign recognition.

Eye-Tracking

Eye-tracking is a technique that uses small cameras to measure eye movements and periods of gaze fixation. The cameras detect infrared light reflected off the cornea or pupil and use it to compute gaze direction. Cameras can be mounted on the head or placed in a fixed location in front of a research participant (see Figure 6.5). (Note that, if the eye tracker is not mounted on the head, then researchers must track head movement in addition to eye movement, or must require participants to hold their head in a fixed position.) This technique is useful for sign language research, because it allows researchers to determine what information a signer is attending to during sign perception or to analyze how eye movements are coordinated with other movements during sign production. Eye-tracking is unique among the techniques discussed here, in that it has been used both as a method for looking at sign perception and as a method for looking at sign production. In the realm of sign perception, eye-tracking can be used to discover what signers attend to while they are perceiving sign language. Further, it can be used to determine how attentional patterns differ with signing skill or language background.

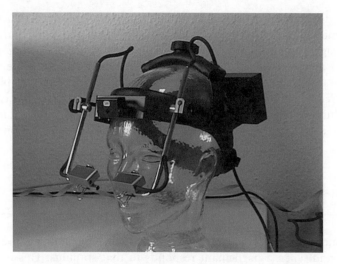

Figure 6.5 A head-mounted eye-tracking system. With permission of William C. Schmidt, SR Research Limited, http://www.sr-research.com/EL_II.html

Muir and Richardson (2005) carried out an eye-tracking study with Deaf users of British Sign Language (BSL). The purpose of the study was to determine which regions of a signer's body carried the most important information for sign perception. Their longer term objective was to optimize standards for videophones, so that they would be well suited to sign language communication. The eye movements of Deaf volunteers were recorded as they watched BSL stories on videotape. To do this, the researchers measured the amount of fixation time at different anatomical regions such as the upper and lower face, the upper and lower body, and the hands. What they found was that signers spent the most time fixating on the face and that most signers looked preferentially at the upper face.

Emmorey, Thompson, and Colvin (2008) compared eye movements during sign perception in native Deaf signers and in hearing beginners. Both groups of signers fixated primarily on the face of the person who was signing. However, the two groups differed in that native signers fixated on the upper face, whereas beginners fixated on the lower face – specifically, the region around the mouth. Both groups made occasional saccades to the signer's hands, but these almost always co-occurred with the signer's fixation on her own hand. In other words, the signer and the interlocutor shared visual attention by fixating on the signer's hands.

Thompson et al. (2006) used an eye-tracking system to examine eye gaze as a component of ASL sign production rather than sign perception. They measured eye gaze during the production of agreeing, non-agreeing, and locative verbs. They found that signers looked toward locative objects and objects of agreeing verbs, but not toward objects of plain verbs. More recently, Thompson, Emmorey, and Kluender (2009) expanded this research to examine eye movements in native signers, non-native beginning signers, and non-native skilled signers during ASL verb production. In this later study they found that beginners did not show a consistent gaze pattern toward one sign type or another and skilled non-native signers showed a gaze pattern similar to that of native signers for locative and agreeing verbs, but not for plain verbs.

The most difficult aspect of using eye-tracking to measure sign production is likely to be the measurement interference created by hand and body movement. For example, a signer might bump into a head-mounted eye tracker while producing a sign located at the forehead. Similarly, a signer's hand might come between an external eye tracker and the eye, such that eye movement data are blocked from being captured. Head motion can also interfere with eye-tracking, if it causes an eye tracker to shift position on the head. This could arise from sign-related movement in a production experiment or from non-signing movement in a perception experiment.

Reaction-Time Studies

Reaction time refers to the time interval between when a stimulus is presented in an experiment and when a participant responds to that stimulus. This is a technique that is used to collect information about sign perception. There is a long history of using reaction times to analyze speech perception (see Studdert-Kennedy, Liberman, and Stevens, 1963), and the technique has also been adopted by researchers who investigate the perception of sign language. In a sign perception experiment participants are typically asked to make judgments about signs by responding to the signed stimuli as quickly as possible. Thus it is not only their responses that are recorded, but also the speed with which they respond. This is thought to reflect the ease or automaticity of the linguistic task. So, for example, if two stimuli are perceived as very similar, it would be expected that the participant takes longer to carry out the judgment task.

The main types of tasks used with reaction-time measures are discrimination tasks, in which a participant has to determine whether two sign tokens are the same or different, and lexical decision tasks, in which a participant has to determine whether a sign token is a real sign or a pseudo-sign. Information about a participant's reaction time is usually collected by means of a button-press on a computer; but the time it takes a participant to initiate a signed response can also be measured. Using this type of paradigm, Dye and Shih (2006) examined phonological priming in BSL. In each experimental trial, participants were shown two signs in sequence and asked to decide whether the second sign was a real sign in BSL. In some cases the first sign was phonologically similar to the second sign, in other cases it was not. In this way the researchers were able to assess the priming effects of the phonological parameters on participants' responses. They found that native signers showed shorter reaction times when the two signs were phonologically similar (specifically, in terms of movement and location). In other words, the phonologically related form primed participants' lexical decision process.

Reaction-time measurements are often interpreted to reflect the ease with which a participant can carry out a perception task; but one difficulty with this is that unusual or unnatural tasks can yield longer reaction times. Thus it is necessary to independently test tasks for naturalness before using reaction time as a measure of phonological processing, for example. Moreover, it is not informative to compare reaction times across studies or across experimental techniques, because different techniques can create variability in the reaction-time values (see Moreno, Stepp, and Turvey, 2011).

Discussion

Like all techniques for studying sign language, instrumentation has its advantages and its disadvantages. The main advantage of instrumented techniques is that they allow precise quantitative measurements. For sign perception, this means that lexical and phonological processing can be examined almost in real time. For sign production, it means that movement trajectories and endpoints for many productions of the same sign can be closely compared in three dimensions, allowing researchers to study, for example, grammatical versus non-grammatical uses of space. Precise measurement by instrumentation can ultimately lead the way to quantitative and objective analyses, which do not rely on language-specific descriptions.

One of the biggest limitations of instrumented measures of sign production and perception currently is that the amount of production and perception data from typical sign language users is very scarce. This is problematic because it impedes researchers' ability to draw inferences about differences related to signing background or language impairment. The data in these areas are so scarce that it is difficult to separate group differences from individual differences. On a related point, for techniques such as motion capture, different signers have different articulators and different anatomical proportions, so it may not be a valid procedure to pool data from different signers, because that might mask real differences or patterns in signing. To date, there have been no attempts to develop an idealized sign articulator set, analogous to the standardized brain tissue maps used by functional MRI studies. As instrumented sign language research evolves, it will be important to develop a reliable normalization procedure for comparing production data across signers. Finally, one point that researchers need to be aware of is the possibility that the equipment used for instrumented sign language research might interfere with normal production and perception processes. This has been a long-standing issue in speech production research, because placing measurement devices inside the mouth can disrupt normal speech movements. Needless to say, the precision that instrumented techniques permit is worth considerably less if they elicit atypical language patterns.

Instrumented measures of sign production are analogous to acoustic phonetics in speech. Descriptive measures are both useful and necessary in sign language research, but quantitative measures of production provide an analytical approach that is less dependent on subjective interpretation. Moreover, quantitative analyses allow researchers to develop measures that are language-independent. As long as sign phonetics relies solely on descriptive measures, it will never be possible to make truly informed cross-linguistic comparisons. Instrumented data capture and analysis can pave the way for universal measures of production and perception, akin to formant frequencies, voice onset time, or fundamental frequency for speech.

Directions for Future Research

Most recent instrumented studies of sign production have focused on phonetics and phonology (Eccarius et al., 2012; Tyrone and Mauk, 2010; Grosvald and Corina, 2012), or on automatic sign recognition (Vogler and Metaxas, 2004; Huenerfauth and Lu, 2010; Karppa et al., 2011.). Instrumented techniques can also be used to examine discourse-level linguistic phenomena such as turn-taking (by recording two signers simultaneously) or the marking of phrase and word boundaries. These phenomena, like phonetic variation, often involve subtle modifications to the timing or size of sign movements, which are most easily measured with instrumentation. Likewise, instrumented techniques can be used to gauge the size and variability of the signing space across individuals or across groups (see Mauk and Tyrone, 2012) – a necessary precursor to a full understanding of the grammatical use of signing space and of how it varies across groups.

Now that instrumented techniques are more widely available, research on sign language would benefit from more studies that combine multiple techniques, such as data gloves and motion capture, or eye-tracking and motion capture. Similarly, it would be useful if there were more direct comparisons of the effectiveness, precision, and reliability of different techniques (Karppa et al., 2011). On a related note, another area to be explored would be the links between the perception and the production of sign language. One could investigate how modifications to production affect perception. For example, does variability in location have a greater effect on perception than variability in handshape? Looking at production and perception together in a systematic way can reveal more about the structure of sign language than looking at the two only in isolation.

Note

1   In this chapter the capitalized form *Deaf* is used to refer to the cultural group of sign language users; the lowercase form *deaf* is used to refer to clinical hearing loss.

Keywords

kinematics; motion capture; sign perception; sign phonetics; sign production

See Also

Chapter 4; Chapter 5

Suggested Readings

Lu, P., and Huenerfauth, M. 2009. Accessible motion-capture glove calibration protocol for recording sign language data from Deaf subjects. In *Proceedings of the 11th international Association for Computing Machinery SIGACCESS conference on computers and accessibility (ASSETS 2009)*. New York: ACM, pp. 83–90.

References

Brentari, D., Poizner, H., and Kegl, J. (1995). Aphasic and Parkinsonian signing: Differences in phonological disruption. *Brain and Language* 48, 69–105.

Dye, M. W. G., and Shih, S.-I. (2006). Phonological priming in British Sign Language. In L. Goldstein, D. H. Whalen, and C. T. Best (Eds.), *Laboratory Phonology 8*. Berlin: Mouton de Gruyter, pp. 241–264.

Eccarius, P., Bour, R., and Scheidt, R. A. (2012). Dataglove measurement of joint angles in sign language handshapes. *Sign Language & Linguistics* 15 (1), 39–72.

Emmorey, K., Thompson, R., and Colvin, R. (2008). Eye gaze during comprehension of American Sign Language by native and beginning signers. *Journal of Deaf Studies and Deaf Education* 14(2), 237–243.

Grosvald, M., and Corina, D. P. (2012). Exploring the movement dynamics of manual and oral articulation: Evidence from coarticulation. *Laboratory Phonology* 3(1), 37–60.

Huenerfauth, M., and Lu, P. (2010). Eliciting spatial reference for a motion-capture corpus of American Sign Language discourse. In P. Dreuw, E. Efthimiou, T. Hanke, T. Johnston, G. Ruiz Martinéz, and A. Schembri (Eds.), *Proceedings of the fourth workshop on the representation and processing of signed languages: Corpora and sign language technologies*. Paris: ELRA, pp. 121–124.

Jantunen, T., Burger, B., De Weerdt, D., Seilola, I., and Wainio, T. (2012). Experiences from collecting motion capture data on continuous signing. In O. Crasborn, E. Efthimiou, E. Fotinea, T. Hanke, J. Kristoffersen, J. Mesch (Eds.), *Proceedings of the fifth workshop on the representation and processing of sign languages: Interactions between corpus and lexicon*. Paris: ELRA, pp. 75–82.

Karppa, M., Jantunen, T., Koskela, M., Laaksonen, J., and Viitaniemi, V. (2011). Method for visualisation and analysis of hand and head movements in sign language video. In C. Kirchhof, Z. Malisz, and P. Wagner (Eds.), *Proceedings of the second gesture and speech in interaction conference*. (GESPIN 2011), Bielefeld, Germany. Accessed September 12, 2014. http://coral2.spectrum.uni-bielefeld.de/gespin2011/final/Jantunen.pdf

Klima, E., and Bellugi, U. (1979). *The signs of language*. Cambridge, MA: Harvard University Press.

Lang, C. E., and Bastian, A. J. (2002). Cerebellar damage impairs automaticity of a recently practiced movement. *Journal of Neurophysiology* 87, 1336–1347.

Lisker, L., and Abramson, A. S. (1964). A cross-language study of voicing in initial stops: Acoustical measurements. *Word* 20(3), 384–422.

Mauk, C. E. (2003). Undershoot in two modalities: Evidence from fast speech and fast signing. PhD thesis, Department of Linguistics, University of Texas at Austin.

Mauk, C. E., and Tyrone, M. E. (2012). Location in ASL: Insights from phonetic variation. *Sign Language & Linguistics* 15(1), 128–146.

Moreno, M. A., Stepp, N., and Turvey, M. T. (2011). Whole body lexical decision. *Neuroscience Letters* 490, 126–129.

Muir, L. J., and Richardson, I. E. G. (2005). Perception of sign language and its application to visual communications for deaf people. *Journal of Deaf Studies and Deaf Education* 10(4), 390–401.

Ostry, D. J., Gribble, P. L., and Gracco, V. L. (1996). Coarticulation of jaw movements in speech production: Is sensitivity in speech kinematics centrally planned? *Journal of Neuroscience* 16(4), 1570–1579.

Poizner, H., Bellugi, U., and Klima, E. S. (1990). Biological foundations of language: Clues from sign language. *Annual Review of Neuroscience* 13, 283–307.

Poizner, H., Klima, E., and Bellugi, U. (1987). *What the hands reveal about the brain*. Cambridge, MA; MIT Press.

Studdert-Kennedy, M., Liberman, A. M., and Stevens, K. N. (1963). Reaction time to synthetic stop consonants and vowels at phoneme centers and at phoneme boundaries. *Journal of the Acoustical Society of America* 35, 1900.

Thompson, R., Emmorey, K., and Kluender, R. (2006). The relationship between eye gaze and verb agreement in American Sign Language: An eye-tracking study. *Natural Language and Linguistic Theory* 24(2), 571–604.

Thompson, R., Emmorey, K., and Kluender, R. (2009). Learning to look: The acquisition of eye-gaze agreement during the production of ASL verbs. *Bilingualism: Cognition and Language* 12(4), 393–409.

Tyrone, M. E., and Mauk, C. E. (2010). Sign lowering and phonetic reduction in American Sign Language. *Journal of Phonetics* 38, 317–328.

Tyrone, M. E., and Mauk, C. E. (2012). Phonetic reduction and variation in American Sign Language: A quantitative study of sign lowering. *Laboratory Phonology* 3, pp. 431–459.

Vogler, C., and Metaxas, D. (2004). Handshapes and movements: Multiple-channel ASL recognition. *Springer Lecture Notes in Artificial Intelligence* 2915, pp. 247–258.

Wilbur, R. B. (1990). An experimental investigation of stressed sign production. *International Journal of Sign Language* 1(1), 41–59.

Wilcox, S. (1992). *The phonetics of fingerspelling*. Philadelphia, PA: John Benjamins.

Part III   Collecting Linguistic Data on Sign Languages

7 Sign Language Fieldwork

Victoria Nyst

Chapter Overview

This chapter addresses the understudied area of sign language fieldwork, taking into account issues that may arise in fieldwork on sign languages outside a context of deaf[1] education and in multilingual and endangered settings. It discusses fieldwork for the purpose of description as well as for that of documentation. The chapter describes practical, interpersonal, and ethical issues in the field that pertain to collaboration with research assistants, consultants, and the larger

Research Methods in Sign Language Studies: A Practical Guide, First Edition.
Edited by Eleni Orfanidou, Bencie Woll, and Gary Morgan.
© 2015 John Wiley & Sons, Inc. Published 2015 by John Wiley & Sons, Inc.

community. Then it turns to more technical issues involved in sign language fieldwork. The use of video and computer technology is briefly touched upon, then followed by the topic of data collection for grammatical analysis. In summary, the chapter discusses the collection of lexical data and of metadata, then the processing and analysis of field data.

Introduction

Linguistic fieldwork concerns the collection of linguistic data in their natural environment, that is, outside of the controlled environments of the laboratory or the library (see Bowern, 2008; Majid, 2012). Linguistic fieldwork is often done for the sake of language documentation and/or description. There is a sound body of studies on fieldwork concerned with spoken languages, including handbooks and guides that address practical, social, and methodological issues. Although they address topics related to the languages of hearing speakers, these studies are in many respects highly relevant for sign language fieldwork (e.g., Newman and Ratliff, 2001; Crowley, 2007; Bowern, 2008; Thieberger, 2011).

There is only a limited number of publications specifically addressing the methodology of fieldwork in sign languages. The first one, Stokoe and Kuschel's (1979) *A Field Guide for Sign Language Research*, is a 30-page paper with checklists for the elicitation of lexical items, grammatical structures, and sociolinguistic metadata as well as with a discussion of how to use them. The second publication is Fischer (2009): a book chapter with a discussion of practical, technical, and ethical issues in sign language fieldwork. Finally, in 2012 Zeshan and Vos edited a volume on rural sign languages that discusses various fieldwork-related issues.

Most of the sign languages studied are majority languages used by large deaf communities that evolved around deaf schools, in industrialized regions. Typically, these sign languages have been studied by linguists based in the countries where the respective languages are used. Most of the data collection for these studies has taken place in well-equipped facilities at universities and deaf organizations.

At the same time a small but growing number of linguists have studied sign languages outside of their own country, in situations that are, in a number of respects, radically different from those of the better studied sign languages – for instance in communities that have limited or no access to deaf education and modern technology, register an unusually high incidence of deafness, or assign a markedly different social position to deaf people and sign languages. Since deaf schools and organizations often provide the natural environment for sign languages, the distinction between natural and controlled environments is not always straightforward. However, the focus of this chapter is on fieldwork in undocumented sign languages in the former type of setting.

I will discuss fieldwork issues for descriptive or documentary purposes. I will give an overview of some of the human, practical, and technical challenges one may face when doing sign language fieldwork, highlighting (1) differences from the existing canon of data collection methods for sign language; and (2) differences from fieldwork on undocumented spoken languages.

Literacy, Bilingualism, and Endangerment

Most sign languages studied so far share a striking number of sociolinguistic features; for instance they are used in highly literate societies, where (residential) deaf schools play a central role in the history of the signing community (see Ladd, 2003); and they are the dominant sign language of their country, being used by a signing community that consists mainly of deaf signers. Undocumented sign languages may crucially differ in these respects, with important implications for fieldwork practices.

When sign languages have evolved and continue to be used outside the context of deaf education, deaf signers are likely to be illiterate, especially when literacy does not play a central role in the wider society and both deaf and hearing signers are typically semi-literate at best. Obviously this situation rules out the use of written stimuli in any form, allowing only non-linguistic or monolingual stimuli. A monolingual approach is seen as desirable for sign language research anyway, because of the risk of transfer of features from the written language (Fischer, 2009); but it is often not fully adhered to for practical reasons. A similar risk of transfer of features exists when a contact sign language is used instead of the target sign language. This may be particularly difficult to avoid when a researcher is not fluent at the onset of the research project, which may be quite typical for fieldworkers from outside the signing community. The inaccessibility of writing not only forces a monolingual approach on the data collection method, but affects virtually all aspects of fieldwork, as will become clear later in this chapter.

One of the reasons why sign languages may remain undocumented for a long time is their coexistence with a larger or more prestigious sign language, which often leads to a negative perception of the local sign language and to a subsequent tendency to not overtly identify with its use and/or to shift to the prestigious sign language. An example of this phenomenon occurs in Israel, where Algerian Jewish Sign Language is used next to Israeli Sign Language by deaf Algerian immigrants and their hearing relatives. Due to negative attitudes toward the language, Algerian Jewish Sign Language is used as an in-group language and as a result its use was not noticed by sign linguists for several decades (Lanesman and Meir, 2012). Similar situations are typically found in countries where a high-prestige sign language is being used in deaf schools (often of foreign origin), and local sign languages are (incorrectly) being perceived as inferior, as for example in the case of Konchri Sain in Jamaica (Cumberbatch, 2012). When signers shift from the low-prestige to the high-prestige sign language, the former often becomes endangered (see Nonaka, 2011). Such unbalanced unimodal bilingualism may affect the fieldwork in various ways. The endangered status of sign languages calls for efforts to document representative samples in order to enable analysis and applied uses in the near or more distant future.

In contrast to most sign languages studied so far, undocumented sign languages may have significant proportions of hearing signers. In the case of communities with a high incidence of hereditary deafness, hearing signers often make up the majority of signers (Nyst, 2012). This situation of balanced bimodal bilingualism exists in tandem with the incidence of hereditary deafness and has important implications for both data collection and analysis.

Descriptive and Documentary Linguistics

For spoken languages, there is a well-established tradition of writing reference grammars that describe the phonology, morphology, and syntax of the language and are optionally accompanied by a word list and samples of text (Ameka, Dench, and Evans, 2006). Such descriptions aim at being data-driven and make use of a repertoire of basic typological notions, which are referred to as "basic linguistic theory" by Dixon (1997).

Writing reference grammars for sign languages is complicated by the shortage of standard methods and tools. First, no convenient phonetic notation system equivalent to the International Phonetic Alphabet (IPA) for spoken languages is available. Second, there is no standard procedure to identify the basic phonological and morphological units of sign languages. Thus there is no standard way to adequately describe the gradient and iconic elements in the lexical and grammatical units or to analyze and describe the phoneme inventory of a given sign language. This makes it hard to describe sign languages in a way that allows for the cross-linguistic comparison that would be necessary for a typology. Recently a collaborative European project has been launched to develop a blueprint for reference grammars of sign languages.[2]

Traditionally, data collection in the field mainly served the purpose of linguistic analysis. More recently the process of data collection has developed into an independent field, in the form of documentary linguistics. Documentary linguistics aims at providing "a comprehensive record of the linguistic practices characteristic of a given speech community ... This ... differs fundamentally from ... language description[, which] aims at the record of a language ... as a system of abstract elements, constructions, and rules" (Himmelmann, 1998: 166).

In view of the endangered state of an increasing number of spoken and signed languages on the one hand and the advance of digital technology on the other, the need was felt to collect representative samples of languages that are accessible to the academic community as well as to the community of users of the language at stake. To this end, data sets need to be representative (e.g., in terms of types of data, but also in terms of language users), accessible (e.g., in terms of annotation, but also practically), and sustainable over time (e.g., in the type of software or tools used). In addition, the involvement of the language community plays a central role in documentary linguistics. Thus ethical issues such as ownership of and access to the language data, reciprocity between the researcher(s) and the community, and language maintenance and/or revitalization are discussed extensively. Language documentation projects may result in representative multimedia corpora (e.g., of discourse, or of stories), lexical databases, and grammatical descriptions. These corpora may also include the documentation of language-related phenomena such as ceremonies, cultural practices, flora and fauna, and so on. Other types of output include materials for use by the community, such as collections of stories and teaching materials. In the past years, large digital corpora have been initiated for a number of majority sign languages, including Sign Language of the Netherlands (Crasborn, Zwitserlood, and Ros, 2008), British Sign Language (Schembri, Fenlon, Rentelis, Reynolds, and Cormier, 2013), and Australian Sign Language (Johnston, 2009). Recently, annotated video corpora of three African sign languages were deposited in online archives: bilingual corpora of Malian Sign Language as used in Bamako (Nyst, Magassouba, and Sylla, 2011) and in the Dogon area of Mali (Nyst, Magassouba, and Sylla, 2012) and a trilingual corpus of Adamorobe Sign Language (Nyst, 2012). (For an updated overview, see the Sign Language Corpora Survey at http://www.sign-lang.uni-ham burg.de/dgs-korpus/index.php/sl-corpora.html).

Practical, Personal, and Interpersonal Issues

Handbooks on linguistic fieldwork address many practical issues. These include the extensive preparations required for the fieldwork itself – trying to get to know as much as possible about the language and culture one is going to study, but also about the practical circumstances of the field site, such as climate, electricity, and so on. One needs to acquire the necessary equipment and become familiar with it. Travelling needs to be prepared (visa, money, health issues), research permits obtained. The practical issues addressed in these handbooks are highly relevant for sign language fieldwork as well: taking one to the field is recommendable (Bowern, 2008; Chelliah and Reuse, 2010; Newman and Ratliff, 2001).

Field guides also typically address the personal and interpersonal challenges that are inevitably part of fieldwork. Many of these challenges are equally encountered in sign language fieldwork. In addition, there are quite a number of interpersonal issues that are specific to this type of fieldwork; they pertain to research assistants, consultants, and the signing community (among other factors), as will be discussed below.

Co-workers: Consultants and research assistants

The active involvement of native language users is indispensible for any fieldwork. A field linguist depends in many ways on the close collaboration with one or more native language users: these act as language consultants, but often also as teachers of the language, interpreters, research assistants, and advisors.

The form that this collaboration takes will vary from one study or from one linguist to another, depending on the type of study. For descriptive studies, a linguist typically works intensively with a small number of language users or consultants. Documentation projects, on the other hand, often aim for large, representative samples of the language; hence a relatively large number of language users will contribute linguistic data. In view of the intended large size of the data set, a lot of assistance is needed for the collection and annotation of the data.

Carrying over part of the responsibility for the data collection to (deaf) native signers automatically traces out quite an elaborate training program for the collectors. This program includes an in-depth exchange on the research project, camera use, interview techniques, and (optionally) literacy and computer skills. The division of roles among deaf collectors in the data collection process may vary according to personal interests and skills. Another significant contribution of native signing research assistants can be their fine-grained intuitions about linguistic variation across a larger group of signers.

When one is not a native signer oneself, it is preferable that data collection be done by (deaf) native signing research assistants. This has a number of important advantages. First of all, the possible linguistic effects of the presence of a (hearing) outside observer on the data collection are avoided. One well-known observer effect in the sign language literature is the signers' tendency to shift toward a signing variety with structures more similar to those of the spoken language in the presence of hearing researchers, irrespective of the latter's command of signing (Fischer, 2009). Sign languages with and without access to deaf education can be expected to differ in this particular observer effect, as a contact variety is not systematically taught to deaf signers in the latter. However, the case of Adamorobe Sign Language shows that contact varieties may exist in the absence of formal education as well (Nyst, 2007); so potential restructuring toward the contact variety – and hence toward the spoken language that shaped it – cannot be ruled out a priori. In the process of collecting data on a low-status sign language that coexists with a higher status one, the presence of a (deaf or hearing) signing researcher from outside during collection may trigger the use of (signs from) the high-status sign language.

Of course, not being present, as a researcher, during data collection also has drawbacks, such as a more limited opportunity to develop the aforementioned intuitions on variation and other interesting phenomena that happen outside the scope of the camera. Also, when natively signing research assistants are not familiar with writing and administration, this may pose challenges related to keeping track of metadata about signers (such as name and age) and about the data collection session.

As native signer co-workers play a pivotal role in the fieldwork, each field linguist faces the task of finding one or more good co-workers who can take part in the project as language consultants and/or research assistants. In some cases it may be difficult to find a good co-worker, but in the communities I have worked in so far, the choice of a particular candidate appeared to be quite straightforward, as everybody seemed to agree on who would be the best collaborator(s), usually because of their outstanding signing skills or because of their participation in earlier sign language projects. Indeed the signers proposed by the community turned out to be invaluably helpful co-workers in most cases.

When one collects data for a corpus, typically, larger numbers of signers are recorded. These consultants are selected in such a way as to come to a sample that is balanced and representative. A common criterion for the selection of signing consultants in sign language studies is, first of all, deafness and, second, native acquisition of the sign language under study (see Fischer, 2009). Thus native signers – that is, deaf signers who acquired their sign language as a first language from their (deaf and ideally natively signing) parents – are generally preferred over others as research subjects. This significantly narrows down the scope of candidate consultants for data collection, as only an estimated 5 percent of the deaf signers seem to fit this profile. In these circumstances, the representativeness of a deaf-of-deaf sampling criterion seems to be limited. For sign languages of communities with mainly hereditary deafness, it is relatively easy to find deaf children with deaf parents; but, in communities with mainly non-hereditary deafness, deaf-of-deaf signers may be extremely hard to find – they may even not exist, as for example in the deaf community of Bamako, the capital of Mali. In fact this may also be the case in smaller deaf communities in industrialized areas, as described for the Basque variety of Spanish Sign Language by Costello, Fernández, and Landa (2008).

Whereas deafness seems a straightforward selection criterion for studies on the structure of sign languages, research on small communities with a high incidence of (hereditary) deafness indicates that the majority of signers are actually hearing. Thus a representative sample of these sign languages should include documentation of the signing of hearing signers as well. In case a sign language has a relatively small number of users, it may be preferable to document the signing of all its signers, rather than of a sample.

Ethics

Sign language fieldwork brings about a host of ethical issues. In the framework of documentary linguistics, the ethics related to data handling and to the language community is given considerable attention. Also discussed there is the usability of ethical guidelines developed for working with human research subjects at several institutions, and particularly the notion of informed consent (for a literature overview, see Rice, 2011). Informed consent is the statement of a research subject that he/she agrees to cooperate in the study, voluntarily informed and fully informed about the uses to which its results will be put. Establishing informed consent with research participants who are unfamiliar with academic practices is challenging, and so is obtaining a meaningful statement of informed consent on paper.

At the same time, as one depends critically on video recordings that cannot be anonymized without loss of information, it is vital to carefully consider how best to come to informed consent in sign language fieldwork. An unproblematic alternative to a statement of consent written on paper is a statement made in sign language and recorded on video. More challenging is the task of clarifying the objectives of the study and the uses to which the data will be put. Thus the initial phase of a large-scale corpus project in Mali consisted of several weeks of discussions and training to make sure we were all on the same page about the necessity to which the recordings would be put, and the uses to which the recordings would be put. Such discussions and trainings were held at various stages of the project, whenever new needs or new questions would come up. The natively signing research assistants would then discuss and clarify the objectives of the study to the over 60 consultants that participated in the data collection for the corpus (Nyst, Magassouba and Sylla, 2011).

For an insightful discussion of the issues pertaining to informed consent in such settings, see Kusters' (2012a) account of her research in Adamorobe.

Another ethical challenge, particularly in the case of communities with a high incidence of deafness, is the question of the extent to which fieldworkers are entitled or obliged to disclose the name and location of their field site. In several cases, anthropological or linguistic research that disclosed the location of such communities has transformed them into destinations for tourists and other interested visitors. The negative effects of this transformation on Adamorobe are described by Kusters (2012b).

Both Stokoe and Kuschel's (1969) field guide and Fischer's (2009) methodological chapter have a section on ethics, which discusses among other things what to do when there are significant restrictions on the use of recorded images and when one records signing children. Stokoe and Kuschel (1969), as well as Kusters (2012a), discuss how the expectations of hearing and deaf people in the field may differ from what the fieldworker can offer.

Community

There are many ways in which the language community can benefit from linguistic research, and the most appropriate way to shape the mutual benefit may differ from one community to another. It is important to plan the community benefit factor into the research design and budget, as it usually requires financial resources.

More traditional ways of giving back to the community include handing out culturally appropriate gifts (e.g., staple food, soap, tools). A perhaps more recent way of giving back consists in offering training and financial support for community projects, such as income-generating and educational ones.

A more long-term way of making sure that the community benefits from the research project is by actively and extensively involving community members in the research project in various functions, such as data collectors, annotators, translators, technical assistants, and the like. In most cases this will require intensive training of the intended co-workers – for instance in filming, interviewing, literacy, general research skills, computer skills, and annotation skills – leading to a transfer of project-related knowledge. To make sure that co-workers become co-owners of the project and also acquire the skills necessary for it, it is vital to plan a preparatory phase, in which the researcher and the co-workers discuss the aims and methods of the project in depth and the necessary training takes place. Both the research and the co-workers will benefit from such a preparatory phase. A similar transfer of project-related knowledge to a larger part of the community can be realized by organizing larger scale training events in which the researcher and the co-workers train together. The aforementioned ways of shaping the benefit for the community are merely a few examples of the various kinds of benefit that research projects may offer to a signing community.

The fruits of the research project – a corpus, a lexical database, or a description – will hopefully benefit the community as well. Research projects and products often improve the status of a sign language and its community. To improve access to digital products, it is recommendable to store a copy in local archives. However, even then, access may be problematic if access to computers and to the corpus software is an issue in general.

Various actions can be undertaken to improve accessibility to research products. If the community so wishes, parts of the research output can be turned into applied materials (e.g., a dictionary, teaching materials, a DVD story). It is good to realize that this often requires extensive human and financial resources, which necessitates finding separate funds. Also, the products of the project can be presented to the community and to government officials in a large event. Another way of facilitating access to the research findings and products is to set up a (multilingual) web-portal.

Learning the language one works on is imperative for communicating with community members and with co-workers. Also, good command of the language facilitates the linguistic analysis of that language. Having a working knowledge of the spoken language (either in speech or in writing) helps a researcher detect traces of language contact, for example in the form of mouthings, loan translations, and grammatical constructions (see Nyst, 2007).

Technical Issues

Ideally, a sign language fieldworker avails her-/himself of the same equipment as her/his colleagues who work in more controlled settings. Typically, however, there are a number of constraints: financial ones (e.g., travel expenses, an already consumed part of the budget), practical ones (limited access to electricity at the field site, or exposure of the equipment to extreme conditions as heat, frost, humidity, or dust). Some of these risks and challenges can be prepared for by bringing sufficient supplies, such as spare batteries and recording space, and perhaps a spare camera.

Documentary linguistics emphasizes the need for high-quality data recordings, which should make sure that the data can be used for various purposes and that loss of quality due to the passing of time will not render the materials useless. To this end, most sign language corpus projects record their data in studios, using extensive equipment to record signers from various angles, the same background for the whole data collection, and several powerful lights for maximum light quality. Corpora recorded in studio conditions of this sort can be used for the development of automated sign language resources, such as signing avatars and machine translation. A professional studio setting is generally not feasible in most field sites, due to practical and budget limitations. Also, signers may be too unfamiliar with such a setting to sign in a natural and relaxed way.[3] An alternative is to record in the daily environment of the signer. This has the added advantage that the natural setting of the sign language is also documented to some extent. This is only possible if everybody in that natural environment is/has become sufficiently familiar with the camera (which in most cases will happen eventually when one carries around and sets up the camera most of the time), so that it does not draw curious crowds. Another possibility is to record at a location relevant to the story being recorded. Thus signers may take the camera on a tour to document and comment on relevant places, animals, plants, and so on.

Grammatical Analysis: Elicitation and Text Collection

The elicitation of linguistic intuitions of consultants is an important tool in the analysis of data in the field. A linguist can ask for intuitions on linguistic features in (recorded) discourse, test the acceptability of constructions made up by the linguist, or translate phrases from a contact language to a target language, for example "How do you say X?" An advantage of elicitation is that one can efficiently elicit complete paradigms.

A drawback of elicitation is that it requires significant metalinguistic awareness from the consultant and/or the language community with regard to the language studied. In my experience, the feasibility of eliciting intuitions is very limited in signing communities where language norms are not strongly defined.

Another disadvantage of elicitation is that one may overlook unexpected features of the language simply by not eliciting them. This is a particularly relevant point, as sign languages of communities with a high incidence of deafness appear to differ significantly in terms of structure, and in an unpredictable way, from the sign languages of large deaf communities studied so far. This drawback of the elicitation method can be circumvented by combining elicitation with textual analysis and long-term to mid-term fieldwork-based observations (see Chelliah, 2001, for a discussion of some benefits of this combination).

Signed texts, such as (semi-)spontaneous monologue and dialogue (as opposed to group discussion) are relatively easy to collect and record and carry a lot of interesting linguistic and non-linguistic information. Sign language consultants often enjoy participating in the collection of (semi-)spontaneous discourse data, for example in the form of personal narratives or open interviews. Spontaneous data have the advantage over elicited data in that they are typically more naturalistic and may bring to light unexpected linguistic features. Working with larger sets of (semi-) spontaneous data requires a corpus-based approach, as target phenomena may be infrequent and dispersed throughout the data. The field of sign language corpus-based analysis is still young, but new tools and approaches are continuously becoming available for the analysis of large sets of digital sign language data.

To aid elicitation and the collection of targeted, semi-spontaneous discourse data, the field linguist can use non-linguistic stimuli. Stimuli used for the elicitation of sign language data typically consist of text, images, props, or a combination of these. (For an overview of elicitation materials, see Hong et al., 2009.)

A popular image-based task is asking signers to retell cartoons or picture stories. Other image-based tasks are "spot the difference" tasks, whereby signers are asked to describe the differences they see between two similar pictures, or "find the right picture" tasks, whereby one signer describes the picture that another signer needs to select out of a set of pictures (e.g., the pictures used by Zwitserlood, 2003).

A perhaps unexpected feature of images is that they require a form of literacy as well. Lack of familiarity with particular types and uses of images makes it difficult to "read" the imagistic codes and conventions used in them. For this reason, most image-based stimuli are hard to use on a representative scale in signing communities with image conventions different from the ones used in the stimuli. Prop-based tasks seem to be particularly frequent in studies on the use of space in sign languages. An example of this is the "man and tree" task (Levinson et al., 1992) as modified by de Vos (2012), which consists of miniature figures that are placed in a particular configuration in space. Pairs of signers are asked to perform various communicative tasks with respect to this configuration.

Collecting Lexical Data

For various purposes, the collection of signs in isolation is useful. Such lexical data may be needed for cross-linguistic comparison (e.g., to asses levels of relatedness between sign languages), for phonological analysis, for documentation, or for (applied) lexicographic purposes.

To collect lexical items, various methods can be used. Lexical items can be elicited with the aid of questionnaires that aim at basic lexical items. The Swadesh list, developed for the elicitation of words for 100–200 concepts in spoken languages, has been adapted by various sign language researchers to be used in their research (Stokoe and Kuschel, 1969; Woodward, 1993; Parkhurst and Parkhurst, 2008). For sign languages that have evolved outside the context of deaf education, it is adamant that these questionnaires use pictures or props instead of written words from the spoken language. However, in view of the problems with pictures mentioned above, props are preferable to pictures. Alternatively, the pictures in the questionnaire can be replaced with locally made pictures of the same object, to maximize recognizability. Collecting a restricted set of basic vocabulary is typically used for the purpose of cross-linguistic comparisons (see Aldersson and McEntee-Atalianis, 2008 for an extensive discussion of lexical comparison studies of sign languages).

To collect as many lexical items as possible, the interviewer may encourage consultants to come up themselves with signs. It often proves a difficult exercise to spontaneously think of a large number of lexical items. To facilitate this process, the interviewer can lead the consultant (or, preferably, the group of consultants) from one semantic field to another: food, family, animals, and so on. Also, going on a "guided tour" or attending events with consultants and the camera can help bring signs to mind.

A general drawback of asking for concepts in isolation is that the resulting set of lexical items will not be informative about their patterns of occurrence in actual usage. An alternative (or complementary) method to counter this effect is to harvest lexical items from a discourse corpus (Crasborn and de Meijer, 2012). The items may consequently be re-recorded in isolation, to be made suitable for phonological analysis or lexicographic purposes.

Metadata

In addition to the linguistic data, one also needs to collect metadata, in other words information about the recorded data. So, for each recording, one needs to collect information about the data collection session, the language(s) involved, the topics, the type of data, the language users, and so on. The IMDI format has been established as a standard for describing multimedia and multimodal language resources (Wittenburg, Broeder, and Sloman, 2000). For sign languages, additional metadata are relevant, such as hearing status, type(s) of school visited, and the like. To cover these additional metadata requirements, a special sign language profile has been developed for IMDI (Crasborn and Hanke, 2003).

Processing and Analysis of the Data

Once the data have been collected, the video data need to be captured and converted, annotated, analyzed, and – especially in the case of endangered languages – deposited in a digital archive. Examples of digital archives containing annotated data of endangered sign languages are the Endangered Language Archive (http://elar-archive. org) and the DoBeS archive (http://dobes.mpi.nl).

The methods for documenting a sign language are in principle the same as for sign language data gathering in controlled settings, as described in this volume. However, a note on annotation is in place. Ideally, annotation of signed texts, for example in ELAN (Crasborn, Sloetjes, Auer, and Wittenburg, 2006), is done by, or in close collaboration with, a native signer. However, when there are no deaf or hearing native signers with the necessary literacy and language and computer skills, an alternative solution is to form annotation teams in which each member has a complementary skill. Thus I worked with three people on the annotation of AdaSL data: one hearing native signer, bilingual in AdaSL and spoken Akan; one non-signer, literate in Akan; and one non-signer, literate in Akan and English. The signer voiced the translation in Akan, which was written down in notebooks by the non-signer literate in Akan, which in turn was translated into English by the third member. The notebooks served as a support for my own annotations of the data (Nyst, 2007). In the meantime, the translations with time codes in the notebooks have been scanned, typed up and imported into ELAN files, leading to the trilingual corpus of AdaSL (Nyst, 2012). In more recent fieldwork in Mali, a team made up of a deaf non-literate signer and a hearing literate non-native signer was trained to annotate directly in ELAN.

The choice of a language or languages of annotation may not be a straightforward matter when a sign language is used in a multilingual country, where the spoken language in contact with the sign language is different from the national spoken language – which may in turn be different from international academic languages. The often great distance between the field site and the researcher's home base impacts the research process in various ways. Annotation is ideally done by native signers in close collaboration with the researcher. If the researcher is a non-native signer based far away from the signing community and the data sets are large, annotators may continue annotating in the absence of the researcher. Although this is also possible when annotators write their annotations on paper, working digitally greatly facilitates collaboration across distance. For this kind of workflow, the annotation team needs to have access to the processed (i.e., captured, cut, and compressed) video clips. Due to the generally large size of the data sets and the sometimes limited Internet facilities, one may need to send the video files by mail or through helpful visitors.

A great distance also means (or at least used to mean) that the researcher, once returned to the home-based office, cannot ad hoc check a new analysis or fill gaps in the data. However, the ever-expanding access to the Internet, together with the continuing development of software tools for linguistic purposes (e.g. ELAN) and for online collaboration, such as Dropbox or Skype, are breaking down the communicative barriers between the office and the field. This allows research assistants from the community to be employed throughout the project, which positively affects the connection between the researcher, the co-workers, and the project.

Conclusion

Since the start of sign language research, a considerable number of studies involved fieldwork in communities of deaf signers but sometimes also in communities of hearing signers, in the country of the fieldwork itself or far away from it, in deaf communities that arose in the context of deaf education or outside of it. In many ways, sign language fieldwork may not differ from fieldwork in spoken languages, where an equally large diversity of user communities and settings is found. However, there are some aspects that are typical for sign language fieldwork. In this chapter I tried to focus on these aspects. Also, mainly because of my own fieldwork record, I tried to outline the kinds of issues that are typical of fieldwork in communities that evolved outside the context of deaf education. But then, again, the difference between fieldwork in communities within and outside of the context of deaf schools is a gradient one.

Fieldwork is challenging and multifaceted. The space permitted for this chapter is not even enough to begin to cover all the relevant issues. Despite the considerable number of studies that are based on data collected in the field, there are relatively few publications addressing the topic of sign language fieldwork. Whereas English is overrepresented as a topic of study in spoken language linguistics, the majority of sign language studies concern ASL and sign languages of European origins. Hopefully, more publications on sign language fieldwork will become available, so that current fieldworkers can learn from each other and aspirant fieldworkers can rely on a body of accounts of good practices. A solid body of literature on various aspects of sign language fieldwork, particularly methodology, is likely to stimulate the study of a more diverse sample of sign languages.

Acknowledgments

I would like to thank Heleen Smits, the editors and an anonymous reviewer for their useful comments on earlier versions of this chapter.

Notes

1   In this chapter I will not follow the convention in the sign linguistic literature of using a capital *D* to signal cultural deafness (as opposed to pathological deafness), because I feel I am not in a position to make this judgment in the case of signers of all sign languages concerned here.
2   "Unraveling the grammars of European sign languages: Pathways to full citizenship of deaf signers and to the protection of their linguistic heritage" (COST SignGram ISCH COST Action IS1006, at http://parles.upf.edu/en/content/cost-signgram).
3   Fischer (2009, p. 6) anecdotally describes a different, but similarly extensive effect of the recording site on the naturalness of signing for American Sign Language. This is a case where a deaf child attending oralist education associated the research lab with school and concluded that signing would not be appreciated in the lab either.

Keywords

endangered sign languages; ethics in sign language research; methodology; rural sign languages; sign language description; sign language documentation; sign language fieldwork

See Also

Chapter 1; Chapter 4; Chapter 9

Suggested Readings

Johnston, T. (1989). Auslan: The sign language of the Australian Deaf community. PhD Thesis, University of Sydney.

Kusters, A. (2012). Being a deaf white anthropologist in Adamorobe: Some ethical and methodological issues. In U. Zeshan, and C. de Vos (Eds.), *Sign languages in village communities: Anthropological and linguistic insights*. Boston, MA/Nijmegen, Nijmegen: Mouton de Gruyter/Ishara Press, pp. 27–52.

Marsaja, I. G. (2008). *Desa Kolok: A deaf village and its sign language in Bali, Indonesia*. Nijmegen, Netherlands: Ishara Press.

Nonaka, A. (2009). Estimating size, scope, and membership of the speech/sign communities of undocumented indigenous/village sign languages: The Ban Khor case study. *Language & Communication* 29(3), 210–229.

Schmaling, C. (2000). *Magannar Hannu- a descriptive analysis of Hausa Sign Language*. Hamburg: Signum Verlag.

References

General

Aldersson, R. R., and McEntee-Atalianis, L. J. (2008). A lexical comparison of signs from Icelandic and Danish Sign Language. *Sign Language Studies* 9(1), 45–87.

Ameka, F., Dench, A., and Evans, N. (Eds.) (2006). *Catching language: The standing challenge of grammar writing*. Berlin: Mouton de Gruyter.

Bowern, C. (2008). *Linguistic fieldwork: A practical guide*. New York: Palgrave Macmillan.

Chelliah, S. L. (2001). The role of text collection and elicitation in linguistic fieldwork. In P. Newman and M. Ratliff (Eds.), *Linguistic fieldwork*. Cambridge: Cambridge University Press, pp. 152–165.

Chelliah, S. L., and de Reuse, W. J. (2010). *Handbook of descriptive linguistic fieldwork*. Dordrecht: Springer.

Costello, B., Fernández, J., and Landa, A. (2008). The non-(existent) native signer: Sign language research in a small deaf population. In R. M. de Quadros (Ed.), *Sign languages: Spinning and unraveling the past, present and future: TISLR9, forty five papers and three posters from the ninth theoretical issues in sign language research conference*. Pétropolis, Brazil: Editora Arara Azul, pp. 77–94.

Crasborn, O., Sloetjes, H., Auer, E., and Wittenburg, P. (2006). Combining video and numeric data in the analysis of sign languages with the ELAN annotation software. In C. Vetoori (Ed.), *Proceedings of the second workshop on the representation and processing of sign languages: Lexicographic matters and didactic scenarios*. Paris: ELRA, pp. 82–87.

Crasborn, O., and Hanke, T. (2003). *Additions to the IMDI metadata set for sign language corpora: Agreements at an ECHO workshop, May 8–9, 2003, Nijmegen University*. Radboud University Nijmegen, Nijmegen, Netherlands. Accessed September 8, 2014. http://www.google.nl/url?sa=t&rct=j&q=&esrc=s&frm=1&source=web&cd=2&ved=0CCsQFjAB&url=http%3A%2F%2Fwww.ru.nl%2Fpublish%2Fpages%2F522090%2Fsignmetadata_oct2003.pdf&ei=kqIWVMe2CMaMO4T1gcAC&usg=AFQjCNG2BylLGxZRfbhB-34utDNbxaK1qA

Crasborn, O., and de Meijer, A. (2012). From corpus to lexicon: The creation of ID-glosses for the Corpus NGT. In O. Crasborn, E. Efthimiou, E. Fontinea, T. Hanke, J. Kristoffersen, J. Mesch (Eds.), *Proceedings of the fifth workshop on the representation and processing of sign languages: Interactions between corpus and lexicon*. Paris: ELRA, pp. 13–17.

Crowley, T. (2007). *Field linguistics: A beginner's guide* (N. Thieberger, Ed.). Melbourne: Oxford University Press.

Cumberbatch, K. (2012). Sociolinguistic sketch of Konchri Sain. In U. Zeshan and C. de Vos (Eds.), *Sign languages in village communities: Anthropological and linguistic insights.* Boston, MA/Nijmegen, Netherlands: Mouton de Gruyter/Ishara Press, pp. 387–388.

Dikyuva, H., Escobedo Delgado, C. S., Panda, S. and Zeshan, U. (2012). Working with village sign language communities: Deaf fieldwork researchers in professional dialogue. In U. Zeshan and C. de Vos (Eds.), *Sign languages in village communities: Anthropological and linguistic insights.* Boston, MA/Nijmegen, Netherlands: Mouton de Gruyter/Ishara Press, pp. 313–344.

Dixon, R. M. W. (1997). *The rise and fall of languages.* Cambridge: Cambridge University Press.

Fischer, S. (2009). Sign language field methods: Approaches, techniques, and concerns. In J. H.-Y. Tai and J. Tsay (Eds.), *Taiwan Sign Language and beyond.* Chia-Yi: Taiwan Institute for the Humanities, National Chung Cheng University, pp. 1–19.

Himmelmann, N. (1998). Documentary and descriptive linguistics. *Linguistics,* 36, pp. 161-195.

Hong, S.-E., Hanke, T., König, S., Konrad, R., Langer, G., and Rathmann, C. (2009). *Elicitation materials and their use in sign language linguistics.* Poster prepared for the workshop "Sign language corpora: Linguistic issues," London, July 24–25, 2009.

Johnston, T. (2009). Creating a corpus of Auslan within an Australian national corpus. In M. Haugh, K. Burridge, J. Mulder, and P. Peters (Eds.), *Selected proceedings of the 2008 HCSNet workshop on designing the Australian national corpus: Mustering languages.* Somerville, MA: Cascadilla Proceedings Project, pp. 87–95.

Kusters, A. (2012a). *Since time immemorial until the end of days: An ethnographic study of the production of deaf space in Adamorobe, Ghana.* PhD Thesis: University of Bristol.

Kusters, A. (2012b). The gong gong was beaten: Adamorobe: A "deaf village" in Ghana and its marriage prohibition for deaf partners. *Sustainability* 4, 2765–2784.

Ladd, P. (2003). *Understanding Deaf culture: In search of deafhood.* Clevedon, UK: Multilingual Matters.

Lanesman, S., and Meir, I. (2012). The survival of Algerian Jewish Sign Language alongside Israeli Sign Language in Israel. In U. Zeshan and C. de Vos (Eds.), *Sign languages in village communities: Anthropological and linguistic insights.* Boston, MA/Nijmegen, Netherlands: Mouton de Gruyter/Ishara Press, pp. 153–180.

Levinson, S. C., Brown, P., Danziger, E., De León, L., Haviland, J. B., Pederson, E., and Senft, G. (1992). Man and tree & space games. In S. C. Levinson (Ed.), *Space stimuli kit 1.2.* Nijmegen, Netherlands: Max Planck Institute for Psycholinguistics, pp. 7–14.

Majid, A. (2012). A guide to stimulus-based elicitation for semantic categories. In N. Thieberger (Ed.), *The Oxford handbook of linguistic fieldwork.* New York: Oxford University Press, pp. 54–71.

Newman, P., and Ratliff, M. (2001). *Linguistic Fieldwork.* Cambridge: Cambridge University Press.

Nonaka, A. (2011). Language endangerment and language socialization. In A. Duranti, E. Ochs, and B. Schieffelin (Eds.), *Handbook of language socialization.* Oxford: Wiley Blackwell, pp. 610–630.

Nyst, V. (2007). *A descriptive analysis of Adamorobe Sign Language (Ghana).* Utrecht, Netherlands: LOT.

Parkhurst, S., and Parkhurst, D. (2003). *Lexical comparisons of signed languages and the effects of iconicity.* Work papers of the Summer Institute of Linguistics, University of North Dakota (47). Accessed September 5, 2014. http://arts-sciences.und.edu/summer-institute-of-linguistics/work-papers/_files/docs/2003-parkhurst-parkhurst.pdf

Rice, K. (2011). Ethical issues in linguistic fieldwork. In N. Thieberger (Ed.), *The Oxford handbook of linguistic fieldwork.* Oxford: Oxford University Press, pp. 407–429.

Schembri, A., Fenlon, J., Rentelis, R., Reynolds, S., and Cormier, K. (2013). Building the British Sign Language Corpus. *Language Documentation and Conservation 7*, 136–154.

Stokoe, W., and Kuschel, R. (1979). *A field guide for sign language research*. Silver Spring: Md. Linstok Press.

Thieberger, N. (Ed.) (2011). *The Oxford handbook of linguistic fieldwork* (Oxford handbooks in linguistics). Oxford: Oxford University Press.

de Vos, C. (2012). Sign-spatiality in Kata Kolok: How a village sign language in Bali inscribes its signing space. PhD Thesis, Radboud University Nijmegen, Nijmegen, Netherlands.

Wittenburg, P., Broeder, D., and Sloman, B., (2000). EAGLES/ISLE: A proposal for a meta description standard for language resources. White Paper, LREC 2000 Workshop, Athens, Greece.

Woodward, J. (1993). The relationship of sign language varieties in India, Pakistan, and Nepal. *Sign Language Studies 78*, 15–22.

Zwitserlood, I. (2003). Classifying hand configurations in Nederlandse Gebarentaal (Sign Language of the Netherlands). PhD Thesis, LOT, Utrecht, Netherlands.

Corpora

Crasborn, O., Zwitserlood, I., Ros, J., and the Centre for Language Studies, Radboud Universiteit Nijmegen (2008). *Het Corpus NGT: Een digitaal* open access *corpus van filmpjes en annotaties van de Nederlandse Gebarentaal* [The corpus of NGT: A digital open access corpus of clips and annotations of the Dutch Sign Language]. Accessed September 4, 2014. http://www.ru.nl/corpusngt

Nyst, V. (2012). *A reference corpus of Adamorobe Sign Language: A digital, annotated video corpus of the sign language used in the village of Adamorobe, Ghana*. Universiteit Leiden: Leiden University Centre for Linguistics.

Nyst, V., Magassouba, M., and Sylla, K. (2011). *Un corpus de référence de la Langue des Signes Malienne, I: A digital, annotated video corpus of the local sign language used in Bamako and Mopti, Mali*. Universiteit Leiden: Leiden University Centre for Linguistics.

Nyst, V., Magassouba, M., and Sylla, K. (2012). *Un corpus de référence de la Langue des Signes malienne, II: A digital, annotated video corpus of local sign language use in the Dogon area of Mali*. Universiteit Leiden: Leiden University Centre for Linguistics.

8 Research Methods for Studying the Form of Signs

Rachel Channon

Chapter Overview

This chapter discusses methodological considerations related to researching the form of a sign – research that can be subsumed to the phonology, phonetics, prosody and iconicity of sign languages. The research process, possible methods, and potential problems are considered in a step-by-step manner, which proceeds from finding a research question to collecting the data, finding signers, determining the equipment needed, and storing, annotating, and analyzing the data.

Research Methods in Sign Language Studies: A Practical Guide, First Edition.
Edited by Eleni Orfanidou, Bencie Woll, and Gary Morgan.
© 2015 John Wiley & Sons, Inc. Published 2015 by John Wiley & Sons, Inc.

Research Question

Sometimes the researcher begins from a research program or a directing theory; other times the researcher begins from nothing more than an observation of something unexpected. In either case, when the phonology, phonetics, iconicity, and prosody of sign languages are at stake, theories and questions are usually related to – or make use of – the notions, definitions, and tools presented below. The examples are from American Sign Language (ASL), unless otherwise specified.

Phonetics

Roughly speaking, the study of linguistic forms branches out into a physical part (phonetics) and a mental part (prosody and phonology). In-between lies iconicity, with characteristics of both.

Phonetics is responsible for the physical aspects of signs, and its primary task is to consider the non-contrastive constraints on phonology – those elements that are not part of the mental representation, but are a necessary part of the physical instantiation of a sign. These constraints are primarily articulatory (extending the ring finger alone is difficult) or perceptual (handshape details are harder to see than gross locations). However, some cognitive constraints would also appear to be phonetic. The obvious example is that different simultaneous movements on each hand are nearly impossible, yet such a constraint cannot be specifically linguistic or phonological, since it obviously applies to many non-linguistic events as well. Phonetics aims to discover these constraints and, in a sense, clear away everything that can be explained, until what is left is what must be included in the phonological/prosodic representations.

The sign FATHER (thumb of the spread hand taps the forehead a few times) shows how phonetic characteristics must be understood to represent a sign correctly. The location of the hand (at the forehead), the shape of the hand (spread, open), and the contact point (tip of thumb) need to be mentally represented in some manner. If phonetics were not considered, it would seem that the orientation of the hand must also be represented. But phonetics shows that there is no reason to include the orientation. Physically, certain orientations are either impossible or extremely awkward. All other orientations are acceptable: the hand may be oriented straight up and down, or the palm may face more or less downward (note that this is not evidence that the orientation of the hand is phonetically determined in every sign).

Iconicity

Iconicity, like phonetics, is rooted in the physical. But, whereas phonetics is concerned with the physical and cognitive characteristics of the signer and of the viewer, iconicity is connected with the physical reality of the world and with human culture. The mind renders iconically some aspect of reality: the shape of a tree, the type of dance performed in some cultures, the outward motion from the self that occurs in giving someone something, the fact that objects, when dropped, fall downward, the cultural belief that heaven is above us, the shape of written letters, and so on. Just as what is phonetic need not be included in a mental representation, it seems likely that what is iconic may not need to be included in a specific representation. Unlike with phonetics, though, with iconicity it has to be the case that there is some mental representation of its content. Without the mental concept that heaven is above, or that, in the act of "giving," something passes from me to you, or that the letter "p" has a specific shape in written language, it would not be possible to use these concepts in the physical sign. Moreover, there are usually multiple ways to represent an object iconically, and there are different choices for different languages.

Additional issues raised by iconicity are:

- Iconic imitation allows substantive and geometric transformations (scaling, skewing, rotating), additions, and deletions. What are the limits?
- Iconicity appears to be optional and unpredictable. In some languages *dog* is iconic, in others arbitrary. Some verbs move in iconically predictable directions, but occurrence is unpredictable: de Beuzeville, Johnston, and Schembri (2009) show that, in two narrative types in Auslan, the occurrence of iconic verb motion is about a half of what is expected. Are there rules governing these processes?
- Why does some iconicity fade away over time, while some remains robust?
- How are grammatical categories related to iconicity?
- Is contrastiveness applicable? Iconicity can produce unsystematic outliers that do not participate in feature contrasts (van der Kooij, 2002).

Prosody

Prosody has two major functions: to group elements and to provide information about intentions and emotional states. Language is a near-continuous stream and prosody is vital to parsing it, to determining the beginnings and ends of signs, phrases, sentences, and larger units. Its second function is to indicate emotions and intentions (statements, questions, or emphasis). In sign languages, prosody is primarily expressed non-manually, by using gestures that typically spread over more than one sign, such as eye gaze direction; widening, narrowing or blinking the eyes; eyebrow raising and lowering; spreading, opening, closing, or pursing the lips; tongue protrusion; and body gestures such as head nods, shoulder shrugs, and turns or leans of body or head. Many non-manual gestures are relatively easy to maintain over periods of manual signing, and therefore they work well for the prosodic goal of pointing out boundaries.

There are a few exceptions to this neat separation of manual and non-manual gestures. Prosody may also be shown manually in the speed or tension of the hands, or in the size of the motion. Contrarily, some non-manual gestures related to a specific sign or to a spoken word are more properly considered part of the phonology. Examples are: (1) mouthing "actress" while signing ACT; (2) opening the mouth while signing OPEN-DOOR or OPEN-WINDOW; and (3) in some versions of the sign COMPARE, holding the hands up on either side of the head while the eyes move back and forth between them (comparing the hands). In these cases, the non-manual gesture adds to the phonologically carried denotational meaning, not to the prosodic intentional meaning. (For a more detailed discussions of sign language prosody than can be given here, see Brentari and Crossley, 2002; Sandler, 2010.)

Phonology

Phonology asks what characteristics must be remembered for a sign to be recognized or produced with all its phonetic variability. The phonological representation of signs is divided into features, hierarchy, and temporal order. In each case, the crucial issue is whether an element is contrastive.

Features

The existence of many current phonological models means that there is no agreed upon feature set, but most models include handshape, location, action, orientation, and global features such as number of hands and type of repetition. Models vary in the level of detail. Stokoe, Casterline, and Croneberg (1965) used broad locations (head, trunk, etc.); other models specify contralateral/ipsilateral, top/bottom, multiple places on the weak hand, and so on. Brentari's (1998) 48-feature system is reasonably representative; Uyechi (1996) and Hansen (2011) are more unusual.

   In spite of the variety of models, phonologists agree that, for something to be considered a feature, it must be contrastive within the system. For example, in most models, FATHER and MOTHER (spread hand contacts location with thumb) show that forehead and chin are contrastive locations. Nevertheless, because contrastiveness only operates within a model, it is possible for contrast to occur in one model but not in another. For example, most systems consider repetition to be a feature; but it is not a feature in Liddell and Johnson (1989), and hence it is not contrastive for them.

Hierarchy

Hierarchical structure shows feature dependencies. There are three possible cases:

   DEPENDENCY   If element y always occurs only when element x occurs but element x can occur without element y, then y depends on x. A hypothetical example: if the pinky extends, then the thumb always extends; but the converse is not true; so, if the thumb extends, sometimes the pinky does not extend. In this case, pinky extension depends on thumb extension. This would be a phonological structure constraint, since physically the pinky can extend without the thumb. Mak and Tang (2011) provide a non-hypothetical but more complex example: they argue that the features [repeat] and [return] depend on a movement feature node.
   NON-DEPENDENCY, SINGLE FEATURE   If element y always occurs only when element x occurs and element x always occurs only when element y occurs, then y and x are the same feature. Example: the relationship of the two smaller (distal) knuckles. Most people cannot flex one of these without the other. Either knuckle predicts the other, so a single feature [distal flexing] controls both.
   NON-DEPENDENCY, TWO FEATURES   If element y sometimes occurs when element x occurs and element x sometimes occurs when element y occurs, then

y and *x* are manifestations of two different and independent features. An example would be the extension of the index and thumb. Sometimes both the index and the thumb are extended, sometimes only the index is, and sometimes only the thumb is. Index and thumb extensions are independent.

Hierarchical structure may be more limited than in spoken languages. What appears to be structure may sometimes be phonetic constraints (Channon, 2004). Much remains to be understood in this area.

Temporal sequence

The notion of temporal order contrast and non-contrast is perhaps most easily understood with syntactic examples: (1) contrast: *Mary sees Jo* contrasts with *Jo sees Mary* because the meaning changes; (2) two kinds of non-contrastiveness: (2a) *Jo and Mary* is not-contrastive with *Mary and Jo* because the meaning does not change; and (2b) *the house* does not contrast with *house the* because only the first sequence is acceptable. Temporal order within a sign may be contrastive or non-contrastive. Examples of contrast and non-contrast are:

1 Contrast: IMPROVE and GET WORSE (the flat hand moves up the arm for IMPROVE and down the arm for GET WORSE).
2 Non-contrast:
   a DEAF can be signed by touching first the ear then the mouth or first the mouth then the ear. The order does not change the meaning;
   b WOMAN first touches the chin and then the chest with the thumb of the flat spread hand. Reversing the order is not acceptable and produces a non-sign.

Channon Crain (1996), Channon (2002a, 2002b), and Channon and van der Hulst (2011) have argued that, although sequences do occur within the sign/segment, they are non-contrastive. Either the meaning does not change because only one sequence is acceptable, or, if the meaning changes with an apparent feature permutation, the variation is not actually caused by feature permutation, but rather by a dynamic feature action (such as closing/opening, pronating/supinating, etc.). However, this viewpoint is controversial, and temporal sequence contrast remains an important question for both spoken language and sign language researchers. For example, some syllable onset sequences are not contrastive in English (*bl* and *str* are allowed, but not *lb* and *trs*). Feature sequence within a segment is not contrastive in spoken languages because even phonemes that appear to be ordered, such as affricates, actually have a fixed and therefore non-contrastive order (Lombardi, 1990).

Refining and clarifying the question

For most research projects, the researcher defines some relatively narrow question that can be answered at least tentatively. One might examine a particular articulatory constraint, or a repetition feature, or the prosodic use of eyebrows. As the project continues, the question may change somewhat, perhaps broadening or swerving aside to some related question, but most likely narrowing to focus even more tightly on some part of the original question. Pilot studies are often useful as part of this process, to determine whether a particular research strategy is likely to be successful.

The researcher will often be working within the framework of some model. The primary test of a model is whether it over- or undergenerates. A desirable model does not undergenerate: it accounts for all observed signs, as well as for potential signs that signers agree are grammatical (accidental gaps). Nor does it overgenerate: it does not permit non-occurring signs that signers agree are impossible and ungrammatical (systematic gaps).

A hypothetical example of undergeneration would be a model that could only represent straight-line motion. If there were only a few signs with circular motion and many sign languages had only straight-line motion, then it might be possible to explain the apparent exceptions through some special stipulations, because one or a few counterexamples are not usually a sufficient counterargument. What is more important is a systematic inability to represent significant elements. In this example, because circular motion is both pervasive and contrastive, such a model would fail to represent reality.

Overgeneration can occur for either signs or representations. For example, a model that allows an unlimited number of location segments within a sign is overgenerating, because it predicts that simple signs with many locations should occur – for example a sign with locations at the forehead, ear, trunk, and hand. Yet sign languages appear to systematically avoid signs with three or more different and distinct locations (Channon, 2002a).

A model that requires that observed physical sequence must always be phonologically represented is overgenerating representations. As noted above, there are signs such as DEAF that can be performed in different sequences without change in the meaning of the sign. If the model requires that this phonetic sequence be represented, the model overgenerates and produces two representation for one sign.

Special rules or constraints can repair overgeneration. But, all other things being equal, a model with fewer added constraints is preferable, especially if the constraint has no clear natural explanation. A natural constraint usually appeals to physical necessity, efficiency, or comfort. Two examples of natural constraints are: (1) signs rarely have locations on the back of the body because the viewer needs to see the sign; and (2) repetition in a sign is usually instantiated as a single repetition, because this is more efficient. Examples of unnatural constraints would be: (1) the index finger must be extended in all signs; and (2) signs have only straight-line motion. These would be arbitrary limitations, with no basis in phonetic reality.

Data and Data Collection

When the researcher has a question and perhaps a model, it is time to collect data, which can be elicited or natural, isolated or connected forms.

Elicitation is more appropriate for type-based questions, such as how many signs in the language are made with a flat hand. Token counts (such as how many times a particular sign occurs) are normally not meaningful, because they would not generalize to natural situations. Preparing prompts is more labor-intensive, but transcribing and analyzing the data is less labor-intensive. The researcher has more control over the output, so systematic sets of responses are possible. Additional information (including material and software) for elicitation can be found on the SIL web site (http://www.sil.org).

Natural data can range from completely natural data outside the researcher's control to semi-natural ones, where the researcher sets up the situation but does not try to control the output. Data of this type are more appropriate for token-based questions, such as what is the most common handshape in conversation. They are usually required when linking phonology/phonetics to syntactic, semantic, sociolinguistic, or discourse information. The type provides frequency data for sign languages, as in Morford and McFarlane (2003) for ASL and Johnston (2012) for Auslan. Naturally, there are gradations between natural and elicited, which are marked by more or less control over the signer's output. An example of intermediate control would be providing a map and asking the signer to describe a path on the map.

Citation forms are what a friendly, relatively equal-status stranger should get when asking a signer *how do you sign X*, or when providing a picture or videoclip and asking the signer to name the prompt. No special phonetic processes have been applied. However, signers' attitudes toward spoken and sign languages and toward the elicitor can create unpredictable *hypercorrections*. Signers might believe that forms influenced by a spoken language should be preferred or avoided. For example, signer A may give an initialized form of LUNCH (fingerspelled L at mouth), while signer B may give a compound (FOOD + NOON). Yet, if the same signers were observed in everyday conversation, signer A might use the compound, and signer B the initialized form.

A related problem is changing citation forms. The citation form for older signers might be a compound form for WOMAN (thumb of the fist–hand strokes side of cheek, then extended spread hand repeatedly contacts center chest). Younger signers may have a simpler citation form (thumb of extended spread hand contacts chin, then chest). Nevertheless, younger signers might still give the compound form if they have seen older, respected signers use it and they equate "citation" with formality and respect. These problems can be reduced (though probably not eliminated) through a non-threatening elicitation process that causes no serious power imbalance between elicitor and elicitee.

Prototypical connected forms occur in group conversations among familiar, fluent signers or when one is using picture book elicitation. Forms will vary both between and within signers. They are labor-intensive to annotate, because they must be identified within a sign stream. Finding enough examples for analysis can be difficult. A variant of connected discourse is the use of carrier phrases – fixed phrases or sentences with sign(s) of interest inserted in order for us to observe the effect of preceding or following material (see Grosvald and Corina, 2012; Emmorey, Gertsberg, Korpics, and Wright, 2009).

Citation and conversational forms are both important. Citation forms provide the benchmark to measure conversational forms against. Conversational forms provide information about the phonetic processes of the language, often replacing more marked with less marked features. For example, in Tyrone and Mauk's (2010) study, the citation form of WONDER occurs on the forehead, but often moves lower in faster signing. Both forms are needed if we want to discover these processes and constraints.

Exceptional data

In any corpus, there will be outliers that the researcher must decide how to handle. The most common types of sign outliers are non-core items (Brentari and Padden, 2001): (a) signs influenced by the spoken or written form of the language of the surrounding community; (b) compounds; and (c) iconic signs.

Spoken language influence adds complexity, as in word mouthing versus mouth gestures. Mouthing for multisyllabic words can include sequences of different mouth movements, which follow the mouth movements of the spoken language gloss (for further discussion of the relationship between mouthing and manual gestures, see Vinson, Thompson, Skinner, Fox, and Vigliocco, 2010). Mouth gestures, in contrast, are usually one (repeated) gesture, such as the mouth opening.

Signs can represent spoken language function words, such as forms of *to be*, articles, prepositions, and affixes. The most obvious effect of using function words is an increase in the number of signs per sentence. Therefore each sentence will probably take longer than usual overall, or each sign will be pronounced more rapidly than usual. In either case, there is likely to be some change in the prosody. The frequency of morphological groups of signs will probably be affected. For example, the use of articles is likely to decrease the use of pointing signs. Written language influence is most commonly seen in initialized signs, fingerspelling, and character signs. Such signs can demonstrate complex iconic handshapes and rare handshapes, as in Turkish fingerspelling (Kubus and Hohenberger, 2011), or Asian character signs (Fischer and Gong, 2011).

Handshape sequences may not follow Corina's (1993) constraint that handshape sequences are one handshape combined with a dynamic feature for opening or closing (see also Lee, 2008). An example of this violation is BACKGROUND: four extended fingers (B) followed by the index extended (G). Two-handed non-contacting signs may have different handshapes, as in TOTAL COMMUNICATION, which is realized with one hand curved (C) and the other in a fist, with thumb protruding between index and middle (T). Contacts may be unusual or difficult: in PERFECT two moving index fingers contact each other, in VERY the fingertips of the spread index and middle contact. More than two places may occur, as in OVERALLS (O at shoulders, then A at high chest, then L at low chest on both hands). This sign also shows that multiple handshapes may co-occur with multiple locations (or with other multiplied characteristic), whereas the core lexicon limits change to a maximum of two simultaneous changes (such as the hand opening while moving forward).

Compounds join two simple signs (rarely three or more), so sequencing markedness increases. Simple signs allow combinations of features, but feature sequences cannot be longer than two (two places, two handshapes, etc.), and the domain of repetition must be the entire sign (Channon, 2002a, 2002b). In contrast, compounds can have a sequenced repetition of two types, such as repeated handshape change followed by repeated location change. They can have more than two distinct locations or handshapes, and so on.

Iconicity (other than that influenced by speech or writing) increases the number of marked but non-complex features (kidney location, contact at bottom of ring finger, etc.). Normally the number of repetitions is non-contrastive (Channon, 2002a), but iconicity allows contrastive repetition (demonstrating two versus four knocks on the door). Signs may be unusually long, and their beginning and ending points unclear. Both signers and viewers are more likely to gaze at the hands (Emmorey, Thompson, and Colvin, 2009).

Handshapes, though not complex, may vary from canonical handshapes. Space is used more systematically, as a three-dimensional map of entities in space (Liddell, 1996).

Exceptional data can be difficult to separate out, if (and when) this is necessary for the research goal. Compounds, for example, may start out as exceptional data, but over time they change sufficiently to become a part of the core lexicon (like DEAF, HOME, WOMAN, and many others), although they do often retain a somewhat unusual double location. Many initialized signs are well-behaved members of the core lexicon (like the days of the week or the names of colors in ASL). Determining what signs are exceptions and can reasonably be excluded from the data is, unfortunately, a judgment call and reasonable people may take different views. One solution is to find another person's data, when these have already been annotated for exception status. Another is to use a neutral referee to judge exceptionality. Alternatively signs can be excluded that meet certain criteria, for instance all the signs that last longer than a certain number of seconds, all the signs with two handshapes and two locations, or all the signs identified in the literature as initialized signs.

Signers

Signer characteristics can affect sign language production and/or perception in many overlapping and complex ways. Obvious characteristics to be considered include the signer's age, sex, and auditory and visual status. Other factors may also be important – for example:

- the signer's language models: auditory status, signers, sign language learners;
- language type: sign language of the deaf,[1] hearing group sign, manually coded sign, cued speech, tactile signing, oral (lip-reading), fingerspelling, gesture system, or spoken;

  Examples of hearing signing are Australian Aboriginal Sign Language (Kendon, 1990), and monastic signing (Umiker-Sebeok and Sebeok, 1987);

- modality:

  Is the signer using both speech and sign (bimodal communication)?

- number of languages known by the signer;
- length of use:

  How long has the signer used the language?

- nativeness:

  The clearest case of native language acquisition is a language acquired from birth. Languages acquired later are less fully native, with a severe decline in competence around puberty, after which few if any individuals acquire native competence (Lenneberg, 1967; Mayberry and Fischer, 1989). The age associated with this decline in competence may vary between speech and sign. Given normal linguistic capabilities, it is rare for a hearing child – but not uncommon for a deaf child born to non-signing hearing parents with subsequent delay in being provided with an accessible language model – to have no native competence from birth in any language;

- associations:

  Signer associations often indicate how much the language is used on a daily basis. A special and interesting case where association is significant is village signing, where an increased percentage of deafness in the population is associated with the development of a sign language used by both deaf and hearing community members;

- cognitive or physical characteristics: any conditions that might affect linguistic development, articulation or perception, such as cerebral palsy.

Number of signers

A final issue is how many signers are needed for the project. Here several questions are important: Is the goal of the project to obtain some representation of the diversity of signers within a particular language? Is the goal to look at cross-linguistic diversity? Is the goal to obtain something that is representative of the community as a whole?

It should be remembered that everyone has a slightly different lexicon, phonology, phonetics, prosody, and so on. This means that, if we collect 1,000 signs in a language, each from a different individual, we are actually collecting from 1,000 slightly different linguistic systems. Depending on the researcher's goals, this may or may not be desirable.

Equipment: Prompts and Cameras

There are several types of equipment to consider: elicitation material or prompts, video cameras, and specialized equipment.

Setting up elicitation material can be a time-consuming process. If there are multiple languages, it can be helpful to be able to reuse material, as is done in the SignTyp2 project. However, using the same material for different languages poses its own problems, since cultures will vary in how they understand the prompt or in whether they will understand it at all. What one culture finds acceptable, another finds offensive. A picture of an American supermarket as an example of "shop/store" may not be appropriate for signers on other continents. At the completion of the SignTyp2 project in 2015, elicitation material will be available for 1,000 concepts, usable cross-linguistically by any interested researcher at SignTyp.uconn.edu.

The second common piece of equipment is one or more video cameras. Setups will range from the simple webcam to complex, expensive multi-camera setups, to capture multiple views of one or more signers. Budget and desired level of detail will dictate the choice. Researchers investigating phonetic or prosodic issues are more likely to need greater detail in the recordings and more elaborate setups, including frequent slow-motion replay. Specialized software will be required for synchronizing multiple cameras or for annotating overlap, synchronization, or disjunction of the sign stream. Bank, Crasborn, and van Hout (2011) use ELAN to annotate overlap variations between manual and mouth gestures in Sign Language of the Netherlands.

Particularly for research in phonetics and prosody, specialized equipment may be needed. Data gloves and other motion capture devices can measure a signer's actions in great detail. Eccarius, Bour, and Scheidt (2012) provide some calibration procedures and techniques for using data gloves to study signing. Special measuring callipers or software can be useful – as in Weast (2011), who used software callipers to measure the degree of eyebrow raising. Cheek (2001) used Vicon, a motion capture system to study handshape variation, and Mauk (2003) used it to look at how fast signing caused signers to undershoot (fail to reach) their target locations. Emmorey et al. (2009) used an Optotrak Certus system for their study of the effect of changing visual feedback for signers. Tyrone and Mauk's (2010) study of WONDER used the Optotrak Certus and Optotrak 3010 systems to capture signers' movement. Grosvald and Corina (2012) used the software package Presentation from Neurobehavioral Systems to display elicitation material and to record participants' responses. These examples are by no means exhaustive.

Although machine production and machine recognition of signs are still at the pilot project stage, they are likely to become useful in the future, for example if one uses sign recognition systems to assist in transcription. At present, however, no consumer system is available. In the absence of large corpora of sign languages, such problems as distinguishing where a sign begins and where it ends or recognizing a large vocabulary of signs are difficult to achieve; and this is only the first step in the far more complex process of recognizing discourse.

Sign production, like speech production, is a simpler task than recognition, and there are some systems approaching the goal of a marketable product; they use software such as Vcom3d, Poser, and Autodesk Maya. Parton (2006) and Lu (2011) provide surveys of the field. Wolfe, Cook, McDonald, and Schnepp (2011) provide a discussion of issues involved in the computer animation of signs and discuss how linguistic models can improve machine production.

Annotation: Transcription and Coding

Once video recordings or other materials have been collected or created, the information must be annotated in order to be organized in a corpus. A corpus has several essential characteristics: it is searchable, it is annotated, and it has a description of how/why/what: how and why it was collected and what is contained within it.

There are many hard-copy sign language dictionaries with pictures and descriptions of how the signs are made. These are annotated, but only in the most primitive sense can they be called searchable (there is usually an index listing the signs by glosses from a spoken language). They usually do include some description of how/why/what. These problems are more obvious for graphic collections of sign languages than for machine-readable text collections of spoken languages, which inherently have at least minimal annotation, are searchable, and usually include how/why/what.

Annotation can be divided into transcription and coding, which are distinct activities, as discussed in van der Hulst and Channon (2010) and summarized here. Transcription is the first step and coding is a second (automatic) step via a conversion table. In transcription quick and easy production is most important, while in coding the researcher's quick and easy understanding of the coding system is most important.

Transcription

The three most important characteristics of transcription systems are bundling, memorability, and physical efficiency. Bundling means that, whatever details are included in the data collection process, they should be incorporated into as few symbols as possible. A common example is the bundling of handshape variables. In Stokoe's system, F is a bundled symbol that represents a handshape with the middle, ring, and pinky spread and extended (all knuckles straight), with the knuckles of the index finger flexed, and with the tip of the thumb contacting the tip of the index finger.

Memorable systems can be created by using either systematic or iconic relationships between symbols. Imagine a transcription system using a numeric keypad for entering letters. Letters randomly assigned to numbers (as in $B = 2$, $C = 24$, $D = 14$, and $A = 17$) would be non-memorable, while $A = 1$, $B = 2$ and so on are systematically memorable. Although each equation is arbitrary, the set of equations is related, and knowing one equation means that others are predictable. Under certain conditions, memorability conflicts with physical efficiency. When this happens, efficiency is often more important for transcription. In the example of the keypad, it might be worthwhile to assign single-digit codes to the ten most commonly used letters and two-digit codes to the rest, in sequence, even though this would partially destroy memorability. If the amount transcribed is small, memorability is more important, while for large amounts efficiency becomes more important.

Another way to make symbols memorable is to use iconicity, as is done in SignWriting and, to a lesser extent, in HamNoSys. Iconic memorability seems especially appropriate for sign languages, because iconicity itself is naturally memorable as well as systematic, and therefore memorable in that way as well. Iconicity does have the drawback of making the transcription system less ergonomic and less computer-friendly, but a well-designed system with appropriate software should reduce these problems to manageable levels.

Ergonomics or physical efficiency depends on the input device. For example, on an ordinary keyboard, assigning the most common symbols to the keys struck by the index or middle fingers is more efficient because these fingers are the strongest. Using the space bar or the enter key as symbols could be efficient, since these are large keys and easier to strike correctly. If one is using a mouse and screen, clickable symbols should be placed fairly close together, to reduce mouse travel time. The keyboard is usually more efficient than the mouse for a given stroke, because the hands are already on the keyboard and a stroke is a single action. In contrast, using the mouse requires three actions: moving the hand to the mouse, moving the mouse to the right place, and then clicking. In addition, for most mice clicking requires more energy than a key click.

Coding

Coding is a separate activity. Unlike a transcription system, which should be bundled and memorable, the coding system should be unbundled and understandable. Where a transcription system ideally has a one-to-many relationship with the data points (one bundled symbol for many variables), a coding system should have an unbundled one-to-one relationship with the data (as well as a many-to-one relationship with the transcription symbols). In a transcription system, "F" can be used to represent a handshape similar in form to the American fingerspelled letter "f." In a coding system, the symbol F would be separated into multiple symbols such as *knuckle bending, thumb contact, extended fingers,* and so on.

The second important characteristic distinguishing transcription and coding is the difference between *memorable* and *understandable.* A memorable symbol is distinct from all other symbols in the system and is systematically or iconically linked to related symbols. Although it takes some time for the transcriber to remember the symbols associated with each variable group, the systematic relationship between the symbols means that, once the transcriber remembers a few of them and what they are linked to, the association of the others are easily derived. An understandable symbol does not necessarily have these kinds of links to related symbols and is usually less distinct. An understandable, but not memorable, coding symbol might be *hand opens.* It is not memorable or distinct, because it is easy to confuse the actual symbol with other potential symbols such as *hand opening, the hand opens, hands open,* and so on.

The different importance of understandability and memorability arises from their different uses in coding and transcription. The transcriber has time to learn and memorize symbols, because (s)he will be repeatedly entering them. Since a transcriber will be presumably transcribing relatively large amounts of data, the effort involved in memorizing symbols that are not immediately obvious but have some kind of internal coherence and are distinct (not confusing) is a reasonable trade-off. The coding system, however, should be transparent and understandable for someone looking at it for the first time. The individuals examining the coded results (i.e., researchers) will usually not be looking at the symbols often enough to memorize them. Their acquaintance with the symbols will be briefer, and will generally not involve the action of creating the symbols. Instead they will be manipulating – counting, sorting, analyzing – already created data, often in aggregate form. Finally, in a coding system physical ease or ergonomics is much less important than in a transcription system. This means that, where a keyboard solution often works better than a mouse for transcription, the reverse is true for a coding system. A mouse-based system is more intuitively obvious because it presents the user with choices instead of requiring the user to remember codes or keys. The more the coding system is skewed to understandability at the expense of memorability, the more important it is to use a mouse-based system with preset choices.

Examples of transcription and coding systems

These examples are from the SignTyp project. Figure 8.1 shows a SignWriting transcription that has only three iconic symbols. These symbols are converted via a table to SignTyp codes. Table 8.1 shows a simplified version of a few of the 20 SignTyp records (=codes) that represent the three SignWriting symbols. SignWriting symbols are bundled and memorable; SignTyp symbols are understandable and unbundled, which means that they are easily sorted, counted, and analyzed.

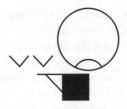

Figure 8.1 SignWriting of BIRD.

Table 8.1 Some SignTyp records (simplified) for BIRD.

Major Category	Subhead1	Subhead2	Value
action	handshape change		closing
action	Repetition		handshape change
hand posture	spreading		unspread
hand posture	finger group	closed fingers	middle–ring–pinky
hand posture	finger group	most extended	index
hand posture	finger group posture	most extended	bent
hand posture	fingers contacted by thumb		index
hand posture	thumb posture		opposed
Location	vertical	head	lower face

Data Storage: Database and Spreadsheet Software

The two most common choices for storage are the spreadsheet and the relational database.

A spreadsheet is appropriate for a small amount of data, perhaps under 10,000 records. Pivot tables (a table that summarizes the data for variables that the researcher selects) are easy to create and access and are an easy way to understand the aggregated data while the non-aggregate data are also quickly accessible. Formulae to manipulate the data can be quickly written and can easily refer to previous and next record – which is important, since most signs are likely to require at least two records (rows). The alternative to a spreadsheet is a *relational database*. Databases are generally faster than spreadsheets and more secure. They allow multiple researchers to access the same data at the same time. However, it is usually not necessary to make a choice between the advantages of spreadsheets and databases. Data can be stored in a relational database and then accessed when one links to them through a spreadsheet. The spreadsheet pivot tables then allow for further manipulation of the data.

Analysis

The final stage in a research project is analysis. Most phonological data are not quantitative but rather qualitative (categorical). They are usually not ordinal – a location on the nose is not greater or smaller than a location on the ear. For categorical non-ordinal data, we can obtain frequencies that include the mode (the most common value). For categorical ordinal data, the median (the middle value) is also obtainable. But, for any categorical data, means (or averages) are meaningless.

Phonetic and prosodic data are more likely to be quantitative. For example, the height of a raised eyebrow can be ordered and measured (as in Weast, 2011). Many characteristics are usefully measured quantitatively, even though the characteristic is actually categorical. For example, categories for finger spreading could be unspread, neutral (neither spread nor unspread), spread, and extremely spread. A possible research project might treat spreading quantitatively and might measure the amount of spreading in various tokens of a handshape. The quantitative information might then help determine how many categories there are, if the researcher can show clustering around multiple modes that can be equated to spreading categories.

A first analysis of data probably uses frequency tables, which provide information about common and rare values, as well as missing values. For example, suppose that the question is what sets of fingers could be extended in a sign. Impossible forms are found by listing all 24 (4 x 3 x 2) logical possibilities and by comparing them with the actually occurring forms. Cross-tabulation examines the relationships between two or more variables and whether certain sets of data are significantly different from a norm – for example, whether the set of the extended fingers influences the type of flexion involved. Some projects will need more complex statistical analyses. Brentari and Eccarius (2011) used ANOVAs to determine whether there were significant differences in responses to different handshape groups, and de Beuzeville et al. (2009) used Varbrul to analyze factors that influence when verbs are inflected in Auslan.

Conclusion

This chapter has looked at the variables that need to be considered in setting up a research project for the forms of signs. The considerations mentioned here are intended to provide a starting point only, since every research project is different. At a minimum, however, the points mentioned here should serve as an initial checklist.

Acknowledgments

This material is based upon work supported by the National Science Foundation under Grant No. BCS-1049510 to the University of Connecticut. Any opinions, findings, and conclusions or recommendations expressed in this material are those of the author and do not necessarily reflect the views of the National Science Foundation.

Note

1   In this chapter I use the lowercase form *deaf* throughout.

Keywords

citation form; coding; contrastiveness; features; iconicity; phonetics; phonological hierarchy; phonology; sign internal sequence; transcription

See Also

Chapter 4; Chapter 5; Chapter 7; Chapter 11

Suggested Readings

Brentari, D. (Ed.) (2001). *Foreign vocabulary in sign languages: Cross-linguistic analysis of word-formation processes*. Mahwah, NJ: Lawrence Erlbaum and Associates.
Brentari, D. (Ed.) (2010). *Cambridge language surveys: Sign languages*. Cambridge: Cambridge University Press.
Channon, R., and van der Hulst, H. (Eds.) (2011). *Formational units in sign language* (Sign Language Typology series, 3). Nijmegen, Netherlands/Berlin: Ishara Press/Mouton de Gruyter.
Grosvald, M. (2009). Long-distance coarticulation: A production and perception study of English and American Sign Language. Dissertation Abstracts International, A: Humanities and Social Sciences.
van der Hulst, H. (1993). Units in the analysis of signs. *Phonology* 10, 209–241.
Meier, R., Cormier, K., and Quinto-Pozos, D. (Eds.) (2002). *Modality and structure in signed and spoken languages*. Cambridge: Cambridge University Press.
Sandler, W. (1987). Sequentiality and simultaneity in American Sign Language phonology. PhD dissertation, University of Texas at Austin. ProQuest Dissertations and Theses.
Sandler, W. (1993). Linearization of phonological tiers in ASL. In G. Coulter (Ed.), *Current issues in ASL phonology*. New York: Academic Press, pp. 103–129.
Sandler, W., and Lillo-Martin, D. (2006). *Sign language and linguistic universals*. Cambridge: Cambridge University Press.
Singleton, J., and Newport, E. (2004). When learners surpass their models: The acquisition of American Sign Language from inconsistent input. *Cognitive Psychology* 49(4), 370–407.

References

Bank, R., Crasborn, O., and van Hout, R. (2011). Variation in mouth actions with manual signs in Sign Language of the Netherlands (NGT). *Sign Language and Linguistics* 14(2), 248–270.
de Beuzeville, L., Johnston, T., and Schembri, A. (2009). The use of space with indicating verbs in Auslan: A corpus-based investigation. *Sign Language and Linguistics* 12(1), 53–82.
Brentari, D. (1998). *A prosodic model of sign language*. Cambridge MA: MIT Press.
Brentari, D., and Crossley, L. (2002). Prosody on the hands and face evidence from American Sign Language. *Sign Language & Linguistics* 5(2), 105–130.
Brentari, D., and Eccarius, P. (2011). When does a system become phonological? Potential sources of handshape contrast in sign languages. In R. Channon and H. van der Hulst (Eds.), *Formational units in sign languages* (Sign Language Typology series, 3). Nijmegen, Netherlands/Berlin: Ishara Press/Mouton de Gruyter, pp. 125–150.

Brentari, D., and Padden, C. (2001). A language with multiple origins: Native and foreign vocabulary in American Sign Language. In D. Brentari (Ed.), *Foreign vocabulary in sign language: A cross-linguistic investigation of word formation*. Mahwah, NJ: Lawrence Erlbaum, pp. 87–119.

Channon, R. (2002a). Signs are single segments: Phonological representations and temporal sequencing in ASL and other sign languages. PhD dissertation, College Park, University of Maryland.

Channon, R. (2002b). Beads on a string? Representations of repetition in spoken and signed languages. In R. Meier, K. Cormier, and D. Quinto-Pozos (Eds.), *Modality and structure in signed and spoken languages*. Cambridge: Cambridge University Press, pp. 110–148.

Channon, R. (2004). The symmetry and dominance conditions reconsidered. *Papers from the Regional Meetings, Chicago Linguistic Society* 40(1), 45–57.

Channon, R., and van der Hulst, H. (2011). Are dynamic features required in signs? In R. Channon and H. van der Hulst (Eds.), *Formational units in sign languages* (Sign Language Typology series, 3). Nijmegen, Netherlands/Berlin: Ishara Press/Mouton de Gruyter, pp. 229–260.

Channon Crain, R. (1996). Representing a sign as a single segment in American Sign Language. In A. D. Green and V. Motopanyane (eds.), *Proceedings of the thirteenth eastern states conference on linguistics*. Ithaca NY: Cornell University, pp. 46–57.

Cheek, D. A. (2001). *The phonetics and phonology of handshape in American Sign Language*. PhD dissertation, University of Texas at Austin.

Corina, D. (1993). To branch or not to branch: Underspecification in American Sign Language handshape contours. In G. Coulter (Ed.), *Current Issues in ASL Phonology*. San Diego: Academic Press, pp. 63–95.

Eccarius, P., Bour, R., and Scheidt, R. A. (2012). Dataglove measurement of joint angles in sign language handshapes. *Sign Language and Linguistics* 15(1), 39–72.

Emmorey, K., Thompson, R., and Colvin, R. (2009). Eye gaze during comprehension of American Sign Language by native and beginning signers. *Journal of Deaf Studies and Deaf Education* 14(2), 237–243.

Emmorey, K., Gertsberg, N., Korpics, F., and Wright, C. E. (2009). The influence of visual feedback and register changes on sign language production: A kinematic study with deaf signers. *Applied Psycholinguistics* 30(1), 187–203.

Fischer, S., and Gong, Q. (2011). Marked hand configurations in Asian sign languages. In R. Channon and H. van der Hulst (Eds.), *Formational units in sign languages* (Sign Language Typology series, 3). Nijmegen, Netherlands/Berlin: Ishara Press/Mouton de Gruyter, pp. 19–42.

Grosvald, M., and Corina, D. (2012). Perception of long-distance coarticulation: An event-related potential and behavioral study. *Applied Psycholinguistics* 33(1), 55–82.

Hansen, K. (2011). ASL movement phonemes and allophones. In R. Channon and H. van der Hulst (Eds.), *Formational units in sign languages* (Sign Language Typology series, 3). Nijmegen, Netherlands/Berlin: Ishara Press/Mouton de Gruyter, pp. 285–314.

van der Hulst, H., and Channon, R. (2010). Notation systems. In D. Brentari (Ed.), *Cambridge language surveys: Sign languages*. Cambridge: Cambridge University Press, pp. 151–172.

Johnston, T. (2012). Lexical frequency in sign languages. *Journal of Deaf Studies and Deaf Education* 17(2), 163–193.

Kendon, A. (1990). Signs in the cloister and elsewhere. *Semiotica* 79, 307–329.

van der Kooij, E. (2002). Phonological categories in Sign Language of the Netherlands: The role of phonetic implementation and iconicity. PhD dissertation, Leiden University, Netherlands.

Kubus, O., and Hohenberger, A. (2011). The phonetics and phonology of the TID (Turkish Sign Language) bimanual alphabet. In R. Channon and H. van der Hulst (Eds.), *Formational units in sign languages* (Sign Language Typology series, 3). Nijmegen, Netherlands/Berlin: Ishara Press/Mouton de Gruyter, pp. 43–64.

Lee, H. (2008). The representation of handshape change in Taiwan Sign Language. *Sign Language and Linguistics* 11(2), 139–183.

Lenneberg, E. H. (1967). *Biological foundations of language*. New York: Wiley.

Liddell, S. (1996). Spatial representations in discourse: Comparing spoken and signed language. *Lingua* 98(1/3) 145–167.

Liddell, S. K., and Johnson, R. E. (1989). American Sign Language: The phonological base. *Sign Language Studies* 64, 195–278.

Lombardi, L. (1990). The nonlinear organization of the affricate. *Natural Language and Linguistic Theory* 8(3), 375–425.

Lu, P. (2011). Data-driven sign language animation generation: A survey. Unpublished manuscript, City University of New York, pp. 1–54.

Mak, J., and Tang, G. (2011). Movement types, repetition, and feature organization in Hong Kong Sign Language. In R. Channon, and H. van der Hulst (Eds.), *Formational units in sign languages* (Sign Language Typology series, 3). Nijmegen, Netherlands/Berlin: Ishara Press/Mouton de Gruyter, pp. 315–337.

Mauk, C. E. (2003). *Undershoot in two modalities: Evidence from fast speech and fast signing*. Dissertation Abstracts International, A: Humanities and Social Sciences.

Mayberry, R. I., and Fischer, S. D. (1989). Looking through phonological shape to lexical meaning: The bottleneck of non-native sign language processing. *Memory and Cognition* 17(6), 740–754.

Morford, J., and MacFarlane, J. (2003). Frequency characteristics of American Sign Language. *Sign Language Studies* 3(2), 213–225.

Parton, B. (2006). Sign language recognition and translation: A multidisciplined approach from the field of artificial intelligence. *Journal of Deaf Studies and Deaf Education* 11(1), 94–101.

Sandler, W. (2010). Prosody and syntax in sign languages. *Transactions of the Philological Society* 108(3), 298–328.

Stokoe, W., Casterline, D., and Croneberg, C. (1965). *A dictionary of American Sign Language on linguistic principles*. Washington, DC: Gallaudet College Press.

Tyrone, M. E., and Mauk, C. E. (2010). Sign lowering and phonetic reduction in American Sign Language. *Journal of Phonetics* 38(2), 317–328.

Umiker-Sebeok, J., and Sebeok, T. A. (Eds.) (1987). *Monastic sign languages*. Berlin: Mouton De Gruyter.

Uyechi, L. (1996). *The geometry of visual phonology* (Dissertations in Linguistics). Stanford, CA: CSLI Publications.

Vinson, D. P., Thompson, R. L., Skinner, R., Fox, N., and Vigliocco, G. (2010). The hands and mouth do not always slip together in British Sign Language: Dissociating articulatory channels in the lexicon. *Psychological Science* 21, 1158–1167.

Weast, T. (2011). American Sign Language tone and intonation: A phonetic analysis of eyebrow properties. In R. Channon and H. van der Hulst (Eds.), *Formational units in sign languages* (Sign Language Typology series, 3). Nijmegen, Netherlands/Berlin: Ishara Press/Mouton de Gruyter, pp. 203–228.

Wolfe, R., Cook, P., McDonald, J. C., and Schnepp, J. (2011). Linguistics as structure in computer animation: Toward a more effective synthesis of brow motion in American Sign Language. *Sign Language and Linguistics* 14(1), 179–199.

9 Methods of Research on Sign Language Grammars

Carol A. Padden

Chapter Overview

Over the last decade or two, sign language research has expanded to include more research with gesture, new sign languages, and cross-linguistic work. This has led to the development of methods that allow elicitation and testing across speakers, hearing gesturers, and signers of different sign languages. Materials such as photographs, illustrations, and video clips are useful as a means of comparing responses and linguistic judgments within similar communicative frames. These tasks also avoid pitfalls with translation-type exercises, which can be difficult or impossible for little-studied sign languages. Some tasks are designed for pairs of signers where one conveys to the other a description that requires a judgment about meaning. Communicative tasks such as these draw the focus to the discursive aspects of language, where signers engage in conversation as well as produce language responses. The easy portability of laptops and lightweight video allows testing and interviews of language users in situ, in their homes and in settings with other language users.

Research Methods in Sign Language Studies: A Practical Guide, First Edition.
Edited by Eleni Orfanidou, Bencie Woll, and Gary Morgan.
© 2015 John Wiley & Sons, Inc. Published 2015 by John Wiley & Sons, Inc.

Much of the work on sign language grammars in the last 50 years has involved established sign languages, many of them "national sign languages," with multiple communities and large numbers of signers (Sandler and Lillo-Martin, 2006). Even when the linguist shares the same language as the consultants or is sufficiently fluent in it and can carry out productive elicitation sessions, it is important to explore different approaches to developing grammatical descriptions. Fischer (2009) provides an excellent guide on how to work with a single signer or with groups of signers eliciting sign language forms and structures. More recently, the SignGram project (www.signgram.eu) has involved collaboration between European researchers to create a blueprint for reference grammars of sign languages; these should include the development of methodological guidelines and common elicitation materials for sign language research.

As the field of sign language research expands in ambition, we see more such research developing across different regions of the world, particularly on "small sign languages" in villages and towns and on larger sign languages in little-researched areas like Eastern Europe and India (Brentari, 2010; Mathur and Napoli, 2011; Zeshan and de Vos, 2012). From these studies new findings emerge on grammars of diverse sign languages, related and unrelated, each having different community characteristics and histories. Many of these studies are carried out outside the laboratory and directly in the field. As it turns out, these methods are also useful in a new area of language research: comparing pantomime and gestures produced by hearing non-signers with home signers and signers of new and established sign languages (Gibson, Brink, Piantadosi, and Saxe, 2011; Goldin-Meadow, So, Ozyurek, and Mylander, 2008; Hall, Mayberry, and Ferreira, 2013; Langus and Nespor, 2010; Padden et al., 2013).

Usually, when linguists begin to work on a spoken language, they already know something about its history, or at least about the history of languages like it. They can identify where the language is spoken; and there may already be published records comparing its grammar to those of other languages in the region. To use an example, a linguist who begins to study a Mayan language in Mexico can find some kind of published work as a starting point for research. There may be a written grammar, or preliminary notes on some aspect of the grammar. She can also use published studies of grammatical features of related languages to guide her work.

But, more often than not, the resources about the history of a particular sign language are limited. For some sign languages, a first step is to identify schools that signers may have attended. From this information the linguist can track the geography of the language, establishing patterns of sign language acquisition, social use, and contact with other language(s) of a region. In the Middle East, Asia, and parts of Africa, schools for deaf[1] children date only to the last half of the twentieth century; this situation results in a different pattern of sign language contact and spread by comparison to that of North American and European sign languages with histories dating to the eighteenth century or earlier (Padden, 2010; Woodward, 1996). In some areas of the Middle East there are unrelated sign languages within a hundred kilometers of each other (Al-Fityani and Padden, 2010), which reflects the political geography of the region.

In this chapter I discuss methods for investigating four areas of sign language grammar: basic vocabulary; lexicon studies; verb classification and grammatical roles; sentence types and discourse structure. The goal here is not to be comprehensive or exhaustive, but to give examples of methods designed for comparative sign language work. Using translation and paradigm studies can be difficult in communities where there are few signers and they are unaccustomed to outsider interest in their language. Such sign languages have long been overlooked in favor of sign languages with long institutional histories and large communities of signers. Now, with more work on sign languages around the world, from the very small to the very large, we see more use of these kinds of testing materials in collecting linguistic data.

Basic Vocabulary

Translation is a time-honored approach to research on an unknown language, and it works if the linguist and the consultants share a common language. If the community is new to any kind of study of its sign language, it may take some time before consultants understand what kind of translation linguists want. Translating with the help of written sentences is a honed skill, which requires literate knowledge and an awareness that sign languages can present small differences in grammatical form and meaning. Metalinguistic knowledge of the kind of detail that linguists want requires time and experience to develop. Asking a signer to read sentences – say, one with a conditional clause and another with a counterfactual – and then to show how they would be signed differently can stump even bilinguals. Susan Fischer (2009) advises against translation, except for basic vocabulary, because signers may inadvertently change their language to more closely mirror the written sentences.

Instead of translation, pictures of objects and videos of actions can be used to develop a basic dictionary. Simple pictures can be used for naming, and then more complex ones can elicit signs for abstract concepts. In communities with little tradition of schooling, signers may give *syntagmatic* responses instead of naming the object in the picture, for example "this tree is tall and leafy like the one outside," or, for a specific type of tree, "a tree that bears the fruit of dates." *Paradigmatic* strategies, or providing a single sign for each picture, is common among those who have attended school. They have more experience of naming tasks, and they also understand how to interpret complex pictures or drawings with movement lines that portray actions as in a cartoon, because these materials are more common at school (Cole, 1996).

Whether you work with the sign language of a village or of a large deaf community, it helps to collect responses across different signers, then to return to the same signer at different points in time to collect the same vocabulary. Paradigmatic responses can be compared to syntagmatic ones to probe variation across generations and groups of signers in a small community. In very small communities, sign variation may appear across families; such sociolects are called "family-lects" (Israel and Sandler, 2012). Families may vary in their signs for the same object. In large national sign languages, sign variation can be related to region, ethnicity, class, generation or age, and gender (Lucas, 2001). Some anthropologists and linguists have used network analyses to track which members of a small community have regular or less frequent contact with one another (Nonaka, 2007) as a way of establishing vocabulary use and conventionalization in the community.

A database of signs from multiple members of a sign language community can be a first step in developing a phonology of that language. Signs can be coded according to features and by phonotactics – for example constraints on one- or two-handed forms (Morgan and Mayberry, 2012), or assimilation across sign segments in a sign and in compounds. There are now large and detailed dictionaries available online (e.g. the *Online Dictionary of New Zealand Sign Language* at http://nzsl.vuw.ac.nz), with illustrations and videos that make it possible to compare lexical variants within sign languages.

Lexicon Studies

One way to explore signs across grammatical categories is to compile pictures of objects that share features and to ask signers to identify them. Linguists have used versions of the Swadesh List, developed by the linguist Morris Swadesh for use with spoken languages. The list is intended as an early "snapshot" of the lexicon of a language (Swadesh, 1950), in preparation for further study. On the basis of what is learned, the linguist can follow up with studies of kinship signs, noun classification, lexical categories, classifier structures, verb classification, as well as inflectional and derivational forms. The Swadesh list includes common objects, actions, colors, and some abstract concepts that one would expect to find in most human communities. James Woodward modified this list for his own comparative studies of sign languages, to avoid eliciting pointing such as for body parts (e.g., ear, eye, nose, mouth) or for personal pronouns (Woodward, 1993). The remaining items on his list include vocabulary relating to color, natural objects, food, animals, number, and intransitive verbs (eat, sleep, walk).

For elicitations, pictures of clothing, animals, or colors can be taken by using local objects; these pictures are then quickly loaded into the laptop for easy presentation on slides (Figure 9.1a–c). Familiar objects in local cultural contexts are more appealing to consultants. Be aware, however, that there are likely constraints and issues of privacy in a small community: you may not be able to show photographs of young women from one family to members (especially young men) of a different family. Instead, generic photographs can be selected from the Internet. Remember, too, that there are cultural issues even for such pictures; for example, animals that are household pets in one culture may not be pets in another; or there is clothing that is judged inappropriate in traditional communities. Before asking members of a community to participate in video actions for testing, be sure there are no privacy risks to the individual who is shown in the video.

Consultants can be asked to provide sign translations of written words across grammatical classes (e.g., nouns, verbs, adjectives), but their responses may not reveal differences between related forms. The difference between the noun "toothbrush" and the verbal counterpart, "brush one's teeth," may be difficult to see or nonexistent (Tkachman and Sandler, 2013). As a strategy for eliciting nouns and related verbs in American Sign Language (ASL), Supalla and Newport (1978) used videos of objects ("toothbrush"), followed by videos of actions featuring those objects ("brushing your teeth with a toothbrush"). They then used videos of unusual

Figure 9.1a–c Examples of photographs of local objects for vocabulary elicitation. Photos courtesy of Rabia Ergin.

actions typically not associated with the object, such as "putting a toothbrush in a cup," to see if the noun in a sentence with a different action would be signed in a distinctive way. They also tested consultants at different times, to see whether signers reliably reproduced forms the same way each time.

Brentari and Padden (2001) discuss a distinction between native vocabulary in sign languages, which includes basic signs and their related forms, and non-native vocabulary which includes borrowed forms such as fingerspelling, initialized signs, and signs from other sign languages. Fingerspelled words are pervasive in some sign languages and play an important role in their lexicons (Padden, 2006; Sutton-Spence, 2006). Wrongly judged as falling outside of lexicon studies, fingerspelled words are broadly used in languages like ASL, British Sign Language (BSL), and Swedish Sign Language. They become embedded in the lexical structure of signs and can be used with signs in compounds – as in the ASL sign BLACK+M-A-I-L, "blackmail"

(Padden, 1998), or in the BSL signs for major cities like G-W, "Glasgow." Foreign borrowings can reveal processes of lexicalization or nativization; thus, for the sign GLASGOW, the handshape of the -W- has been partially assimilated to that of -G-. Borrowed vocabulary in a sign language can be found in brand names, towns and cities, commercial entities, and signs for new technologies. Pictures of new technologies, maps, and commercial advertisements can be used to see what resources sign languages use for these concepts.

For classifier structures, including size and shape specifiers, a common approach is to use pictures or illustrations of objects in various arrangements. Zwitserlood (2003) used illustrations of objects in common classificatory schemata as a way of mapping classifier types for Sign Language of the Netherlands (NGT). She added illustrations of nonexistent entities to explore productive strategies for using classifier handshapes (Figure 9.2).

Brentari, Coppola, Mazzoni, and Goldin-Meadow (2012) compared pantomimic gestures of hearing non-signers and classifiers used by signers, focusing on (1) their use of "handling handshapes" in order to depict an agent moving an object, or (2) their use of "object handshapes" in order to describe the shape or dimension of objects without reference to an agent. They used pictures of an object (or objects) on a flat surface, then they presented the same objects in a video that showed a human hand touching or manipulating them in the picture (Figure 9.3a–b). They video-recorded gesturers' and signers' responses and coded for types of handshapes and movements.

Davidson (2011) asked English speakers and ASL signers to judge the meaning of spoken and ASL sentences containing quantifiers such as "some" and "all." Her question was whether the word or the sign meaning "some" is understood to mean a quality applying to some objects in a set, but not to all of them. These pragmatic evaluations by language users are called "scalar implicatures." After consulting with ASL signers, Davidson developed an experiment that compared speakers and signers by using Psyscope software on a laptop. First the program showed, on the left side of the screen, a photograph with an array of objects; then a video window appeared

Figure 9.2a–b Illustrations of nonexistent or alien entities for elicitation of classifier structures. Zwitserlood, 2003, with permission of Inge Zwitserlood.

with a model speaking (for English speakers) or signing (for ASL signers) a sentence with the concept "some" or "all." Participants were asked to evaluate the acceptability of the sentence by touching either a key with a smiling face sticker or a key with a frowning face sticker (Figure 9.4). Using a task that requires a key-press for judging a signed sentence allows ASL signers to rate acceptability in ASL without influence from written English.

(a)   (b)

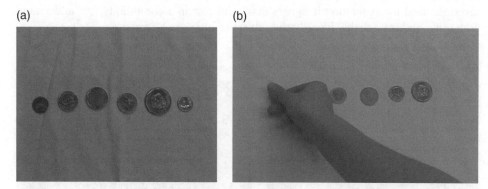

Figure 9.3a–b Photograph (left) and frame of video (right) for eliciting classifier structures for objects and agents handling objects. Courtesy of Diane Brentari.

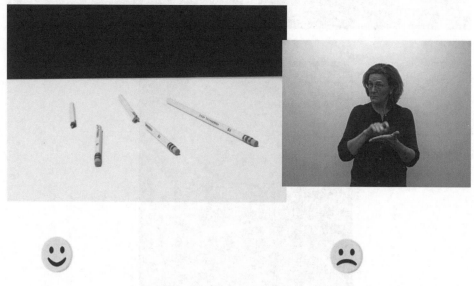

Figure 9.4 Screenshot of an ASL experimental trial eliciting judgments of quantifiers. Signers are asked to judge whether the signer's description matches (smiling face) or does not match (frowning face) the picture. From Davidson, 2011 with permission of Kathryn Davidson.

Verb Classification and Grammatical Roles

Some studies of sign language word order and grammatical roles use video clips to elicit basic sentence structure with intransitive and transitive actions (Sandler, Meir, Padden, and Aronoff, 2005; Senghas, Coppola, Newport, and Supalla, 1997). Signers are asked to describe an action in a video clip to another signer, who is then asked to repeat the description or to identify a picture that corresponds to the action. Paired communicative tasks are ideal for evaluating if signers in a cohort or in a community can understand each other and can reliably identify the subject or object in a sentence.

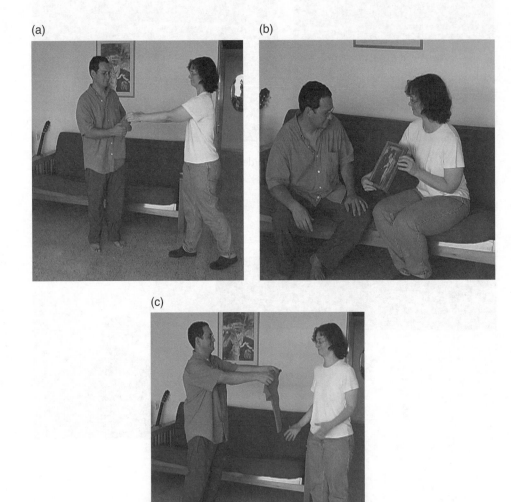

(a)

(b)

(c)

Figure 9.5a–c Response sheet for addressees in paired communication tasks: "The woman gives the man a shirt." From Shai Davidi and Sign Language Research Lab, University of Haifa, Israel.

Sandler, Aronoff, Meir, and Padden (2011) asked signers to describe an action in a video clip to another signer, who then had to identify one out of three pictures. For example, in a video showing a woman giving a man a shirt, the signer first observes a partner describing the video, then sees on the screen three pictures: a correct picture; the man showing the woman a picture (different action); and the man giving the woman a shirt (different subject) (Figure 9.5a–c). Signers' responses to these videos have been used to demonstrate argument structure in sign languages (Meir, 2010a; Padden, Meir, Sandler, and Aronoff, 2010), how the body marks a lexical subject (Meir, Padden, Aronoff, and Sandler, 2007), and how the competing iconicities of person and subject are resolved in a sign language (Meir, Padden, Sandler, and Aronoff, 2013).

Senghas (2003) studied spatial modulations and directional verb forms in Nicaraguan Sign Language (NSL). Signers view a video with three actors seated adjacently to each other. One actor turns to the side and taps the person next to her on the shoulder. The signer is then asked to provide a sign description of what happened to a second signer, who has to choose from an array of pictures featuring different actions. Different combinations of interactions between the three actors were designed to elicit various possibilities of marking grammatical roles and of representing them in space. Sign forms across cohorts of NSL signers were coded for the use of spatial modulation.

Sentence Types and Discourse Structure

Elicitation guided by using video clips, described earlier, is a good starting point for the analysis of sentence types in a sign language. Video clips can be designed to probe different kinds of sentences: with intransitive and transitive verbs, with one object and two objects (ditransitive), with inanimate and animate objects. They can elicit verbs involving path and motion and verbs involving transfer from one human to another. For example, signers may represent verbs of transfer by using separate sentences instead of one: instead of "the woman gave the man a shirt," the signer produces two sentences: "the woman gave a shirt and the man took it." Photographs of models with different characteristics can assist in examining the use of descriptive adjectives in a sentence. Generally, sentences used for face-to-face interaction differ from the types represented in written language (Miller, 2006) – which is another reason why signed translation from written sentences can be misleading for linguistic analysis. For more complex structures, signed narratives can have examples of direct or quoted speech, conditionals or topic structures, and they can provide data beyond what can be found in guided elicitations.

To elicit narratives, signers can be asked to describe picture books (Morford, 2003) or to view a cartoon (Brentari, Nadolske, and Wolford, 2012; Senghas and Coppola, 2001) featuring complex actions performed by an animated character.

Senghas (2010) used pictures of figures in spatial arrangements relative to each other to explore how signers position referents in signing space; these pictures were drawn from available materials developed by Levinson et al. (1992) (Figure 9.6a–c). Two signers had the same set of pictures, which showed a figure facing a tree or (a)　　　　　　　　　　　　　　　　　　(b)

(c)

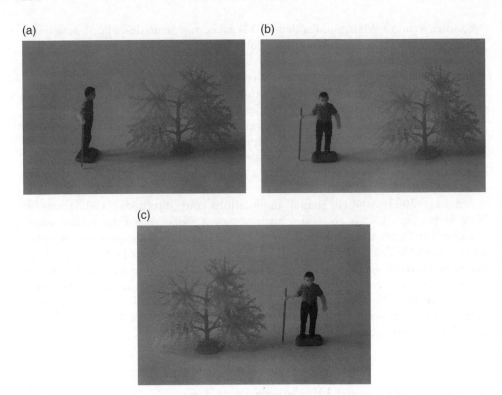

Figure 9.6a–c Photographs of figures in various spatial arrangements (Levinson et al. 1992). From http://fieldmanuals.mpi.nl/volumes/1992/man-tree-space-games

standing next to it on either the left or the right. One signer on the other side of a screen between the two described one picture to another signer, who then selected a picture that corresponded to the description. This elicitation evaluates whether signers provided a spatial description from their own point of view – that is, whether the figure was to the left of the signer, in which case it was called "unrotated," or to the left of the addressee, in which case it was to the right of the signer and was called "rotated." Senghas and her colleagues have used multiple measures, including photographs and video clips of actors performing actions, to evaluate spatial modulation across cohorts of signers.

When analyzing complex structures, it is crucial to be able to view both the grammatical structure and the prosody in sign language sentences. Cues to sentence boundaries, including the difference between coordinate and complex structures (which have embedded dependent clauses), are often found not entirely on the hands, but on the face and in movements of the head and body. Often, though not always, the eyes blink at a clause boundary, the head moves forward or tilts, and the body may also shift position. At points where these cues are aligned together, they can signal a shift to a new sentence or clause (Sandler, 2011). The body can mark a new subject of a clause with a body shift to the side (though not all sign languages have body shift) (Meir et al., 2007). The body is also the locus for predicates referring to bodily functions and emotions, which are called plain verbs (Meir, 2010b; Taub, 2001) and can be themselves used as a location and a map of the body itself, for instance to do surgery or to do other things involving the body (such as putting clothes on).

Any study of sentences and narratives needs to make sure that sign language data are visually accessible through clear lighting and sharp focus of the face and body of the signer. A frequent mistake is to try to video-record the entire body instead of the signer's face and upper torso. Using split-screen technology where both signers in a conversation are simultaneously aligned together allows for the comparison of both production and comprehension. It also makes it possible to observe live sign language forms and structures, with interruptions, clarifications, and repetitions that are characteristic of normal online conversations. These data can be used for comparisons with elicited material, both to confirm and to clarify claims made with the help of more focused data.

As sign language studies expand to explore the continua of visual–gestural forms between gesture and conventionalized sign languages, research methods can be adapted to this purpose. Pictures and videos of the type used to elicit word order and lexical categories in established and in small sign languages can also be used with other populations. Research materials can anticipate flexibility – a feature that allows them to be used with signers and non-signers, with signers of established and signers of small sign languages, *and* with hearing non-signers who speak different languages and belong to different cultures. Some examples of this work have adapted materials to the study of word order in signers of new sign languages (Sandler et al., 2005; Senghas et al., 1997) or to the study of cognitive ordering strategies in hearing non-signers (Gibson et al., 2011; Goldin-Meadow et al., 2008; Hall et al., 2013; Langus and Nespor, 2010; Meir, et al., 2010). Cartoons have been used to compare face and body movements during speech in hearing speakers to prosody in signers' descriptions of the same cartoon (Brentari et al., 2012).

Coding Strategies

Coding strategies for sign language material are closely tied to what is possible to do with annotation systems and technologies. Developed at the Max Planck Institute at Nijmegen, ELAN has emerged as a popular annotation software for many sign language research teams (Crasborn and Sloetjes, 2008). In addition to being available for free download, ELAN has enormous flexibility and functionality for almost any purpose in sign language transcription. Annotation sequences are linked to individual video frames, permitting varying degrees of detail for notation – from individual features to signs, sentences, and discourse frames. Sequences can be matched with as many tiers or levels as is needed for simultaneous analysis – for example, a tier for coding handshapes in two-handed signs, another tier for glosses of individual signs, and yet another for a translation of the sign sentence. The use of body shift, eye blinks, and eye gaze can be represented on additional tiers, all tiers being synchronized to individual video frames.

After a narrative has been translated by using a tier tied to the video segment, a clip can be pulled out and the translation tier can be converted into subtitles for use during academic presentations. Any series of coded video segments can be retrieved, listed, and stored for playback as examples of signing featuring – say, all the sentences with transitive clauses, or all the sentences with handling handshapes. Coded data can be exported to Excel for purposes of basic statistical analysis as well as to make graphs for visible display of the data. As studies of human language acknowledge the vital role of gesture and of the visible body in communication, there will be even more development of technologies like the lightweight and high-definition video camera or of annotation software like ELAN, which can code both audible and visible material.

   To summarize, here are the major considerations in research methods for sign language grammar:

1   The social and cultural contexts of signers' communities should guide the design of materials for language study. This presupposes identifying networks of contact in smaller communities and institutions of social interaction in larger communities. This information can be used to evaluate the history of a sign language, including influence from other sign languages.
2   In many parts of the world, signers have little or no access to schooling. Research methods need to be selected and designed to accommodate signers' cultural and literacy experiences. Researchers need to be mindful of signers' work lives and to use methods that do not demand large amounts of their time. An ambitious research agenda can be divided up into smaller encounters over time, at the signers' convenience.
3   Elicitation methods can use pictures, illustrations, and video clips of various types to prompt the use of various types of structures. Communicative tasks, where signers are paired with each other, show language as it is used interactively. The linguist learns not only the vocabulary and the grammar of the language, but also how signers correct, repeat, clarify, and use language in conversational contexts.

Note

1   The standard lowercase form *deaf* is used in this chapter to refer to signers in different communicative contexts.

Keywords

elicitation methods in sign languages; field research in sign languages; new sign languages

See Also

Chapter 7

Suggested Readings

Bowern, C. (2008). *Linguistic fieldwork: A practical guide*. New York: Palgrave Macmillan.
Newman, P., and Ratliff, M. (Eds.) (2001). *Linguistic fieldwork*. Cambridge: Cambridge University Press.

References

Al-Fityani, K., and Padden, C. (2010). Sign languages in the Arab world. In D. Brentari (Ed.), *Sign Languages: A Cambridge Language Survey*. New York: Cambridge University Press, pp. 433–450.

Brentari, D. (Ed.) (2010). *Sign Languages*. Cambridge: Cambridge University Press.

Brentari, D., and Padden, C. (2001). Native and foreign vocabulary in American Sign Language: A lexicon with multiple origins. In D. Brentari (Ed.), *Foreign vocabulary in sign languages: A cross-linguistic investigation of word formation*. Mahwah, NJ: Lawrence Erlbaum Associates, pp. 49–85.

Brentari, D., Nadolske, M., and Wolford, G. (2012). Can experience with co-speech gesture influence the prosody of a sign language? Sign language prosodic cues in bimodal bilinguals. *Bilingualism: Language and Cognition* 15(2), 402–412.

Brentari, D., Coppola, M., Mazzoni, L., and Goldin-Meadow, S. (2012). When does a system become phonological? Handshape production in gesturers, signers, and homesigners. *Lingua* 30, 1–31.

Cole, M. (1996). *Cultural psychology : A once and future discipline*. Cambridge, MA: Harvard University Press.

Crasborn, O., and Sloetjes, H. (2008). Enhanced ELAN functionality for sign language corpora. Paper presented at the sixth international conference on language resources and evaluation, Marrakech, Morocco.

Davidson, K. (2011). *The nature of the semantic scale: Evidence from sign language research*. PhD dissertation, University of California, San Diego.

Fischer, S. (2009). Sign language field methods: Approaches, techniques and concerns. In J. H.-Y. Tai and J. Tsay (Eds.), *Taiwan Sign Language and beyond*. Taiwan: Taiwan Institute for the Humanities, National Chung Cheng University, pp. 1–19.

Gibson, E., Brink, K., Piantadosi, S., and Saxe, R. (2011). Cognitive pressures explain the dominant word orders in language. Paper presented at the CUNY Sentence Processing Conference, Stanford, California.

Goldin-Meadow, S., So, W. C., Ozyurek, A., and Mylander, C. (2008). The natural order of events: How speakers of different languages represent events non-verbally. *Proceedings of the National Academy of Sciences* 105(27), 9163–9168. doi: 10.1073/pnas.0710060105

Hall, M. L., Mayberry, R. I., and Ferreira, V. S. (2013). Cognitive constraints on constituent order: Evidence from elicited pantomime. *Cognition* 129(1), 1–17.

Israel, A., and Sandler, W. (2012). Phonological category resolution: A study of handshapes in younger and older sign languages. In R. Channon and H. van der Hulst (Eds.), *Formational units in sign language*. Nijmegen/Berlin: Ishara Press/Mouton de Gruyter, pp. 177–202.

Langus, A., and Nespor, M. (2010). Cognitive systems struggling for word order. *Cognitive Psychology* 60(4), 291–318. doi: 10.1016/j.cogpsych.2010.01.004

Levinson, S., Brown, P., Danziger, E., De León, L., Haviland, J., Pederson, E., and Senft, G. (1992). Man and tree & space games. In S. Levinson (Ed.), *Space stimuli kit 1.2*. Nijmegen: Max Planck Institute for Psycholinguistics, pp. 7–14. Accessed September 3, 2014. http://fieldmanuals.mpi.nl/volumes/1992/man-tree-space-games

Lucas, C. (2001). *The sociolinguistics of sign languages*. New York: Cambridge University Press.

Mathur, G., and Napoli, D. J. (Eds.) (2011). *Deaf around the world : The impact of language*. New York: Oxford University Press.

Meir, I. (2010a). The emergence of argument structure in two new sign languages. In M. Hovav, E. Doron, and I. Sichel (Eds.), *Syntax, lexical semantics and event structure*. Oxford: Oxford University Press, pp. 101–123.

Meir, I. (2010b). Iconicity and metaphor: Constraints on metaphorical extension of iconic forms. *Language* 86(4), 865–896.

Meir, I., Lifshitz, A., Ilkbasaran, D., and Padden, C. (2010). The interaction of animacy and word order in human languages: A study of strategies in a novel communication task. In A. Smith, M. Schouwstra, B. de Boer, and K. Smith (Eds.), *Eighth evolution of language conference*. Utrecht, Netherlands: World Scientific, pp. 455–456.

Meir, I., Padden, C., Aronoff, M., and Sandler, W. (2007). Body as subject. *Journal of Linguistics* 43, 531–563.

Meir, I., Padden, C., Sandler, W., and Aronoff, M. (2013). Competing iconicities in the structure of sign languages. *Cognitive Linguistics* 24(2), 309–343.

Miller, J. (2006). Relative clauses in spoken discourse. In K. Brown (Ed.), *Encyclopedia of Language & Linguistics* (2nd ed.). New York: Elsevier, pp. 508–511.

Morford, J. (2003). Grammatical development in adolescent first-language learners. *Linguistics* 41(4), 681–721.

Morgan, H., and Mayberry, R. (2012). Complexity in two-handed signs: Evidence for sublexical structure in a young sign language. *Sign Language and Linguistics* 15(2), 147–174.

Nonaka, A. (2007). Emergence of an indigenous sign language and a speech/sign community in Ban Khor, Thailand. PhD dissertation, University of California, Los Angeles.

Padden, C. (1998). The ASL lexicon. *Sign Language & Linguistics* 1(1), 39–60.

Padden, C. (2006). Learning fingerspelling twice: Young signing children's acquisition of fingerspelling. In B. Schick, M. Marschark, and P. Spencer (Eds.), *Advances in the sign language development of deaf children*. New York: Oxford University Press, pp. 189–201.

Padden, C. (2010). Sign language geography. In G. Mathur and D. J. Napoli (Eds.), *Deaf around the world: The impact of language*. New York: Oxford University Press, pp. 19–37.

Padden, C., Meir, I., Sandler, W., and Aronoff, M. (2010). Against all expectations: The encoding of subject and object in a new language. In D. Gerdts, J. Moore, and M. Polinsky (Eds.), *Hypothesis A/Hypothesis B: Linguistic explorations in honor of David M. Perlmutter*. Cambridge, MA: MIT Press, pp. 383–400.

Padden, C. A., Meir, I., Hwang, S. O., Lepic, R., Seegers, S., and Sampson, T. (2013). Patterned iconicity in sign language lexicons. *Gesture* 13(3), 287–308.

Sandler, W. (2011). Prosody and syntax in sign language. *Transactions of the Philological Society* 108(3), 298–328.

Sandler, W., and Lillo-Martin, D. (2006). *Sign language and linguistic universals*. Cambridge, MA: Cambridge University Press.

Sandler, W., Aronoff, M., Meir, I., and Padden, C. (2011). The gradual emergence of phonological form in a new language. *Natural Language and Linguistic Theory* 29, 503–543.

Sandler, W., Meir, I., Padden, C., and Aronoff, M. (2005). The emergence of grammar: Systematic structure in a new language. *Proceedings of the National Academy of Sciences* 102(7), 2661–2665.

Senghas, A. (2003). Intergenerational influence and ontogenetic development in the emergence of spatial grammar in Nicaraguan Sign Language. *Cognitive Development* 18, 511–531.

Senghas, A. (2010). The emergence of two functions for spatial devices in Nicaraguan Sign Language. *Human Development* 53(5), 287–302.

Senghas, A., and Coppola, M. (2001). Children creating language: How Nicaraguan Sign Language acquired a spatial grammar. *Psychological Science* 12(4), 323–328.

Senghas, A., Coppola, M., Newport, E., and Supalla, T. (1997). Argument structure in Nicaraguan Sign Language: The emergence of grammatical devices. In E. Hughes and A. Greenhill (Eds.), *Proceedings of the twenty-first Boston University conference on language development*. Boston: Cascadilla Press, pp. 550–561.

Supalla, T., and Newport, E. (1978). How many seats in a chair? The derivation of nouns and verbs in American Sign Language. In P. Siple (Ed.), *Understanding language through sign language research*. New York: Academic Press, pp. 91–132.

Sutton-Spence, R. (2006). Fingerspelling. In K. Brown (Ed.), *Encyclopedia of language and linguistics* (2nd ed.). Oxford: Elsevier, pp. 468–473.

Swadesh, M. (1950). Salish internal relationships. *International Journal of American Linguistics* 16, 157–167.

Taub, S. F. (2001). *Language from the body : Iconicity and metaphor in American sign language*. New York: Cambridge University Press.

Tkachman, O., and Sandler, W. (2013). The noun–verb distinction in two young sign languages. *Gesture* 13(3), 253–286.

Woodward, J. (1993). Lexical evidence for the existence of South Asian and East Asian sign language families. *Journal of Asian Pacific Communication* 4(2), 91–106.

Woodward, J. (1996). The relationship of sign language varieties in India, Pakistan and Nepal. *Sign Language Studies* 78, 15–22.

Zeshan, U., and de Vos, C. (Eds.) (2012). *Sign languages in village communities*. Berlin: Mouton de Gruyter.

Zwitserlood, I. (2003). *Classifying hand configurations in Nederlandse Gebarentall (Sign Language of the Netherlands)*. PhD dissertation, University of Utrecht, Netherlands.

10 Documentary and Corpus Approaches to Sign Language Research

Jordan Fenlon, Adam Schembri, Trevor Johnston, and Kearsy Cormier

Chapter Overview

In this chapter we discuss some key aspects of the methodology associated with sign language documentation and corpus-based approaches to sign language research. We first introduce the field of sign language corpus linguistics, carefully defining the term "corpus" in this context and discussing the emergence of technology that has made this new approach to sign language research possible. We then discuss specific details of the methodology involved in corpus-building, such as the recruitment of participants, the selection of language activities for the corpus, and the set-up for filming. We move on to a discussion of annotation for corpora, with a focus on the use of ID glossing. We close with a brief discussion of online archiving and accessibility.

Research Methods in Sign Language Studies: A Practical Guide, First Edition.
Edited by Eleni Orfanidou, Bencie Woll, and Gary Morgan.
© 2015 John Wiley & Sons, Inc. Published 2015 by John Wiley & Sons, Inc.

Introduction

A modern linguistic corpus is understood to refer to a large collection of spoken, written, or signed language data (with associated metadata) that is in machine-readable form, is (as far as possible) maximally representative of the language and its users, and can be consulted to study the type and frequency of constructions in that language. One well-known example of a modern linguistic corpus is the British National Corpus (BNC) of English. At 100 million words, this corpus consists of samples of spoken and written British English that have been carefully selected from a wide range of sources so as to be representative of British English during the late twentieth century and is often consulted by researchers for linguistic analysis (Rayson, Wilson, and Leech, 2002). Like most modern linguistic corpora, the texts within the BNC have, appended to them, linguistic annotations in the form of grammatical tags that provide another level of detail to the corpus (although other types of linguistic annotation are often available in modern corpora; see McEnery, Xiao, and Tono, 2006). Subsequently researchers can use the BNC to examine not only the frequency with which a given word occurs, but also the relative frequencies of each of its grammatical functions – in order to gain a better picture of language use in British English.

Sign language linguists (like their spoken language counterparts) have generally used the term "corpus" to refer to any kind of data set upon which a linguistic description or analysis has been based, or to any collection of video recordings (Lucas, Bayley, and Valli, 2001; Neidle and Vogler, 2012). These uses of the term are at odds with the description given above; and none of the data sets they refer to can be said to constitute a linguistic corpus in the modern sense. For instance, the data set subjected to linguistic analysis in these cases sometimes consists of elicited examples from a comparatively small number of native signers and, as such, cannot be said to be representative of everyday sign language. Other – larger, more spontaneous – collections of video recordings have often not been digitized or appropriately annotated and thus are not currently machine-readable in the sense explained above.

Although sign language corpora are now being developed, they and subsequent studies based on these corpora represent an emerging practice in sign language research; thus the field of corpus-based approaches to sign language linguistics is still very much in its infancy. Most sign language corpora are currently works in progress: they are primarily large data sets consisting of spontaneous and elicited signing that have been digitized and are currently undergoing linguistic annotation – the latter proving to be the most laborious stage in the creation of a sign language corpus. Depending on how much work has been completed for their respective sign language lexicons (i.e., whether a lexical database is available to support annotation), sign language corpus projects are at different stages in the annotation process, some having to take on the task of developing a lexical database concurrently with corpus creation.

The Need for Corpora

Why do we need sign language corpora? One important reason is that there is much work that needs to be done within the field of sign language linguistics to further our understanding of the structure and use of these languages. There is a pressing need to test the claims made by many existing linguistic descriptions and analyses of sign languages, because they have often been based on limited data sets from a small number of signers. This reliance on small data sets is problematic when one considers that sign language use is commonly reported to be highly variable (Schembri and Johnston, 2012). The variability owes much to the fact that sign languages exist in unique sociolinguistic circumstances: they are young, minority languages, with few native signers and with an interrupted pattern of intergenerational transmission. As a consequence, it is often difficult even for native signers to be certain about what is and is not an acceptable construction in their language. The justification for corpora is supplied in this case by the assumption that the processing of large amounts of annotated texts can reveal patterns of language use and structure not available to everyday user intuitions, or even to expert detailed analysis.

There are also potential benefits to the deaf[1] community in the creation of sign language corpora. Further empirical research on sign language structure and on the documentation of signs used in the language (e.g., via a corpus-based dictionary or lexical database) will inform and improve sign language teaching materials – which will, in turn, lead to the improvements in the training of sign language teachers and interpreters and in the education of deaf children. In some cases sign language corpora have themselves been used as tools in educational settings, in the training of interpreters or teaching linguistics students, both groups being invited to explore and annotate texts from within corpora for specific sign language phenomena (e.g., Leeson, 2010; Mesch, Nilsson, Wallin, and Bäckström, 2010). These corpora also provide an important means of recording sign languages as they are used today for posterity, particularly since they are now increasingly recognized as endangered languages (Johnston, 2004; Nonaka, 2004; Schembri, 2010). Furthermore, if some texts are oriented toward specific topics relevant to the field of Deaf studies (e.g., if participants are encouraged to describe their educational experience), this will also enhance the status of a corpus as an important and valuable resource with wide-ranging applications.

The Emergence of Sign Language Corpus Linguistics

Modern sign language corpora have not been possible until relatively recently, due to the absence of a widely recognized and favorable transcription system for sign language data and the lack of suitable technology for sign language capture and secondary processing (see Crasborn, Efthimiou, Hanke, Thoutenhoofd, and Zwitserlood, 2008). In recent years advancements in technology have gone some way toward addressing these shortcomings. Coupled with a growing recognition, among the sign language research community, of the role that larger empirical data sets can play for testing hypotheses about sign language structure and use, this has led to the rapid emergence of a number of sign language corpus projects worldwide, as described below.

Prior to this, few sign language texts of any kind could be subjected to linguistic annotation (e.g., be tagged for parts of speech) for the purposes of studying the frequency of occurrence of specific signs or grammatical constructions. The absence of such texts reflected the fact that sign languages do not have a widely accepted writing system (although Sutton SignWriting is used by some for this purpose: see www.signwriting.org), or even a standardized specialist notation system that can be used for transcription (a number of such systems exist, such as the Hamburg Notation System, but are time-consuming to use and require special font software; see Prillwitz, Leven, Zienert, Hanke, and Henning, 1989). Instead, researchers have often used contextually based glosses in place of such systems, particularly for studies of sign language grammatical structure. This practice is not without its disadvantages, since contextually based glosses do not provide information on a sign's form, do not have standardized ways to accurately represent some key formational aspects involved in articulation (e.g., the spatial and non-manual features of sign language utterances), and are likely to be inconsistent across studies, as one cannot be certain which specific lexical variant a particular gloss represents in each case (the disadvantages of relying on glossing in sign language research have long been recognized; see Johnston, 1991; Pizzuto and Pietrandrea, 2001; Frishberg, Hoiting, and Slobin, 2012). Furthermore, the use of glosses (or even a dedicated notation system) in these cases is also a major problem, since one sacrifices any connection with the primary data source, which, in itself, is far more likely to be informative for sign language research.

The development of time-aligned video annotation software, together with more widely available computer capacity for the capture and storage of large amounts of digital video, provided a solution for the "transcription problem" described above and set the scene for the emergence of corpus-based approaches to sign language linguistics. One multimedia annotation software program in widespread use among sign language researchers is ELAN (Wittenburg, Brugman, Russel, Klassmann, and Sloetjes, 2006). Using software like ELAN, transcriptions can be directly time-aligned with a media file representing a signed segment. Overlapping annotations can also be stored on separate tiers that represent a different level of analysis or a different articulator (e.g., tiers can be specifically devoted to grammatical tags denoting a sign's function or to a non-manual articulator such as the eyebrows). The use of such video annotation software also means that the source of the digital video material can remain the primary data rather than being replaced by a transcription that is less transparent (one needs only to look at the media file linked to an ELAN annotation file to see a specific sign's form). This innovation also meant that researchers could now systematically use glosses as annotations rather than transcriptions to which further linguistic annotations are appended. A systematic approach to glossing within sign language corpora, known as ID glossing (Johnston, 2010), involves identifying conventional linguistic units and types with the help of unique sign identifiers (i.e., ID glosses). We discuss ID glosses and their importance in more detail in the section on corpus methods below.

Further developments to ELAN over the years have enhanced capacity for working on sign language corpora (Crasborn and Sloetjes, 2008). In ELAN it is now possible to extract frequency statistics for any annotation on any tier and to examine the environments in which the frequencies occur. These searches can be modified further by specifying co-occurring annotations within tiers, which may include metadata values associated with each individual ELAN file (such as age, gender, or region). With these capabilities, the possibilities available to sign language researchers who use ELAN are numerous. For example, one can search multiple files that represent a wide cross-section of a given sign language community for all tokens of a specific sign (glossed on one tier), co-occurring with a particular grammatical function (annotated on a grammatical category tier), and/or certain social factors (e.g., age) in order to gain a more thorough picture of patterns in sign language use.

Other video annotation software has also been developed for use with sign language corpora. In particular, iLex has been created by the team at the Centre for German Sign Language at the University of Hamburg, and, while it is similar to ELAN, it has the additional advantage of making it possible to link glosses in the annotation file to entries in a lexical database (Hanke and Storz, 2008). Work is currently underway to facilitate links between ELAN annotation files and lexical database tools such as LEXUS (Crasborn, Hulbosch, and Sloetjes, 2012).

Data Collection

The first sign language corpus project began in Australia in 2004 with a digital video archive of recordings of 100 deaf native or early learner/near-native signers of Auslan; the expectation was that it would later become a large machine-readable corpus in the modern linguistic sense. A similar project on a smaller scale began in Ireland in the same year to collect Irish Sign Language (ISL) data. Since then a number of other sign language corpus projects have begun (e.g., Netherlands Sign Language (NGT), British Sign Language (BSL), German Sign Language (DGS), Swedish Sign Language, and Polish Sign Language). For most of these projects, at the time of writing, the first stage (i.e., data collection and archiving) has been completed and, for NGT and BSL, the video data and some ELAN annotation files have been made openly available online (some of the Auslan corpus video data and ELAN annotation files are available online through the Endangered Languages Archive at the University of London, but they have restricted access). In this section we elaborate on the design criteria for these corpus projects, with a specific focus on the BSL and Auslan corpora. We also discuss specific issues unique to the design of sign language corpora, such as representativeness and the problem of the observer's paradox (Schembri, 2010; Schembri, Fenlon, Rentelis, Reynolds, and Cormier, 2013).

Sites and participants

One of the key criteria used to define a linguistic corpus is that it should be representative of a language's variety (McEnery and Wilson, 2001). This is important if the corpus is to be used as a basis for making generalizations about language. Sampling provides a way to ensure as wide a representation as possible and is based on explicit linguistic criteria. However, there are challenges facing those involved in sign language corpus design when representativeness is to be achieved. It is very likely that not enough is known about the size of the deaf community and its distribution in order to create a representative data set. For all sign languages, published estimates as to the size of the signing population are known to vary or are unreliable, if they exist at all (Johnston, 2004). Faced with this lack of information, sign language corpus projects have tended to favor the methodology employed in studies investigating sociolinguistic variation (e.g., Lucas et al., 2001), where participants are selected as part of a quota sample, according to a set of demographic variables (e.g., gender, age, region, ethnicity, socioeconomic class, and age of sign language acquisition) that are considered relevant to deaf communities. Although the resulting data set may or may not be representative of the wider deaf community (considering that many deaf signers learn to sign in later childhood, or even in adulthood), recruiting participants via a quota sample with these demographic variables does take us some way toward capturing the full range of variability in the deaf community.

Sign language corpus projects have sought to recruit participants from a number of cities across their respective countries, partly as a way to achieve representativeness generally, but also because regional variation within sign language communities is known to be significant (Johnston and Schembri, 2007; Sutton-Spence and Woll, 1999). For the BSL corpus, eight cities in the United Kingdom were selected (Belfast, Birmingham, Bristol, Cardiff, Glasgow, London, Manchester, and Newcastle) that broadly represented the major countries within the United Kingdom (England, Scotland, Wales, Northern Ireland) and five of the most important regions in England (the country in the United Kingdom with the largest population). For Auslan, the five largest cities were selected (Sydney, Melbourne, Brisbane, Perth and Adelaide), because this is where both the general population and the deaf community are concentrated (Australia is a highly urbanized country, with half of its total population in these five urban centers). For both projects, the selection of these regions was motivated partly by the fact that they were all sites of centralized deaf schools (although in some cases these schools have now closed due to the trend to mainstream deaf children in schools with their hearing peers) and partly by the fact that they contain thriving adult deaf communities that have developed around these schools. The decision to recruit from major cities is also strategic, since it is easier to find a sufficient number of signers from a variety of backgrounds (e.g., of different ages, from deaf and hearing families, and so on) in these areas. In the BSL project, which drew on methodology employed in previous sociolinguistic studies of American Sign Language (ASL) and Auslan, care was taken to ensure that participants had lived or worked in a given region for a minimum amount of time (10 years) so that they could be considered representative of the signing used in that region.

It is well known that the age at which a child is exposed to sign language as a first language can affect language proficiency in adulthood (Cormier, Schembri, Vinson, and Orfanidou, 2012; Emmorey, 2002). With this in mind the Auslan and BSL corpus projects aimed to recruit only signers who reported having learned to sign by 7 years of age. Each project also aimed to recruit a large number of native signers (i.e., signers who learnt to sign from birth from deaf parent(s) or an elder sibling). Native signers represent nearly a third of the participants in the BSL corpus (31 percent or 76–249 signers) and more than three quarters in the Auslan corpus (79 percent or 79–100 signers). One could argue that these figures represent a disproportionately large sample of native signers, given estimates for the total number of native signers in the deaf community: the actual figure is widely thought to be around 5 percent (see Mitchell and Karchmer, 2004). This focus is motivated, however, by a desire to document the most proficient sign language users in the community, and this is standard practice in collecting language samples in linguistics.

Age-related variation is also given important consideration in corpus design. In many corpus projects, the selection of participants according to age is motivated partly by a need to document language change as the result of changes in language policy in deaf education. For example, participant selection for the BSL corpus was balanced across four age groups that roughly reflect different periods in deaf education. In the oldest age group, participants are likely to have been educated in residential schools for deaf children that focused on the use of fingerspelling and/or the development of speech-reading skills in the classroom, while BSL may have been used among school children in dormitories or on the playground. In contrast, participants in the youngest group (18–30 years of age) are much more likely to have been educated in mainstream school settings with few (if any) deaf peers, although some may have been educated in schools that used BSL as the medium of instruction (some schools in the UK have introduced bilingual approaches, using BSL together with English since the 1980s).

Other variables that have been given consideration in sign language corpus design are gender, ethnicity, and social class. These variables have all been found to be relevant for spoken languages, and there is evidence to suggest that they are significant for sign languages too (Lucas et al., 2001; McKee, Schembri, McKee, and Johnston, 2011; Schembri et al., 2009).

Although each of these corpus projects has clearly defined criteria regarding participant selection, some flexibility is often required. First, many deaf community members may be understandably nervous about being filmed for an open-access archive and may decline invitations to participate; this concern can significantly reduce the pool of potential participants. Second, the research design criteria may not be realistic, because – in the absence of specific statistics such as census information – they are based on guesswork about the composition of deaf communities. For example, the BSL corpus aimed to recruit 10 percent non-white participants in each of its eight regions. However, this proved difficult, as few non-white signers (e.g., black and South Asian deaf people) could be recruited in the smaller urban centers. Additionally, when one is faced with an increasingly mobile deaf community (and a small one too), fulfilling some quotas can prove a challenging task. In some of the smaller cities in the BSL corpus it was often difficult to find early learners in the youngest age group who had remained within their region for at least 10 years and who were willing to participate. Lastly, some demographics traditionally applied to the wider community are much more difficult to define within the deaf community. For example, in the BSL project, participants were identified according to two broad social classes – working class or middle class – on the basis of their educational background and occupation. However, the emergence of a professional class is a relatively recent phenomenon for most western sign language communities, following recent improvements in access to university education, and this means that it is difficult to achieve a balance of social classes across age groups. To overcome these problems in future, it is advised that projects either attempt to recruit more signers in the more populous regions known to contain a higher concentration of a specific group (e.g., non-white or middle-class signers) or adjust their design criteria slightly in some cases (e.g., by allowing participants who report learning to sign later or living in the area for a shorter period of time to be recruited), so that other key criteria that are underrepresented may be fulfilled. A sensitive awareness of these issues and of how they may affect the recruitment process is therefore required of the team in the planning stages of corpus-building, so that concessions may be made and alternatives quickly sought (e.g., less insistence on the recruitment of middle-class signers may be required in the older age groups).

Using the methodology outlined above, the Auslan corpus project recruited 100 deaf signers from Sydney, Melbourne, Brisbane, Perth and Adelaide, namely 20 participants at each site; this data set has been combined with other data from previous projects to create a total collection of data from 256 deaf Australians. The BSL corpus consists of a data set collected from 249 signers; 30 signers were filmed in Belfast, Birmingham, Cardiff, Glasgow, Manchester and Newcastle, 32 in Bristol, and 37 in London. The DGS corpus consists of an even larger data set, collected from 330 deaf signers in 13 German regions (Langer, 2012). The ISL corpus is based on data collected from 40 deaf signers (Leeson and Saeed, 2012), and the Swedish Sign Language corpus is based on data collected from 42 deaf signers (Mesch and Wallin, 2012). When these corpora are compared to one another, the difference in participant numbers between some of them may reflect the relative size of the general population in these countries and, consequently, the estimated size of the signing community. For example, the general population of the Republic of Ireland is much smaller than that of the United Kingdom and, consequently, a smaller number of deaf signers are said to use ISL (Leeson and Saeed, 2012).

Recruitment and filming

In order to ensure the recruitment of large numbers of participants from many regions, many of the sign language corpus projects mentioned so far have employed local members of the deaf community in the role of "fieldworkers," to locate suitable participants – a methodology first used by Ceil Lucas and colleagues (see Lucas et al., 2001). For both the BSL and the Auslan corpus projects, fieldworkers were deaf signers who were well known and respected members of their local deaf community, and nearly all were native signers from deaf families. Fieldworkers were also present on the day of filming, to assist with data collection and to lead on some tasks given to the participants. An important reason for having deaf fieldworkers present on the day of filming to perform these functions, instead of a hearing researcher, is that they would assist in keeping language contact influences to a minimum (as reported by Lucas and Valli, 1992). Furthermore, it is important for *local* deaf community fieldworkers to lead on lexical elicitation, particularly if elicitation of regional variants is expected. Deaf fieldworkers also provide a key link to the local community that can be maintained long after the data collection stage has been completed; thus deaf fieldworkers on the BSL corpus were also involved in a series of local community presentations delivered in each region involved in data collection.

The BSL corpus fieldworkers were also on hand to explain the project's aims to participants before filming commenced and to assist with the collection of background information about the participants. This was obtained through a questionnaire consisting of 39 questions that aimed to elicit comprehensive background information on each participant's language experience. These questions followed metadata standards for sign language corpora proposed in Crasborn and Hanke (2003), which also serve as the basis for metadata categories in the NGT and DGS corpora. Questions covered a range of topics that included the participant's general language preference (e.g., signing, sign with speech) with different members of their family, the language used at school in and out of the classroom, the language used during childhood, where else the participant may have lived in the UK, and the extent to which (s)he interacted with the deaf community.

Figure 10.1 Screenshots from BSL Corpus Project video data (pair view and individual view). Schembri, Fenlon, Rentelis, and Cormier, 2011.

It is also necessary to give serious consideration to the layout and location of the filming studio and to the pairing of participants in order to maximize the quality and range of the data collected. For the BSL corpus, participants were filmed in pairs, with two high-definition cameras focused respectively on each member of the pair and a third one focused on both, as shown in Figure 10.1. In the DGS corpus project five cameras were used, two additional ones being positioned above the signers, to give a bird's eye view of their hands as they moved in the signing space around their body (Hanke, König, Wagner, and Matthes, 2010). BSL corpus participants were seated in chairs without arms (so they could not rest their elbows during signing, which may have interfered with sign language production), in front of a blue background screen with appropriate studio lighting, and wearing plain colored clothing on the upper body in order to ensure the best possible capture of the sign language data. Participants were always filmed in same-sex or mixed pairs made up of people of similar ages. They were also paired with someone familiar to them – friends or acquaintances – as one of the tasks required them to engage in spontaneous conversation for 30 minutes. Pairs of participants in a long-term relationship (particularly retired married couples) were not filmed together, because in these cases the conversational data obtained was often not natural due to a high level of familiarity. Filming sessions were always located in settings familiar to the participants, such as deaf social clubs or the offices of deaf organizations, to ensure that participants felt comfortable and that it was appropriate to use a relatively informal variety of BSL.

Data types

While there are some differences between projects in the type of data collected, there is a clear consensus among projects that different genre types should be sampled in order to maximize representativeness. The type of texts contained in sign language corpora is often linked to a project's overall aims and to the initial studies intended/ proposed. For the BSL corpus, data collection was limited to four situational varieties which are considered the bare minimum for studies on sociolinguistic variation and language change: a personal experience narrative, free conversation, an interview, and a word list. The personal experience narratives (primarily intended as a warm-up, to acquaint participants with the filming studio) lasted no more than five minutes and featured the retelling of an amusing, poignant, or significant event in the participants' lives. This was followed by a 30-minute conversation where participants were left to themselves and were free to talk about anything they wanted. A short 15-minute interview on language attitudes and awareness, led by the deaf fieldworker, followed the conversation session. Lastly, participants took part in a lexical elicitation task in which they were asked to produce signs that they used for 102 concepts chosen for their known or suspected high level of sociolinguistic variation.[2]

Other corpus projects have used a variety of elicitation tasks in order to elicit language that included specific grammatical constructions. The Auslan corpus project used the video stimuli from two tests in the test battery for ASL morphology (Supalla et al., n.d.): the verbs of motion production (VMP) and the noun–verb production (NVP) tasks. The VMP involves 40 stop-animation movies that are intended to elicit representations of a subset of motion events with a selected number of referent types; this is a very useful way to elicit classifier/depicting verbs of motion. The NVP was selected because the video material not only elicited short sentences that involved descriptions of various types of transitive events, but also often resulted in the production of noun–verb pairs (i.e., related lexical items in which the nominal and the verbal forms are distinguished by movement and/or non-manual features).

A number of narratives were also elicited using methods widely employed in the sign language literature. The "Canary Row" video stimulus from the Warner Brothers' *Tweety and Sylvester* cartoon series was employed as a way to elicit a story from the participants. This methodology was originally borrowed from gesture studies (see McNeill, 1992), but it is also used in sign language research (e.g., Emmorey, Borinstein, Thompson, and Gollan, 2008). Written stimuli to elicit narratives were also used: written English versions of two Aesop's fables – "The Boy Who Cried Wolf" and "The Hare and the Tortoise" – were given to the participants, who were then asked to retell the stories in Auslan (see Crasborn et al., 2007). An additional narrative was also elicited by using the children's picture story book *Frog, Where Are You?* (see Engberg-Pederson, 2003). The DGS corpus project collected deaf community jokes in addition to elicited narratives.

Discussions, exchanges of different viewpoints, and argumentation were also elicited in the Auslan and NGT corpora through the use of an interview that focused on issues of concern or controversy in the deaf community. Discussion in the DGS corpus was stimulated by informants looking at warning signs collected from different places in the world and talking about what they may or may not mean. Also in the DGS corpus data collection, negotiation was elicited through a calendar task in which participants agreed on dates for separate meetings at times that did not clash with other timetabled tasks. A barrier game task in which participants had to identify a number of differences in two related pictures was also used with similar results in the Auslan corpus project. Explanatory discourse was involved in the Auslan and DGS projects, where participants had to explain the meaning and origin of their name signs.

Observer's paradox, audience design, and consent

Data collected for sign language corpora are at risk of the observer's paradox – i.e., the fact that the vernacular form of a language, used by speakers when they are not being observed, can only be studied by observation. In order to lessen the effects of this paradox (whereby signers may adjust their signing style because they are being observed/filmed), participants in the BSL corpus were reassured during the process of obtaining informed consent that the conversational data would form part of a restricted-access corpus: it would not be made publicly available on the Internet but would only be shared with other university researchers who have declared an academic interest in the data. It was hoped that participants would relax and converse freely as a result and that the data collected would be as close to the vernacular variety as possible. Additional measures, such as pairing participants with someone well known to them and filming in settings conducive to spontaneous conversation, also ensured that the effects of the observer's paradox were lessened. The remaining three situational varieties – the personal narratives, the interviews, and the lexical elicitation data – all formed part of the open access archive, although access to the interview data was later restricted, as issues arose over the content and its appropriateness within the public domain (for details, see Schembri et al., 2013). The results of a subsequent phonological variation study (Fenlon, Schembri, Rentelis, and Cormier, 2013) suggests that phonological variation in the conversational data is not too dissimilar to phonological variation in the data collected by Bayley, Lucas, and Rose (2002), which was not intended to be part of an online open access collection.

Annotation and Translation

Once the data have been collected and converted into a digital video archive, the next stage of corpus-building can begin. It is after this stage, where annotation work is undertaken, that the digital video archive becomes a modern linguistic corpus. Here it is important to prioritize the type of annotation most appropriate for allowing one to search the corpus effectively – particularly since the process of annotation for sign language corpora is a time-consuming one. Johnston (2010) stresses that two types of annotation are essential for all sign language corpora: ID glossing and a written translation. It is only these two types of annotation at a minimum that will allow the video data set to become a searchable and machine-readable resource. By contrast, transcription – i.e., a notation system adopted in order to describe a sign's form – is likely to take much longer and will not necessarily result in a corpus that can be readily searched by others. In this section we discuss in more detail ID glossing, written translations, and their rationale – with reference to the BSL and Auslan corpora.

ID glossing refers to the practice of using one unique identifying gloss or "ID gloss" for each sign. This ID gloss is used to represent the sign in its citation form along with all its phonological and morphological variants. The procedure and principles of grouping sign variants together under a single lemma form what is called "lemmatization" and are outlined, for signed languages, in Johnston and Schembri (1999), Cormier, Fenlon, et al. (2012), and Fenlon, Cormier, and Schembri (under review). One such principle (which applies equally to spoken languages) is that all inflectional morphological variants of a sign are identified as a single lemma (e.g., the directional verb GIVE is always assigned the same ID gloss regardless of how it has been modified spatially for person or number). Both the

BSL and the Auslan corpora use English words as ID glosses, the choice of the English word being often motivated by its strong association with a particular sign form (e.g., the English word "like" may be one of the primary meanings that signers associate with the sign LIKE). Therefore the choice of an English word as a surrogate marker for a sign's form aids in consistent glossing and is strongly preferred over notation systems for corpus-based approaches to sign language research.

The practice of using ID glossing is made considerably easier if this lemmatization work has already been completed for each sign language and if these groupings have been recorded in a lexical database that can be said to be representative of all the signs that make up a sign language's core lexicon. Annotators can then consult this database to find a form's corresponding ID gloss and possible meanings (via English translation equivalents) linked to this ID gloss. For the Auslan corpus, a lexical database that follows such principles was already in place prior to annotation work (see Johnston, 2001). Such a resource has given the Auslan corpus an advantage that has resulted in its becoming the largest annotated sign language corpus that is based on a lemmatized lexical database (c. 105,000 sign token annotations at the time of writing). In contrast, no such resource existed for BSL prior to the BSL corpus project. Available dictionaries for BSL (e.g., Brien, 1992) had not followed lemmatization practices: many homonyms are grouped together as a single entry, and many phonological variants are often presented as separate, unrelated entries. As a result, lemmatization work had to take place concurrently with annotation work, as part of a lexical frequency study of approximately 25,000 tokens. This has resulted in a database of approximately 1,800 entries, each entry showing, at a minimum, the sign's form, its ID gloss, and English keywords associated with its meaning. At the time of writing, this lexical database is being converted into BSL SignBank, an online dictionary for BSL (see Cormier, Fenlon, et al., 2012 and Fenlon et al., under review).

Johnston (2010) also advocates a written translation as a second type of annotation that should be prioritized in order to enhance usability and to maximize access to the corpus. This is because the act of ID glossing is unlike that of context-based glossing, which is often seen as a type of translation in itself. Since the same ID gloss is consistently applied to a sign form regardless of any variation in grammatical use (i.e., GIVE labels one sign regardless of whether it functions as a verb "give" or as a noun "gift") or in its particular meaning/sense (e.g., EXCITED labels a particular sign even where the English words "motivate," "interest," "interesting," or "eager" would appear to be a better translation), it is difficult to get a sense of the intended meaning of a signed utterance from ID glosses. The task of translation is instead assigned to a separate tier in the ELAN annotation viewer, which is also time-aligned with the ID glosses and the corresponding media file. Therefore anyone accessing the corpus can use both the ID gloss tier and the English translation to gain a full understanding of what is being signed via which lexical items. Although both ID glossing and translation are needed for a corpus, a written translation is much faster to achieve than ID glossing and can render a larger proportion of the corpus accessible in a shorter space of time than ID glossing alone.

The annotation stage is the most time-consuming and laborious stage in the creation of sign language corpora. For most sign language corpus projects, this is because the task of annotation must be conducted concurrently with the creation of a lexical database. Furthermore, the process of annotation cannot be automated, as the technology required to do so is still in its formative years. Thus it may be some time before any sign language corpus is minimally complete – in the sense that ID glossing and translation have been completed for the entire corpus. For example, work on ID glossing and translation of the Auslan corpus began in 2006 and is expected to take at least five more years before a basic reference corpus of the entire video archive is achieved. Detailed multi-tier annotation beyond ID glossing and translation (e.g., to the level of detail described in Johnston, 2011) would take even longer. For the BSL corpus, after the first two years of lexical annotation work carried as part of a lexical frequency study, only 5 percent of the conversational data had been glossed. Although this seems very little, the creation of these sign language corpora signals in fact the beginning of a period of corpus-based research in sign language linguistics, in which questions that are difficult or impossible to answer in any other way can finally be addressed. This is certain to lead to a much better understanding of the structure and use of sign languages.

Archiving, Interfaces, and Access

Today it is possible to access some sign language corpus data over the Internet. However, this access is often restricted to the video data alone; annotation data are limited or not available at all (depending on the amount of annotation work completed). The first stage of the NGT corpus was completed in 2008, in the sense that the archived video recordings had been edited and catalogued and were made openly accessible through a digital video archive on the Internet. However, at the time of writing, only a small percentage of the NGT video files have been annotated and/or translated into a parallel written text. Similarly, video files for the Swedish Sign Language corpus are now openly available online but only a small percentage have been annotated and translated (see Mesch, Wallin, Nilsson, and Bergman, 2012). From 2012 the Auslan corpus videos have been available on the SOAS Endangered Languages Documentation Archive (University of London); most recordings are openly accessible, though some have limited or restricted access. Registered users may apply for increased access if they agree to SOAS and deposit-specific conditions. ELAN annotation files are also available for a limited set (only about half of the Auslan corpus has been annotated with ID glosses and translations). The Auslan deposit at SOAS is updated yearly, as additional annotations become available. Since 2011 the BSL corpus video data have been made available online via CAVA (human Communication Audio-Visual Archive), a secure system that allows anyone to view and download the open access corpus data – that is, narratives and lexical elicitation data – and allows researchers access to the restricted corpus data – conversations and interviews – via a user license that includes a confidentiality agreement. An initial set of ELAN annotation files (containing lexical annotations from conversation data from four regions) has been available online since September 2014. For the NGT, Auslan, and BSL corpora, it is possible to search the video data by using the participant metadata collected.

Conclusion

Corpus methods can (and, we argue, should) be used in any kind of language documentation. Sampling sign language data from a variety of signers with different backgrounds and different text types helps ensure that the data set is as representative as possible, even if it is not large for whatever reason (e.g., due to lack of resources). The use of ID glossing via a lexical database in particular is crucial for any kind of language documentation. Without ID glossing, no claims can be made about the nature of the lexicon (e.g., lexical frequency), and ultimately the study of any other level of language structure (phonology, syntax) is also compromised. The use of ID glossing, coupled with translation into one or more written languages, ensures maximum searchability and accessibility, in addition to machine readability.

Notes

1   In this chapter we do not make a distinction between the spellings *deaf* and *Deaf*: we are using *deaf* throughout, because we wish not to make assumptions about individual deaf people's identity.
2   For a list of the 102 concepts that were included in the lexical elicitation task and the list of questions asked during the interview, see http://www.bslcorpusproject.org/cava/activities

Keywords

annotation; corpora; ELAN; ID glossing; lexical database; machine readability; observer's paradox; representativeness; sampling; translation

See Also

See Chapter 4 for more information on technical requirements and the use of annotation software when collecting sign language data.

Suggested Readings

For more on the background that led to the beginnings of sign language corpora, see Johnston and Schembri (2013). For more about the observer's paradox, audience design, and issues surrounding consent and confidentiality in sign language corpus studies, and about multiple interfaces and access levels for different audiences in the BSL corpus, see Schembri et al. (2013).

References

Bayley, R., Lucas, C., and Rose, M. (2002). Phonological variation in American Sign Language: The case of the 1 handshape. *Language Variation and Change* 14(1), 19–53.
Brien, D. (Ed.) (1992). *Dictionary of British Sign Language/English*. London: Faber & Faber.

Cormier, K., Schembri, A., Vinson, D., and Orfanidou, E. (2012). First language acquisition differs from second language acquisition in prelingually deaf signers: Evidence from grammatical processing of British Sign Language. *Cognition* 124, 50–65.

Cormier, K., Fenlon, J., Johnston, T., Rentelis, R., Schembri, A., Rowley, K., Adam, R., Woll, B. (2012). From corpus to lexical database to online dictionary: Issues in annotation of the BSL corpus and the development of BSL signbank. In O. Crasborn, E. Efthimiou, E. Fotinea, T. Hanke, J. Kristoffersen, and J. Mesch (Eds.), *Proceedings of the fifth workshop on the representation and processing of sign languages: Interactions between corpus and lexicon*. Paris: European Language Resources Association, pp. 7–12.

Crasborn, O., and Hanke, T. (2003). *Additions to the IMDI metadata set for sign language corpora*. Paper presented at the ECHO workshop, Nijmegen University.

Crasborn, O., and Sloetjes, H. (2008). Enhanced ELAN functionality for sign language corpora. In O. Crasborn, E. Efthimiou, T. Hanke, E. D. Thoutenhoofd, and I. Zwitserlood (Eds.), *Proceedings of the third workshop on the representation and processing of sign languages: Construction and exploitation of sign language corpora*. Paris: European Language Resources Association, pp. 39–43.

Crasborn, O., Hulbosch, M., and Sloetjes, H. (2012). Linking Corpus NGT annotations to a lexical database using open source tools ELAN and LEXUS. In O. Crasborn, E. Efthimiou, E. Fotinea, T. Hanke, J. Kristoffersen, and J. Mesch (Eds.), *Proceedings of the fifth workshop on the representation and processing of sign languages: Interactions between corpus and lexicon*. Paris: European Language Resources Association, pp. 19–22.

Crasborn, O., Efthimiou, E., Hanke, T., Thoutenhoofd, E. D., and Zwitserlood, I. (Eds.) (2008). *Proceedings of the third workshop on the representation and processing of sign languages: Construction and exploitation of sign language corpora*. Paris: European Language Resources Association.

Crasborn, O., Mesch, J., Waters, D., Nonhebel, A., Van Der Kooij, E., Woll, B., and Bergman, B. (2007). Sharing sign language data online: Experiences from the ECHO project. *International Journal of Corpus Linguistics* 12(4), 535–562.

Emmorey, K. (2002). *Language, cognition, and the brain: Insights from sign language research*. Mahwah, NJ: Lawrence Erlbaum.

Emmorey, K., Borinstein, H. B., Thompson, R., and Gollan, T. H. (2008). Bimodal bilingualism. *Bilingualism: Language and Cognition* 11(1), 43–61.

Engberg-Pederson, E. (2003). How composite is a fall? Adults' and children's descriptions of different types of falls in Danish Sign Language. In K. Emmorey (Ed.), *Perspective on classifier constructions in sign languages*. Mahwah, NJ: Lawrence Erlbaum, pp. 311–322.

Fenlon, J., Cormier, K., and Schembri, A. (under review). Building BSL SignBank: The lemma dilemma revisited.

Fenlon, J., Schembri, A., Rentelis, R., and Cormier, K. (2013). Variation in handshape and orientation in British Sign Language: The case of the "1" hand configuration. *Language and Communication* 33, 69–91.

Frishberg, N., Hoiting, N., and Slobin, D. I. (2012). Transcription. In R. Pfau, M. Steinbach, and B. Woll (Eds.), *Sign language: An international handbook*. Berlin: Mouton de Gruyter, pp. 1045–1075.

Hanke, T., and Storz, J. (2008). iLex: A database tool for integrating sign language corpus linguistics and sign language lexicography. In O. Crasborn, T. Hanke, E. Efthimiou, I. Zwitserlood, and E. D. Thoutenhoofd (Eds.), *Proceedings of the third workshop on the representation and processing of sign languages: Construction and exploitation of sign language corpora*. Paris: European Language Resources Association, pp. 64–67.

Hanke, T., König, L., Wagner, S., and Matthes, S. (2010). DGS corpus & Dicta-Sign: The Hamburg studio set-up. In P. Dreuw, E. Efthimiou, T. Hanke, T. Johnston, G. Martinez-Ruiz, and A. Schembri (Eds.), *Proceedings of the fourth workshop on the representation and processing of sign languages: Construction and exploitation of sign language corpora.* Paris: European Language Resources Association, pp. 106–109.

Johnston, T. (1991). Transcription and glossing of sign language texts: Examples from Auslan (Australian Sign Language). *International Journal of Sign Linguistics* 2(1), 3–28.

Johnston, T. (2001). The lexical database of Auslan (Australian Sign Language). *Sign Language & Linguistics* 1(2), 145–169.

Johnston, T. (2004). W(h)ither the deaf community? Population, genetics and the future of Australian Sign Language. *American Annals of the Deaf* 148(5), 358–375.

Johnston, T. (2010). From archive to corpus: Transcription and annotation in the creation of signed language corpora. *International Journal of Corpus Linguistics* 15(1), 106–131.

Johnston, T., and Schembri, A. (1999). On defining lexeme in a signed language. *Sign Language & Linguistics* 2(2), 115–185.

Johnston, T., and Schembri, A. (2007). *Australian Sign Language: An introduction to sign language linguistics.* Cambridge: Cambridge University Press.

Johnston, T., and Schembri, A. (2013). Corpus analysis of sign languages. In C. A. Chapelle (Ed.), *Encyclopedia of applied linguistics.* Oxford: Wiley Blackwell, pp. 1312–1319.

Langer, G. (2012). A colorful first glance at data on regional variation from the DGS-corpus: With a focus on procedures. In O. Crasborn, E. Efthimiou, E. Fotinea, T. Hanke, J. Kristoffersen, and J. Mesch (Eds.), *Proceedings of the fifth workshop on the representation and processing of sign languages: Interactions between corpus and lexicon.* Paris: European Language Resources Association, pp. 101–108.

Leeson, L. (2010). *From theory to practice: Sign language corpora in teaching and learning.* Paper presented at the sign linguistics corpora network: Workshop 4 (Exploitation), Berlin, Germany.

Leeson, L., and Saeed, J. I. (2012). *Irish Sign Language.* Edinburgh: Edinburgh University Press.

Lucas, C., and Valli, C. (1992). *Language contact in the American deaf community.* San Diego: Academic Press.

Lucas, C., Bayley, R., and Valli, C. (2001). *Sociolinguistic variation in American Sign Language* (vol. 7). Washington, DC: Gallaudet University Press.

McEnery, T., and Wilson, A. (2001). *Corpus linguistics* (2nd ed.). Edinburgh: Edinburgh University Press.

McEnery, T., Xiao, R., and Tono, Y. (2006). *Corpus-based language studies: An advanced resource book.* London: Routledge.

McKee, R., Schembri, A., McKee, D., and Johnston, T. (2011). Variable subject expression in Australian Sign Language and New Zealand Sign Language. *Language Variation and Change* 23(3), 375–398.

McNeill, D. (1992). *Hand and mind: What gestures reveal about thought.* Cambridge: Cambridge University Press.

Mesch, J., and Wallin, L. (2012). From meaning to signs and back: Lexicography and the Swedish Sign Language corpus. In O. Crasborn, E. Efthimiou, E. Fotinea, T. Hanke, J. Kristoffersen, and J. Mesch (Eds.), *Proceedings of the fifth workshop on the representation and processing of sign languages: Interactions between corpus and lexicon.* Paris: European Language Resources Association, pp. 123–126.

Mesch, J., Nilsson, A.-L., Wallin, L., and Bäckström, J. (2010). *Using corpus data for teaching purposes.* Paper presented at the sign linguistics corpora network: Workshop 4 (Exploitation), Berlin, Germany.

Mesch, J., Wallin, L., Nilsson, A.-L., and Bergman, B. (2012). Datamängd: Projektet Korpus för det svenska teckenspråket 2009–2011 (version 1). Avdelningen för teckenspråk, Institutionen för lingvistik, Stockholms universitet. Accessed September 16, 2014. http://www.ling.su.se/teckensprakskorpus

Mitchell, R. E., and Karchmer, M. A. (2004). Chasing the mythical ten percent: Parental hearing status of deaf and hard of hearing students in the United States. *Sign Language Studies* 4(2), 138–163.

Neidle, C., and Vogler, C. (2012). A new web interface to facilitate access to corpora: Development of the ASLLRP Data Access Interface (DAI). In O. Crasborn, E. Efthimiou, E. Fotinea, T. Hanke, J. Kristoffersen, and J. Mesch (Eds.), *Proceedings of the fifth workshop on the representation and processing of sign languages: Interactions between corpus and lexicon*. Paris: European Language Resources Association, pp. 137–142.

Nonaka, A. M. (2004). Sign languages: The forgotten endangered languages: Lessons on the importance of remembering. *Language in Society* 33(5), 737–767.

Pizzuto, E., and Pietrandrea, P. (2001). The notation of signed texts: Open questions and indications for further research. *Sign Language & Linguistics* 4(1/2), 29–45.

Prillwitz, S., Leven, R., Zienert, H., Hanke, T., and Henning, J. (1989). *HamNoSys Version 2.0. Hamburg notation system for sign languages: An introductory guide*. Hamburg: Signum.

Rayson, P., Wilson, A., and Leech, G. (2002). Grammatical word class variation within the British National Corpus sampler. In P. Peters, P. Collins, and A. Smith (Eds.), *New frontiers of corpus research: Papers from the twenty-first international conference on English language research on computerized corpora, Sydney 2000*. Amsterdam: Rodopi, pp. 295–306.

Schembri, A. (2010). Documenting sign languages. In P. Austin (Ed.), *Language documentation and description* (vol. 7). London: School of African and Oriental Studies, pp. 105–143.

Schembri, A., and Johnston, T. (2012). Sociolinguistic aspects of variation and change. In R. Pfau, M. Steinbach, and B. Woll (Eds.), *Sign language: An international handbook*. Berlin: Mouton de Gruyter, pp. 788–816.

Schembri, A., Fenlon, J., Rentelis, R., and Cormier, K. (2011). British Sign Language Corpus Project: A corpus of digital video data of British Sign Language 2008–2011 (1st ed.). London: University College London. Accessed September 17, 2014. http://www.bslcorpusproject.org.

Schembri, A., Fenlon, J., Rentelis, R., Reynolds, S., and Cormier, K. (2013). Building the British Sign Language corpus. *Language Documentation and Conservation* 7, 136–154.

Schembri, A., Mckee, D., Mckee, R., Pivac, S., Johnston, T., and Goswell, D. (2009). Phonological variation and change in Australian and New Zealand Sign Languages: The location variable. *Language Variation and Change* 21(02), 193–231.

Supalla, T., Newport, E. L., Singleton, J., Supalla, S., Metlay, D., and Coulter, G. (n.d.). *The test battery for American Sign Language morphology and syntax*. Unpublished manuscript, University of Rochester, New York.

Sutton-Spence, R., and Woll, B. (1999). *The linguistics of British Sign Language: An introduction*. Cambridge: Cambridge University Press.

Wittenburg, P., Brugman, H., Russel, A., Klassmann, A., and Sloetjes, H. (2006). ELAN: A professional framework for multimodality research. In *Proceedings of the fifth international conference on language resources and evaluation, LREC 2006*. Nijmegen, Netherlands: Max Planck Institute for Psycholinguistics, The Language Archive. Accessed September 17, 2014. http://tla.mpi.nl/tools/tla-tools/elan

11 Methods in Carrying out Language Typological Research

Nick Palfreyman, Keiko Sagara, and Ulrike Zeshan

Chapter Overview

This chapter introduces readers to the field of sign language typology, which undertakes systematic comparisons of linguistic structures in different sign languages to assess cross-linguistic variation. The underlying aim of typology is to chart linguistic diversity by identifying patterns of variation and language universals (characteristics that languages have in common). Sign language typologists use theories and frameworks from language typology to analyze samples of many different sign languages in order to uncover previously hidden patterns. This involves building upon the documentation of diverse sign languages.

Given the relatively recent emergence of sign language typology as a discipline, only a handful of substantial cross-linguistic studies have been conducted

Research Methods in Sign Language Studies: A Practical Guide, First Edition.
Edited by Eleni Orfanidou, Bencie Woll, and Gary Morgan.
© 2015 John Wiley & Sons, Inc. Published 2015 by John Wiley & Sons, Inc.

thus far. Nevertheless, we present an overview of methodological issues in sign language typology, including a discussion of some of the key decisions that must be made when conducting a cross-linguistic typological study. These issues concern the choice of research domain, the identification of parameters for investigation, and the collection and analysis of data from a wide range of sign languages.

Along the way we note some of the solutions to the challenges that are associated with this kind of research, as well as issues of research ethics. We conclude with some thoughts on what we believe to be an important goal for the further development of sign language typology research: a cross-modal typology that includes both signed and spoken languages.

Linguistic Diversity and Sign Languages

It is still commonplace for those with no knowledge of sign languages to suppose that these languages are the same around the world. Those who are proficient in a sign language and meet someone using a different sign language know that this is not the case. They may also know about the similarities and differences between sign languages and spoken languages, which are becoming ever clearer (e.g. Meier, Cormier, and Quinto-Pozos, 2002). Yet even sign language researchers have asked whether, *within* the visual–gestural modality, it can be said that sign languages are generally similar to one another, or at least much more similar among themselves than spoken languages are (Newport and Supalla, 2000: 100). One of the central tenets of sign language typology is that sign languages around the world exhibit much more diversity than is often assumed and that systematic investigation is the key to identifying variation through cross-linguistic study. In other words, sign language typology offers the tools and theoretical frameworks for researchers to look at sign languages afresh and to assess the degree to which these languages are similar to and different from one another. Given that theories and methodologies from fields such as sociolinguistics and psycholinguistics have been fruitfully applied to sign language data, the application of language typology to sign languages is an even more obvious choice, as the field of typology is, by its very nature, concerned with the diversity of all human language, both in its spoken and in its signed modalities.

Language typologists are concerned with mapping the diversity of languages and with discovering patterns across them through comparative research in various domains. The aims of sign language typology are threefold: to document individual sign languages; to compare structures, systems and constructions across different sign languages; and to determine the extent to which patterns of variation are modality-specific. Cross-linguistic comparison of sign languages depends upon the documentation of individual languages, which enables the creation of the kind of database that is necessary for rigorous sign language typology research. It is usually unfeasible for one typologist to collect primary data from a large number of languages, and because of this typologists usually rely on several data sources.

The documentation of individual sign languages is essential for language typology. It is particularly helpful if descriptive work is informed by a typological perspective. This means producing fine-grained documentation with information that is reliable and well structured, taking into account the different parameters and categories that exist across languages within various domains. Examples of such typologically informed documentation are Lutalo-Kiingi (2013), whose work on Ugandan Sign Language includes a grammatical profile alongside descriptions of domains such as number and quantification, the pronoun system, and several clause types; and the description of Jordanian Sign Language by Hendriks (2008).

Sign language typology has developed at the confluence of two disciplines – sign linguistics and linguistic typology – that have previously had little contact with each other. Even now, it is unusual for spoken language typologists to mention the findings of sign language research; this is not necessarily because spoken language typologists are unaware of sign languages, but it may stem from a lack of familiarity with signed languages that reflects the inaccessibility of sign language data (see Haspelmath, 1997, p. 17). Conversely, the documentation of sign languages has seldom been informed by linguistic typology.

Interestingly, both sign linguistics and linguistic typology emerged as modern disciplines at around the same time, and, as this chapter demonstrates, they have much to offer to each other. Greenberg's (1963) seminal work on spoken language typology has had a lasting influence on subsequent spoken language typologists, who have continued to use and refine central notions such as substantive and implicational universals (see Comrie, 1989; Whaley, 1997). Around the same time, Stokoe (1960) realized that the structure of sign language contained meaningless elements in much the same way as the structure of spoken language; and he published a phonological analysis of American Sign Language (ASL). Much of the early research on sign language focused on ASL, although the number of sign languages that have been studied has steadily increased. ASL research has been very important for the development of sign linguistics, but its dominance has at times led to overt or covert assumptions that what is true for ASL must be true of (all) other sign languages. More significantly, this research has constrained what scholars look for in other sign languages; and this is not dissimilar to the way in which western field linguists have sometimes been influenced by the linguistic structures of Indo-European languages (Gil, 2001).

Language typology offers the framework to generate a more balanced assessment of the range and limits of sign language variation, aiming for increasingly refined and valid generalizations on the basis of a broadening database. Some spoken language typologists, such as those who contributed to Dryer and Haspelmath (2011), have used surveys that include hundreds of languages; but this is not yet possible for sign languages, for reasons that are discussed in the next section. Of the sign language typological studies that have been conducted so far, there have been only a handful of large-scale surveys, such as Zeshan (2006), Zeshan and Perniss (2008), and Wilkinson (2009); and most studies have been smaller in scale. However, all typological studies make an important contribution to our understanding of sign languages. In this chapter we focus more on the large-scale surveys that have been conducted, but most of our comments are applicable to smaller scale projects too, since many of the methodological questions that sign language typologists face are similar regardless of how many sign languages are included.

Before moving on to look at some of these methodological questions, it is worth briefly mentioning some of the other, non-academic reasons for engaging with typology. The quest to show how sign languages are similar to and different from spoken languages is helpful in reinforcing the understanding that sign languages are equal in value to spoken languages, while the commitment of typology to the documentation of minority languages can lead to the empowerment of sign communities, especially those whose sign languages are endangered and devalued. Both of these benefits are particularly valuable in countries where recognition of equality between spoken and signed languages is not yet widespread. There is also much potential for supporting the development of metalinguistic awareness and research skills among deaf[1] people through data collection activities, and such ethical goals are increasingly becoming a non-negotiable part of sign language research (Dikyuva, Escobedo Delgado, Panda, and Zeshan, 2012). The involvement of deaf communities in research can be actively promoted by providing accessible information, effective communication, and mentoring schemes for deaf researchers around the world. We touch upon some of these opportunities here.

Domains and Parameters

The first methodological challenge in a typological study of sign languages is how to identify suitable parameters of variation within a promising domain of investigation. Many of the subsequent methodological issues are influenced by these initial decisions. Research on spoken language typology has covered different levels of linguistic organization (see Dixon, 2010), and the same is true for typological research on sign languages. At the grammatical level, the first large-scale sign language typology projects compared negative and interrogative constructions across 37 sign languages (Zeshan, 2006) and possessive and existential constructions across 28 sign languages (Zeshan and Perniss, 2008). Other grammatical typology studies have included domains such as constituent ordering (Johnston, Vermeerbergen, Schembri, and Leeson, 2007), negation and modals (Pfau and Quer, 2007), first-person plural pronouns (Cormier, 2007), interrogatives (Šarac, Schalber, Alibašić, and Wilbur, 2007), classifiers (Eccarius and Brentari, 2007) and numerals (Zeshan, Escobedo Delgado, Dikyuva, Panda, and de Vos, 2013). Lexical typology studies include Wilkinson (2009) on kinship terms and Zeshan and Sagara (2014), who are conducting a collaborative survey of numerals and of color and kinship terms in over thirty sign languages. The third volume in the *Sign Language Typology* series (Channon and van der Hulst, 2011) focuses on the level of phonology; its authors are currently preparing the SignTyp Database, which will hold approximately 1,000 signs from 15 sign languages (see Suggested Readings for more details).

When conducting cross-linguistic comparisons, it is important to be as sure as possible that target structures in different languages are comparable. This is very difficult to determine internally, by looking at morphosyntactic or phonological structure alone, and so cross-linguistic comparisons are founded on external, functional definitions (Croft, 2003), which require the selection of a particular semantic/pragmatic structure, situation type, or domain. It makes sense to choose a research domain that appears to be cross-linguistically interesting, where sign languages are known to use a number of different forms or strategies to express a given function. A review of published studies on signed and spoken languages is a good starting point for identifying potentially suitable domains, and it is preferable to choose a domain that is well documented in the literature on spoken languages, so that some useful analytical tools and concepts are potentially available for application – often in a modified way – to the sign language data. There is no set process that ensures the selection of a suitable research domain, but first-hand experience in field-work, ideally on an undocumented sign language, is often crucial in terms of generating helpful observations and intuitions. Sometimes only after going through further steps – such as developing lists of parameters and testing them out on smaller sets of pilot data – will it become apparent that a domain is unlikely to yield interesting results.

Once a domain has been selected, it is necessary to determine the parameters of investigation (see Figure 11.1 for an example of parameters in the domain of negation). A scan of the literature on sign languages may quickly present some obvious parameters, although theories and concepts from the literature on spoken language typology can also be useful. Where frameworks already exist for a given domain, they have usually been created with spoken languages in mind and may not account for properties that are unique to sign languages. It can be useful therefore to think of typological research as operating in a cyclical way, starting from a linguistic and cognitive domain (such as negation or possession) and collecting systematic sign language data that can in turn lead to a revision of the initial parameters.

For example, the parameters for Zeshan and Perniss (2008) drew in part upon the ideas of Heine (1997) concerning possessive constructions such as "have" and "belong" constructions in spoken languages. Data analysis leads to bottom-up inductive generalizations, which can then be compared with results yielded by spoken language data. Ultimately a contribution is made to the development of

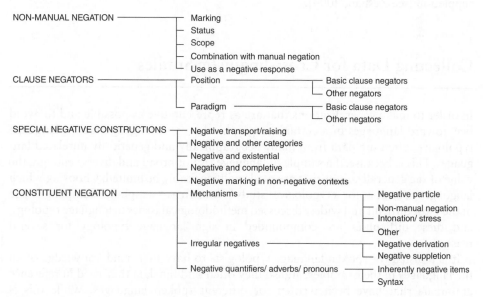

Figure 11.1 Parameters of investigation for negation. From Zeshan, 2004, p. 7.

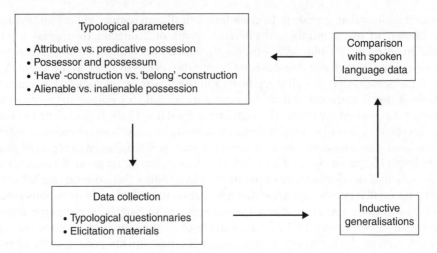

Figure 11.2 The cyclical nature of typological research. From Zeshan and Perniss, 2008, p. 14.

understanding of the linguistic and cognitive domain in question, and generalizations can be refined; this becomes the basis for new lines of enquiry, and so on. This cyclical process is illustrated in Figure 11.2.

Another example of the cyclical nature of defining parameters of investigation can be shown in the area of negation. One may start with a certain list of grammatical distinctions to consider – such as the difference between negation with a separate particle and morphological negation through what is known in sign language as "irregular negative" predicates – and then realize, upon analyzing the data, that the latter category needs to be replaced by several subparameters, in order to represent the difference between morphological negation (by clitics and affixes) and negative suppletion (see Zeshan, 2004).

Collecting Data for Cross-linguistic Studies

In order to make generalizations that are as representative as possible and to avoid bias toward languages of a certain geographical area or language family, language typologists often use data from many geographically and genetically unrelated languages. This is because, if a sample of languages is not broad and diverse enough, the value of the generalizations that are made will inevitably be limited. Choosing which languages to look at for a typological study is known as "sampling." Sampling is one of the most difficult and widely discussed methodological issues in language typology, and these difficulties are compounded in sign language typology for several reasons.

It is unusual for spoken language typologists to have first-hand knowledge of all the languages in their samples, and so they often find the data they need in reference grammars that have been written for different spoken languages. While this is common practice in language typology, the prospect of using a large sample is problematic for sign language typologists. Compared with spoken languages, sign languages are severely underdocumented, which means that the amounts of data needed to conduct a large-scale typological research project are simply not readily available. To date, not a single reference grammar of a sign language has been published that meets the common standards set by spoken language reference grammars.

In sign language typology it is often impossible to create a geographically balanced sample because the data needed are simply not available for a sufficient number of sign languages. Geographically, the spread of sign languages that have been documented in some detail to date is skewed toward sign languages of urban deaf communities in North America and Western Europe, although recent publications have started to redress this situation (Brentari, 2010; Pfau, Steinbach, and Woll, 2012).

One of the ways in which sign language typologists have significantly broadened the sample beyond these western sign languages has been to include sign languages that are used in small-scale rural communities. Recently several linguistic analyses of such sign languages have been undertaken; and these languages have striking linguistic features, which challenge some of the assumptions that have been made of sign languages (Nyst, 2007; Nonaka, 2011; de Vos, 2012). While most sign languages have developed in the urban centres where deaf people gather, rural sign languages have usually developed in clearly circumscribed small-scale communities, often with limited external contact, where an atypically large number of deaf people live, usually due to endogamous marriages that have resulted in hereditary deafness (Zeshan and de Vos, 2012).

Given the unique features that village sign languages exhibit, it is worth including them in typological studies where this is possible, in order to maximize the diversity of the sample. Zeshan and Perniss (2008) included two rural sign languages – Kata Kolok and Adamorobe Sign Language – while the sample used by Zeshan et al. (2013) includes rural sign languages from three countries, along with the corresponding national sign languages (see Table 11.3 for some of the findings of this study).

Obtaining a genetically balanced sample of sign languages is also a major challenge. To start with, it is not clear what constitutes a "genetic relationship" between sign languages. While it is certain that not all sign languages are related to one another, the genetic affiliations of most of them are not known. Even the notion of "language families" is not well defined in sign linguistics, and not enough is known about historical change or about the results of contact between sign languages. No principled or robust methods have been developed for ascertaining family membership for a particular sign language, for reconstructing its earlier forms, or for deducing its family tree. With these limitations, it is difficult to see how a genetically balanced sample of sign languages could be created.

Finally, it is also important to have clarity concerning the varieties that are being referred to. For example, the distinction between languages and dialects is notoriously difficult to define and may be of no typological relevance (although typological approaches have much to offer to the field of dialectology, and vice versa; see Kortmann, 2004). However, in some domains, such as numerals, dialectal variation can be considerable, and in such cases it may be preferable to include several regional varieties in a typological study. This issue also applies at a transnational level. For instance, it has been argued that British Sign Language (BSL), Auslan in Australia, and New Zealand Sign Language could be regarded as dialects rather than separate sign languages (Johnston, 2003), and the same has been argued for sign language varieties in the Levantine Arab area (Hendriks and Zeshan, 2009). These issues need not cause concern, but it is advisable to be as clear as possible in describing the language varieties that are being included in the sample.

Although a long-term aim for sign language typologists has to be to produce surveys with representative samples like those in spoken language typology, given the comparatively small number of documented sign languages and the limited information that we have at present on language families, a degree of compromise is necessary. Representative sampling has not been used in most of the large-scale surveys undertaken so far (such as Zeshan, 2006), because excluding geographical or genetic bias would have resulted in the comparison of only a handful of sign languages. Instead these studies aimed to include as many data from as many sign languages as possible, thus maximizing the potential diversity of features in the data. In samples of sufficient geographical diversity, and with some knowledge of the history of the sign languages involved, it is possible to be confident that at least some of the sign languages will not be genetically related – even in the absence of robust proof in each individual case.

So far as collecting data for a particular study is concerned, there are various different options. Although no sign language reference grammars have been published thus far, probably the first will appear before long, and the COST SignGram project team is currently creating a framework for such work (again, see the Suggested Readings section). However, it is unlikely that the next few years will produce enough reference grammars to enable a typological study based on them alone.

An alternative source of data is sign language corpora, which are being created in several countries such as Australia, Britain, Sweden, Germany, Italy, and the US. The recent rise of sign language corpora is particularly exciting for the field of sign language typology, as it eliminates the need to film new sign language data in some cases and creates the possibility of finding relevant data more quickly, from existing corpora. The problem of bias remains, as the vast majority of corpora are based in western countries; only a few are in non-western areas – like those used in de Vos (2012) for Kata Kolok, in Lutalo-Kiingi (2013) for Ugandan Sign Language, and in Palfreyman (forthcoming) for Indonesian varieties of sign language. Furthermore, even if a corpus is optimally annotated (and few are), the time required to access it and to search for and analyze structures in the target domain is not inconsiderable. In spite of this, the emergence of sign language corpora is a very positive and welcome development for typology and will make cross-linguistic studies ever more feasible.

Given the scarcity of data, sign language typology cannot currently proceed in quite the same way as spoken language typology. In most cases it is necessary to go beyond simply collecting and systematizing the existing data and to actually generate them for the project. For this reason Zeshan (2006), Zeshan and Perniss (2008), and Zeshan and Sagara (2014) worked with many research participants from around the world to collect data through questionnaires and other materials that cover the parameters of investigation and can be distributed to sign language linguists, native consultants, and fieldworkers worldwide. In working with international research partners, there will always be a trade-off between quality and quantity of information. The aforementioned projects included research partners who responded to an open call for participation: this has been the only feasible way to include a sufficiently large number of different sign languages. Therefore the collected information predictably varies in terms of quality, level of detail, and reliability. Not all respondents have extensive training as linguists. However, all receive guidance materials, which may include different versions to choose from, for example shorter and longer versions of the questionnaire or translations into different languages. Given the complex nature of materials collected in this way, it is imperative that the linguists undertaking comparative analyses of these data have extensive first-hand experience with data collection, fieldwork, and the diversity of sign languages. Without such experience it is very difficult to make judgments as to the likely reliability of the information provided and to do effective follow-up with international participants.

The participation of deaf communities in typological research is very important, and this can be actively supported by translating the questionnaires and other materials into International Sign, thereby increasing access for deaf researchers and assistants (see Zeshan and Sagara, 2014). Translations into each individual sign language are not feasible given the large number of participating countries, and in our opinion International Sign is an adequate lingua franca for the purposes of exchange with diverse deaf communities. As long as one contact person in the target country is fluent in International Sign, the content of the project materials can be relayed to other deaf participants in local research groups. Arrangements can also be made to pair novice researchers with more experienced mentors based in different locations, to promote shared learning and mutual support.

In terms of content, questionnaires need to be open enough to be able to accommodate unusual structures, which may be hitherto undocumented, but cannot be so abstract as to be unusable; external research participants need illustrative examples of the potential diversity of structures. It is essential for the research team collectively to have some knowledge of diverse sign languages, so that these examples can be presented in the questionnaire, allowing where appropriate for an option labelled "Other" to accommodate novel structures. The following is an abbreviated example from a questionnaire on color terms:

Q.2 Sign for abstract expression "color"
- There is no sign or expression referring to color in general. → *Proceed to Q.3*
- Yes, there is a single sign for "color." *Provide a picture or video of the sign*
- Yes, there is a complex expression meaning "color":
- A sign for a specific color and a sign meaning "etc.," "various," or something similar, e.g. RED VARIOUS in Indian Sign Language.
- Several signs for specific colors, with or without other additions/modifications, e.g. RED WHITE BLACK in Kata Kolok.
- Any other combination of signs (specify) _____

Q.8 The semantic origin of color signs
- The sign is non-iconic. → *List the signs(s) in this category and provide a picture or video example*
- The sign is semantically related to an object, e.g. TEETH for "white," or ORANGE for "the color orange." → *List the signs(s) in this category, provide a picture or video example, and name the relevant body part/object.*
- The sign is linked to the spoken/written language, e.g. fingerspelling in ASL color signs → *List the signs(s) in this category, provide a picture or video example, and name the relevant word(s) from the spoken/written language*
- Other kind of motivation, namely _____ → *Describe and provide a picture or video example*

The combination of a typological questionnaire with elicitation materials such as those used in Zeshan and Perniss (2008) and Zeshan and Sagara (2014) has proven to be particularly effective, because targeted elicitation creates relevant data, from which examples can then be extracted to illustrate responses to the questionnaire. This is helpful especially where target structures are unlikely to occur frequently in spontaneous data, as is the case with a large range of color terms. Moreover, the use of the same materials for different sign languages is likely to result in data that are more equivalent functionally, since the structures that emerge have been used to deal with similar situations.

Elicitation materials should have a clear goal – and it is worth considering a goal that is ostensibly unrelated to the underlying aim of data collection, so that participants relax and use natural structures. Sentence elicitation, if used at all, should be

Table 11.1 Examples of elicitation materials for possession and existence. Based on Zeshan and Perniss, 2008, Appendix B.

Name	Goal	Linguistic targets
Family tree game	Player A gets information about player B's family or about the family of a friend of player B and uses this information to create a family-tree chart.	• inalienable possession with kinship terms and possessive pronouns • predicative possessive structures • quantified possessive nominals ("I have two sisters") • first-, second-, and third-person forms
Doctor–patient game	Player A must diagnose player B's illness (headache, weakness, skin rash, etc.) on the basis of the symptoms on a chart.	• body part possession ("my head"), one of the core examples of inalienable possession • predicative possession ("have a headache") • first- and second-person reference
Picture matching game	There are pictures of 15 items and three people, and players A and B decide which items belong to which person.	• alienable possession • third-person reference • may elicit "belong" constructions (in contrast to "have" constructions)
Picture comparison game	Players A and B each have pictures that differ from each other in a number of respects; looking at their own picture only, they must identify the differences.	• possessed items • modified and quantified possessed items • existential statements (positive and negative)

used very cautiously. Basing elicitation activities on real-life situations has proven to be very successful, and informants have responded well to games that require role play. For example, asking participants to bargain for objects (such as a shirt, a cow, or a house) has worked well in eliciting examples of numerals in different sign languages (Dikyuva et al., 2012; Zeshan and Sagara, 2014).

Facilitators must be culturally aware and asked to use elicitation materials flexibly. The precise nature of a task can usually be varied in order to keep elicitation fresh and interesting for the participants, as well as culturally appropriate (for instance, by avoiding materials based on mathematics in contexts where there is no deaf education or where schooling has strong negative connotations for participants). Table 11.1 describes four of the elicitation activities that were used by Zeshan and Perniss (2008).

Typological Analysis: Uncovering Ranges and Patterns

There are two different stages of analysis for typology studies. In the first stage – the initial analysis – data are analyzed according to the parameters of investigation by the individuals or groups of linguists who collected the data and have direct knowledge of the sign language through fieldwork. This work may also be undertaken by participants who are not linguists, so long as they receive instructions and guidance from the lead researcher(s). It may be that those involved in the primary analysis stage collect data expressly for the typology project, or they may be able to refer to data that have already been collected as part of a corpus. For instance, in a questionnaire section about numeral incorporation, the available options might be numeral incorporation with time units, with monetary units, with school grades, with any other units, or not at all. For each sign language, this can serve as a checklist; and, if any instances exist, they are reported along with examples in the form of videos, pictures, and/or glossed utterances, and ideally with the range of numerals that can be incorporated.

At this first stage, the aim is to identify the target structures and categorize them, so as to account for the full range of corresponding forms that can be found in each sign language. In some instances it may be the (principal) typologist(s) who conduct the initial analysis, because they either have access to the sign languages themselves or are working in partnership with the researcher. Of course, where a sufficient number of analyses have already been published – descriptive work, articles, and the like – typologists can work with them directly.

The second stage – comparative typological analysis – involves analyzing target structures across the sample. For instance, evaluating the occurrence of numeral incorporation across 21 sign languages has shown that it is very rare to have no numeral incorporation at all, and that its use is most widespread with time units such as "month," "year," and "week." Moreover, the analysis shows that there is an implicational hierarchy: whenever numeral incorporation is used with respect to money, school systems, or any other domain, it is also used with time units. The fact that all sign languages in the data conform to this implicational hierarchy can be "read off" straightforwardly from a data table into which the findings from each sign language have been entered (see Table 11.2). Identifying such patterns is one of the main goals of typological analysis.

It is crucial, wherever possible, to retain a close link with real examples from the cross-linguistic data samples, and always to bear in mind that reinterpretation and re-evaluation may be necessary in light of the cross-linguistic patterns that start to emerge. However, one of the challenges of using multiple parties to collect and analyze data is the inevitable variation in the coding schemes used. Naturally, researchers use their own schemes, but discrepancies in notation can be confusing at the comparison stage. It is not advisable to circulate a rigid coding schema in advance, since this could be restrictive and could suppress real cross-linguistic variation. In any case, the categories for coding may not always be obvious – the whole point of a typological study is to identify linguistic heterogeneity, not to "enforce" homogeneity by applying predetermined categories or labels.

Typologists often display the presence or absence of features in the form of tables or graphs, so that patterns can be identified more easily. Where values are binary, as in the case of numeral incorporation, tables can be used to show the presence (+) or absence (−) of the phenomenon in question (see Table 11.2 for an example). Table 11.3 shows another example of a binary-values table for numbers up to 100 in six different sign languages. From this table it becomes clear that the three rural sign languages in the sample (Alipur, Chican, and Mardin) use strategies that are not available in the urban sign languages (see the highlighted cells).

The presence or absence of a feature is the most basic distinction, but the outcomes of typological analysis may also be concerned with interrelationships between features, relative frequencies, the hierarchical organization of linguistic features, or abstract observations about the properties of linguistic subsystems. For instance, Table 11.3 also shows that Indo-Pakistani Sign Language is monosystemic with respect to these numerals, using only one of the available numeral strategies (digital). Various graphs can be used to illustrate non-binary findings. For instance, Figure 11.3 shows the frequency of negative particles across all sign languages in the data sample.

Another way to compare parameters in different sign languages is to use data spreadsheets, where each sheet may include multiple parameters per sign language, as in Figure 11.4, or a single parameter expressed in all available sign languages. This has the advantage of producing an automated sorting if data sets are large. In

Table 11.2   Data table on numeral incorporation. Based on data collected for the iSLanDS Sign Language Typology Project, 2010–2014, in Zeshan and Sagara, 2014.

Sign Language	Time	Money	School
Chinese	+	+	+
Hungarian	+	+	+
Icelandic	+	−	−
Indian	+	+	+
Indonesian	−	−	−
Israeli	+	+	−
Japanese	+	+	−
Kosovo	+	−	+
Mexican	+	+	+
Sri Lankan	+	+	+
Ugandan	+	+	−

Table 11.3 A binary values table showing the properties of numeral systems for numerals up to 100 in different sign languages. Adapted from Zeshan et al., 2013.

	Alipur Sign Language	Chican Sign Language	Mardin Sign Language	Turkish Sign Language	Indo-Pakistani Sign Language	Mexican Sign Language
Base-20 numerals	−	+	+			
Base-50 numerals	+	+	+		Ø	
Subtractive	+	−	+			
Spatial modification	+	−	−			
Additive	+	+	+	+	−	+
Numeral incorporation	+	−	+	+	−	+
Digital	+	−	−	+	+	−

Figure 11.3 A chart showing the frequency of various negative particles across sign languages (n = 37). Based on Zeshan, 2006, p. 48.

addition to notes that concern what is known about the parameters in each variety, it is also important to identify gaps in the data that can be supplemented or, in accordance with a circular approach, it might be possible to combine or redefine subparameters. If suitable expertise is available within a typological project, a database with multiple search functionalities may be ideal, as has often been implemented successfully in spoken language typology.

Whatever tools are used, the aim of the typological analysis is to abstract away from the data on individual sign languages so as to uncover patterns in the domain and the range of structural variation.

PHENOMENON	VALUE	WRITTEN EXAMPLE	PICTURE EXAMPLE	VIDEO EXAMPLE
I. Attributive possession				
A. *Pronominal possessors*				
A1. Personal pronouns	yes	yes; 2 examples	no	yes; 2 examples
A2. Possessive pronouns	yes	yes; 13 examples	yes; 2 examples	yes; 2 examples
B. *Nominal possessors*				
B1. Juxtaposition	yes	yes; 4 examples	no	yes; 1 example
B2. Overt marking	yes	yes; 8 examples	no	yes; 2 examples
C. *Spatial marking*	no	-	-	
C1. How used for possession?	-	-	-	
C2. Restriction to few signs?	-	-	-	
II. Predicative possession				
D. *Basic 'have'-construction*				
D1. Existential pattern	yes	yes; 13 examples	yes; 1 example	yes; 1 example
D2. Locative pattern	no	-	-	
D3. Action pattern	no (but similar)	yes; 3 examples	no	
D4. Zero-marking	no	-	-	
D5. Other pattern	no (no comment)	-	-	
D6. Use of more than one pattern	no (no comment)	-	-	
E. *Extended patterns for 'have'-constr.*				
E1. Possessum categories	same as 'have'	yes; 7 examples	no	yes; 4 examples
E2. Modified possessum	same as 'have'	yes; 6 examples	no	yes; 1 example
E3. Inanimate possessor	yes	yes; 7 examples	no	
E4. Other clause types ('have'-constr.)	no (no comment)	-	-	yes; 3 examples

Figure 11.4 Section from a spreadsheet used to record and compare data from different sign languages.

If the focus of analysis is likely to involve areal typology, it can be helpful, in addition to some of the methods here, to plot the geographical distribution of structures on a map. For example, Zeshan (2011) looks at question particles – signs that indicate that an utterance is a question – in 37 sign languages from different parts of the world. Plotting the data on a map of the world reveals a high incidence of these particles in East Asia, while the sign languages used in Southeast Asia and the South Asian subcontinent do not have any question particles. Furthermore, the four sign languages where the presence of more than one question particle could be established are all in East Asia (Hong Kong, mainland China, Taiwan, and South Korea).

Once such patterns have been identified, it is possible to try and explain them. For instance, the high incidence of question particles in East Asia corresponds to the presence of question particles in the spoken languages of the region, for instance *ka* in Japanese and *ma* in Mandarin, which raises the possibility that spoken languages may have had structural influence on sign languages in the domain of interrogatives (Zeshan, 2011, p. 565). For other patterns it may be viable to form only tentative hypotheses, and often existing work from spoken language typology, for example frameworks of grammaticalization, can be helpful in understanding the data.

Toward a Cross-modal Typology

So far we have focused on sign language typology; we now turn to cross-modal typology, which describes studies that include data from both spoken and signed languages. Cross-modal typology is an important syncretic development for linguistics, marking a point where signed and spoken language linguists come together. Indeed, the word "cross-modal" could be considered redundant; we use it to emphasize the inclusion of both modalities, highlighting the fact that what is traditionally called "typology" has hitherto excluded sign languages and is better described as "spoken language typology." One of the key questions is whether or not universals are modality-dependent. Are the "universals" that have been identified so far applicable only to spoken languages ("spoken language universals") or only to sign languages ("sign language universals") – or are they genuine, cross-modal universals that are true of all languages, signed and spoken?

Approaches to cross-modal typology have only recently begun to take shape (see Pfau and Steinbach, 2006; Zeshan et al., 2013). Zeshan (2004) compares sign languages with spoken languages and notes that the former "differ strikingly" in terms of the negation strategies that are used (see Table 11.4). For example, sign languages prefer negative particles in post-predicate or clause-final positions, whereas preverbal particles are prevalent in spoken languages. Another notable example is the use of head movements to express negation suprasegmentally, which is universal across sign languages; conversely, suprasegmental marking of negation in spoken languages (via intonation) is extremely rare. Thus it could

Table 11.4   Negation in signed and spoken languages. Zeshan, 2004, p. 51.

Parameter	Spoken languages	Sign languages
Frequency of negation strategies	• morphological negation (affixing) is general across a word class and common across languages • negative particles are common • intonation is extremely uncommon	• morphological negation is limited • negative particles are very common • intonation is extremely common
Morphological negation	• almost always affixation (both prefixes and suffixes), other morphological processes are very rare	• only suffixation, no prefixes, plus simultaneous internal modification of signs
Syntactic position of negative particles	• predominantly preverbal	• predominantly clause-final
Double marking of negation	• relatively uncommon, especially as a combination with negative intonation, but some instances of double particle constructions	• extremely common, especially with manual and non-manual negation, but no double particle construction
Form of negative morpheme	• arbitrary and not recurrent in unrelated languages	• often iconic and recurrent in unrelated languages

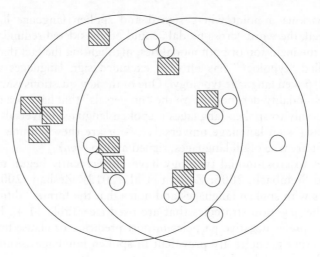

Figure 11.5 The patterning of linguistic features in cross-modal typology. From Zeshan et al., 2013.

be argued that sign languages and spoken languages constitute two different typological groupings.

In other domains, however, a different picture emerges. Zeshan and Perniss (2008) find no evidence that sign languages can be grouped together as a type with respect to possession and existence. Similarly, Zeshan et al. (2013) compare the expression of cardinal numerals in rural sign languages, urban sign languages, and spoken languages and conclude that typological diversity across sign languages is far greater than previously recognized. As shown in Table 11.3, each sign language has its own unique system, and again, neither sign languages nor rural sign languages emerge as a homogeneous subtype. For instance, the numeral system of Mardin Sign Language is, in some ways, more similar to spoken languages that have multiple bases and vigesimal numerals than to sign languages that use a decimal system.

In other words, while typological features may be modality-dependent and thus appear only in spoken languages or only in sign languages, other features may appear in both modalities (see the schematic representation in Figure 11.5). It cannot be assumed that features will always pattern according to modality, and inductive generalizations need to be obtained separately for each domain.

Conclusion

Sign language typology invites linguists to look at patterns of variation both within sign languages and across sign languages and spoken languages. Despite the challenges that sign language typologists face, it is not unfeasible to collect sufficient quantities of data for the purpose of making inductive generalizations that are empirically substantiated. Once a larger number of studies have been conducted, the results of these studies can be synthesized into a theory of variation across sign languages. Within such a theory, it will be possible to look at the question of *why* the observable patterns occur across sign languages in the way they do (see Zeshan and Perniss, 2008, p. 14). Finding explanations for these patterns depends in turn on reaching a better understanding of the structures and processes that affect sign languages. In this way sign language typology can help identify and frame the questions that sign language linguists need to address.

All these studies work with primary data from sign languages, using a combination of the methodologies discussed in earlier sections, and they rely on published literature for spoken language data. The parallel collection of primary data from both signed and spoken languages is in its infancy and currently represents a methodological gap, explicit approaches to the methodologies of such cross-modal typological studies being almost absent.

Typologists believe that cross-linguistic comparison opens doors to our knowledge of languages, but we believe it is cross-modal typology that offers the most exciting possibilities in terms of developing the field of sign linguistics. The question of how linguistic features interact within and between the two modalities – signed and spoken languages – will inevitably continue to prompt new lines of enquiry in unexpected and fruitful areas. It is largely down to sign language linguists to champion cross-modal approaches and to effect new transformations in our understanding of human languages.

Note

1   No textual differentiation between *Deaf* and *deaf* is made in this chapter. Our use of *deaf* refers to culturally and linguistically deaf signers, and a distinction between this and medical deafness is not relevant to the discussion.

Keywords

cross-linguistic; cross-modal; elicitation; ethics; linguistic domains; linguistic parameters; linguistic research methods; sign language typology

See Also

Chapter 6; Chapter 9

Suggested Readings

Croft (2003) situates typology within broader linguistic traditions and gives many examples of how spoken languages can be compared through terminology and methods that, with care, can be applied successfully to sign languages. Lutalo-Kiingi (2013) examines many aspects of the morphosyntax of Ugandan Sign Language, including how it expresses possession, negation, and number. Zeshan (2004) gives an overview of negative constructions in sign languages and compares sign languages with spoken languages in this domain. Zeshan and Perniss (2008) is a typological study of possessive and existential constructions in 28 sign languages around the world, including village sign languages in Ghana and Indonesia. Zeshan et al. (2013) look at cardinal numerals in rural sign languages from a cross-modal typology perspective.

As for web resources, COST SignGram (http://parles.upf.edu/en/content/cost-signgram) is the website of a project entitled "Unravelling the Grammars of European Sign Languages." The aim of the project is "to design a blueprint for the creation of reference grammars of individual sign languages which is descriptively thorough and theoretically grounded." The website includes more information and a signed introduction. The SignTyp database, which is currently under development, will hold approximately 1,000 signs for 15 sign languages. It will enable typological analysis of location, handshape characteristics, contact types and locations, path shapes, directions, and orientations. The World Atlas of Language Structures (http://wals.info; see Dryer and Haspelmath, 2011) is an online database of the structural properties of languages, compiled from the descriptive materials of over 50 authors. It contains two chapters on sign languages.

References

Brentari, D. (Ed.) (2010). *Sign languages.* Cambridge: Cambridge University Press.

Channon, R., and van der Hulst, H. (Eds.) (2011). *Formational units in sign languages.* Berlin: Mouton de Gruyter / Ishara Press.

Comrie, B. (1989). *Language universals and linguistic typology* (2nd ed.). Oxford: Basil Blackwell.

Cormier, K. (2007). Do all pronouns point? Indexicality of first person plural pronouns in BSL and ASL. In P. Perniss, R. Pfau, and M. Steinbach (Eds.), *Visible variation: Comparative studies on sign language structure.* Berlin: Mouton de Gruyter, pp. 63–101.

Croft, W. (2003). *Typology and universals* (2nd ed.). Cambridge: Cambridge University Press.

Dikyuva, H., Escobedo Delgado, C. E., Panda, S., and Zeshan, U. (2012). Working with village sign language communities: Deaf fieldwork researchers in professional dialogue. In U. Zeshan and C. de Vos (Eds.), *Sign languages in village communities: Anthropological and linguistic insights.* Berlin: Mouton de Gruyter / Ishara Press, pp. 313–344.

Dixon, R. M. W. (2010). Doing typology. In R. M. W. Dixon (Ed.), *Basic linguistic theory.* Oxford: Oxford University Press, pp. 242–263.

Dryer, M. S., and Haspelmath, M. (Eds.) (2011). *The world atlas of language structures online,* http://wals.info. Munich: Max Planck Digital Library. (Accessed July 1, 2012).

Eccarius, P., and Brentari, D. (2007). Symmetry and dominance: A cross-linguistic study of signs and classifier constructions. *Lingua* 117, 1169–1201.

Gil, D. (2001). Escaping Eurocentrism: Fieldwork as a process of unlearning. In P. Newman and M. Ratliff (Eds.), *Linguistic fieldwork.* Cambridge: Cambridge University Press, pp. 102–132.

Greenberg, J. H. (1963). Some universals of grammar with particular reference to the order of meaningful elements. In J. H. Greenberg (Ed.), *Universals of language.* Cambridge, MA: MIT Press, pp. 73–113.

Haspelmath, M. (1997). *Indefinite pronouns.* Oxford: Clarendon Press.

Heine, B. (1997). *Possession: Cognitive sources, forces, and grammaticalisation.* Cambridge: Cambridge University Press.

Hendriks, B. (2008). Jordanian Sign Language: Aspects of grammar from a cross-linguistic perspective. PhD dissertation, LOT, Utrecht, Netherlands.

Hendriks, B., and Zeshan, U. (2009). Sign languages in the Arab world. In K. Versteegh, M. Woidich, A. Elgibali, and A. Zaborski (Eds.), *Encyclopedia of Arabic language and linguistics.* Leiden: Brill.

Johnston, T. (2003). BSL, Auslan and NZSL: Three signed languages or one? In A. Baker, B. van den Bogaerde, and O. Crasborn (Eds.), *Cross-linguistic perspectives in sign language research: Selected papers from TISLR 2000*. Hamburg: Signum Verlag, pp. 47–69.

Johnston, T., Vermeerbergen, M., Schembri, A., and Leeson, L. (2007). Real data are messy: Considering the cross-linguistic analysis of constituent ordering in Australian Sign Language, Vlaamse Gebarentaal and Irish Sign Language. In P. Perniss, R. Pfau, and M. Steinbach (Eds.), *Visible variation: Comparative studies on sign language structure*. Berlin: Mouton de Gruyter, pp. 163–206.

Kortmann, B. (Ed.) (2004). *Dialectology meets typology: Dialect grammar from a crosslinguistic perspective*. Berlin: Mouton de Gruyter.

Lutalo-Kiingi, S. (2013). A descriptive grammar of morphosyntactic constructions in Ugandan Sign Language (UgSL). PhD dissertation, University of Central Lancashire, UK.

Meier, R. P., Cormier, K., and Quinto-Pozos, D. (Eds.) (2002). *Modality in language and linguistic theory*. Cambridge: Cambridge University Press.

Newport, E. L., and Supalla, T. (2000). Sign language research at the millennium. In K. Emmorey and H. Lane (Eds.), *The signs of language revisited: An anthology to honor Ursula Bellugi and Edward Klima*. Malwah, NJ: Erlbaum, pp. 103–114.

Nonaka, A. M. (2011). Interrogatives in Ban Khor Sign Language: A preliminary description. In D. J. Napoli and G. Mathur (Eds.), *Deaf around the world: The impact of language*. Oxford: Oxford University Press, pp. 194–220.

Nyst, V. (2007). A descriptive analysis of Adamorobe Sign Language (Ghana). PhD dissertation, LOT, Utrecht, Netherlands.

Palfreyman, N. (forthcoming). Sign language varieties in Indonesia: a linguistic and sociolinguistic investigation. PhD dissertation, University of Central Lancashire, UK.

Pfau, R., and Quer, J. (2007). On the syntax of negation and modals in German Sign Language (DGS) and Catalan Sign Language (LSC). In P. Perniss, R. Pfau, and M. Steinbach (Eds.), *Visible variation: Comparative studies on sign language structure*. Berlin: Mouton de Gruyter, pp. 129–161.

Pfau, R., and Steinbach, M. (2006). Pluralization in sign and speech: A cross-modal typological study. *Linguistic Typology* 10, 135–182.

Pfau, R., Steinbach, M., and Woll, B. (2012). *Sign language: An international handbook*. Berlin: Mouton de Gruyter.

Šarac, N., Schalber, K., Alibašić, T. and Wilbur, R. B. (2007). Crosslinguistic comparison of sign language interrogatives. In P. Perniss, R. Pfau, and M. Steinbach (Eds.), *Visible variation: Comparative studies on sign language structure*. Berlin: Mouton de Gruyter, pp. 207–244.

Stokoe, W. C. (1960). Sign language structure: An outline of the visual communication systems of the American deaf. *Studies in linguistics: Occasional papers 8*. Buffalo: Department of Anthropology and Linguistics, University of Buffalo. (Later published by Linstok Press.)

de Vos, C. L. G. (2012). Sign-spatiality in Kata Kolok: How a village sign language of Bali inscribes its signing space. PhD dissertation, MPI, Nijmegen, Netherlands.

Whaley, L. J. (1997). *Introduction to typology: The unity and diversity of language*. London: Sage.

Wilkinson, E. L. (2009). Typology of signed languages: Differentiation through kinship terminology. PhD dissertation, University of New Mexico.

Zeshan, U. (2004). Hand, head and face: Negative constructions in sign languages. *Linguistic Typology* 8(1), 1–58. http://www.degruyter.com/

Zeshan, U. (Ed.) (2006). *Interrogative and negative constructions in sign languages*. Nijmegen, Netherlands: Ishara Press.

Zeshan, U. (2011). Sign languages. In M. S. Dryer and M. Haspelmath (Eds.), *The world atlas of language structures online*. Max Planck Digital Library. Accessed July 1, 2012. http://wals.info/supplement/9. Munich

Zeshan, U., and Perniss, P. (Eds.) (2008). *Possessive and existential constructions in sign languages*. Nijmegen, Netherlands: Ishara Press.

Zeshan, U., and de Vos, C. (Eds.) (2012). *Sign languages in village communities: Anthropological and linguistic insights*. Berlin: Mouton de Gruyter / Ishara Press.

Zeshan, U., and Sagara, K. (Eds.) (2014). *Semantic fields in sign languages*. Berlin: Mouton de Gruyter and Nijmegen, Netherlands: Ishara Press.

Zeshan U., Escobedo Delgado, C. E., Dikyuva, H., Panda, S., and de Vos, C. (2013). Cardinal numerals in village sign languages: Approaching cross-modal typology. *Linguistic Typology* 17(3). http://www.degruyter.com/

12 Data Collection in Sociolinguistics

Joseph C. Hill

Chapter Overview

During the data collection phase of sociolinguistic projects, sign language researchers face some challenges that are unique to the deaf and hard of hearing communities; and these challenges may affect the process of collecting targeted data. The challenges are related to the set of social characteristics of the communities, the visual nature of sign languages that require video recordings, which compromise the nature of confidentiality, and the sensitive social relationship between sign language researchers and deaf and hard of hearing individuals. This chapter highlights the methodological strategies applied in the studies of sign languages that addressed the challenges.

Research Methods in Sign Language Studies: A Practical Guide, First Edition.
Edited by Eleni Orfanidou, Bencie Woll, and Gary Morgan.
© 2015 John Wiley & Sons, Inc. Published 2015 by John Wiley & Sons, Inc.

The main areas of sociolinguistics that researchers can pursue with their studies of sign languages are variation, bilingualism and multilingualism, language contact, discourse, and language policy and planning. The most recent comprehensive socio-linguistic review on sign languages is *The Sociolinguistics of Sign Languages* edited by Ceil Lucas (Lucas, 2001): each chapter in the volume is dedicated to a sociolinguistic area, complete with the discussion of relevant studies and methodologies. For all the differences between areas, data collection methods are similar with respect to the distinct focus placed on the social characteristics of Deaf[1] communities and on the nature of data collection in sign languages. The similarities may apply to all areas, except for that of language policy and planning, which usually focuses on governmental and non-governmental organizations and their communication artifacts with respect to policies and planning, whereas the other areas largely focus on individuals' use of language in their respective communities.

As in all sociolinguistic studies, researchers must consider their goals and interests when they design their research studies; but that is only half the battle. Researchers must also consider the geographical and social characteristics of a community that have defined language varieties (in an inclusive sense, languages and dialects) when it comes to determine the appropriate data collection methods. If two researchers have the same goals and interests but the communities in which they are interested have completely different geographical and social characteristics, the researchers must design data collection methods that are appropriate for their respective communities. In other words, one method is as successful as the other if they are truly designed to accommodate the targeted communities and their particular geographical and social characteristics. With the Deaf communities, sociolinguistic researchers face special challenges through the different phases of the sociolinguistic projects: recruitment, data collection, and data presentation. In this chapter only recruitment and data collection will be discussed. The challenges are related to the set of social characteristics that are unique to Deaf communities, the visual nature of sign languages, which requires high-quality video recordings that compromise the nature of confidentiality, and the sensitive relationship between sign language researchers and Deaf community members, which is based on social status.

This chapter addresses the special challenges outlined in the previous paragraph and provides a description of data collection methods that are used in the sociolin-guistic studies of deaf and hard of hearing people whose primary means of commu-nication are sign languages in their respective communities. The recent and refined data collections methods described in the chapter are derived from selected variation and corpus studies (variation studies typically require sign language corpora of var-ious sizes) produced in the recent decade on the following sign languages by the following teams: American Sign Language (ASL) by a team of Ceil Lucas, Robert Bayley, and Clayton Valli (2001); African American variety of ASL (hereafter Black ASL) by a team of Carolyn McCaskill, Ceil Lucas, Robert Bayley, and Joseph Hill (2011); Italian Sign Language (LIS) by a team of Carlo Geraci, Katia Battaglia, Anna Cardinaletti, Carlo Cecchetto, Caterina Donati, Serena Giudice, and Emiliano Merghetti (2011); British Sign Language (BSL) by Gary Quinn (2010) and by a team of Kearsy Cormier, Jordan Fenlon, Ramas Rentelis, and Adam Schembri (2011); and New Zealand Sign Language (NZSL) by a team of Rachel and David McKee and their associate, George Major (2011). BSL and NZSL are in the same language family, on the basis of their histories and linguistic constructions, and the researchers have collaborated with each other in some ways, but ASL and LIS are very different from these sign languages, and they are different from each other as well. Even with ASL and LIS as mutually unintelligible languages, the researchers of ASL and LIS may consult each other on the shared methods and data interpretations and can communicate with the researchers of BSL and NZSL as well. Furthermore, some of the research groups have developed websites that store sign language corpora, for the purpose of sharing their data and methodologies worldwide. Here are examples of such websites: the British Sign Language corpus project (www.bslcorpusproject. org), the Australian Sign Language (Auslan) Sign Bank (www.auslan.org.au), the Black ASL project (blackaslproject.gallaudet.edu), and Progetto corpus LIS (Italian Sign Language corpus project, w3.uniroma1.it/progettolis).

Nature of Social Characteristics of Deaf Communities

In the sociolinguistic literature, a certain set of geographical and social characteristics have been identified as factors of language variation; the factors are typical in variation studies, but they could apply in other areas of sociolinguistics that deal with the use of language in targeted communities. The geographical and social factors that are described as external constraints in the literature – as opposed to internal constraints, which are linguistic factors – have been repeatedly shown to be significantly correlated with linguistic variation in the respective communities. Region, gender, age, ethnicity, and socioeconomic status are the typical external constraints under observation in sociolinguistic studies. The typical external constraints are observed in the sociolinguistic studies of Deaf communities as well, but, due to the unique histories of these communities, sign language researchers are compelled to include other external constraints, which are typical of them and have a significant correlation with linguistic variation: language use in the home, age of sign language acquisition, and type of education.

Deaf communities are the microcosm of the larger communities – namely the hearing ones – in their respective countries; so it makes sense to observe the typical external constraints in the sociolinguistic studies of sign languages. These are region, gender, age, ethnicity, and socioeconomic status. The Deaf communities reflect the social diversity that exists in the larger societies. Geographical and social factors, which explain the natural or man-made boundaries between existing communities, often play a role in the formation of language varieties (see Wolfram and Schilling-Estes, 2006, pp. 28–43). The geographical and social factors can also be compounded by others, particular to the communities. In the geographical sense, communities can be separated by natural or man-made boundaries, for example by natural geographic barriers (rivers, mountains, or swamps), settlement patterns, political borders, social stratification, and economic ecology – that is, geographic concentrations of occupations (Wolfram and Schilling-Estes, 2006). As communities are in relative isolation from one another, language varieties arise naturally and are defined by their communities' culturally bound communication practices, which are passed down through generations. However, the main difference between spoken languages and sign languages is in how the languages are transmitted and in how the population, environmental, regional, and educational factors play a role in this process; thus the social characteristics that are of particular interest in the Deaf communities are language use at home, age of sign language acquisition, and type of education.

Generally speaking, spoken languages are practiced in different units of the hearing communities, from individuals to families to institutions, and they are widely available for children to acquire. But sign languages are not as widely practiced in the hearing communities in which deaf and hard of hearing people are members. National censuses may not contain a direct question about disability, much less one about deafness, but if such a question is included, deafness may not be distinguished from the other disabilities and there may be no question of sign language use. For instance, there is no systematic data collection on sign language or ASL use in the general US population (Mitchell, Young, Bachleda, and Karchmer, 2006, p. 307). With no direct data available, researchers often resort to their own sources to make an estimate of the deaf and hard of hearing population. The population estimates of deaf and hard of hearing people can vary and one should exercise caution and investigate the methods of population estimate (Mitchell et al., 2006). However, deafness being a low-incidence disability, with the number of deaf people who are proficient in sign language, the proportion of deaf and hard of hearing people is expected to be extremely low. For example, the United States has a population of nearly 313 million, and the general but unconfirmed estimate of deaf people who use sign language is 500,000 (Mitchell et al., 2006, p. 328), but there are other estimates, reported elsewhere, that run between 100,000 and 15,000,000 (p. 307). The large variation in these estimates is attributed to anecdotal evidence, methodological differences, and a conflation of the estimates for the population of deaf people who use ASL and for people with various degrees of hearing loss regardless of their communication preferences. In New Zealand, out of 4 million New Zealand citizens, the estimate of the deaf population is between 4,500 and 7,700 (McKee, McKee, and Major 2011, p. 490). In Australia the deaf population is estimated to be of 7,000 out of 22,685,018 (Johnston 2004, p. 367).

It is safe to say that in the most parts of the world communities have a similar proportion of deaf and hard of hearing members who use sign language. In 2012 the World Federation of the Deaf estimated the number of deaf people in the world at 70 million; in the context of the world's population, this figure is well below 7 billion people as projected by the US Census Bureau in 2012. In other words, around 1 percent of the world's population are deaf or hard of hearing. Even though sign languages are generally limited to communities of deaf and hard of hearing people, it is important to know that not all of them use sign language. There are various natural and accidental causes of deafness; it can happen at any age. If we are to focus on deaf and hard of hearing people who have acquired sign language, the proportion is even smaller. Hearing people with personal or professional connections to someone in the Deaf community (a family member, friend, teacher, interpreter, or researcher) and can converse comfortably in sign language can be considered members; but, even so, it is unlikely that there is a large segment in the hearing population of people who are skilled in sign language and maintain connection with Deaf communities on a regular basis.

The percentage of deaf and hard of hearing people born to families of deaf and hard of hearing adults who use sign language as a primary means of communication tends to be very small by comparison to the percentage of deaf and hard of hearing people born to non-signing families with normal hearing. For example, in the United States approximately 8 percent of deaf children have at least one parent who is deaf or hard of hearing (Mitchell and Karchmer, 2005, p. 243). About 4.8 percent of the deaf children have one hearing and one deaf or hard of hearing parent, and approximately 3.5 percent have two deaf or hard-of-hearing parents (p. 243). Moreover, deaf and hard of hearing children who have at least one deaf parent are more likely to use sign language at home and at school than those who have hard of hearing parents, but unfortunately the number of homes that use ASL as the home language is not available (Mitchell and Karchmer 2004). In contrast, 92 percent of the deaf children were born to hearing parents, and it is very likely that many of those children are exposed to alternative communication forms, which exclude ASL at home with their families (Mitchell and Karchmer 2004). There are some cases where hearing parents may be fluent in sign language; but the evidence is largely anecdotal and, as has been mentioned above, there is no systematic data collection concerning the language used at home by deaf children. With deafness as a low-incidence disability and the genetic factor that affects a minor proportion of deaf population, there is a strong possibility that the percentages are similar in the different Deaf communities around the world with the majority of deaf and hard of hearing people born to hearing parents. In this context, the population factor functions as a constraint on the transmission of sign language for deaf and hard of hearing people. And yet what contributes to the success of sign language transmission among deaf and hard of hearing people is the environmental factor, which is typically related to education.

Deaf communities have been typically formed in regions where special schools or education programs for deaf children were established. This is the case for ASL (Lucas et al., 2001), Black ASL (McCaskill et al., 2011), NZSL (McKee et al., 2011), and LIS (Geraci et al., 2011). Some Deaf communities can be formed in regions where there are no special schools but where deaf people gather for an employment, residential, or social reason. For example, BSL users live in Lancaster and Morecambe, where there are no special schools for the deaf, and some of them attended such schools out of town (Quinn, 2010, p. 477). Although there is a university in the town of Lancashire within half-hour's drive from both towns that offers courses on BSL and deaf studies, the university is not one of the typical institutional settings where deaf and hard of hearing children acquire sign language. For deaf people who have attended special schools for their education, the schools provide a rich language environment, sign language being used among deaf and hard of hearing peers and school staff. Deaf students who had little or no knowledge of sign language prior to the beginning of their formal education usually acquired sign language in the company of older deaf peers. This is known as "horizontal transmission," which is normal for the cohorts of deaf and hard of hearing children at special schools – as opposed to "vertical transmission," which is normal in hearing communities, where hearing children typically acquired their language from the preceding generation.

Schools for the deaf have long been considered to be the crucibles for the acquisition and maintenance of sign language (Lucas et al., 2001, p. 52); but, since the advent of mainstreaming,[2] whereby deaf and hard of hearing students attend regular schools with or without accommodation, the role of the schools for the deaf has diminished as a source of sign language input for such children. For example, before the 1960s, almost 80 percent of the deaf children in the US attended residential schools for the deaf; by 2010, the percentage had declined to 24.3 percent (Gallaudet Research Institute, 2011). The type of education is the decisive factor in whether deaf and hard of hearing children acquired sign language during the course of their schooling, and it should be observed in the sociolinguistic projects on sign languages.

The type of education also correlates with the age of the participants. In sociolinguistic literature, the age of a generation is normally one of the social variables observed in linguistic community studies (Eckert, 1997, p. 152). But in the case of Deaf communities the educational and age factors are clearly related due to the passage of mainstreaming laws that encourage the placement of deaf and hard of hearing students in regular educational settings. In the large-scale sociolinguistic study of ASL, Lucas et al. (2001) put down the age factor as an external constraint based on the division of three generational age groups (15–25, 26–54, and 55+). This age division has been motivated by developments in the language policy of deaf education in the early 1970s with the passage of Public Law 94–142 (the Education of All Handicapped Children Act of 1975) and by the change in communication methods from oral to signed, which may not include ASL (Lucas et al., 2001, p. 35). In Italy a similar trend emerged in late 1970s with the passage of legislation on the mainstreaming of children with disabilities, including deaf and hard of hearing children (Geraci et al., 2011, p. 532). The same happened in New Zealand from the 1980s, when the mainstream placement of deaf and hard of hearing children was increasingly favored (McKee et al., 2011, p. 492). These developments in deaf education have produced a clear effect on the communication background of the generations of deaf and hard of hearing people.

With the educational effect on the language acquisition of deaf and hard of hearing signers, it can be very difficult to find a desired group of signers who acquired sign language during the critical period of their language development, as well as meeting the criteria of extensive and continued involvement in a Deaf community and choice of sign language as a primary means of communication. A particular recruitment method that proves to be useful is the employment of deaf local contact persons who possess the local network knowledge, have good social standing in Deaf communities, and can help recruit deaf individuals with the target social characteristics (Lucas, 2013, pp. 282–284). This method is commonly used in sign language projects such as the ASL, the Black ASL, the LIS, the NZSL, and the BSL projects under discussion here.

The Visual Nature of Sign Language

There are two aspects of language ability displayed by language users in general: linguistic competence and linguistic performance. Linguistic competence is the knowledge that language users have about a language and their ability to use it; in contrast, linguistic performance is the production of actual utterances, which may include errors or forms that language users deny using. If questionnaires are used in the data collection, the self-reported data from language users may be helpful in an analysis designed to reveal how participants perceive their own language use; this ties to linguistic competence, but often these users' linguistic performance contradicts their perceived knowledge of the language. This is the main reason why sign language corpora are essential for sociolinguists; it helps them analyze actual utterances.

Sociolinguists interested in capturing utterances that are spontaneously produced in a specific context have to be cautious with the interview portion in a data collection. When language users are aware that they are being observed, they may exhibit self-consciousness in their language production and adjust their language to the perceived preference of a researcher. The presence of a recording device can make language users feel self-conscious. Even with the recording device concealed, the mere presence of a researcher influences language users' linguistic behavior. This phenomenon has been addressed by sociolinguists starting with Labov (1972), who discussed it as the "observer's paradox" (see McCaskill et al., 2011, p. 51). In any sign language project, capturing the targeted data in a natural form is already a challenge because of the visual nature of sign languages and because of a set of social characteristics that are unique to Deaf communities. The researchers have also to consider the problem of the observer's paradox and the sensitivity of signers to the audiological status and ethnicity of interviewers or interlocutors.

The modalities of languages – spoken and signed – are the key factor that affects the use of a recording device in data collection. With spoken language in the oral-and-aural modality, researchers enjoy flexibility in the choice of recording format, which can be audio only or audio-visual. With advances in audio recording technology, powerful audio recording devices have become increasingly portable, affordable for sociolinguistic researchers, and less distracting to interviewees. With sign language in the visual and kinetic modality, however, a video recording device is an absolute necessity and the filming process is usually more overt. To ensure visual clarity in the filming of a signing production, signers must be in a well-lit setting and with their heads, hands, and torsos entirely visible to a camera. Also, the seating must be arranged to help with the clarity of the signing: for the interlocutors to see each other and the camera to be able to record, a pair of signers must be seated next to each other, with their fronts turned slightly toward each other, and a group of signers must be seated in a semi-circle (see Figure 12.1). In some cases a video camera must be placed close to the signers, to capture a full view of the signing. A backdrop may be necessary to help with the clarity of the signing and the face and body movements. With these arrangements and the use of video recording devices that feel intrusive to the participants, the problem of the observer's paradox becomes much more acute.

To address the problem of the observer's paradox and the fact that language users may be inhibited in their language production when they are aware of being observed, Labov (1972) developed the sociolinguistic interview, which encourages speakers to use the vernacular – their everyday language. Since the goal is to gather as much informal language production as possible, the sociolinguistic interview is designed to reduce the power differential between the interviewer and the interviewee by avoiding a formal language variety, by keeping questions brief, and by including topics (such as childhood games, dating patterns, marriage and family, dreams) designed to encourage an informal language production. Also, the chance of getting informal language production may improve if the interviewer has similar social characteristics with the interviewee(s). The sociolinguistic interview technique has shown to be effective in sign language projects (see McCaskill et al., 2011; Lucas et al., 2001; Lucas and Valli, 1992).

The location is another thing to consider when planning an interview. In Geraci et al.'s (2011) study, the researchers filmed their LIS signers in an environment familiar

Figure 12.1 An example of signers sitting in a semi-circle with a deaf interviewer facing them. Frame grab from video clip. Courtesy of Black ASL project.

to them, at a club for the Deaf or in a restaurant where the deaf signers were patrons. In the study of ASL, Lucas and her associates (2001) collected their data from a number of groups at community centers, at schools for deaf students, in private homes, and, for three groups, in a public park (p. 40). In the study of NZSL, McKee, McKee, and Major recruited signers at a Deaf school reunion, a Deaf youth camp, and a Deaf club and interviewed them in a semi-secluded area (2011, pp. 76–77).

Sensitivity to the Social Characteristics of Interviewers and Interlocutors

Normally sociolinguistic researchers in sign language projects conduct free and structured conversations to collect data from participants with target social characteristics. During a free conversation, participants can sign among themselves without a researcher being present. This is designed to help them be less inhibited in their signing and it encourages spontaneity in their discussion. While it is a good way to gather natural data, the free conversation has its limitations. Typically the conversation lasts about 20–30 minutes, depending on how well the participants know each other and the topics of conversation; but it may last for only a few minutes if the participants know each other very well and feel no need to continue the conversation. Also, the number of tokens that appear in the free conversation might not be enough, depending on the choice of statistical methods (see Aguilar-Sánchez,

2011) and on the goal of the research. For that reason a structured conversation is conducted to capture target data. The typical forms of structured conversation are interviews and lexical and phrasal elicitations. For the lexical or phrasal elicitations, an interviewer uses cue cards with pictures, as used in McCaskill et al. (2011), in Geraci et al. (2011), and in McKee et al. (2011), or written words from the spoken languages, as used in the BSL study and in the NZSL study to get the participants to produce their own signs. If the interviewer signs a certain concept, it is very likely that the interviewer's sign would influence the participants' choice of sign; so the use of cue cards is the safe way to elicit target signs or phrases.

One thing that sign language researchers are always conscious about when conducting free and structured conversations is to manage the social sensitivity of participants. The participants' social sensitivity can manifest itself in their conscious or unconscious choice of signing when they are in the presence of an interviewer. It is true that participants may be sensitive even to each other's social characteristics. For example, in Lucas and Valli's (1992) study of contact signing (which is cited frequently in the context of the effect of social sensitivity on communication), social sensitivity often manifested itself in switchings between ASL, Signed English (an invented manual code for English), and contact signing (a mixed system combining core features of ASL and Signed English along with the continuous voiceless mouthing, which is a common feature) when deaf signers experienced change from a deaf interviewer to a hearing one. Even in the company of deaf ASL native signers, a few signers chose to use contact signing or Signed English instead of ASL. The signers' self-consciousness (which led them not to use ASL) could be caused by the relative formality of the interview situation, which included the presence of a video camera and the lack of familiarity with the interviewer and other interviewees (Lucas and Valli, 1992).

Sign language users can be sensitive to a signer's audiological status (e.g., hearing or deaf). The Deaf/hearing dichotomy is a relevant criterion in defining in-groups and out-groups in a Deaf community and is used as a guide in determining a signer's language preference or skills. The terms "Deaf" and "hearing" have particular meanings in the Deaf community: "Deaf" is used to describe someone who is a skillful ASL signer and who understands and observes the values, behavior, and customs of the Deaf community, while "hearing" is used to describe someone who is not as skillful in his/her use of ASL and is less familiar with the Deaf community. Although a signer's audiological status is included as a trait of the Deaf and hearing identities, the audiological status is not visible; so the signing skills are used instead as an indicator of one's audiological status. Even though a number of identities are relevant in the Deaf community – hard of hearing, late deafened, mainstreamed student, cochlear implant user, hearing child of deaf adult (CODA), hearing sibling of deaf person – the identities of "Deaf" and "hearing" have a particularly powerful influence on language production (Hill, 2012, p. 160).

The social considerations of racial/ethnic background and audiological status can also interact to affect interview situations. It is suggested that interviewers share the same ethnicity as their interviewees, so the production of informal language can be encouraged. For example, some black deaf participants in McCaskill et al.'s (2011) Black ASL study explain that they stylistically shift their signing when engaging in a conversation with a white signer. These instances of style-shifting can be explained by Giles' (1973) accommodation theory, which accounts for how language behavior may change according to the perceived language preference of an interlocutor. Another example in the Black ASL project is that, at some point during the data collection, a white hearing researcher who was skillful in ASL was mindful of the influence of her racial identity and audiological status on the sociolinguistic interview between a black deaf researcher and a black deaf interviewee; she managed to lessen her influence by staying in the background during the interview. At the conclusion of the interview, the interviewee met with the white hearing researcher and signed with her. When the interviewee asked about the researcher's audiological status, the interviewee made a dramatic shift across modalities, from signing to speaking, even though they had understood each other's signing perfectly prior to the discovery of the white researcher's audiological status as hearing. This is a striking example of how the researcher's audiological status can influence the participant's language use; but it is in fact quite common for deaf signers to switch to contact signing or to Signed English when they learn the audiological status of a hearing person (see Lucas and Valli, 1992, pp. 53–66). Depending on their research goals, researchers and interviewers should always consider the potential effects on language exchange when exercising their discretion in revealing or concealing their social characteristics in a language situation during data collection.

It is in the best interest of sign language researchers to make sure that a group of participants have similar social characteristics – depending on the kinds of data the researchers aim to have. The researchers also need to make sure that an interviewer has similar social characteristics, so that participants may feel comfortable in relating with the interviewer. In different sign language projects, deaf interviewers are typically employed; they can be local contact persons, research assistants, or researchers, although researchers tend to avoid acting as interviewers due to the power imbalance generated by their educational and social status.

Considerations for the Future

Researchers who are conducting sign language projects must always be mindful of the geographical and social constraints that define Deaf communities. The constraints can be similar to those of the greater societies of which the Deaf communities are a part, but researchers should also be aware of the unique characteristics that describe Deaf communities in their regions. In any case, researchers should be careful about the social characteristics of interviewers and interlocutors, particularly audiological status and racial/ethnic identity, in relation to the researcher's goal of obtaining targeted language samples. It is always a challenge to make signers comfortable in a setting with a video camera, but researchers can overcome the problem of the observer's paradox by following the design of the sociolinguistic interview and by using an interviewer who shares the same audiological status and racial/ethnic background as the interviewees.

Traditionally, one key criterion is that signers have to have native knowledge of sign language. Sign language researchers prefer to observe deaf and hard of hearing signers who acquired sign language during the critical period of language development – that is, during their childhood. For the majority of deaf and hard of hearing signers who were born to hearing parents with little or no knowledge of sign language, the acquisition of sign language largely took place at special schools for the deaf. As long as they acquired sign language during the critical period, those are the kind of people that are qualified to participate in sign language studies. Another, albeit smaller, group of deaf and hard of hearing signers – those who were born to parents with the native knowledge of sign language – are also qualified. But in these days the recent developments in deaf education have affected the kinds of communication that deaf and hard of hearing children are exposed to and have widened the social gap between a group of people whose educational experience includes sign language as a primary medium of instruction and a group whose experience does not. Also, the number of mainstreamed deaf and hard of hearing children is larger than the number of those who attended special schools for the deaf. So a wide variety of communication and language experience is expected in most deaf and hard of hearing children, and it is highly likely that this has affected the way sign language is practiced today. In the future, the key criterion that signers have a native knowledge of sign language may be difficult to apply; and this is where employing local contacts to find native signers can be of advantage. However, focusing only on native signers does not reflect the reality of language practices in the Deaf communities. It is time to accept that variety of communication and of language experience has become the norm for deaf signers and that sociolinguistic studies of signers whose sign language exposure was delayed are highly encouraged, for the sake of capturing the linguistic and cultural realities.

Given the rate of change in sign language due to educational developments, the archival practice of collecting language samples is strongly encouraged; in this way the researchers can have access to data produced by native and non-native signers and can also investigate language change within Deaf communities. The advance in video and storage technology has made it affordable for sign language researchers to obtain recording equipment and to archive language samples. In addition, the technological advances have produced different kinds of new data – face-to-face video chatting and user-generated video-sharing on personal computers and on mobile devices – and such data can be included in sign language corpora as well (see Lucas et al., 2013 for a further discussion of the effects of new technologies on sign language research). The last decade has seen the apparition of large-scale sign language corpus projects such as the one discussed in this chapter. At the time of writing, the ASL corpus project is under development and will be added to the list of corpora that lend themselves to sociolinguistic treatment, helping researches to produce more findings and to contribute to better understandings of how sign language (and language in general) is used in the social-bound practices of a community with targeted social characteristics at a given time.

Notes

1   The difference between uppercase D and lowercase d in the word *deaf* makes much sense to those who are familiar with Deaf culture. Uppercase D is used to describe communities of sign language users with various degrees of hearing loss who subscribe to cultural values, beliefs, and behaviors related to deafness. Lowercase d describes deafness as a physical deficiency, in medical contexts and from the medical viewpoint. Individuals who are *deaf* may not necessarily be *Deaf*. The lowercase *deaf* is a good catch-all term for a population of deaf people who may or may not be culturally Deaf and may

or may not use sign language as their primary language. But throughout this chapter, for the purpose of simplicity, I will use the lowercase *deaf* when I talk about individual people with deafness and capitalized *Deaf* with reference to places or communities that function as cultural institutions.

2 Mainstreaming is the practice of integrating deaf and hard of hearing students, as well as students with disabilities, with non-disabled students and having them participate in regular classrooms, with appropriate accommodation.

Keywords

accommodation theory; data collection methods; deaf education; interview; observer's paradox; recruitment; sign languages; sign language corpus projects; sociolinguistics

See Also

Chapter 2; Chapter 7

Suggested Readings

de Beuzeville, L., Johnston, T., and Schembri, A. (2009). The use of space with indicating verbs in Auslan. *Sign Language & Linguistics* 12(1), 53–82.

Johnston, T. (2010). From archive to corpus: Transcription and annotation in the creation of signed language corpora. *International Journal of Corpus Linguistics* 15(1), 106–131.

Lane, H., Hoffmeister, R., and Bahan, B. (1996). A journey into the DEAF-WORLD. San Diego: Dawn Sign Press.

Lucas, C., and Schembri, A. (Eds.) (2015). *Sociolinguistics and deaf communities*. Cambridge: Cambridge University Press.

References

Aguilar-Sánchez, J. (2011, October). Sample size planning in sociolinguistic research: How many subjects? How many tokens? Which statistical analysis? Paper presented at the New Ways of Analyzing Variation 40 (NWAV), Washington, DC.

Cormier, K., Fenlon, J., Rentelis, R., and Schembri, A. (2011). Lexical frequency in British Sign Language conversation: A corpus-based approach. In P. K. Austin, O. Bond, L. Marten, and D. Nathan (Eds.), *Proceedings of the third conference on language documentation and linguistic theory*. London: School of Oriental and African Studies, pp. 81–90.

Eckert, P. (1997). Age as a sociolinguistic variable. In F. Coulmas (Ed.), *The* Oxford *handbook of sociolinguistics*. Oxford: Blackwell, pp. 151–167.

Gallaudet Research Institute (2011). *Regional and national summary report of data from the 2009–2010 Annual survey of deaf and hard of hearing children and youth*. Washington, DC: GRI, Gallaudet University. Accessed March 4, 2012. http://gri.gallaudet.edu/Demographics/2010_National_Summary.pdf

Geraci, C., Battaglia, K., Cardinaletti, A., Cecchetto, C., Donati, C., Giudice, S., and Merghetti, E. (2011). The LIS corpus project: A discussion of sociolinguistic variation in the lexicon. *Sign Language Studies* 11(4), 528–574.

Giles, H. (1973). Accent mobility: A model and some data. *Anthropological Linguistics* 15, 87–105.

Hill, J. (2012). *Language attitudes in the American Deaf community*. Washington, DC: Gallaudet University Press.

Johnston, T. (2004). W(h)ither the Deaf community? Population, genetics, and the future of Australian Sign Language. *American Annals of the Deaf* 148(5), 358–375.

Labov, W. (1972). *Sociolinguistic patterns*. Philadelphia: University of Pennsylvania Press.

Lucas, C. (Ed.) (2001). *The sociolinguistics of sign languages*. Cambridge: Cambridge University Press.

Lucas, C. (2013). Methods for studying sign languages. In R. Bayley, R. Cameron, and C. Lucas (Eds.), *The Oxford handbook of sociolinguistics*. Oxford: Oxford University Press, pp. 280–298.

Lucas, C., and Valli, C. (1992). *Language contact in the American Deaf community*. San Diego: Academic Press.

Lucas, C., Bayley, R., and Valli, C. (2001). *Sociolinguistic variation in American Sign Language*. Washington, DC: Gallaudet University Press.

Lucas, C., Mirus, G., Palmer, J. L., Roessler, N. J., and Frost, A. (2013). The effects of new technologies on sign language research. *Sign Language Studies* 13(4), 541–564.

McCaskill, C., Lucas, C., Bayley, R., and Hill, J. (2011). *The hidden treasure of black ASL: Its history and structure*. Washington, DC: Gallaudet University Press.

McKee, D., McKee, R., and Major, G. (2011). Numeral variation in New Zealand Sign Language. *Sign Language Studies* 12(1), 72–160.

Mitchell, R. E., and Karchmer, M. A. (2004). When parents are deaf versus hard of hearing: Patterns of sign use and school placement of deaf and hard-of-hearing children. *Journal of Deaf Studies and Deaf Education* 9(2), 133–152.

Mitchell, R. E., and Karchmer, M. A. (2005). Parent hearing status and signing among deaf and hard of hearing students. *Sign Language Studies* 5(2), 231–244.

Mitchell, R. E., Young, T. A., Bachleda, B., and Karchmer, M. A. (2006). How many people use ASL in the United States? Why estimates need updating. *Sign Language Studies* 6(3), 306–335.

Quinn, G. (2010). Schoolization: An account of the origins of regional variation in British Sign Language. *Sign Language Studies* 10(4), 476–505.

US Census Bureau (2012). US & world population clocks. Accessed September 25, 2012. http://www.census.gov/main/www/popclock.html

Wolfram, W., and Schilling-Estes, N. (2006). *American English* (2nd ed.). Oxford: Wiley Blackwell.

World Federation of the Deaf (2012). *About us*. Accessed September 25, 2012. www.wfdeaf.org/about

Part IV   Collecting Cognitive Data on Sign Languages

13 Research Methods in Psycholinguistic Investigations of Sign Language Processing

Jill P. Morford, Brenda Nicodemus, and Erin Wilkinson

Chapter Overview

This chapter provides an overview of methods used to investigate the comprehension and production of signed languages. In a methodological review of 61 published studies, we found that psycholinguistic studies have been carried out on a very restricted range of signed languages. The majority of investigations were conducted in laboratory settings. The populations studied consisted primarily of proficient adult deaf[1] signers, with some inclusion of hearing signers. The methods used were best suited for testing specific hypotheses about signed language processing, rather than for documenting or discovering norms and preferences for language use within social contexts. We conclude our review with a discussion of the challenges researchers face when conducting psycholinguistic investigations of signed language processing.

Research Methods in Sign Language Studies: A Practical Guide, First Edition.
Edited by Eleni Orfanidou, Bencie Woll, and Gary Morgan.
© 2015 John Wiley & Sons, Inc. Published 2015 by John Wiley & Sons, Inc.

Introduction

Psycholinguistic studies of signed languages have provided significant insights into language comprehension and production. A central outcome of psycholinguistic research is that we can now better distinguish modality-specific and modality-independent aspects of language processing. In all domains of language processing, commonalities across signed and spoken languages have been found; however, some of the most insightful findings on signed languages to date concern how language processing is impacted by modality differences. Critically, research findings on the comprehension and production of signed languages have deepened our understanding of the nature of all human language. Conducting studies of signed languages has challenged psycholinguists to revise traditional research methods, for instance by adapting materials and paradigms to the visual modality and by taking prior linguistic analyses of signed languages into account.

In this chapter we provide a methodological review of the current literature of psycholinguistic studies on signed languages. To aid the reader in gaining an overview of studies in this domain, we include four tables in which we summarize the research questions, methods, participants, and findings of a selection of psycholinguistic studies on signed languages. Our hope is that these tables will serve the reader in two ways. First, the tables offer new investigators a means to quickly gain a sense of the breadth of the field in terms of both research questions and methods – which may then be used in their own study design. Second, investigators who have already selected a research method can use the tables to easily identify prior studies that have also used the method in question. We are not attempting in this chapter to prescribe specific methods for conducting signed language psycholinguistic research, although there are many issues – both scientific and ethical – that will become apparent through this review. We encourage readers to supplement their consideration of these issues by also reading the first three chapters in this volume. Our chapter covers the psycholinguistic methods most frequently used to study signed languages to date, as well as the methodological challenges faced by researchers who investigate signed language processing.

To select articles for the tables, we completed a search of the PsycInfo database using the search terms "sign language" and "language processing." The results were disparate and too numerous for inclusion in this chapter, so we narrowed the selection to areas not covered in other chapters of this volume. Thus we eliminated studies that investigated spoken language use, children,[2] reading, and studies that used neuroimaging methods. We further restricted our selection by excluding chapters that described studies that had been previously published as peer-reviewed articles, or chapters that did not provide a full description of the study methods. However, we did include many of the early, classic psycholinguistic studies of signed languages that were published as chapters and not in peer-reviewed publications. The resulting selection of 61 publications on the psycholinguistics of signed languages is comprehensive, but not exhaustive. We apologize for any omissions that would have been appropriate given our criteria for inclusion.

As in the broader field of psycholinguistics, studies on signed language comprehension vastly outnumber studies on signed language production. Three domains pertaining to language comprehension are well represented in current research on signed languages and are provided in Table 13.1, Table 13.2, and Table 13.3:

perception; lexical access;[3] and grammatical processing. Table 13.4 summarizes studies investigating signed language production. We first explore methodological issues common to all four domains of research, then address unique aspects of the methodology in each of these domains.

Standard Methods in Psycholinguistic Research

Psycholinguistic studies have a well-established tradition of reporting the details of the research method according to a prescribed format. The method section of over 90 percent of the articles and chapters included in our tables include three subsections: participants, materials, and procedures. All three of these areas raise special considerations that distinguish research on signed languages from research on spoken languages.

Considerations regarding the participants

The participants in studies of signed language processing almost invariably included deaf individuals. Many hearing individuals also use signed languages, and this is apparent from the participant groups investigated in psycholinguistic studies. Further, hearing people who do not know a signed language are frequently recruited as members of control groups. The studies reviewed in this chapter almost always distinguished whether participants were hearing or deaf. As discussed in Chapters 1 to 3 of this volume, signed language research is likely to be more reliable and to have a greater impact when the Deaf community is consulted and integrated into the research approach, as opposed to research that includes deaf participants without respecting the social and ethical implications for members of this community.

Signed language proficiency is an important factor in selecting the participants. Due to a lack of signed language assessment tools, investigators have generally relied on the age of acquisition to estimate proficiency level. Numerous studies have documented the impact of the age of acquisition of a signed language on language processing (for reviews, see Emmorey, 2002 and Mayberry, 2010). To minimize the variability related to age of acquisition, some studies recruit only native signers, although the operational definition of this group is not consistent across studies. Alternatively, researchers tend to group signers according to their age of acquisition. Unfortunately, the ages used to group signers differ across studies, making comparisons difficult. Further, treating age of acquisition as a categorical rather than a continuous variable may obscure important distinctions in the way age impacts language processing if the age groups selected by the researcher do not correspond to the disparities in participant performance. The most frequent way to use age of acquisition to form groups in the studies reviewed here is:

1   native signers (exposure from birth);
2   childhood signers (exposure by age 5);
3   adolescent signers (exposure by age 9).

Hearing signers are less frequently divided into groups according to their age of exposure to a signed language, although most studies do distinguish between CODAs (children of deaf adults) who were exposed to a signed language from birth and hearing signers who acquired a signed language as a second language. Like deaf signers, these groups can be highly variable in their proficiency level, and thus should have their proficiency directly assessed if assessment tools are available. At the very least, specifying the criteria used to select participants, including native signers, would facilitate comparison of results across studies.

Another population included in two of the studies we reviewed consists of late deafened adults (Mayberry, 1993; Provine and Emmorey, 2006). These individuals have a unique language acquisition history in that full competency in a spoken language was achieved prior to acquisition of a signed language. While this is also the case with many hearing signers, late deafened adults may have greater access to signed language interaction as deaf individuals, and thus are not comparable to hearing second-language signers.

Several other factors are used as selection criteria in the studies reviewed here – for example hearing level (only participants with a hearing loss of 70 dB or greater are included), education level, and parental hearing status. None of the studies we reviewed reported socioeconomic status (SES) of their participants or included it as a selection criterion. Controlling these factors – or at least reporting them – is essential, given the high degree of variability in signed language proficiency among deaf and hearing signers, particularly when the language proficiency level cannot be directly assessed.

A final point about participants concerns the use of control groups. The nature of the research question determines the appropriate type of control group for studies of signed language processing. In the domain of signed language perception, for example, 12 of 18 studies included a control group of hearing non-signers. Because hearing non-signers can make visual judgments about sign stimuli without having knowledge of a signed language, they provide an excellent control group for distinguishing signed language perception from visual perception.[4] By contrast, only five of 18 studies of lexical access included a control group of non-signers, because most lexical access tasks require some proficiency with the language. Studies of lexical access typically compare performance of native and non-native signers. No studies of grammatical processing or language production included non-signers as a control group.

Considerations regarding materials

Developing materials for empirical investigations of signed languages is an area of methodology that is ripe for innovation. Psycholinguistic studies of spoken languages rely primarily on text for stimuli as opposed to using audio recordings of speech. Clearly this is an aspect of psycholinguistic research methods that does not transfer easily to the study of signed languages. In order to present signed language stimuli to participants in experimental settings, most researchers have relied on line drawings, still photographic images, and video recordings. However, some creative solutions have been developed in order to allow investigators to isolate specific parameters of signed language stimuli or to manipulate the visual features of the stimuli. These novel methods will be covered in the discussion of each subdomain of psycholinguistic research.

In a few early studies, researchers presented stimuli as *glosses*, printed words that approximate the spoken language translations of signs (e.g., Hanson and Feldman,

1989), presumably because presenting signs as stimuli was more technologically complex. However, using signs instead of glosses as stimuli has the important advantage that the process under investigation can be examined in the absence of translation. No study published since 1990 has used glosses – one indication that this approach has been abandoned in favor of direct presentation of signed stimuli.

The most common way to present signed stimuli in experimental tasks is with digital recordings of live signers. Implementing video stimuli is changing rapidly, as the technology undergoes advancements resulting in variance in the size and quality of the stimuli. It may not be possible to standardize the size and quality of video stimuli under such dynamic conditions, but the field would benefit from reporting these characteristics, so that this can be taken into consideration in interpreting results. One means of controlling the realization of signed stimuli is the increasing use of avatars. As in the use of video, avatars vary in size and quality; these factors are not likely to be standardized until the technology is more uniform and more widely available.

In order to isolate form- and meaning-processing in signed languages, investigators use nonce signs or signs of a foreign sign language as stimuli. Nonce signs are phonologically permissible forms that do not occur in the language under investigation. Because phonological constraints on specific signed languages are still under investigation, the creation of nonce signs requires careful consideration of the acceptable combinations of the selected parameters. The most frequently used approach to the generation of nonce signs is to begin with standard signs and replace one parameter (see Best, Mathur, Miranda, and Lillo-Martin, 2010; Brentari, 2006; Hildebrandt and Corina, 2002, Orfanidou, Adam, Morgan, and McQueen, 2010). The use of authentic signs, such as foreign signs, allows researchers to avoid inadvertently creating infelicitous stimuli, but there is also the possibility that what is phonologically common in one signed language is restricted or forbidden in another. To explore issues in grammatical processing, some investigators have also used agrammatical signed utterances (see Boudreault and Mayberry, 2006; Emmorey, Bellugi, Friederici, and Horn, 1995; Mayberry and Fischer, 1989). Again, caution should be taken when manipulating the grammaticality of signed utterances, since investigations of signed language grammar are ongoing.

In the following section we describe the primary research procedures or tasks used in each of the four domains of psycholinguistic research covered in this chapter, as well as any aspects of participants and materials that are specific to that research subdomain.

Methodological Considerations: Four Sub-domains of Signed Language Psycholinguistics

Language comprehension: Signed language perception

Studies of language perception investigate how sensory information is mapped to perceptual categories. The question of modality effects is particularly central to language perception studies, because the sensory cues associated with signed and spoken languages are fundamentally different. Yet, even in this domain, parallels between the perception of signed and of spoken languages have been found. While the materials used for sign perception studies differ radically from the materials used in speech perception studies, the tasks used are largely the same. Three types of tasks have been used to date in sign perception studies (see Table 13.1):

1   identification and discrimination tasks;
2   phonological similarity judgment tasks;
3   monitoring tasks.

Studies using *identification* and *discrimination tasks* compare how participants identify or categorize sensory stimuli into perceptual categories at sublexical or lexical levels, in relation to how they discriminate stimuli drawn from within a single perceptual category or from different perceptual categories. For example, signers may be presented with a sequence of signs that vary gradually from using the U handshape to using the V handshape (Best et al., 2010). Even though there might be ten visually unique versions of the sign, signers can categorize each signed production into two categories: U or V. This paradigm is used to investigate the extent to which perception is language-specific, or whether linguistic signals are perceived in much the same way as non-linguistic signals such as gestures, facial expressions, or other visual stimuli. In a *phonological similarity judgment task*, participants view multiple signs or nonce signs that differ only in one or two parameters or in certain dimensions of a single parameter, and decide which stimuli look most similar (see Figure 13.1). These studies seek to determine how the different phonological parameters or dimensions of them contribute to sign perception. In *phoneme monitoring tasks*, participants are asked to view a sequence of signs or nonce signs and to respond when a target is observed. For example, participants might be asked to press a response button each time the sign is made with a fist or is located at the chin. This task is the only perception task we reviewed to incorporate reaction time, and thus it can inform us about the efficiency of perceptual processing. One way this task has been used was to isolate effects of language acquisition history on perceptual processing of specific sublexical components of signs (Grosvald, Lachaud, and Corina, 2012; Morford and Carlson, 2011).

Studies of signed language perception require a great deal of control over the experimental materials, since these studies evaluate how signers perceive sensory cues. One way to control the exact form of a sign is to use synthetic sign, or signing avatars, to present the signed stimuli. Synthetic sign can be either static (Emmorey, McCullough, and Brentari, 2003) or dynamic (Morford, Grieve-Smith, MacFarlane, Staley, and Waters, 2008). Another way to create signed stimuli for perception experiments is to use visual morphing of video recordings (Best et al., 2010).

More than half of sign perception studies involve the investigation of handshape perception. Very few studies, by contrast, have investigated movement perception, presumably due to the technological challenges in measuring and controlling the dynamic properties of signs. And yet one of the most innovative approaches to materials development came about as a result of investigating movement perception. Poizner placed light-emitting diodes on the hands of signers and then filmed them signing in the dark (Poizner, 1981; cf. Tartter and Fischer, 1982). The resulting videos show patterns of movement without any information pertaining to handshape and location. Finally, several investigators have modulated the visual information presented to subjects in order to explore the impact on perception, for example by adding *visual noise* – a random pattern of small dots that disrupts the visual cues

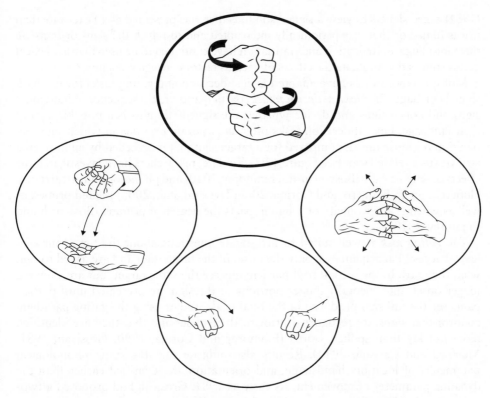

Figure 13.1 Phonological similarity judgment task. Participants select from the three lower fields one response that matches the upper field most closely. Actual videos are used instead of line drawings. Line drawings courtesy of Bill Vicars and www.lifeprint.com

associated with the sign (Lane, Boyes-Braem, and Bellugi, 1976) – or by inversion of the video image (Corina and Grosvald, 2012).

Language comprehension: Lexical access in signed languages

Lexical access in comprehension concerns the process that links language form to meaning in the mental lexicon. Psycholinguistic studies of spoken language lexical access have relied heavily on the use of priming and lexical decision. By contrast, no single task has dominated the research on signed language lexical access. Of the many tasks used in the studies we reviewed, only three tasks were used by independent groups of researchers (see Table 13.2):

1 sign repetition or translation;
2 primed lexical decision;
3 gating.

The earliest studies of lexical access investigated how modifications to the sign signal impacted sign recognition, and thus lie at the border between sign perception and lexical access studies. Tweney, Heiman, and Hoemann (1977) and Heiman and Tweney

(1981) asked signers to view a signed stimulus that was presented at a faster rate than it was filmed or that was periodically interrupted and to *repeat* the signs or *translate* them into English. Repetition and translation have continued to be used in other lexical access studies that evaluate the effects of various factors on sign recognition.

Multiple laboratories have adapted lexical decision and gating tasks for use with signed languages. In a *lexical decision task*, participants view a sequence of individual signs and nonce signs and decide whether the signed stimulus is a possible sign in their language. Lexical decision tasks often incorporate *priming*, in which sign recognition response time is compared for a target sign that is preceded by an unrelated sign versus a related sign (see Figure 13.2). To date, researchers have investigated the effects of semantically (Bosworth and Emmorey, 2010) and phonologically (Carréiras, Gutierrez-Sigut, Baquero, and Corina, 2008; Dye and Shih, 2006) related primes, as well as whether the iconicity of a sign impacts the degree of priming (Bosworth and Emmorey, 2010).

The *gating task* is well suited to investigate questions about the time course of lexical access. Participants see only the onset of the target sign and are asked to sign what they saw. In the second trial participants see the same target, but are shown a longer onset. Incrementally longer portions of the sign are presented until participants see the full sign produced in the final trial. Studies using the gating paradigm confirm that signs are recognized prior to their offset and that they are identified more quickly than spoken words (Emmorey and Corina, 1990; Grosjean, 1981; Morford and Carlson, 2011). Results also indicate that the static phonological parameters of location, handshape, and orientation are identified earlier than the dynamic parameter of movement. As early as 1981, Grosjean had proposed a two-stage model of lexical access to account for this difference.

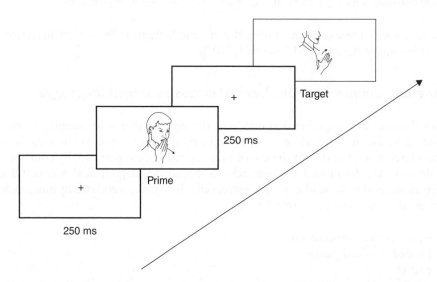

Figure 13.2 Primed lexical decision task. Participants view a sequence of signs and decide for each sign whether or not it is a real sign. Half of the stimuli are nonce signs. Targets can be preceded by semantically or phonologically related primes. Actual videos are used instead of line drawings. Line drawings courtesy of Bill Vicars and www.lifeprint.com

In addition to repetition, lexical decision, and gating, a variety of other tasks have been used in isolated studies. These are:

4   sign-spotting – that is, identifying a sign embedded in continuous signing;
5   deciding whether a signed stimulus is one or two signs;
6   deciding whether the handshape is straight or curved;
7   deciding whether a sign is made with one or two hands;
8   deciding whether a sign and a picture match.

With the exception of Hanson and Feldman's (1989) use of glosses as stimuli, all of the remaining lexical access studies reviewed used video recordings of signs as stimuli.

Language comprehension: Signed language grammatical processing

Several indicators suggest that grammatical processing is a less developed area of signed language processing research than sign perception or lexical access (see Table 13.3). The earliest study in this subdomain was not published until 1989 (Mayberry and Fischer, 1989). Further, only 11 studies that investigate grammatical processing were identified. These studies employed five tasks:

1   grammaticality judgment task;
2   probe recognition;
3   sign monitoring;
4   sentence or narrative shadowing;
5   sentence recall.

In a *grammaticality judgment task*, participants view signed sentences and have to decide whether they are grammatically acceptable or not. Researchers control which aspects of grammar are investigated by disrupting the target grammatical morpheme or construction in the agrammatical sentences. In a *probe recognition task*, participants view a signed sentence, and then are asked to decide whether a target sign occurred in the sentence or not. *Sign monitoring tasks*, like phoneme monitoring, can be completed with lists of signs, but studies investigating grammatical processing present participants with sentences and ask them to respond when they see a target sign. For both probe recognition tasks and sign monitoring tasks, sign detection or recognition can potentially be affected by the grammatical context in which the sign occurred, allowing investigators to evaluate the effects of grammatical manipulations (see, e.g., Emmorey, Bellugi, et al., 1995).

Sentence-shadowing and recall tasks require participants not only to respond to a single sign, but to reproduce full sentences. In a *sentence shadowing task*, participants reproduce the target sentence while watching it. In *sentence recall*, participants must wait until a sentence is completed before trying to reproduce it exactly. If the signed stimuli are long and complex, then participants will invariably generate errors in trying to recall the sentences verbatim. These errors provide insights into the comprehension process (see Figure 13.3). Further, the modified responses can be evaluated for their grammaticality. Mayberry and colleagues have used these tasks

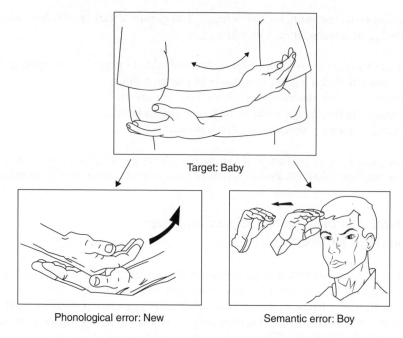

Target: Baby

Phonological error: New   Semantic error: Boy

Figure 13.3 Error types generated in a sentence recall task. Phonological errors demonstrate surface-level processing of the target signs, while semantic errors demonstrate deeper processing of the target signs. Line drawings courtesy of Bill Vicars and www.lifeprint.com

to demonstrate that the age at which signers are first exposed to sign language has lifelong consequences for language comprehension (Mayberry, 1993; Mayberry and Fischer, 1989; Mayberry and Eichen, 1991).

Materials for studies of grammatical processing to date have consisted of video recordings of grammatically complex signs, sentences, and narratives. In one study, Mayberry and Fischer (1989) added visual noise to the signed stimuli by mixing randomized black and white dots with the visual image, such that only 41 percent of the original video image was visible. This manipulation was disruptive to language comprehension.

Signed language production

Our survey of language production studies resulted in 14 studies spanning the time period of 1979 to 2011 (see Table 13.4). Language production studies have provided insights into underlying cognitive processes by evaluating *intact production*, on the one hand, and *production errors*, on the other. There was more consistency in the tasks used to investigate language production than in the other three areas of signed language processing reviewed. The tasks used can be categorized into two subsets. One approach is to analyze corpora; the other is to elicit language production through picture naming, storytelling, or translation. Both approaches are used to investigate intact language production and production errors.

In 1979 Klima and Bellugi published the first known study on signed language production, analyzing a corpus of naturally occurring errors produced by signers.

Their analysis became the classic study on *slips of the hand* produced by ASL signers (available online at lcn.salk.edu; see Newkirk, Klima, Canady Pedersen, and Bellugi, 1980). Almost twenty-five years later, a group of German researchers took up the tradition of investigating slips of the hand, but switched to using *elicited production* under cognitively stressful conditions, or requiring sign reversal, in order to induce signers of German Sign Language (DGS) to produce slips of the hand in a laboratory environment (Hohenberger, Happ, and Leuninger, 2002; Leuninger, Hohenberger, Waleschkowski, Menges, and Happ, 2004). Despite differences in methodology, the conclusions reached in the early studies on ASL and in the later studies on DGS are similar. Both groups found that handshape is the most likely phonological parameter to be substituted in forms during signed language production, demonstrating that signs have sublexical structure. More generally, the groups conclude that language production errors provide evidence of separate processing of form and meaning, as is found for spoken language production.

The earliest study of intact sign production that we were able to identify was published by Boyes-Braem in 1999. She compared elicited narratives of native and non-native signers of Swiss German Sign Language (DSGS) to determine whether the impression reported by her deaf research assistants was correct that the rhythmic characteristics of the signing of these two groups differed. More recently, several groups of investigators have published analyses of corpora, including publicly available corpora (Neidle, 2001), to investigate issues such as how videophone technology impacts the use of space in signed language production (Keating, Edwards, and Mirus, 2008), how movements of the mouth and hands are coordinated in signing (Kröger, Birkholz, Kannampuzha, Kaufmann, and Mittelberg , 2011) or how laughter is controlled so as not to interfere with signed language production (Provine and Emmorey, 2006).

In laboratory settings, production of single signs has been elicited through *picture-naming tasks* in order to examine lexical retrieval (Baus, Gutiérrez-Sigut, Quer, and Carréiras, 2008; Corina and Knapp, 2006; Thompson, Emmorey, and Gollan, 2005). These studies aim to determine how and when semantics and phonology contribute to lexical retrieval. Materials for corpus studies consist of the corpus itself and, for elicitation studies, materials generally consist of pictures. The only time when signs are presented as stimuli in the language production studies we reviewed was when participants were asked to name pictures that were superimposed on signs that were semantically or phonologically related to the target sign (Baus et al., 2008; Corina and Knapp, 2006), or when participants were asked to watch a two-sign sequence and reverse the order of signs in their response (Leuninger et al., 2004).

Methodological Challenges

In this section we address challenges facing signed language researchers that were revealed by this review of psycholinguistic research methods. Great progress has been achieved in our understanding of signed language processing with the help of the methods reviewed here, but these methods have by no means been perfected. In some cases the field would be helped tremendously by standardization of methods. In other cases actual changes to methods and study populations are needed.

Generalizability of findings

A brief perusal of Tables 13.1 to 13.4 is sufficient for us to conclude that the range of signed languages studied to date is much too narrow. The most frequently asked research question is how modality impacts language processing. Yet the data used to evaluate this question come from a narrow range of Western European signed languages and from ASL. Clearly more signed languages need to be studied before generalizations across them can be made with confidence.

Efforts to increase psycholinguistic research across a range of signed languages may be supported through transnational research partnerships with initiatives such as scholarship funds to attend psycholinguistic conferences, scholar exchange programs between institutions, and structured mentoring opportunities for new researchers. Further, establishing linguistic web sites that provide International Sign and/or translations in written languages may be helpful in disseminating information (for example, see www.signlinguistics.org and dsdj.gallaudet.edu).

Study population

A related concern is that study populations are highly variable, and yet sample sizes in past studies of signed language processing are generally quite small. This is almost inevitable, given the low incidence of deafness and the many factors that impact language proficiency in the signing population. Standardizing how participants are described (e.g., by age of signed language acquisition, gender, educational level, or socioeconomic status) is necessary in order to enable comparisons across studies. Directly assessing language proficiency would be even better.

Few standardized assessment tools to measure signed language proficiency in adults are available at this time (Haug and Mann, 2008); this makes direct assessment a challenge, particularly in contexts where signed language research is still emerging. Progress is being made; for example, a sentence reproduction test has been developed for both ASL, the ASL-SRT (Hauser, Paludnevičienė, Supalla, and Bavelier, 2008), German Sign Language (DGS), the DGS-SRT (Kubus and Rathmann, 2012), and is currently under development for British Sign Language (BSL; Cormier, Adam, Rowley, Woll, and Atkinson, 2012). There are also plans to adapt the SRT for Swiss German Sign Language (DSGS; Tobias Haug, personal communication). In addition, the Aachen Test for German Sign Language Competence (ATG) has been developed by an interdisciplinary team in Aachen for the assessment of DGS competence in both children and adults (Fehrmann, Huber, Jäger, Sieprath, and Werth, 1995a, 1995b). These assessment tools are so recent that most investigations using them are not yet published, and none of these tools is publicly available. All of the studies reviewed for this chapter relied upon acquisition history rather than direct assessment as a way to establish sign language proficiency.

Developing assessment tools for signed languages is facilitated by several interrelated factors: the ongoing development of signed language grammars, continued study of language acquisition in Deaf individuals, and creating corpora of the world's sign languages. These efforts will provide the foundation necessary to assess signed language proficiency with accuracy. Further, it would be useful to create programs of study within psychology or linguistics departments in which signed language assessment is a recognized specialty.

Analysis methods

The vast majority of studies reviewed relied on standard parametric analysis methods, such as ANOVAs and correlations, to evaluate their results. A few studies relied on more descriptive and distributional analyses. One type of data analysis clearly lacking in this domain of inquiry is the use of *multilevel modeling*. Given the heterogeneity of the signing population, particularly with respect to language experience, the use of multilevel modeling and of other methods that can demonstrate the interaction of multiple factors on language processing would be particularly well suited to the population under investigation (Traxler, 2013). Further, when variability caused by individual characteristics and group-level characteristics is distinguished, psycholinguistic studies are less likely to report significant results that are actually driven by factors that were not controlled. An online course in multilevel modeling is available free of charge online (at http://www.bristol.ac.uk/cmm/learning/course.html).

Stimulus selection

Psycholinguists who study spoken languages rely on published corpora and resources to control variables known to affect language production and comprehension. Lexical frequency is the best example of a factor that is easily controlled in spoken language studies, but that is, to date, challenging to control in studies of signed language processing. Studies that controlled for sign frequency relied on familiarity ratings (e.g., Carréiras et al., 2008). Familiarity ratings have now been published for 300 BSL signs (Vinson, Cormier, Denmark, Schembri, and Vigliocco, 2008), but most signed language researchers must collect these ratings prior to running a study. A new development that will be helpful to sign language psycholinguists in the future is the recent investment in signed language corpora. If these corpora are machine readable, it should be possible for psycholinguists to calculate lexical frequencies. Where these resources are lacking, researchers can use within-subject experimental designs, in which participants see the same signs across different conditions. When this is not an option, collecting familiarity ratings is still the best alternative.

Likewise, controlling for the type or degree of iconicity of a sign can be a challenge to investigators. Bosworth and Emmorey (2010) asked 68 hearing non-signers to rate the degree of iconicity of their sign stimuli on a scale from 1 to 5. Campbell, Martin, and White (1992), by contrast, asked just two signers (one native and one non-native) to rate the degree of iconicity of their stimuli on a scale from 1 to 3. Standardizing such scales would be beneficial, but having access to published iconicity ratings would truly facilitate experimental design. One question that needs to be addressed before iconicity ratings can be standardized is how to interpret the iconicity ratings of non-signers versus signers. If investigators assume that iconicity is a characteristic of the sign, independent of linguistic experience, then ratings of non-signers would be useful, as they are impartial. Some researchers, however, have argued that iconicity is construed through linguistic experience, and thus is never independent of signed language knowledge (Adam, Iversen, Wilkinson, and Morford, 2007). If this is the case, then iconicity ratings by non-signers could be considered irrelevant to the effect of iconicity on signed language processing.

Measuring reaction times

Reaction time is the most frequently used dependent variable in studies of signed language processing. Yet measuring reaction time in response to signs is quite challenging, since it is not always clear when a sign begins and ends. Reaction time must be measured from sign onset, since signs are recognized well before they are complete, but signers may tend to wait until the end of a sign to respond, making it more difficult to determine the time course of various subprocesses in signed language processing. Carréiras and colleagues (2008, p. 112) found that participants responded more quickly to stimuli in a lexical decision task when signs were extracted from a signed sentence than when signed stimuli were filmed in isolation, with the hands beginning in the signer's lap. This finding suggests that investigators should be careful to measure the onset of reaction time close to the actual articulation onset of the sign, and to consider how sign length may be contributing to reaction time. By reducing variability in response time that is not directly related to language processing, psycholinguistic studies are more likely to generate meaningful results. For language production studies, the use of reaction time could also be implemented, but this may require the development of innovative ways of detecting sign onsets, such as using laser triggers at the beginning of an utterance.

Conclusion

Signed language researchers are on a new frontier among psycholinguists. Though many methods have been borrowed from spoken language processing studies, signed language researchers have found innovative ways to adapt these methods for use with visual languages. Relying on psycholinguistic methods from spoken language studies has provided a grounding for signed language research but could also result in reliance on approaches that do not exploit the inherent nature of signed languages. Richer conceptualizations of the linguistic properties of signed languages can motivate new approaches. Advances in video technology and software are also a boon to investigators interested in creating new paradigms for the investigation of signed language processing. The methodological future of this field will be found in improvements in experimental control combined with innovations in the development of materials and paradigms uniquely suited for visual languages.

Acknowledgments

Jill P. Morford and Erin Wilkinson received support from the National Science Foundation Science of Learning Center Program, under cooperative agreement number SBE-0541953 and SBE-1041725 at the time of the writing of this chapter. Any opinions, findings, and conclusions or recommendations expressed are those of the authors and do not necessarily reflect the views of the National Science Foundation.

Table 13.1 Summary of publications investigating signed language perception

Author(s)	Research question(s)	Task(s)	Participants	Findings
Baker, Idsardi, Golinkoff, and Petitto (2005)	Is perception of signs and speech modality-specific? Is handshape perception mediated by linguistic experience?	Handshape identification and discrimination	15 deaf native American Sign Language (ASL) signers and 15 hearing non-signers	Deaf signers exhibited better discrimination of across-category handshape pairs than of within-category handshape pairs for two of three handshape continua, but hearing non-signers did not.
Best, Mathur, Miranda, and Lillo-Martin (2010)	Is perception of signs and speech modality-specific? Is handshape perception mediated by linguistic experience?	Discrimination and categorization with goodness ratings	10 deaf native ASL signers, 10 deaf non-native ASL signers, 10 hearing non-native ASL signers, and 10 hearing non-signers	All participants showed a psycho-physical effect of better discrimination of spread than unspread handshape variation, but experience also affected performance, deaf non-native signers showing better discrimination than the other three groups.
Bochner, Christie, Hauser, and Searles (2011)	Can adult learners discern when differences in sign formation are contrastive?	Discrimination of minimal pairs	10 deaf native signers and 127 hearing non-native signers	Native signers were able to discriminate all contrasts better than non-native signers. Location contrasts were the easiest and movement contrasts the hardest for both groups.

(Continued)

Table 13.1 (Continued)

Author(s)	Research question(s)	Task(s)	Participants	Findings
Campbell, Woll, Benson, and Wallace (1999)	Can face actions that carry significance within sign language be perceived categorically?	Identification and discrimination of facial expression	16 deaf native and non-native British Sign Language (BSL) signers, 12 hearing non-native BSL signers, and 34 hearing non-signers	No effect of language background on perception of emotional face contrast, but signers tended to perceive the grammatical distinction categorically while only few of the non-signers did. Age of acquisition of sign did not influence performance.
Corina and Grosvald (2012)	Does the processing of sign forms diverge from the processing of human actions?	Continuous categorization of signs and self-grooming actions incorporating 180° inversion and repetition priming	13 deaf native ASL signers, 9 deaf early ASL signers, 21 deaf late ASL signers, and 33 hearing non-signers	Deaf signers categorized signs and self-grooming gestures more rapidly and more accurately than hearing non-signers. Signers experienced greater disruption from inversion than non-signers for ASL signs, which indicates that signers may rely on the configuration of the articulators for sign recognition instead of decomposing signs into parts.

Study	Research question	Task	Participants	Findings
Corina, Grosvald, and Lachaud (2011)	When and how does the processing of sign forms diverge from the processing of human actions?	Categorization of signs and self-grooming actions with primes that varied in perspective (front, left, or right view)	22 deaf native and early ASL signers, 21 deaf late ASL signers, and 33 hearing non-signers	Deaf signers were faster and more accurate to categorize signs vs. actions than hearing non-signers, but viewpoint priming impacted signers and non-signers similarly, suggesting that the earliest stages of sign processing are not sign-specific.
Emmorey, McCullough, and Brentari (2003)	Do signers exhibit categorical perception effects for distinctions in handshape or location?	Identification and discrimination of handshape (Exp 1) and location (Exp 2)	Exp 1: 14 deaf native ASL signers, 1 deaf non-native ASL signer, and 17 hearing non-signers. Exp 2: 22 deaf native ASL signers and 20 hearing non-signers	Signers and non-signers categorized the stimuli similarly, but only signers showed categorical perception of contrastive handshape. No one showed categorical perception of allophonic handshape contrasts or of any location contrast.
Grosvald, Lachaud, and Corina (2012)	Does handshape recognition rely on specialized linguistic processing or on factors that are common to human action recognition?	Handshape monitoring	19 deaf native ASL signers, 17 deaf non-native ASL signers, and 20 hearing non-signers	Deaf signers were faster than hearing non-signers to detect handshape in isolated signs; both groups responded faster to marked handshapes in one-handed signs and to unmarked handshapes in two-handed signs.

(Continued)

Table 13.1   (*Continued*)

Author(s)	Research question(s)	Task(s)	Participants	Findings
Hildebrandt and Corina (2002)	Does linguistic experience shape judgments of sign similarity?	Phonological similarity judgments	Exp 1: 21 deaf native ASL signers, 20 deaf non-native ASL signers, and 42 hearing non-signers Exp 2: 29 deaf native ASL signers, 33 deaf non-native ASL signers, and 51 hearing non-signers	Exp 1: All groups judged nonce signs overlapping in movement and location with the target nonce signs as most similar in form. Exp 2: Judgments of which nonce sign was most similar to the target sign differed across groups, deaf native signers preferring signs overlapping in movement, deaf non-native signers preferring signs overlapping in handshape, and hearing non-signers equally preferring signs overlapping in movement or location.
Lane, Boyes-Braem, and Bellugi (1976)	Are handshapes perceived according to distinctive features?	Handshape identification in noise	Exp 1: 4 deaf early ASL Signers Exp 2: 2 deaf non-native ASL signers	Participants' handshape confusions as well as prior reports of slips of the hand and allophonic variation in handshape can be accounted for within a distinctive feature model.

Morford, Grieve-Smith, MacFarlane, Staley, and Waters (2008)	How does age of acquisition affect handshape and location perception?	Handshape, location identification and discrimination	9 deaf native ASL signers, 9 deaf non-native ASL signers, and 9 hearing non-native ASL signers	Identification functions were similar for all groups for both handshape and location contrasts. Discrimination of handshape but not of location differed as a function of language background. Signers' discrimination declined close to the category prototype.
Poizner (1981)	Does knowledge of a signed language modify perception of sign movement?	Triadic similarity judgments of point-light displays	5 deaf native ASL signers and 5 hearing non-signers	Four dimensions best account for variability in performance, but signers weighted repetition more heavily than non-signers, indicating that knowledge of a signed language does modify visual perception.
Poizner (1983)	What dimensions underlie the perception of ASL lexical movement?	Triadic similarity judgments of point-light displays	5 deaf native ASL signers and 5 hearing non-signers	Four dimensions best account for variability in performance for both lexical and grammatical movement, but signers weighted repetition for lexical movement and cyclicity for grammatical movement more heavily than non-signers did.

(Continued)

Table 13.1   *(Continued)*

Author(s)	Research question(s)	Task(s)	Participants	Findings
Poizner, Bellugi, and Lutes-Driscoll (1981)	How does the perception of movement impact the perception of ASL?	Identification and discrimination of movement in normal vs. point-light display conditions	Exp 1: 9 deaf childhood ASL signers Exp 2: 6 deaf native ASL signers Exp 3: 19 deaf native ASL signers Exp 4: 8 deaf native ASL signers	Participants were highly accurate in matching signs to point light displays for both lexical and inflectional movement and were also able to identify signs on the basis of movement trajectory alone when handshape was held constant. The most distal articulators contributed the most information to discrimination of movement.
Poizner and Lane (1978)	Is each location perceptually distinct from every other location, or do locations form classes based on shared features?	Location identification	5 deaf native ASL signers and 5 hearing non-signers	Identification errors were similar across the two groups, suggesting that the perception of location is determined by psychophysical factors.
Richards and Hanson (1985)	What dimensions underlie the perception of handshape?	Handshape sorting and similarity judgments	10 deaf native ASL signers and 10 deaf non-native ASL signers	Handshapes were sorted on the basis of compactness and orientation in both tasks. Language experience did not influence performance.

Study	Research question	Task	Participants	Results
Stungis (1981)	Is handshape perceived according to distinctive features as proposed by Lane et al. (1976)?	Handshape identification and discrimination	3 deaf native ASL signers and 3 hearing non-signers	Signers and non-signers showed similar patterns of performance on both tasks. Performance was consistent with Lane et al.'s model, but more variability in performance was captured with a two-dimensional continuous model of handshape similarity.
Tartter and Fischer (1982)	What low-level information do signers use to discriminate minimal pairs?	Discrimination of signs embedded in sentences in normal and point-light display conditions	14 deaf native and childhood ASL signers	Discrimination performance was higher under normal viewing conditions than when point-light displays were presented. Signs differing in location or orientation were more easily discriminated than signs differing in movement or handshape.

Table 13.2 Summary of publications investigating lexical access in signed languages

Author(s)	Research question(s)	Task(s)	Participants	Findings
Baus, Carreiras, and Emmorey (2013)	Does iconicity enhance translation performance for novice and proficient second language signers?	Translation task	15 hearing non-native ASL signers and15 hearing non-signers	New learners benefited from sign iconicity, recognizing iconic translations faster and more accurately and exhibiting faster forward and backward translation times for iconic signs. Proficient bimodal bilinguals exhibited slower recognition and translation times for iconic signs.
Bosworth and Emmorey (2010)	Does iconicity enhance semantic priming effects?	Primed lexical decision	20 deaf native ASL signers	Significant facilitation for target signs when preceded by semantically related primes; however, iconicity did not increase priming effect.
Brentari (2006)	What cues do signers rely on for word segmentation in signed languages?	Decide whether nonce sign is actually one or two signs	13 deaf native ASL signers and 13 hearing non-signers	Changes in all parameters increased likelihood to judge two signs instead of one sign. Signers and non-signers relied most heavily on movement and place of articulation parameters to make segmentation judgments. Signers were more sensitive to handshape than non-signers.

Study	Research question	Method	Participants	Findings
Carreiras, Gutiérrez-Sigut, Baquero, and Corina (2008)	Do the properties of lexical familiarity and phonological neighborhood influence lexical access in sign language?	Primed lexical decision	Exp 1 and Exp 2: 15 deaf native Spanish Sign Language (LSE) signers (16 for Exp 2) and 30 deaf non-native LSE signers
Exp 3 (a and b): 13 deaf native LSE signers	Lexical familiarity and phonological neighborhood impact the speed and accuracy of lexical access in both native and non-native signers.
Clark and Grosjean (1982)	What is the role of context on lexical sign recognition?	Gating paradigm and confidence ratings	10 deaf native and non-native ASL signers	Context significantly affects sign recognition with the amount of a sign required for recognition reduced in context. Context also increased participants' confidence in their responses. Two-stage process of parameter narrowing was supported: orientation, location, and handshape parameters were isolated first, followed by movement.
Dye and Shih (2006)	What elements of language input are used for mapping incoming language data onto a sign language lexicon?	Primed lexical decision	12 deaf native BSL signers and 12 deaf non-native BSL signers	Both native and non-native signers used phonological information to access their mental lexicon; however, the native signers were faster and used different parameters (location plus movement) than the non-native signers.

(*Continued*)

Table 13.2 (Continued)

Author(s)	Research question(s)	Task(s)	Participants	Findings
Emmorey and Corina (1990)	What is the time course of sign recognition for monomorphemic and morphologically complex signs?	Gating paradigm and confidence ratings	Exp 1 and 2: 8 deaf native ASL signers and 8 deaf non-native ASL signers	Sign identification was much faster than previously found for spoken languages. Morphologically complex signs had longer identification times than matched monomorphemic signs. Handshape and location parameters were identified first. Identification of a sign's movement then led to lexical recognition.
Fischer, Delhorne, and Reed (1999)	What is the effect of production rate on sign and sentence identification?	Sign and sentence repetition tasks	14 deaf native ASL signers	A breakdown in identification accuracy occurred when stimuli were presented at 2.5–3 times the normal rate of production. Better performance was achieved on isolated signs than on sentences. The pattern of errors shifted from semantic to formational errors under faster rates.
Grosjean (1981)	Which aspects of lexical access are comparable in speech and sign and which are specific to each of the two language modalities?	Gating paradigm	5 deaf native ASL signers	The recognition of a lexical item involved two distinct states in both signed and spoken modalities: the isolation of the item from the other candidates, and the acceptance or recognition of the lexical item.

Source	Research question	Method	Participants	Findings
Hanson and Feldman (1989)	Are the lexicons of ASL and English organized in the same way in deaf ASL–English bilinguals, or in accordance to their respective morphological structures?	Exp 1: sign decision task (1 or 2 hands) Exp 2: primed lexical decision of English words	Exp 1: 12 deaf native ASL signers and 7 deaf non-native ASL signers Exp 2: 17 deaf native ASL signers and 2 deaf non-native ASL signers	Exp 1: Deaf ASL–English bilinguals responded more quickly to morphologically related prime-target pairs than to morphologically unrelated pairs, indicating that the organization of the ASL lexicon relies on morphological principles. Exp 2: Lexical decision of English prime-target pairs did not reflect morphological characteristics of ASL translation equivalents.
Heiman and Tweney (1981)	How does time compression affect the comprehension and intelligibility of signed narratives and individual signs within those narratives?	Comprehension of 1-min narratives filmed at 12 fps and presented at 24 fps and sign translation	80 deaf native and non-native ASL signers	Comprehension and intelligibility of narratives and individual signs extracted from the narratives was negatively impacted by time compression but not completely disrupted.
Morford and Carlson (2011)	Do non-native signers have difficulty with both sign perception and lexical access?	Handshape and location monitoring task and gating paradigm	Exp 1 and 2: 12 deaf native ASL signers, 12 deaf non-native ASL signers, and 12 hearing non-native ASL signers	Deaf non-native signers differed from native signers more on the lexical access task than on the perceptual processing task. Hearing L2 signers differed from native signers on both tasks, but were more similar to native signers on the lexical access task than non-native signers.

(Continued)

Table 13.2 (Continued)

Author(s)	Research question(s)	Task(s)	Participants	Findings
Orfanidou, Adam, McQueen, and Morgan (2009)	Do all components of a sign contribute equality to its recognition?	Sign-spotting task	29 deaf native BSL signers, 10 deaf childhood BSL signers and 13 deaf adolescent BSL signers	Form-based parameters in sign language models have consequences for online processing; specifically movement, handshape, and location parameters contributed differentially to sign recognition.
Orfanidou, Adam, Morgan, and McQueen (2010)	Do signers avoid creating impossible words when segmenting signs from two-sign sequences?	Sign-spotting task	34 deaf native BSL signers (native = before age 5), 13 deaf childhood BSL signers, and 13 deaf adolescent BSL signers	Signers were faster and made fewer errors when segmenting real signs from possible nonce signs than when segmenting them from impossible nonce signs. No effects of age of acquisition were found.
Reed, Delhorne, Durlach, and Fischer (1995)	How accurate is tactual reception of sign language?	Sign and sentence repetition tasks	10 deaf–blind users of ASL or Pidgin Sign English	Participants were 87% accurate when repeating isolated signs. In sentences, performance ranged from 60% to 85% correct repetition of key signs. The most frequent type of perception error in isolated signs involved location, whereas handshape was most often mistaken during sentence repetition.

Study	Research question	Task	Participants	Findings
Thompson, Vinson, and Vigliocco (2009)	Does a close form–meaning relationship as seen in iconic signs affect language processing? Is there any difference between L1 and L2 signers?	Picture–sign matching	5 deaf native ASL signers, 9 deaf childhood ASL signers, 17 hearing non-native ASL signers, and 17 hearing non-signers	Native ASL signers were faster to respond when a specific property iconically represented in a sign was made salient in a corresponding picture. Second-language learners did not show the same facilitation effect as native signers.
Thompson, Vinson, and Vigliocco (2010)	To what extent does iconicity affect a phonological decision task in which the meaning of the sign is irrelevant?	Phonological decision task	13 deaf native BSL signers, 12 deaf non-native BSL signers, 1 hearing native BSL signer, and 15 hearing non-signers	Iconicity slowed response time for signers but not for non-signers, which indicates that iconicity effects are derived from language experience, are automatic, and are not dependent on tasks requiring access to semantic representations.
Tweney, Heiman, and Hoemann (1977)	Can signs be recognized despite temporal interruptions?	Sign repetition task	Exp 1: 24 deaf native and non-native ASL signers and 24 hearing non-signers Exp 2: 24 deaf native and non-native signers	Temporal interruptions impacted the intelligibility of signs, but less than the interruptions impacted speech for the temporal durations and frequencies tested. Intelligibility improved for semantically or grammatically related lists of words.

Table 13.3 Summary of publications investigating signed language grammatical processing

Author(s)	Research question(s)	Task(s)	Participants	Findings
Boudreault and Mayberry (2006)	What is the effect of late exposure to a primary language on adult grammatical processing?	Grammaticality judgment task	10 deaf native ASL signers, 10 deaf childhood ASL signers, and 10 deaf adolescent ASL signers	Error rates increased and sensitivity to grammaticality decreased with age of acquisition for six different grammatical structures. Adolescent L1 learners exhibited sensitivity scores close to chance for some syntactic structures.
Emmorey (1991)	Is morphological priming a modality-independent process? Does early language experience influence morphological priming in ASL?	Primed lexical decision	Exp 1: 14 deaf native ASL signers and 12 deaf non-native ASL signers Exp 2: 16 deaf native ASL signers and 12 deaf non-native ASL signers	Stronger facilitation was found with aspect morphology than with agreement morphology. Repetition priming was not observed for non-signs. Both native and late signers showed weak priming with agreement morphology, but only native signers showed evidence of morphological priming with aspect morphology.
Emmorey (1997)	Is the lack of suppression of non-antecedents during the production of signed pronouns due to morphological ambiguity in the spatial reference of the pronoun?	Probe recognition task	Exp 1: 18 deaf native ASL signers and 6 deaf non-native ASL signers Exp 2: 11 deaf native ASL signers and 7 deaf non-native signers	In a probe recognition task, neither repeated nouns nor pronouns suppressed the activation of non-antecedents. In a "before anaphor" baseline condition, both pronouns and repeated nouns suppressed the activation of non-antecedents.

Study	Research question	Task	Participants	Findings
Emmorey, Bellugi, Friederici, and Horn (1995)	What is the effect of late exposure to a primary language on adult grammatical processing?	Sign monitoring task and grammaticality judgment task	Exp 1: 11 deaf native ASL signers and 10 deaf non-native ASL signers Exp 2: 10 deaf native ASL signers and 10 deaf non-native ASL signers	Native signers, but not non-native signers, were slower to detect target signs that followed errors in verb agreement. Both native and non-native signers were slower to detect target signs that followed errors in aspect morphology. In off-line grammaticality judgment, all groups were able to detect the grammatical errors.
Emmorey, Corina, and Bellugi (1995)	What are the neural underpinnings of topographic and referential spatial functions in sign language? What is the online processing of these different uses of space? How are they encoded in memory?	Exp 1: story retell Exp 2: probe recognition task Exp 3: continuous recognition memory task	Exp 1: 1 hearing ASL signer with a mesial superior occipital–parietal lesion Exp 2: 12 deaf native ASL signers and 12 deaf non-native ASL signers Exp 3: 13 deaf native ASL signers	Signs can be located in space for referential or topographic functions. Changes in the spatial locus of such signs disrupt signers' recognition and recall more when space is functioning topographically than when space is functioning referentially.
Emmorey and Lillo-Martin (1995)	Do overt and null pronouns similarly reactivate their referents during online sentence comprehension?	Probe recognition task	Exp 1: 18 deaf native ASL signers and 12 deaf non-native ASL signers Exp 2: 8 deaf native ASL signers and 10 deaf non-native ASL signers	Participants responded faster to probe signs that were referents of either an overt pronoun or a null pronoun than to control probes that had no prior referent.

(Continued)

Table 13.3 (Continued)

Author(s)	Research question(s)	Task(s)	Participants	Findings
Emmorey, Norman, and O'Grady (1991)	How are pronominal references processed in signed language? Does the pronoun also activate a representation of the spatial locus associated with the referent?	Probe recognition task	Exp 1: 16 deaf native ASL signers and 16 deaf non-native ASL signers Exp 2: 12 deaf native ASL signers and 12 deaf non-native ASL signers	Pronoun activation was not immediate, and no strong evidence for the inhibition of non-referents was found. There was no interference effect when a pronoun was present by comparison to a neutral sentence condition.
Emmorey, Thompson, and Colvin (2008)	Where do deaf native signers and hearing beginning signers look while comprehending a short narrative and spatial description?	Narrative comprehension task and eye tracking	9 deaf native ASL signers and 10 hearing novice signers	Both groups fixated primarily on the signer's face but differed with respect to fixation location. Beginning signers fixated on or near the signer's mouth, whereas native signers fixated on or near the signer's eyes.
Mayberry (1993)	Is the outcome of delayed first language acquisition comparable to second language acquisition?	Sentence recall	9 deaf native ASL signers, 9 deaf childhood ASL signers, 9 deaf adolescent ASL signers, and 9 late deafened L2 ASL signers	Native signers had better recall of lexical stems than late learners and L2 learners, but L2 learners' recall errors were more similar to native signers' than late learners' errors, preserving semantics of the stimulus sentences. Adolescent learners' errors were typically phonologically related to target signs but semantically unrelated. Adolescent learners' responses were grammatically less acceptable than the other groups' responses.

Study	Research question	Method	Participants	Results
Mayberry and Eichen (1991)	What is the effect of late exposure to a primary language on adult grammatical processing?	Sentence recall	16 deaf native ASL signers, 20 deaf childhood ASL signers, and 13 deaf adolescent ASL signers	Native signers recalled more signs and produced more grammatically intact responses than non-native signers. Native signers' errors consisted primarily of semantically appropriate lexical substitutions, while the non-native signers' errors consisted primarily of phonologically similar signs to the target signs.
Mayberry and Fischer (1989)	What is the effect of late exposure to a primary language on adult grammatical processing?	Exp 1: ASL narrative shadowing with and without visual noise. Exp 2: ASL shadowing and immediate recall of grammatical and ungrammatical sentences	Exp 1: 8 deaf native ASL signers and 8 deaf adolescent ASL signers. Exp 2: 11 deaf native ASL signers, 11 deaf early childhood ASL signers, 11 deaf late childhood ASL signers, 11 deaf adolescent signers, and 11 deaf adult (age 18) ASL signers	Exp 1: Native signers more accurately shadowed narratives than non-native signers. Native signers' errors consisted primarily of semantically appropriate lexical substitutions, while the non-native signers' errors consisted primarily of phonologically similar signs to the target signs. Exp 2: Native signers more accurately shadowed and recalled sentences than non-native signers. Error types replicated Exp 1.

Table 13.4 Summary of publications investigating signed language production

Author(s)	Research question(s)	Task(s)	Participants	Findings
Klima and Bellugi (1979)	Are signs formed holistically or are they composed of sublexical units similar to those of spoken languages?	Corpus analysis of naturally occurring sign production errors	Not specified	Signers' production errors demonstrated sublexical structure, including substitutions of handshape (65%), location (13%), and movement (11%). This classic study refuted the traditional view that signs are iconic and holistic, concluding instead that signs are composed of sublexical units.
Baus, Gutiérrez-Sigut, Quer, and Carreiras (2008)	Does sign retrieval involve distinct stages of semantic and phonological processing similar to those of spoken languages?	Picture naming interference task	12 deaf native Catalan Sign Language (LSC) signers and 12 deaf non-native LSC signers	Semantic interference effects were independent of phonological interference effects, suggesting that the distinction between semantic and phonological levels in language production holds across modalities. Modality-specific effects in phonological encoding were found.
Boyes-Braem (1999)	What rhythmic elements might distinguish the signing of native and non-native signers?	Elicited narrative and conversational interaction	2 deaf native Swiss German Sign Language (DSGS) signers, 1 deaf childhood DSGS signer, and 3 deaf adolescent DSGS signers	All DSGS signers exhibited temporal balancing to match the final phrase duration to the previous phrase. Only native and early signers also exhibited a side-to-side swaying to mark larger chunks of discourse.

Corina and Knapp (2006)	What is the timing of semantic and phonological form retrieval in sign production?	Picture naming interference task	28 deaf native ASL signers	Semantic distractors inhibited production earlier but not later in the picture naming process. Phonological distractors facilitated production both early and late in the naming process when target-distractor pairs overlapped in movement and location.
Emmorey, Gertsberg, Korpics, and Wright (2009)	How do changes in visual feedback and in register impact the size of signing space during sign language production?	Elicited sign production with restricted visual feedback	9 deaf native or early ASL signers	Signers used a larger sign space in the "shouted" register, but not for restricted visual feedback. Signers used a smaller signing space with tunnel vision but differed only on duration for blind vs. citation signing.
Grossman and Kegl (2006)	Can facial expressions in sign language be quantitatively analyzed?	Elicited sentence production	2 deaf native ASL signers	A novel method for quantifying group differences in facial expressions is presented. The novel method allows for computations over complex, multilevel, and dynamic features of facial expressions while also generating a summary format accessible to individuals unfamiliar with the coding process.

(*Continued*)

Table 13.4 (Continued)

Author(s)	Research question(s)	Task(s)	Participants	Findings
Hohenberger, Happ, and Leuninger (2002)	What is the impact of modality on language production?	Elicited slips of the hand: story production under cognitive stress	10 deaf German Sign Language (DGS) signers	As in spoken languages, the most frequent slips of the hand were phonological anticipation and perseveration errors, followed by semantic substitutions and blends. Errors were more likely to occur within words than within phrases and repairs were much faster in sign than in speech, indicating that modality differences are related to speed of production.
Keating, Edwards, and Mirus (2008)	How does digital technology impact the use of space?	Analysis of corpus of spontaneous videophone conversations	13 deaf and deaf-blind native and non-native ASL signers	Use of videophone technology leads to innovations in the use of signing space and to alterations in sign production and discourse structure, to enhance the visibility and contrast in signs and to adjust signs to generate spatial referencing within the 2-D image on the videophone.

Reference	Research question	Method	Participants	Findings
Kröger, Birkholz, Kannampuzha, Kaufmann, and Mittelberg (2011)	Are movements of the lips, face, and non-dominant hand governed by movements of the dominant hand in sign language?	Analysis of publicly available corpus of signed sentences	Native signers of ASL (number unspecified)	No manual holds were identified in 100 signed sentences for the dominant hand, but 22% of oral actions exhibited holds and 100% of facial actions exhibited holds, demonstrating that the timing of actions is determined by the dominant articulatory system.
Leuninger, Hohenberger, Waleschkowski, Menges, and Happ (2004)	What is the impact of modality on language production?	Elicited slips of the hand: 2-sign repetition/ reversal task	10 deaf DGS signers	Stem exchanges with morpheme stranding can be elicited in signed languages despite the use of non-concatenative morphology.
Newkirk, Klima, Pedersen, and Bellugi (1980)	Are signs formed holistically or are they composed of sublexical units?	Corpus analysis of naturally occurring sign production errors	Not specified	Signers interchanged individual parameters when they produced lexical errors. The most frequent lexical error was handshape substitution, but form-based errors with other parameters also occurred at much lower frequencies, suggesting that signs are composed of sublexical units.

(Continued)

Table 13.4 (Continued)

Author(s)	Research question(s)	Task(s)	Participants	Findings
Provine and Emmorey (2006)	How is laughter coordinated with ASL sign production, given that it does not have the same articulators as speech?	Elicited conversation	24 deaf or late-deafened native ASL signers and 14 deaf or late-deafened early ASL signers	Deaf signers produce laughter at phrase boundaries and during pauses more frequently than during language production, which is similar to the coordination of laughter with speech production.
Thompson, Emmorey, and Gollan (2005)	Do signers experience a tip of the fingers (TOF) state similar to the tip of the tongue (TOT) state for speakers?	Exp 1: Picture naming task Exp 2: Word translation task	Exp 1: 18 deaf native signers Exp 2: 15 deaf non-native signers	Signers experienced a tip of the fingers state in which they access semantic information but only partially retrieve phonological information. Signers were more likely to retrieve a target sign's handshape, location, and orientation than its movement.
Vinson, Thompson, Skinner, Fox, and Vigliocco (2010)	Are manual components and mouthing patterns of signs associated, and, if so, what is the role of language experience in shaping these associations?	Picture naming and word translation	8 deaf native BSL signers and 7 hearing native BSL signers	Both deaf and hearing signers retrieved English mouthing patterns separately from manual signs, which suggests that mouthing patterns are stored separately from signs.

Notes

1 Padden and Humphries (1988) introduced the terminological distinction between lowercase *deaf* to refer to audiological deafness and capitalized *Deaf* to refer to deafness as a sociolinguistic construct. We follow this distinction here.

2 Language processing studies have almost exclusively focused on adults. One notable exception is Virginia Swisher's (1993) work on the perception of signs in the peripheral vision of adolescent signers. One reason for the dearth of research investigating processing in young signers may be that the latter are more variable in their use of language, given that they are still developing competency. For the sake of consistency, we excluded all studies involving children, both experimental and observational, no matter whether acquisition was the stated purpose of the study or not.

3 Only two studies of sign segmentation were identified in our review. These studies are included in Table 13.2 (grouped with studies of lexical access).

4 Deaf non-signers would provide an even better control group, but this population was not included in any of the studies reviewed.

Keywords

comprehension; deaf signers; grammatical processing; hearing signers; language processing; lexical access; perception; psycholinguistics; segmentation; signed language assessment

See Also

Chapter 1; Chapter 2; Chapter 3; Chapter 4; Chapter 11; Chapter 14; Chapter 15; Chapter 16; Chapter 17

Suggested Readings

Field, J. (2004). *Psycholinguistics: The key concepts*. London: Routledge.

Garrod, S. (2006). Psycholinguistic research methods. In K. Brown (Ed.), *Encyclopedia of language and linguistics* (2nd ed., vol. 10). Oxford: Elsevier, pp. 251–257.

Wilcox, S., and Morford, J. P. (2007). Empirical methods in signed language research. In M. Gonzalez-Marquez, I. Mittelberg, S. Coulson, and M. J. Spivey (Eds.), *Methods in cognitive linguistics*. Amsterdam: John Benjamins, pp. 173–202.

References

Adam, M., Iversen, W., Wilkinson, E., and Morford, J. P. (2007). Meaning on the one and on the other hand: Iconicity in native vs. foreign signed languages. In E. Tabakowska, C. Ljungberg, and O. Fischer (Eds.), *Insistent images*. Amsterdam: John Benjamins, pp. 209–225.

Baker, S. A., Idsardi, W. J., Golinkoff, R., and Petitto, L. (2005). The perception of handshapes in American Sign Language. *Memory & Cognition* 33(5), 887–904.

Baus, C., Carreiras, M., and Emmorey, K. (2013). When does iconicity in sign language matter? *Language and Cognitive Processes* 28(3), 261–271.

Baus, C., Gutiérrez-Sigut, E., Quer, J., and Carreiras, M. (2008). Lexical access in Catalan Signed Language (LSC) production. *Cognition* 108, 856–865.

Best, C. T., Mathur, G., Miranda, K. A., and Lillo-Martin, D. (2010). Effects of sign language experience on categorical perception of dynamic ASL pseudosigns. *Attention, Perception & Psychophysics* 72(3), 747–762.

Bochner, J. H., Christie, K., Hauser, P. C., and Searls, J. (2011). When is a difference really different? Learners' discrimination of linguistic contrasts in American Sign Language. *Language Learning* 61(4), 1302–1327.

Bosworth, R. G., and Emmorey, K. (2010). Effects of iconicity and semantic relatedness on lexical access in American Sign Language. *Journal of Experimental Psychology: Learning, Memory, and Cognition* 36(6), 1573–1581.

Boudreault, P., and Mayberry, R. I. (2006). Grammatical processing in American Sign Language: Age of first-language acquisition effects in relation to syntactic structure. *Language and Cognitive Processes* 21(5), 608–635.

Boyes-Braem, P. (1999). Rhythmic temporal patterns in the signing of deaf early and late learners of Swiss German Sign Language. *Language and Speech* 42(2/3), 177–208.

Brentari, D. (2006). Effects of language modality on word segmentation: An experimental study of phonological factors in a sign language. In L. M. Goldstein, D. H. Whalen, and C. T. Best (Eds.), *Papers in laboratory phonology* (vol. 8). Berlin: Mouton de Gruyter, pp. 155–164.

Campbell, R., Martin, P., and White, T. (1992). Forced choice recognition of sign in novice learners of British Sign Language. *Applied Linguistics* 13(2), 185–201.

Campbell, R., Woll, B., Benson, P., and Wallace, S. B. (1999). Categorical perception of face actions: Their role in sign language and in communicative facial displays. *The Quarterly Journal of Experimental Psychology A: Human Experimental Psychology* 52A(1), 67–95.

Carreiras, M., Gutiérrez-Sigut, E., Baquero, S., and Corina, D. (2008). Lexical processing in Spanish Sign Language (LSE). *Journal of Memory and Language* 58, 100–122.

Clark, L. E., and Grosjean, F. (1982). Sign recognition processes in American Sign Language: The effect of context. *Language and Speech* 25(4), 325–340.

Corina, D. P., and Grosvald, M. (2012). Exploring perceptual processing of ASL and human actions: Effects of inversion and repetition priming. *Cognition* 122(3), 330–345.

Corina, D., and Knapp, H. (2006). Lexical retrieval in American Sign Language production. In L. M. Goldstein, D. H. Whalen, and C. T. Best (Eds.), *Papers in laboratory phonology* (vol. 8). Berlin: Mouton de Gruyter, pp. 213–240.

Corina, D., Grosvald, M., and Lachaud, C. (2011). Perceptual invariance or orientation specificity in American Sign Language? Evidence from repetition priming for signs and gestures. *Language and Cognitive Processes* 26(8), 1102–1135.

Cormier, K., Adam, R., Rowley, K., Woll, B., and Atkinson, J. (2012, March). The British Sign Language Sentence Reproduction Test: Exploring age-of-acquisition effects in British deaf adults. Paper presented at the workshop "Experimental studies in sign language research" at the annual meeting of the German Linguistics Society (DGfS), Johann-Wolfgang Universität, Frankfurt, Germany.

Dye, M. W. G., and Shih, S. (2006). Phonological priming in British Sign Language. In L. M. Goldstein, D. H. Whalen, and C. T. Best (Eds.), *Papers in laboratory phonology* (vol. 8). Berlin: Mouton de Grutyer, pp. 241–263.

Emmorey, K. (1991). Repetition priming with aspect and agreement morphology in American Sign Language. *Journal of Psycholinguistic Research* 20, 365–388.

Emmorey, K. (1997). Non-antecedent suppression in American Sign Language. *Language and Cognitive Processes* 12(1), 103–119.

Emmorey, K. (2002). *Language, cognition, and the brain: Insights from sign language research*. Mahwah, NJ: Lawrence Erlbaum.

Emmorey, K., and Corina, D. (1990). Lexical recognition in sign language: Effects of phonetic structure and morphology. *Perceptual and Motor Skills* 71, 1227–1252.

Emmorey, K., and Lillo-Martin, D. (1995). Processing spatial anaphora: Referent reactivation with overt and null pronouns in American Sign Language. *Language and Cognitive Processes* 10(6), 631–653.

Emmorey, K., Corina, D., and Bellugi, U. (1995). Differential processing of topographic and referential functions of space. In K. Emmorey and J. Reilly (Eds.), *Language, gesture, and space*. Hillsdale, NJ: Lawrence Erlbaum, pp. 43–62.

Emmorey, K., McCullough, S., and Brentari, D. (2003). Categorical perception in American Sign Language. *Language and Cognitive Processes* 18(1), 21–45.

Emmorey, K. E., Norman, F., and O'Grady, L. (1991). The activation of spatial antecedents from overt pronouns in American Sign Language. *Language and Cognitive Processes* 6(3), 207–228.

Emmorey, K., Thompson, R., and Colvin, R. (2008). Eye gaze during comprehension of American Sign Language by native and beginning signers. *Journal of Deaf Studies and Deaf Education* 14(2), 237–243.

Emmorey, K., Bellugi, U., Friederici, A., and Horn, P. (1995). Effects of age of acquisition on grammatical sensitivity: Evidence from on-line and off-line tasks. *Applied Psycholinguistics* 16, 1–23.

Emmorey, K., Gertsberg, N., Korpics, F., and Wright, C. E. (2009). The influence of visual feedback and register changes on sign language production: A kinematic study with deaf signers. *Applied Psycholinguistics* 30(1), 187–203.

Fehrmann, G., Huber, W., Jäger, L., Sieprath, H., and Werth, I. (1995a). *Linguistische Konzeption des Aachener Tests zur Basiskompetenz in Deutscher Gebärdensprache (ATG)*. Unpublished manuscript, RWTH-Aachen, Germanistisches Institut und Neurologische Klinik, Projekt DESIRE.

Fehrmann, G., Huber, W., Jäger, L., Sieprath, H., and Werth, I. (1995b). *Aufbau des Aachener Tests zur Basiskompetenz in Deutscher Gebärdensprache (ATG)*. Unpublished manuscript, RWTH-Aachen, Germanistisches Institut und Neurologische Klinik, Projekt DESIRE.

Fischer, S. D., Delhorne, L. A., and Reed, C. M. (1999). Effects of rate of presentation on the reception of American Sign Language. *Journal of Speech, Language and Hearing Research* 42(3), 568–582.

Grosjean, F. (1981). Sign and word recognition: A first comparison. *Sign Language Studies* 32 195–220.

Grossman, R. B., and Kegl, J. (2006). To capture a face: A novel technique for the analysis and quantification of facial expressions in American Sign Language. *Sign Language Studies* 6(3), 273–305.

Grosvald, M., Lachaud, C., and Corina, D. (2012). Handshape monitoring: Evaluation of linguistic and perceptual factors in the processing of American Sign Language. *Language and Cognitive Processes* 27 (1), 117–141.

Hanson, V., and Feldman, L. (1989). Language specificity in lexical organization: Evidence from deaf signers' lexical organization of American Sign Language and English. *Memory & Cognition* 17, 292–301.

Haug, T., and Mann, W. (2008). Developing tests for sign language assessment: A review of common problems and other related issues. *Journal of Deaf Studies and Deaf Education* 13(1), 138–147.

Hauser, P. C., Paludnevičienė, R., Supalla, T., and Bavelier, D. (2008). American Sign Language: Sentence reproduction test. In R. M. de Quadros (Ed.), *Sign languages: Spinning and unraveling the past, present and future*. Petrópolis, Brazil: Editora Arara Azul, pp. 160–172.

Heiman, G. W., and Tweney, R. D. (1981). Intelligibility and comprehension of time compressed sign language narratives. *Journal of Psycholinguistic Research* 10(1), 3–15. doi:10.1007/BF01067358

Hildebrandt, U. C., and Corina, D. P. (2002). Phonological similarity in American Sign Language. *Language and Cognitive Processes* 17(6), 593–612.

Hohenberger, A., Happ, D., and Leuninger, H. (2002). Modality-dependent aspects of sign language production: Evidence from slips of the hands and their repairs in German Sign Language. In R. P. Meier, K. Cormier, and D. Quinto-Pozos (Eds.), *Modality and structure in signed and spoken languages*. New York: Cambridge University Press, pp. 112–142.

Keating, E., Edwards, T., and Mirus, G. (2008). Cybersign and new proximities: Impacts of new communication technologies on space and language. *Journal of Pragmatics* 40(6), 1067–1081.

Klima, E., and Bellugi, U. (1979). *The signs of language*. Cambridge, MA: Harvard University Press.

Kröger, B. J., Birkholz, P., Kannampuzha, J., Kaufmann, E., and Mittelberg, I. (2011). Movements and holds in fluent sentence production of American Sign Language: The action-based approach. *Cognitive Computation* 3(3), 449–465.

Kubus, O., and Rathmann, C. (2012, March). Degrees of difficulty in the L2 acquisition of morphology in German Sign Language. Poster presented at the annual meeting of the German Linguistics Society, Johann-Wolfgang Universität, Frankfurt, Germany.

Lane, H., Boyes-Braem, P., and Bellugi, U. (1976). Preliminaries to a distinctive feature analysis of American Sign Language. *Cognitive Psychology* 8, 263–289.

Leuninger, H., Hohenberger, A., Waleschkowski, E., Menges, E. and Happ, D. (2004). The impact of modality on language production: Evidence from slips of the tongue and hand. In T. Pechman and Ch. Habel (Eds.), *Multidisciplinary approaches to language production*. Berlin: Mouton de Gruyter, pp. 219–277.

Mayberry, R. I. (1993). First-language acquisition after childhood differs from second-language acquisition: The case of American Sign Language. *Journal of Speech and Hearing Research* 36, 1258–1270.

Mayberry, R. I. (2010). Early language acquisition and adult language ability: What sign language reveals about the critical period for language. In M. Marshark and P. Spencer (eds.), *The Oxford handbook of deaf studies, language, and education* (vol. 2). New York: Oxford University Press, pp. 281–291.

Mayberry, R. I., and Eichen, E. (1991). The long-lasting advantage of learning sign language in childhood: Another look at the critical period for language acquisition. *Journal of Memory and Language* 30, 486–512.

Mayberry, R. I., and Fischer, S. D. (1989). Looking through phonological shape to lexical meaning: The bottleneck of non-native sign language processing. *Memory & Cognition* 17(6), 740–754.

Morford, J. P., and Carlson, M. L. (2011). Sign perception and recognition in non-native signers of ASL. *Language Learning & Development* 7(2), 149–168.

Morford, J. P., Grieve-Smith, A. B., MacFarlane, J., Staley, J., and Waters, G. S. (2008). Effects of language experience on the perception of American Sign Language. *Cognition* 109, 41–53.

Neidle, C. (2001). SignStream™: A database tool for research on visual-gestural language. *Sign Language and Linguistics* 4(1/2), 203–214.

Newkirk, D., Klima, E. S., Canady Pedersen, C., and Bellugi, U. (1980). Linguistic evidence from slips of the hand. In V. A. Fromkin (Ed.), *Errors in linguistic performance: Slips of the tongue, ear, pen and hand*. New York: Academic Press, pp. 165–197.

Orfanidou, E., Adam, R., McQueen, J. M., and Morgan, G. (2009). Making sense of nonsense in British Sign Language (BSL): The contribution of different phonological parameters to sign recognition. *Memory & Cognition* 37, 302–315.

Orfanidou, E., Adam, R., Morgan, G., and McQueen, J. M. (2010). Recognition of signed and spoken language: Different sensory inputs, the same segmentation procedure. *Journal of Memory and Language* 62(3), 272–283.

Poizner, H. (1981). Visual and "phonetic" coding of movement: Evidence from American Sign Language. *Science* 212(4495), 691–693.

Poizner, H. (1983). Perception of movement in American Sign Language: Effects of linguistic structure and linguistic experience. *Perception & Psychophysics* 33, 215–231.

Poizner, H., and Lane, H. (1978). Discrimination of location in American Sign Language. In P. Siple (Ed.), *Understanding language through sign language research.* New York: Academic Press, pp. 271–288.

Poizner, H., Bellugi, U., and Lutes-Driscoll, V. (1981). Perception of American Sign Language in dynamic point-light displays. *Journal of Experimental Psychology: Human Perception and Performance* 7(2), 430–440.

Provine, R. R., and Emmorey, K. (2006). Laughter among Deaf signers. *Journal of Deaf Studies and Deaf Education* 11(4), 403–409.

Reed, C. M., Delhorne, L. A., Durlach, N. I., and Fischer, S. D. (1995). A study of the tactual reception of sign language. *Journal of Speech & Hearing Research* 38(2), 477–489.

Richards, J. T., and Hanson, V. L. (1985). Visual and production similarity of the handshapes of the American manual alphabet. *Perception & Psychophysics* 38(4), 311–319.

Stungis, J. (1981). Identification and discrimination of handshape in American Sign Language. *Perception & Psychophysics* 29(3), 261–276.

Swisher, M. (1993). Perceptual and cognitive aspects of recognition of signs in peripheral vision. In M. Marschark, and M. Clark (Eds.), *Psychological perspectives on deafness.* Hillsdale, NJ: Lawrence Erlbaum, pp. 209–227.

Tartter, V. C., and Fischer, S. D. (1982). Perceiving minimal distinctions in ASL under normal and point-light display conditions. *Perception & Psychophysics* 32(4), 327–334.

Thompson, R., Emmorey, K., and Gollan, T. H. (2005). "Tip of fingers" experiences by deaf signers: Insights into the organization of a sign-based lexicon. *Psychological Science* 16(11), 856–860.

Thompson, R. L., Vinson, D. P., and Vigliocco, G. (2009). The link between form and meaning in American Sign Language: Lexical processing effects. *Journal of Experimental Psychology: Learning, Memory, and Cognition* 35, 550–557.

Thompson, R. L., Vinson, D. P., and Vigliocco, G. (2010). The link between form and meaning in British Sign Language: Effects of iconicity for phonological decisions. *Journal of Experimental Psychology: Learning, Memory, and Cognition* 36, 1017–1027.

Traxler, M. (2013, November). Individual differences in literacy skills among Deaf readers. Invited presentation in the VL2 Presentation Series. Washington, DC: Gallaudet University.

Tweney, R. D., Heiman, G. W., and Hoemann, H. W. (1977). Psychological processing of sign language: Effects of visual disruption on sign intelligibility. *Journal of Experimental Psychology: General* 106(3), 255–268. doi: 10.1037/0096-3445.106.3.255

Vinson, D., Cormier, K., Denmark, T., Schembri, A., and Vigliocco, G. (2008). The British Sign Language (BSL) norms for age of acquisition, familiarity, and iconicity. *Behavior Research Methods* 40(4), 1079–1087.

Vinson, D. P., Thompson, R. L., Skinner, R., Fox, N., and Vigliocco, G. (2010). The hands and mouth do not always slip together in British Sign Language: Dissociating articulatory channels in the lexicon. *Psychological Science* 21(8), 1158–1167.

14 Methods in Bimodal Bilingualism Research: Experimental Studies

*Ronice Müller de Quadros, Deborah
Chen Pichler, Diane Lillo-Martin,
Carina Rebello Cruz, L. Viola Kozak,
Jeffrey Levi Palmer, Aline Lemos Pizzio,
and Wanette Reynolds*

Chapter Overview

This chapter presents experimental methods for investigating the bilingual development of signed and spoken language. We begin with an introduction to a research project for which these methods were developed. Next we describe

Research Methods in Sign Language Studies: A Practical Guide, First Edition.
Edited by Eleni Orfanidou, Bencie Woll, and Gary Morgan.
© 2015 John Wiley & Sons, Inc. Published 2015 by John Wiley & Sons, Inc.

the process of selection, adaptation, or development of parallel test batteries for target languages. These test target children between the ages of 4 to 7 years in the areas of general language, vocabulary, morphosyntax, phonology, and non-verbal intelligence. We describe each test, including information on how the test was developed and how it is administered, as well as suggestions for the set-up of camera(s) during filming. The chapter concludes with a discussion of the advantages of the data collection fair concept (an innovative technique for child data collection designed to improve on traditional piecemeal collection) and with a list of best practices for optimizing test effectiveness.

Introduction

This chapter will present an overview of methods in bilingualism and bimodal bilingualism research, focusing on experimental studies conducted by Lillo-Martin, Chen Pichler, and Quadros between 2009 and 2014 as part of a project called Development of Bimodal Bilingualism. In those studies we focused on the linguistic development of two groups of bilingual children exposed to one sign language and one spoken language: hearing children of Deaf[1] parents (Coda children or "kodas"); and signing Deaf children with a cochlear implant (CI) who have either Deaf or hearing parents. This chapter describes the use of experimental studies to investigate the simultaneous acquisition of sign language and speech by these children.

Important Considerations When Collecting Bimodal Bilingual Data

There are many challenges that must be approached carefully when setting out to collect bimodal bilingual data. Several of these challenges apply to the collection of unimodal bilingual data as well, and have been detailed in various publications regarding bilingual research (e.g. Moyer and Li Wei, 2008; Bhatia and Ritchie, 2004; Grosjean, 2008; Marian, 2008; de Houwer, 2009). In this section we will introduce general challenges related to collecting and evaluating bimodal bilingual data; a more detailed discussion of specific tests will follow in subsequent sections. Although our tests focus on American Sign Language (ASL), Brazilian Sign Language (Libras), and English and Brazilian Portuguese (BP), the practices we describe are applicable to other sign and spoken language combinations as well.

Studying bilinguals requires first and foremost the acceptance that bilingualism is not a static phenomenon. For instance, we have observed that the kodas in our longitudinal studies display very different developmental patterns as they grow out of toddlerhood and enter school, where they are immersed into a spoken language environment. We also noted a continual evolution of the roles played by the children's sign language and spoken language in their lives, and these changes impact children's use of these languages. It is important to identify the language experiences of the child, considering the persons with whom the child interacts during the period when the data are collected. Following Grosjean (2008), this includes gathering information on the child's language history and typical use (for instance, when the child was first exposed to each language, or the language(s) typically used with individuals in his/her everyday life); language stability (current skills in the languages currently being acquired and/or language attrition phenomena); language function (the typical context in which the child uses one language or the other); language proficiency; language mode (the amount of time spent in monolingual and bilingual modes); and general biographical data. In our project, we collect some of this information through a very detailed background form that we fill out together with the parent, in an informal interview format. Although time-consuming, this practice gives us the greatest assurance that parents (many of whom, in the US, are second-language users of ASL and English, having only learned them upon immigrating) understand the questions we are asking and answer them as accurately as possible. Other options include distributing the background form electronically, with an accompanying video that explains each section of the form in sign language. This material can be sent to parents to read/watch ahead of time, which reduces the amount of time needed to fill out paperwork on the day of testing.

Another consideration is that bilingual people must be evaluated in both languages. Marian (2008) points out that it is not always appropriate to use monolingual norms as the baseline for assessing bilingual development. This is especially clear in the case of vocabulary development (for discussion of this point with respect to speech bilinguals, see Pearson, Fernandez, and Ollder, 1993). A monolingual child with 20 words compared with a bilingual child with 10 words in each language should be considered as equivalent, although the bilingual has fewer words in the common language than her monolingual counterpart. Looking at only one language usually puts the bilingual child at a disadvantage, and this can lead to an inaccurate evaluation of his/her linguistic development.

Some researchers advocate for children's being tested by monolinguals for each of their languages (Grosjean, 2006; Cantone, 2007). In our specific case, since we are interested in bimodal bilingual production, to study how and when transfer and blending take place, we also encourage bimodal bilinguals to interact with the children. Our tests clearly target either the spoken language or the signed language, and they are administered by hearing or by Deaf/Coda researchers, respectively; but almost all of our experimenters are bilingual to varying extents. Thus the children are usually in bilingual mode (in the sense discussed by Grosjean, 2006, 2008). This favors normal access to both languages, even though there is a specific language target for each test.

Our discussion so far underlines a general but very important point raised by Grosjean with respect to bilingual status: we must remember that a bilingual person is not the equivalent of two monolinguals in one person. Having two languages in a single brain invariably leads to interaction, potentially of a kind not observed in monolinguals, so it follows that "bilinguals will not give exactly the same kinds of results as monolinguals" (Grosjean, 2008, p. 246). In our research we are seeing that this general rule also applies to bimodal bilinguals, whose patterns are similar to those of monolinguals in some areas, similar to those of unimodal bilinguals in other areas, and unique to them in yet other areas, with productions specific to bimodals, such as code-blending (Emmorey, Borinstein, Thompson, and Gollan, 2008).

The development of stimuli for bilingual projects is another area that deserves much careful consideration. Grosjean raises three potential issues related to stimuli: "differences in the stimuli used across studies, differences in stimuli used within studies, and factors that need to be controlled for in stimulus selection" (Grosjean, 2008, p. 259). In developing tests for a bimodal bilingual population, consideration must be given to how to compare children's development of phonotactic constraints and language-specific phonetics, since signed and spoken languages employ different articulators. It is crucial to take great care to ensure that the stimuli used would be as comparable as possible, despite differences in modality – as will be detailed in the following section.

Finally, it is very important to provide adequate training for experimenters (de Houwer, 2009). It is relevant to pay special attention to the sociolinguistic contexts of each setting for the experimental studies, especially with respect to each language. This is one of the reasons for prioritizing the presence of Deaf/Coda and hearing experimenters in our study, depending on the target language for each test.

Data Collection Fairs

The traditional model of experimental data collection involves testing children during the school day. To minimize disruption to the children's instructional time, data collection is typically spread over a prolonged period of weeks or months. Such an arrangement is acceptable if all the children to be tested attend the same school or live in the same general area. However, bimodal bilingual children are relatively difficult to find and are normally scattered across a broad geographical area, which requires extensive travel time for multiple visits to each child. We thus devised a new model for data collection: weekend "data collection fairs" held once or twice a year at various central locations with a particularly high density of children who meet our inclusion criteria.

Each fair targets either a sign language or a spoken language and consists of 5–8 hours of testing, interspersed with games, food, and free play with other signing children. At the start of each fair, we give the children "game cards" that list the tests they are scheduled to take on that day. Each test is represented on the card with an animal that matches an animal on one of the doors of the different testing rooms. The children's objective is to complete their game card by the end of the day – a task they take to with considerable enthusiasm.

The main advantage of the fair model is that it allows the collection of a large amount of data all at once, in conditions that are as consistent as possible across children and across tests. Because all the tests are administered on the same day, they offer us a useful snapshot of each child's total linguistic development at a single point in time, something that we could not achieve if data collection were drawn out over an extended period of time. Despite the long hours of testing, the children enjoy the fairs immensely. Another advantage is the chance to interact and exchange information with a large group of Deaf parents of bimodal bilingual children – for example, by including an informational program for parents to share project updates, answer questions, and discuss issues related to raising bimodal bilingual children. This interaction is very important, as families are critical long-term partners in such a research program.

General Principles of Test Development

Tests for a bimodal bilingual population need to target common areas of linguistic ability in both sign and spoken languages. Tests should give a good overview of the children's languages, and also go into some detail in areas of morphosyntax that are of particular interest for sign languages. Tests need to be as comparable as possible across target languages, especially in studies where different sign languages are compared. In cases where comparable tests are not available across the languages being studied, the focus should be on developing tests that are comparable within a single modality (e.g. across Libras and ASL, or across BP and English). In our study, when a test was available in one of the two sign languages only, we adapted a parallel version for the other sign language. For spoken languages, where standardized tests are more common, published, normed tests should be used whenever possible, adaptations should be developed as necessary, or completely new tests should be designed. Existing tests that have already been used with bimodal bilingual children, especially with CI children, should also be considered, so that results may be compared with those reported in the literature; for example our choice of the pseudo-word test developed by Dillon, Cleary, Pisoni, and Carter (2004) to study speech development in children with cochlear implants falls in this category.

Test adaptation begins with translation but also involves important language-specific modifications, which require careful work. For example, English morphology tests include the singular–plural distinction but no gender distinctions, whereas gender distinctions are included in Brazilian Portuguese tests. Similarly, in adapting the standardized Expressive Vocabulary test (EVT) of English vocabulary, we replaced several items that were culturally inappropriate or lacked a clear lexical equivalent in the target languages of BP, Libras, and ASL.

Also, some flexibility is needed where there is substantial regional linguistic variation. It is important to consult with local adults, especially the parents of the participant children, to ensure awareness of any local variants of the signs or words used.

The adaptation of tests involving different languages and cultures is a complex task, and the task is even more challenging when the target languages are in different modalities, as mentioned earlier. This challenge is most notable in sign language adaptations of phonological awareness tests, because signed and spoken languages have very different sublexical units: there are sign parameters (handshapes, locations and movements) in sign languages versus phonemes in spoken languages. Even if we assume that spoken and sign languages share aspects of internal, abstract phonological organization, phonological awareness tests designed for spoken languages generally focus on the sequence of phonetic segments, and this leads to an experimental methodology that is not clearly appropriate for sign language. For instance, the experimenter typically produces a word, then asks the child to take out, insert, or substitute a phoneme or a syllable in different parts of the word. In sign languages, the handshape(s), location(s), and movement(s) that compose a sign primarily occur simultaneously (although many signs are organized sequentially as well, for example when there is a change from one handshape to another). This difference between spoken and signed languages makes phonological awareness evaluation very complex (see also Cruz and Lamprecht, 2011). Considering this fact, we have adopted strategies such as the use of pictures associated with parts of the handshapes.

After running the tests, we evaluated the test administration process and contrasted the results with those of various comparison groups: Coda adults, Deaf children of either Deaf or hearing parents but with very early exposure to sign language (as controls for sign language tests only), and hearing children (as controls for spoken language tests only).

The Test Battery in the Bibibi Project

The goals of the project Development of Bimodal Bilingualism, also known as the Binational Bimodal Bilingual (Bibibi) project, are to understand the nature of conditions for cross-language influence, the mechanisms by which two separate grammars interact, and the feasibility of accounting for bilingual phenomena without appealing to any special machinery. Readers interested in details of our theoretical motivations and findings that are not discussed here are referred to earlier publications (Lillo-Martin, Quadros, Koulidobrova, and Chen Pichler, 2010; Lillo-Martin, Koulidobrova, Quadros, and Chen Pichler, 2012; Quadros, Lillo-Martin, and Chen Pichler, 2010; Quadros, Lillo-Martin, and Chen Pichler, 2013; Quadros, Lillo-Martin, and Chen Pichler, forthcoming; Quadros and Karnopp, 2004). Our test battery is organized across four different linguistic areas, for both spoken and sign language. As previously mentioned, we test each language individually, at separate fairs. We summarize the tests below according to the area of language examined[2]:

general language tests:

- the Kendall Conversational Proficiency test;
- the Preschool Language Scales test;
- the Sign Language Receptive Skills test;
- narrative samples;

vocabulary tests:

- the Expressive Vocabulary test (EVT);

morphosyntax tests:

- verbal morphology;
- modifier noun order;
- wh-questions;

phonology tests:

- picture-naming;
- phonological discrimination (minimal pairs);

- phonological awareness;
- non-word repetition (pseudo-signs and pseudo-words);

additional tests:

- Leiter Non-verbal IQ (selected subtests);
- parent–child interaction sample.

All tests targeting BP and English are administered by hearing experimenters, while tests targeting Libras and ASL are administered by experimenters who are either Deaf or native hearing signers (Codas). Tests are recorded on video for subsequent coding and analysis. Some tests, particularly those targeting sign language, require specific camera angles to capture all the information necessary for coding; in our descriptions of individual tests below, we include several photos to illustrate these optimal camera angles.

General Language Tests

The Kendall Conversational Proficiency test (French, 1999)

This is a general communicative development instrument. It consists of a written checklist that defines levels of communicative competency with respect to various communicative features that may or may not be present in the child's language use. The checklist is completed by an evaluator who is a proficient signer and is also familiar with the child's current language use – typically, with the child's parents or teachers. It was developed in the US by French (1999) and adapted for use in Brazil (administered in written BP) for the purposes of this research. The advantage of this tool is that it gives a global sense of the child's communicative abilities in both sign and speech, which serves as context for interpreting children's scores on tests that target specific linguistic abilities.

The Preschool Language Scales (PLS4) test for English (Zimmerman, Steiner, and Pond, 2002) and BP

This test measures both comprehension and expression for a variety of language structures. Tasks vary according to the age of the subject at the time of testing, as subjects pass from one level to the next if they achieve a minimal score. An experimenter both administers this test and records the child's responses on a special answer sheet. A BP adaptation of the test was developed for the purposes of this project.

We selected this test because it has previously been used for children with cochlear implants, and it was also recommended by speech language therapists who work with kodas. The example below, from the BP version of the test, is designed to elicit specific verbal morphology.

67. *Usar formas verbais irregulares* [use of irregular verbal forms]
PRÁTICA: *Vamos brincar de completer a frase seguindo a primeira frase apresentada*
[Let's play! I will present a phrase, and then you complete it.]
A primeira palavra é "fazer", eu começo a frase e você continua.
[The first word is "to make." I will start a phrase and you continue it.]
Por exemplo, "Joana fez um bolo. A Maria ... (fez um bolo)".
[For example, "Joana made a cake. Mary .... (made a cake)".]
a. *Eu faço biscoitos. A Maria ...* [I make cookies. Mary ...]
b. *Eu fiz um desenho. Matias ...* [I made a drawing. Matias ...]

The disadvantage of the PLS is that it is a fairly long test, which may be difficult to administer to young children. However, its major advantage is the availability of standardized norms for monolingual English-speaking children. Additionally, the test items cover a number of grammatical domains, allowing the researcher to examine the child's performance in these areas.

The Sign Language Receptive Skills test (Herman, Holmes, and Woll, 1999; Enns and Zimmer, 2009; Enns and Herman, 2011)

This test is based on the British Sign Language (BSL) Receptive Skills test (Herman et al., 1999). It was developed to monitor the sign language development of deaf children enrolled in bilingual programs. This tool offers a standardized measurement of sign language skills and represents a significant departure from sign language checklists and non-standardized experiments. The BSL version was carefully adapted for ASL by Enns and colleagues (Enns and Zimmer, 2009; Enns and Herman, 2011), who took into consideration linguistic differences between the two sign languages. Currently adaptations also exist for German Sign Language (Haug, 2011) and for Italian Sign Language (Surian and Tedoldi, 2005); there is also a pilot version for Australian Sign Language (Johnston, 2004). The ASL version is currently available on DVD, having been developed by Northern Signs Research as the Assessing ASL Development Receptive Skills test (see Enns and Zimmer, 2009; Enns and Herman, 2011). For our project, we made a further adaptation for Libras.[3] All versions contain 45 items and test number and distribution, negation, noun–verb distinctions, spatial verbs, size and shape classifiers, handling classifiers, role shift, and conditionals. For each item the child watches a signed sentence, then chooses one of four pictures that best corresponds to what was signed (an example is shown in Figure 14.1).

The Receptive Skills test is easy and straightforward to administer. In agreement with the pilot test results reported by Enns and Herman (2011), we found a high degree of variability in test scores among our participants.

Narrative samples

Co-constructed narrative samples between the child and either a parent or a researcher are elicited by using various wordless picture books (including *Good Dog, Carl* by Alexandra Day and *Tuesday* by David Wiesner). The same general

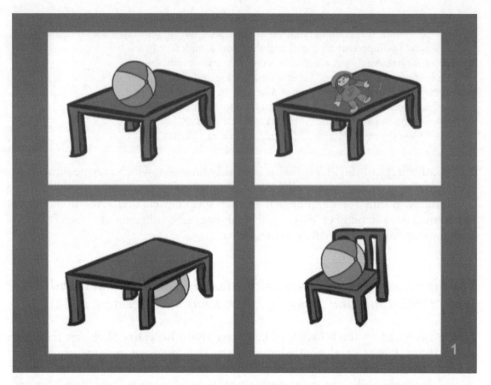

Figure 14.1 Card showing answer choices for the Sign Language Receptive Skills test.

approach is used for all four target languages during different sessions. One experimenter talks/signs with the child in the target language and reviews the book with the child. Then a second experimenter enters the room and interacts with the child, inviting him/her to retell (or at least comment on) the stories (s)he saw in the stimuli. The children interact with Deaf experimenters for the sign narratives and with hearing experimenters for the spoken language narratives. In a third and separate session, short film clips from wordless videos (including the *Minuscule* and the *Shaun the Sheep* series) are used in order to prompt short narratives in both languages during the same session. Narratives are filmed with the camera angled, so as to include both the child and the interlocutor's signing; the latter provides important additional context for analyzing the child's production (see Figure 14.2).

Precautions are necessary to ensure that comparable narratives are collected in both of the children's languages. For instance, to prevent effects of presentation order and practice, we provide multiple video stimuli and vary the order of the target language across children (Pavlenko, 2008). Our video elicitation task thus comprises four short video clips; the first two clips are elicited in the signed language first, then in the spoken language, while the second set of clips is presented in the reverse order. Furthermore, in order to encourage narratives that would be as comprehensive as possible, we wanted to emphasize to children that their interlocutors had not seen the stimulus pictures/videos. Thus we asked the

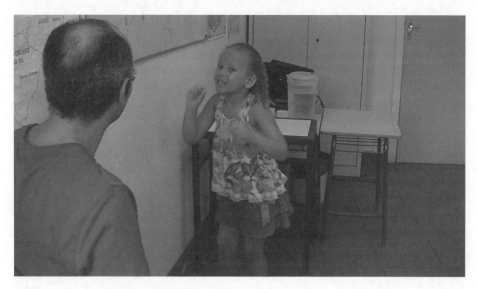

Figure 14.2 Camera angle for narrative task.

first experimenter to leave the room at the moment when the second (naïve) experimenter entered.

We score the narrative samples using the Index of Productive Syntax (IPSyn; Scarborough, 1990), which was developed for English and adapted by us for ASL, Libras, and BP. Analysis of narrative structure was conducted on the Brazilian data by Neves (2013). Naturally, other types of analyses can also be applied, as narrative data are an extremely rich resource for investigating the development of a broad range of syntactic and discourse structures.

Vocabulary Tests

The Expressive Vocabulary test (EVT) (Williams, 1997)

In this test vocabulary is elicited with the help of a set of pictures organized at different levels of difficulty, according to age. An experimenter shows the pictures to the child and asks him/her to produce the appropriate spoken or signed label. During administration of the EVT the camcorder should face the child and should include the elicitation picture, as shown below in Figure 14.3, so that coders may know which item is being tested.

We chose the EVT rather than a vocabulary comprehension test, reasoning that an expressive test would allow us to use essentially the same stimuli across all four target languages. This is a considerable advantage for research groups conducting cross-linguistic comparisons. On the other hand, the researchers must establish a list of acceptable responses for each item, and for this reason ensuring comparable scoring across languages can be challenging.

Figure 14.3 Camera angle for EVT.

Morphosyntax Tests

ASL and Libras verbal morphology

We designed this test of comprehension of ASL or Libras verbal morphology employing the truth-value judgment task methodology (Crain and McKee, 1986; Crain and Thornton, 1998). We have used this methodology in previous studies of both signed and spoken language, and we have modified it slightly from the original versions to make it more suitable for administration in ASL or Libras. Children watch a series of short video vignettes in which a cat, a pig, and a duck perform various actions to each other. After each vignette, the cat appears and signs a sentence summarizing what he thinks occurred in the vignette. The child must judge whether the verb agreement marking produced by the cat corresponds to the action presented in the preceding vignette.

The original version of this test included 32 items, but experimenters have reported that this number was too large for most children, who lost interest halfway through. As a result, the test has been shortened to roughly half of the original items.

English and BP verbal morphology

This test elicits production of verbal agreement – specifically, third-person agreement. For each item, the child sees a set of four pictures, one of which is highlighted by a bright red border. The child must describe the highlighted action to an experimenter, who then tries to pick out the same picture from a matching set of pictures in which the target picture is not highlighted. For each test item, the four pictures vary according to how many characters are depicted (one or two) and which of two actions is depicted (action A or action B).

The advantages of this test are that it is quite easy to administer and elicits common agreement forms for each target language. However, for researchers conducting an in-depth study of specific verbal forms, a more extensive study would be required.

Modifier noun order

We designed this elicitation test for English, BP, ASL, and Libras. It evaluates whether the child can produce sentences matching a situation shown in pictures, with an emphasis on the order of placement of adjective and noun within a subject or object noun phrase. An experimenter delivers instructions in sign or speech, depending on the test. The child and another experimenter each look at duplicate pairs of pictures, which are identical except for the fact that, in the child's pair, one of the pictures is highlighted (see Figure 14.4). The child must describe (in either sign or speech, depending on the target language) the highlighted picture to the experimenter, who in turn tries to determine which picture of the pair the child is describing. All the items in this test target adjective/noun word order. The target sentence in English for the highlighted picture in the sample below would be: "A fat cat and a fat dog are eating." The test is filmed capturing the child only, as shown in Figure 14.5; there is no need to film the experimenter in this test.

Because we use the same stimuli across all four languages for this test, each child sees the full set of pictures twice. However, the specific pictures that they are required to describe in the first testing differ from those in the second: on each card, the picture highlighted for the spoken language version of the test is the opposite of the one highlighted for the sign language version of the test. Additionally, since Libras and English are more restrictive than BP and ASL in terms of modifier–noun word order, we test children in the less restrictive language first, then in the more restrictive language after a month (or even later). This practice serves as a precaution against the possibility that test items in the first test would bias the children's word order choices in the second test.

Figure 14.4 Sample prompt from word order test.

Figure 14.5 Camera angle for word order test.

Wh-questions

We designed this production test targeting various types of wh-questions (see Lillo-Martin, 2000). It is administered by two experimenters: one story-teller and one "cat." The storyteller explains to the child that the cat is very knowledgeable about many things, but unfortunately very shy and afraid of interacting directly with adults. For this reason, the child is needed to ask questions on behalf of the storyteller and to relay the cat's answers back to her. The storyteller then uses toy props to tell a series of short stories, ending each one with a prompt for the child to ask the cat about some aspect of the story. An example is given below.
   (Props: Woody, Buzz, Lotso, dog, cat)

STORYTELLER	Woody has a pet dog (Spot) and a pet cat (Fluffy). He's going on a trip and wants someone to help him out. Someone will have to feed Fluffy.
	Ask the cat who.
TARGET RESPONSE	Who will feed Fluffy?

The wh-test is filmed at an angle that captures the child head-on and both experimenters obliquely, as illustrated in Figure 14.6.
   As is the case with the modifier noun order test, we use the same wh-test stimuli for the signed and the spoken languages. Thus we apply the precautions discussed above: we test children in the language with the less restrictive word order (in the case of wh-questions, these are Libras and ASL) before testing in those with the more restrictive word order, with sufficient time elapsed in between.

Figure 14.6 Camera angle for the wh-test.

Phonology Tests

BP picture naming (Andrade, Befi-Lopes, Fernandes, and Wertzner, 2004)

This is a phonological test for BP that includes a selection of the whole spectrum of phonological forms that are targeted in the analysis. The experimenter elicits words on the basis of 34 pictures, to determine the phonetic inventory of the child and to verify the occurrences of phonological processes that involve the types of syllabic structure used by the child and their distribution. An experimenter presents the child with pictures and asks him/her to name each one. If the child does not know a picture's name, the experimenter names it and continues through the next five items before returning to the unnamed picture and prompting the child again to name it. This test is simple and quick to administer.

English picture-naming (Goldman and Fristoe, 2000)

This is a very common, standardized test of English articulation that has been used in previous studies examining children with CIs. It is valid for individuals between the ages of 2 and 21 years. The experimenter shows children a series of pictures for which the child must provide English labels designed to cover a wide range of English phonemes. When scoring the Goldman–Fristoe test, it is recommended that researchers also use the Khan–Lewis Phonological Analysis (Pearson) for more comprehensive error analysis.

Figure 14.7 Camera angle for sign picture-naming test.

Libras and ASL picture-naming (Cruz, 2008)

These tests follow the same methodology as the BP picture-naming test described earlier. The ASL version was adapted from Cruz's original Libras test for the purposes of the Bibibi project. This test evaluates articulation of signs with various handshapes, locations, movements, and orientations. An experimenter presents a picture to the child and asks him/her to produce the corresponding sign. This test always precedes the tests of phonological awareness and phonological perception, since it introduces the items used in those tests, ensuring that the child knows the corresponding signs. If a child does not know the sign for a given picture, we follow the same technique as in the spoken BP test: the experimenter provides the sign, continues through the next five items, then returns to the picture that the child was unable to name and prompts him/her to try again. If the child still has problems, the experimenter will teach the child the sign, so that (s)he knows it for the phonological awareness test.

This test is filmed at an angle that captures the child head-on, as shown in Figure 14.7. In order to film each picture as it is being tested, the experimenter should turn each picture card toward the camera before presenting it to the child. There is a total of approximately 40 test items in the picture-naming test, but children in our target age range were able to name them easily and progressed fairly quickly through this task.

Phonological discrimination/minimal pairs (Pronovost and Dumbleton, 1953 for English; Carvalho, 2007 for BP)

This test uses minimal pairs to evaluate the child's perception of minimal phonological differences in English or BP. The experimenter produces a pair of words consisting of either the same word, repeated twice, or two words that differ by only a single

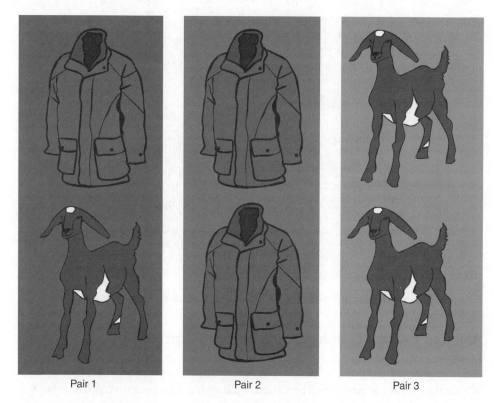

| Pair 1 | Pair 2 | Pair 3 |

Figure 14.8 Sample prompt for English phonological discrimination.

phoneme (i.e., a minimal pair). The child must select from three possible picture pairs the correct pair that matches the words produced by the experimenter. For instance, if the experimenter says "coat" and "goat" (a minimal pair in English), the child should pick Pair 1 from the three pairs illustrated in Figure 14.8. If the experimenter says "goat" and "goat," the child should pick Pair 3.

Our phonological discrimination tests include 40 items that are generally quite straightforward to administer and easy for the children to answer.

ASL and Libras phonological discrimination/minimal pairs

For ASL and Libras, we designed tests parallel to the English and BP phonological discrimination tests described above. For each sign language, we collected minimal pairs that can be identified through picture pairs. The signs are presented by a Deaf signer on video (see Figure 14.9 for setup and camera angle). These minimal pairs differ in handshape only, in location only, in movement only, or in orientation only. The child watches a video in which an adult signer produces either the same sign twice or two signs that constitute a minimal pair. Then the child is instructed to pick from three pairs of pictures the one that matches the signs just produced. As for the English and BP phonological discrimination tests, the sign versions are simple to administer and produce dependable results.

Figure 14.9 Camera angle for phonological discrimination/minimal pairs test.

ASL and Libras phonological awareness (Cruz and Lamprecht, 2008)

We use the Libras test developed by Cruz and Lamprecht and our own ASL adaptation to evaluate children's awareness of the handshape parameter; a similar test is currently under development for ASL (McQuarrie, 2012) as part of the VL2 sign assessment toolkit (cited below). The test is organized into sections on the basis of research on sign well-formedness (Quadros and Karnopp, 2004), sign language phonology, and sign language acquisition by Deaf children (Karnopp, 1999; Quadros, 1997). For each test item, the child sees one target picture plus three additional pictures below it. From these three pictures below the target, the child must pick the one whose sign matches the target in handshape. The three options include at least one foil, that is, an item whose sign has either the same location or the same movement as the target sign. The pictures selected are related to familiar contexts for children (family, toys, colors, animals, foods, etc.). For example given in Figures 14.10 and 14.11, the child sees a target picture of a snake and must think of the sign for SERPENTE (*snake*) in Libras (children are permitted to sign to themselves as a memory aid), then considers each of the three lower pictures, picking the one whose sign uses the same handshape (in this example, the "bent V" handshape). The correct answer in this case is CINCO (*five*). (Note that the child does not see a video of any signs, only pictures of each item. The signs are shown here solely for the purpose of illustrating these Libras signs for the reader.)

Although the child is not shown video for any of the signs represented by the pictures, all the signs that appear in this awareness test will have been previously elicited from the child in the earlier production test (see the description above for the Libras and ASL picture-naming test), ensuring that (s)he is familiar with all the relevant signs and can correctly associate them with the picture prompts.

For both phonological discrimination and awareness tests in Libras and ASL, the child selects answers by pointing to a computer screen, so the camera must be angled

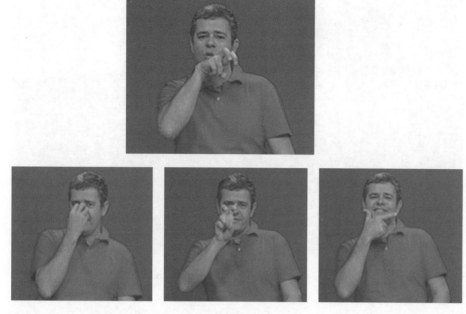

Figure 14.10 Libras signs for SERPENTE (*snake*), PALHAÇO (*clown*), CINCO (*five*), and SORRIR (*smile*).

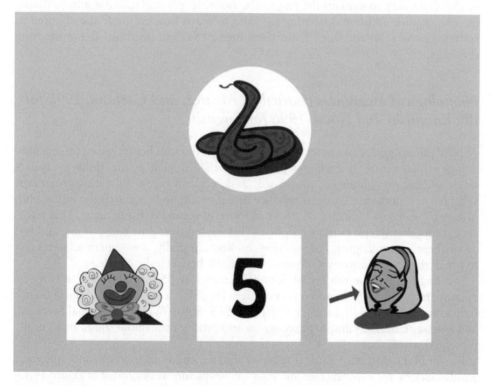

Figure 14.11 Sample prompt from Libras phonological awareness test.

Figure 14.12 Camera angle for sign phonological awareness test.

so as to capture clearly the direction of the child's pointing, as illustrated in Figure 14.12. It is also important to include the experimenter, who can reconfirm children's selections, if these are not clearly articulated.

The ability of children to complete this test is especially dependent on the ability of experimenters to explain the test instructions. In particular, those administering the test require additional training in order to learn how to guide the children in retrieving the relevant signs from their mental lexicon without demonstrating the signs.

Phonological awareness (Carvalho, Alvarez, and Caetano, 1998 for BP; Kaminski and Good, 1996 for English)

This BP phonological awareness test (Perfil de Habilidades Fonológicas) targets phonological processing. It evaluates phonological skills such as the ability to isolate single syllables or phonemes in a word, to detect and repeat rhymes, to rearrange syllables in a nonsense word to produce a real word, and to match the initial phoneme of a word to a picture of a human mouth forming that phoneme. This test is very comprehensive; it contains 56 items distributed over nine subsections, and it is consequently very lengthy. For younger children especially, it is sometimes necessary to break the testing into two sessions, with a rest between the sessions.

For English, we use the Initial Sound Fluency test (ISF), a phonemic awareness measure for children from 4 to 6 years of age. The ISF is a component of the Dynamic Indicators of Basic Early Literacy Skills (DIBELS; Sopris West Educational Services), and assesses children's ability to recognize and produce the initial sound in an orally presented word.

For all BP/English phonological tests, we film the child's face closely, and optionally we also include the experimenter and the stimulus picture as illustrated in Figure 14.13.

Figure 14.13 Camera angle for speech phonological awareness test.

We also film with an additional microphone and in a quiet room. If the child speaks very softly, experimenters should ask the child to repeat his/her answer more loudly, or the experimenter may repeat the child's answer, to help with later coding.

English non-word repetition/pseudo-words (Carter, Killon, and Pisoni, 2002; Dillon et al., 2004) and BP non-word repetition/ pseudo-words (Santos and Bueno, 2003)

The English pseudo-word repetition task developed by Carter et al. (2002) was designed to investigate the ability of English-speaking children with CIs to reproduce novel sound patterns that nevertheless display phonological patterns typical of English; we use this test with both hearing and deaf participants. Pseudo-words are grouped according to number of syllables; they range from two to five syllables. Upon hearing a pseudo-word, children must be able to hold it in their phonological memory in order to reproduce it accurately. Their reproduced forms are scored with respect to overall correctness/incorrectness, number of syllables, and stress placement, with the option of more detailed phonetic coding.

The BP pseudo-word task was developed on the basis of studies of word frequency in Brazilian TV shows and analysis of recurring phonological patterns across the most frequently occurring words. Items in this test have the following stress and syllable properties: a basic strong/weak stress pattern in two-syllable words; a weak/strong/weak stress pattern in three-syllable words; a weak/weak/ strong/weak stress pattern in four-syllable words; and a weak/weak/weak/strong/ weak stress pattern in five-syllable words. As in the English pseudo-word test, BP pseudo-words can be scored for overall (in)correctness, number of syllables, and word-likeness, with the option of coding for more detailed phonetic information as needed.

To ensure consistency in presentation, the pseudo-word stimuli are pre-recorded. Children generally find this repetition task entertaining and easy to do. While their overall reproduction is good, the finer-grained analyses of segmental accuracy reveal interesting errors (Quadros, Cruz, and Pizzio, 2012). Many children also volunteer their intuitions about real words that sound like the pseudo-words, and we noted these intuitions for future reference.

ASL and Libras non-word repetition/Pseudo-signs (Mann, Marshall, Mason, and Morgan, 2010)

We designed the pseudo-sign tests with the same goals as the pseudo-word described above, following a procedure similar to that reported in Mann et al. (2010) for pseudo-signs in BSL. The sign versions include pseudo-signs that resemble real ASL and Libras signs in that they display common patterns of internal sign structure. They vary across several parameters – such as the number of hands involved in articulation, whether there is handshape change during the sign, the type of sign movement, and whether or not the sign is a compound. The signs are presented by a Deaf signer on video, and the child is instructed to repeat each item after it is presented. Figure 14.14 illustrates an example of a non-sign item from the first category (one hand, one handshape, no path movement):

The pseudo-sign test can be filmed at the angle shown in Figure 14.15, capturing both the stimulus video and the child's production.

Figure 14.14 Sample prompt from the ASL pseudo-sign test.

Figure 14.15 Camera angle for pseudo-sign test.

The ASL (39 items) and Libras (33 items) versions of the pseudo-sign test are rather lengthy, and some younger subjects have difficulty staying on task for the entire test. Generally, however, children appear to find this task easy and enjoyable, and they volunteer phonologically similar real signs, as described above for the pseudo-word task. The only notable challenge encountered during administration was that, because stimuli were pre-recorded and played automatically (alternating with a brief blank screen during which the child reproduces the sign), children sometimes missed seeing stimuli. For this reason it was very important to remind experimenters to pay close attention to the task, so that they could stop the video and repeat a stimulus if the child failed to see it.

Additional Tests

Non-verbal IQ: Leiter International Performance Scale, Revised (Roid and Miller, 1997)

This standardized test is a non-verbal measure of intelligence designed to assess the child's IQ independently of language. We use only the figure ground, form completion, sequential order, and repeated patterns subtests, which comprise the Leiter Brief IQ Screener. Tests are administered through gestures and demonstration rather than in any particular language (although many gestures permitted by the test designers, such as pointing and "pantomime," resemble signs). Each child takes this test only once.

Despite the fact that we used only a small subset of the possible tasks included in the Leiter, this test is still quite lengthy to administer, and some younger children are not able to complete it. Generally, however, participants scored above the average for their ages on this task. Again, it is worth noting that, while the test instructs experimenters to use gesture and pantomime in order to avoid giving the child "verbal" (i.e. linguistic) cues, these cues may be perceived as linguistic by bimodal bilingual children, who have been acquiring a visual language from birth.

Parent–child interaction sample

We use a series of pictures showing scenes from familiar contexts (at the grocery store, at the zoo, etc.) to help elicit a short sample of naturalistic interaction between each child and a parent. No target language is imposed in this task; the child and the parent are free to use whichever language(s) they wish, with the goal of capturing a sample of typical language input that the child receives from the parent. The parent and the child are seated at the angles shown in Figure 14.16, to record a clear video capture.

Parents vary widely in how comfortable and spontaneous they are during this task. Some appear nervous in front of the camera and unsure how to proceed. For these parents, it is helpful to have ready a list of other common activities they might find easier to discuss with their child than those portrayed in the provided pictures. For this reason, an experimenter can remain in the room during filming, sitting discretely behind the camera but available to facilitate conversation if needed.

Figure 14.16 Camera angle for parent–child interaction sample.

Adjusting the Tasks and the Details of the Applications

Following the first round of testing, we met with experimenters to evaluate the effectiveness of each test and to modify it if necessary. This step is useful, as it identifies both positive aspects and problems with regard to the experimental approach. Some problems are language- or culture-specific, for instance the higher degree of nervousness of Brazilian children in front of the camera by comparison to their American counterparts. We attribute this difference to the relative absence of a testing culture in Brazilian schools. However, the Brazilian children were distinctly more at ease in the second round of testing, which suggests that children are able to acclimatize to testing and filming fairly quickly.

Post-testing evaluations also generated a list of best practices for optimal test administration, a practical resource that resulted in more effective testing at subsequent data fairs. The list had the following points:

1 Experimenter preparation must include explicit training related to the goal of each test, as well as very specific instructions on the kinds of help and clarification that experimenters can and cannot give to the child. Experimenters must know their test very well before administering it.

2 When creating tests, tasks should be simple enough to be quickly grasped, yet challenging enough to engage children's interest.

3 Parents sign informed consent and video release forms before their children can participate in testing. It is most effective to either fill the forms out with the parents or create an explanation in sign language, then post it as a YouTube video prior to the data collection fairs. This allows parents to review the video ahead of time, so they can be ready to ask any questions or express any concerns they might have on the day of testing.

4 Testing rooms should be carefully prepared prior to testing, following standardized instructions for the arrangement of test materials and the placement of the camera. All experimenters must be trained in proper use of the camcorder and of the microphone (if used).

5 Some children are nervous upon entering the testing room and would benefit from a bit of light chatting designed to break the ice and set them at ease before the testing begins. Showing children themselves on camera as they make funny faces is also a useful way of making them comfortable with being filmed.

6 Children should be asked for verbal assent before test-taking begins and should understand that they can stop the test at any time. If a child shows signs of anxiety mid-test, the experimenter should stop testing and return the child to the playroom to rest. The child will be given the chance to resume the test later.

7 At the beginning of each videotaped test session, experimenters should write the participant's pseudonym, the test name, and the date on a mini-whiteboard held up to the camera before filming begins.[4] Training the camera on the whiteboard contents before hitting the Record button results in this information appearing as the thumbnail image for that video session, which makes it easier to identify the film when it is copied from the camera and transcribed.

8 All instructions and clarifications should be presented to the child together with the practice items rather than later, during the actual test. The experimenter

should not proceed with the actual test until it is clear that the child understands the task. If the child does not understand the task, the experimenter must explain it again; and, if the child still does not understand, testing should be suspended and reattempted at a later time.

9   Experimenters should try to maintain positive, encouraging facial expressions during testing, even when a child answers a test question incorrectly. Regardless of whether a child gives a correct or an incorrect answer, the experimenter should respond with a neutral-to-positive comment like "Good job."

10   During tests in which the child selects an answer by simply pointing at some stimulus, the experimenter should always reiterate the child's answers in some way, for example by pointing or commenting on which item was selected, to clarify the child's choice for later coding.

11   Some children respond in speech only, even when they are being tested on their sign language by Deaf experimenters. In such cases the experimenter should gently remind the child that (s)he did not understand the spoken response because (s)he is deaf and should ask the child to repeat his/her response in sign. Alternatively, the presence of a Deaf parent in the testing room might encourage the child to sign. Speech-only responses are not necessarily a reason to abandon testing, unless the child is repeatedly unable to produce signed responses. In the Bibibi study all the children were able to switch to the appropriate language after prompting.

12   Scheduling individual children for specific tests at set blocks of time is not the most effective method for fair testing. A fluid organization is more effective, allowing children to decide after finishing one test whether they want to return to the playroom to rest or continue with the next test. To keep track of which child has finished (or simply attempted) which tests, all experimenters should check in with a central "schedule keeper" as they take each child to be tested, and again as they return that child to the playroom. The experimenters should also keep track of the children who have participated in their room on a participant checklist with notes and other information.

Transcribing Experimental Data

We transcribe our experimental data using ELAN (EUDICO Linguistic Annotator, http://www.lat-mpi.eu/tools/elan) (Crasborn and Sloetjes, 2008), a tool for multimedia annotation. ELAN is also widely used by researchers for linguistic annotation of sign language video data. Annotated utterances in ELAN are linked to their corresponding points in the video data, and researchers can view an utterance of interest by simply clicking on its annotation. ELAN also allows searches of multiple annotated files simultaneously, greatly facilitating data analysis.

Brief responses can be coded directly in ELAN, as can longer utterances or dialogues (such as the narrative and conversation samples). The advantage of using ELAN for bilingual data is that both languages are annotated in the same document and, when the participants produce blending, the speech and sign annotations are shown connected and aligned in timing to each other, in accordance with the video (see Figure 14.17). All annotations should be entered by trained bilinguals who are

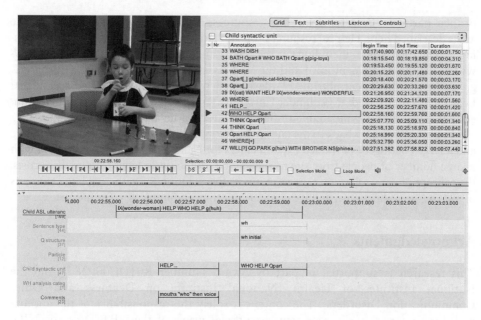

Figure 14.17 Screen shot of a test video coded in ELAN.

native users of at least one of the two languages of the child on video. Transcribers follow standardized notational and glossing conventions developed through frequent meetings with other transcribers (Chen Pichler, Hochgesang, Lillo-Martin, and Quadros, 2010). Sections of finished transcripts are reliably checked by other bilingual researchers and stored on a server with restricted access.

All the data from our experimental studies are stored in a shared FileMaker Pro database. Formats were created for inputting answers from each child on each test, so that reports can be generated and compared. All ELAN files, videos, participant background information, and scanned answer sheets from data collection fairs are also linked to the FileMaker Pro database.

Conclusion

The data collection fair methodology has allowed the collection of a wide range of experimental data in a short time, in a manner that is comparable across testing sites. The tests described here are only a selection of the growing number of tasks designed to investigate language development. This test battery was developed with the goal of obtaining as much information as possible about bimodal bilingual children's overall linguistic development, since there are so few existing publications on this population. Specific areas of linguistic development that have been the focus of previous studies on relevant comparison groups (Deaf children without cochlear implants, Coda adults, and unimodal bilingual children) have also been prioritized. Those who with to collect experimental data from bimodal bilinguals should choose tests on the basis of their particular research focus and resources; it is not necessary to test all of the areas described here. Helpful resources for sign language assessment tools are increasingly available online, including on the Sign Language Assessment web site (http://www.signlang-assessment.info) and the VL2 Assessment Toolkit web site (http://vl2.gallaudet.edu/document.php?id=14) developed by the Visual Language and Visual Learning Center based at Gallaudet University. Our project's web site (bibibi.uconn.edu) also includes downloadable resources related to our research and findings.

The only major drawback to the fair methodology is that it requires extensive planning and a large contingent of trained experimenters for each fair. The costs of traveling with a large number of people from site to site can be prohibitively high. Despite these costs, the concept of data collection fairs is an innovative solution for gathering large amounts of test data in a short time, and we continue to refine and improve it for future use.

Acknowledgments

This research is supported in part by Award Number R01DC009263 from the National Institutes of Health (National Institute on Deafness and Other Communication Disorders). The content is solely the responsibility of the authors and does not necessarily represent the official views of the NIDCD or the NIH. Support is also provided by awards from the Gallaudet Research Institute and from CNPq (Brazilian National Council of Technological and Scientific Development) Grant #200031/2009-0 and #470111/2007-0.

Notes

1 Capitalized *Deaf* is used with reference to a specific, self-defined cultural group with a common history and language. Lowercase *deaf* is used with reference to the deafness in general.
2 We would be pleased to share those test materials we developed with other interested researchers. Please feel free to contact us if you are interested in making such an arrangement.
3 The Libras adaptation is considered to be still at the pilot stage, as we are currently collecting data from native signing children.
4 Thanks to Marie Coppola for suggesting this practice to us.

Keywords

bimodal bilingual corpora; bimodal bilingual development; experimental studies; research in sign language acquisition methods; sign language acquisition

See Also

Chapter 4; Chapter 5; Chapter 17; Chapter 18; Chapter 19

Suggested Readings

Baker, A., van den Bogaerde, B., and Woll, B. (2009). Methods and procedures in sign language acquisition studies. In A. Baker and B. Woll (Eds.), *Sign language acquisition* Amsterdam: John Benjamins, pp. 1–49.

Chen Pichler, D. (2012). Language acquisition. In R. Pfau, B. Woll and M. Steinbach (Eds.), *Handbook of linguistics and communication science: Sign language*. Berlin: de Gruyter, pp. 647–686.

Chen Pichler, D., Lee, J., and Lillo-Martin, D. (2014). Language development in ASL–English bimodal bilinguals. In D. Quinto-Pozos (Ed.), *Multilingual aspects of signed language communication and disorder*. Bristol: Multilingual Matters.

Chen Pichler, D., de Quadros, R. M., and Lillo-Martin, Diane (2010). Effects of bimodal production on multi-cyclicity in early ASL and LSB. In J. Chandlee, K. Franich, K. Iserman, and L. Keil (Eds.), *A supplement to the proceedings of the 34th Boston university conference on language development*. Somerville, MA: Cascadilla Press. Accessed September 12, 2014. http://www.bu.edu/bucld/proceedings/supplement/vol34

Chen Pichler, D., Hochgesang, J., Lillo-Martin, D., de Quadros, R. M., and Reynolds, W. (2014). Best practices for building a bimodal bilingual child language corpus. Manuscript submitted for publication.

Chen Pichler, D., Kuntze, M., Lillo-Martin, D., de Quadros, R. M., and Stumpf, M. (forthcoming). *Sign language acquisition by Deaf and hearing children: A bilingual introductory digital course*. Washington, DC: Gallaudet University Press.

Karnopp, L. B. (1994). Aquisição do parâmetro configuração de mão dos sinais da LIBRAS: Estudo sobre quatro crianças surdas filhas de pais surdos. MA dissertation, Pontifícia Universidade Católica do Rio Grande do Sul, Porto Alegre, Brazil.

Lillo-Martin, D. (2009). Sign language acquisition studies. In E. Bavin (Ed.), *The Cambridge handbook of child language*. Cambridge: Cambridge University Press, pp. 399–415.

McDaniel, D., McKee, C., and Kerns, H. (Eds.) (1996). *Methods for assessing children's syntax*. Cambridge, MA: MIT Press.

Quadros, R. M. (2013). Contextualização dos estudos linguísticos da libras no Brasil. In R. M. de Quadros, M. Stumpf, and T. A. Leite (Eds.), *Série estudos de línguas de sinais*. Volume 1: *Programa de pós-Graduação em Linguística*. Florianópolis, Brazil: Universidade Federal de Santa Catarina, pp. 15–36.

References

Andrade, C. R. F., Befi-Lopes, D. M., Fernandes, F. D. M., and Wertzner, H. F. (2004). *Teste de linguagem infantil nas áreas de fonologia, vocabulário, fluência e pragmática* (2nd ed.). Bauru, Brazil: Pró-Fono Departamento Editorial.

Bhatia, T. K., and Ritchie, W. C. (2004). *The handbook of bilingualism*. Malden, MA: Blackwell.

Cantone, K. (2007). *Code-switching in bilingual children* (Studies in Theoretical Psycholinguistics, 37). Dordecht: Springer.

Carter, A. K., Killon, C. M., and Pisoni, D. B. (2002). Imitation of nonwords by hearing impaired children with cochlear implants: Suprasegmental analyses. *Clinical Linguistics & Phonetics* 16(8), 619–638.

Carvalho, B. (2007). *Teste de figuras para discriminação fonêmica: Proposta e aplicação*. Dissertação de Mestrado. Programa de Pós-Graduação em Distúrbios da Comunicação. Santa Maria, Brazil: Universidade Federal de Santa Maria.

Carvalho, I. A. M., Alvarez A. M. A., and Caetano, A. L. (1998). *Perfil de habilidades fonológicas: Manual*. São Paulo, Brazil: Via Lettera.

Chen Pichler, D., Hochgesang, J., Lillo-Martin, D., and de Quadros, R. M. (2010). Conventions for sign and speech transcription of child bimodal bilingual corpora in ELAN. *Language, Interaction and Acquisition* 1, 11–40.

Crain, S., and McKee, C. (1986). Acquisition of structural restrictions on anaphora. In S. Berman, J.-W. Choe, and J. McDonough (Eds.), *Proceedings of the North Eastern Linguistic Society* (vol. 16). Amherst, MA: GLSA, pp. 94–110..

Crain, S., and Thornton, R. (1998). *Investigations in universal grammar: A guide to experiments on the acquisition of syntax and semantics*. Cambridge, MA: MIT Press.

Crasborn, O., and Sloetjes, H. (2008). Enhanced ELAN functionality for sign language corpora. In O. Crasborn, E. Efthimiou, E. Fotinea, T. Hanke, J. Kristoffersen, J. Mesch (Eds.), *Proceedings of the third international conference on language resources and evaluation: Interactions between corpus and lexicon*. Paris: ELRA, pp. 39–43.

Cruz, C. R. (2008). *Proposta de instrumento de avaliação da consciência fonológica, parâmetro configuração de mão, para crianças surdas utentes da Língua de Sinais Brasileira*. Porto Alegre: Programa de Pós-Graduação em Letras da Faculdade de Letras da Pontifícia Universidade Católica do Rio Grande do Sul.

Cruz, C. R., and Lamprecht, R. (2008). Proposta de instrumento de avaliação da consciência fonológica, parâmetro configuração de mão, para crianças surdas utentes da Língua de Sinais Brasileira. *Letras de Hoje: Estudos e debates em linguística, literatura e língua portuguesa* 43, 98–106.

Cruz, C. R., and Lamprecht, R. (2011). A phonological awareness test for deaf children using Brazilian Sign Language. In R. Channon and H. van der Hulst (Eds.), *Formational units in sign languages*. Berlin: Mouton de Gruyter, pp. 151–176.

Dillon, C. M., Cleary, M., Pisoni, D. P., and Carter, A. K. (2004). Imitation of nonwords by hearing-impaired children with cochlear implants: Segmental Analyses. *Clinical Linguistics & Phonetics* 18(1), 39–55.

Emmorey, K., Borinstein, H. B., Thompson, R., and Gollan, T. H. (2008). Bimodal bilingualism. *Bilingualism: Language and Cognition* 11(1), 43–61.

Enns, C., and Herman, R. (2011). Adapting the assessing British Sign Language development: Receptive Skills test into American Sign Language. *Journal of Deaf Studies and Deaf Education* 16(3), 362–374.

Enns, C., and Zimmer, K. (2009). Research study: Adapting the British Sign Language Receptive Skills test into American Sign Language. Summary Report, University of Manitoba, Canada.

French, M. M. (1999). *The toolkit appendices for starting with assessment: A developmental approach to deaf children's literacy*. Washington, DC: Gallaudet University Pre-College National Mission Programs.

Goldman, R., and Fristoe, M. (2000). Goldman–Fristoe Test of Articulation 2. San Antonio, TX: Pearson.

Grosjean, F. (2006). Studying bilinguals: Methodological and conceptual issues. In T. K. Bhatia and W. C. Ritchie (Eds.), *The handbook of bilingualism*. Oxford: Blackwell, pp. 32–64.

Grosjean, F. (2008). *Studying bilinguals* (Oxford Linguistics series). New York: Oxford University Press.

Haug, T. (2011). *Adaptation and evaluation of a German Sign Language test: A computer-based receptive skills test for deaf children ages 4–8 years old*. Hamburg: Hamburg University Press.

Herman, R., Holmes, S., and Woll, B. (1999). *Assessing British Sign Language development: Receptive Skills test*. Gloucestershire: Forest Bookshop.

de Houwer, A. (2009). *Bilingual first language acquisition*. Bristol: Multilingual Matters.

Johnston, T. (2004). The assessment and achievement of proficiency in a native sign language within a sign bilingual program: The pilot Auslan Receptive Skills test. *Deafness and Education International* 6(2), 57–81.

Kaminski, R. A., and Good, R. H., III (1996). Toward a technology for assessing basic early literacy skills. *School Psychology Review* 25(2), 215–227.

Karnopp, L. B. (1999). Aquisição fonológica na Língua Brasileira de Sinais: Estudo longitudinal de uma criança surda. PhD dissertation, Pontifícia Universidade Católica do Rio Grande do Sul, Porto Alegre, Brazil.

Lillo-Martin, D. (2000). Aspects of the syntax and acquisition of Wh-questions in American Sign Language. In K. Emmorey and H. Lane (Eds.), *The signs of language revisited: An anthology in honor of Ursula Bellugi and Edward Klima*. Mahwah, NJ: Lawrence Erlbaum, pp. 401–413.

Lillo-Martin, D., Koulidobrova, H., de Quadros, R. M., and Chen Pichler, D. (2012). Bilingual language synthesis: Evidence from Wh-questions in bimodal bilinguals. In *Proceedings of the 36th annual Boston University conference on language development*. Somerville, MA: Cascadilla Press, pp. 301–314.

Lillo-Martin, D., de Quadros, R. M., Koulidobrova, H., and Chen Pichler, D. (2010). Bimodal bilingual cross-language influence in unexpected domains. In J. Costa, A. Castro, M. Lobo, and F. Pratas (Eds.), *Language acquisition and development: Proceedings of GALA 2009*. Newcastle upon Tyne: Cambridge Scholars Press, pp. 264–275.

Mann, W., Marshall, C., Mason, K., and Morgan, G. (2010). The acquisition of sign language: The impact of phonetic complexity on phonology. *Language Learning and Development* 6, 1–27.

Marian, V. (2008). Bilingual research methods. In J. Altarriba and R. R. Heredia (Eds.), *An introduction to bilingualism: Principles and processes*. Mahawah, NJ: Lawrence Erlbaum, pp. 13–37.

McQuarrie, L. M. (2012). The American Sign Language Phonological Awareness Test (ASL-PAT). Unpublished manuscript, University of Alberta, Edomonton, Canada.

Moyer, M., and Wei, L. (2008). *The Blackwell guide to research methods in bilingualism*. Oxford: Wiley Blackwell.

Neves, B. (2013). Competência narrative: Uma análise das produções das crianças bilíngues bimodais. MA dissertation, Universidade Federal de Santa Catarina,. Florianópolis, Brazil.

Pavlenko, A. (2008). Narrative analysis in the study of bi- and multilingualism. In M. Moyer and L. Wei (Eds.), *The Blackwell guide to research methods in bilingualism*. Oxford: Wiley Blackwell, pp. 311–325.

Pearson, B. Z., Fernandez, S. C., and Ollder, D. K. (1993). Lexical development in bilingual infants and toddlers: Comparison to monolingual norms. *Language Learning* 43, 93–120.

Pronovost, W., and Dumbleton, C. (1953). A picture-type speech sound discrimination test. *Journal of Speech and Hearing Disorders* 18, 258–266.

de Quadros, R. M. (1997). *Educação de surdos: A aquisição da linguagem*. Porto Alegre, Brazil: ArtMed.

de Quadros, R. M., and Karnopp, L. B. (2004). *Língua de Sinais Brasileira: Estudos linguísticos*. Porto Alegre, Brazil: Editora ArtMed.

de Quadros, R. M., Cruz, C. R., and Pizzio, A. L. (2012). Memória fonológica em crianças bilíngues bimodais e crianças com implante coclear. *ReVEL* 10(19). Accessed September 12, 2014. www.revel.inf.br

de Quadros, R. M., Lillo-Martin, D., and Chen Pichler, D. (2010). Desenvolvimento bilíngue intermodal. *Anais do IX congresso internacional de educação de surdos*. Rio de Janeiro, Brazil: Intituto Nacional de Educação de Surdos, pp. 146–150.

de Quadros, R. M., Lillo-Martin, D., and Chen Pichler, D. (2013). Early effects of bilingualism on Wh-question structures: Insight from sign-speech bilingualism. In Stavroula Stavrakaki, Marina Lalioti and Polyxeni Konstantinopoulou (Eds.), *Language acquisition and development: Proceedings of GALA 2011*. Newcastle upon Tyne: Cambridge Scholars Press, pp. 300–308.

de Quadros, R. M., Lillo-Martin, D., and Chen Pichler, D. (forthcoming). Methodological considerations for the development and use of sign language acquisition data. In T. Raso, H. Mello, and M. Pettorino (Eds.), *Spoken corpora and linguistic studies*. John Benjamins, pp. 84–102.

Roid, G. H., and Miller, L. J. (1997). Leiter International Performance Scale, Revised (Leiter-R). Wood Dale, IL: Stoelting Co.

Santos, F. H., and Bueno. O. F. A. (2003). Validation of the Brazilian children's test of pseudo-word repetition in Portuguese speakers aged 4 to 10 years. *Brazilian Journal of Medical and Biological* Research 36, 1533–1547.

Scarborough, H. (1990). Index of productive syntax. *Applied Psycholinguistics* 11(1), 1–22.

Surian, L., and Tedoldi, M. (2005). *Adaptation of BSL Receptive Skills test to Italian Sign Language (LIS)*. Unpublished manuscript, University of Trento, Italy.

Williams, K. T. (1997). *Expressive vocabulary test*. San Antonio, TX: Pearson.

Zimmerman, I. L., Steiner, V. G., and Pond, R. E. (2002). *Preschool language scale (PLS-4)* (4th ed.). San Antonio, TX: Harcourt Assessment.

15   Studying Sign Language Acquisition

Amy M. Lieberman and Rachel I. Mayberry

Chapter Overview

The study of sign language acquisition has revealed important insights regarding the acquisition of language in the visual modality, the impact of delayed first-language exposure on language ability, and the relationship between language and cognitive processes. Unique challenges arise in studying sign language acquisition due to the low incidence and heterogeneity of the population and the need for inclusion in all aspects of the research of highly skilled native and near-native language users who are deaf.[1] Despite these challenges, a range of methodological approaches have been applied to sign language acquisition, including longitudinal and cross-sectional sampling of

Research Methods in Sign Language Studies: A Practical Guide, First Edition.
Edited by Eleni Orfanidou, Bencie Woll, and Gary Morgan.
© 2015 John Wiley & Sons, Inc. Published 2015 by John Wiley & Sons, Inc.

the population, case studies, adaptation of assessment instruments, standardized measures, analyses of naturalistic language, and elicited language samples. Through these methods, researchers are able to conduct rigorous studies whose findings have made invaluable contributions to theories of language acquisition and development in a number of sign languages and populations.

Introduction: Key Questions Motivating Sign Language Acquisition Research

The field of language acquisition has a long and fertile history. It begins with diary entries of researchers' children (e.g. Preyer, 1889; Tomasello, 1992) and extends to large-scale studies designed to garner generalizations about how children talk as they grow (Templin, 1957) and to studies and experiments aimed at teasing apart how children master a given language structure or cognitive phenomenon (Bloom, 1970; Brown, 1973). The more recent field of sign language acquisition research asks similar questions using similar methods, but with a complicating overlay of issues. These issues include the possible effects of sensory–motor modality on language acquisition, namely whether the acquisition of visual–manual languages looks similar to or different from that of auditory–oral languages. Then there are the a priori issues of whether and how the age of onset of language acquisition and the amount and quality of language input affect the trajectory and outcome of this universal process of child development. Understanding sign language acquisition is also essential to educators and clinicians who work with deaf children as well as with other populations, but here we focus primarily on the key questions that researchers have asked about sign language acquisition and how they have gone about answering them.

A fundamental question motivating sign language research is this: How is sign language acquisition similar to and/or different from spoken language acquisition? Typically this question is asked assuming that the circumstances surrounding acquisition of the two kinds of language are parallel, in other words that language is acquired in a typically untutored fashion, from birth, in an environment in which the parents are the primary transmitters of that language to their children (Mayberry and Squires, 2006). Thus the underlying question becomes what differences – if any – arise in the processes and content of language acquisition as a result of the fact that it is produced manually and perceived visually. Assuming that spoken and signed language acquisition are not identical and that some modality-based differences exist, a related question asks what the study of sign language acquisition reveals about language, modality, and acquisition in general. These questions address the extent to which the learning processes that underlie language acquisition are supramodal in nature.

The study of sign acquisition has led to lively discussion regarding the visuospatial nature of sign language and its potential effects on acquisition. For example, studies of the timing of the onset of sign production have sought to determine whether first signs appear before the first spoken words; evidence suggests that there is little if any difference in the onset of the two kinds of language, and any difference is short-lived (Meier and Newport, 1990; Anderson and Reilly, 2002). Studies of complex morphological structures such as classifiers have contributed to theoretical perspectives regarding the nature of sign versus gesture, the role of iconicity in acquisition (Thompson, Vinson, Woll, and Vigliocco, 2012), and the degree to which children perceive and acquire such structures holistically or as multi-unit combinations (Schick, 1990; Slobin et al., 2003). Underlying all these debates is the question of what constitutes word learning and how it can be distinguished from gesture. The need to think deeply about this issue arises from the fact that language and gesture occur within the same modality when language is signed but are expressed cross-modally when language is spoken.

One particular factor in language acquisition that is hypothesized to be impacted by modality is the nature of parent–child interactions. Specifically, given the highly visual nature of joint attention interactions in early parent–child communication, researchers have explored the ability of deaf and hearing parents to obtain and maintain joint attention with their young deaf children. This is typically approached through naturalistic observations of dyadic interaction between caregivers and their children, which are videotaped and later coded and analyzed for specific features such as eye gaze, attention-getting, and joint focus on objects. In studies of how deaf parents sign to their deaf children, research encompassing several different sign languages has identified a visual equivalent to child-directed speech, known as child-directed signing (Erting, Prezioso, and O'Grady Hynes, 1990; Holzrichter and Meier, 2000; Masataka, 1992). This sign language register includes many parallels to child-directed speech: a slower rate of signing, greater repetition, shorter utterances, larger signs, and positive facial affect. In addition, deaf parents have been shown to make modifications in their signing in order to make signs more visually accessible to deaf children. Examples of such modifications are the use of overt attention-getters, moving objects into the child's line of vision, signing on objects, or signing on the child's body (Spencer, Bodner-Johnson, and Gutfreund, 1992; Harris, Clibbens, Chasin, and Tibbitts, 1989; Masataka, 1992; 2000). Deaf children also exhibit a developing ability to shift their gaze rapidly and meaningfully between their mother and an object or book of interest, and they have sophisticated abilities to do so from an early age, provided they are exposed to sign language from birth (Lieberman, Hatrak, and Mayberry, 2014).

Beyond the question of modality, one of the unique characteristics of sign language learners in comparison to spoken language learners is the degree to which they vary in the age of first-language exposure. A very small proportion (roughly 5–10 percent) of deaf children have deaf parents and thus are exposed to sign language from birth (Mitchell and Karchmer, 2004). The remaining 90–95 percent of deaf children have hearing parents with no prior experience with deafness or sign language; thus language acquisition among these children follows a large range of alternative trajectories. The introduction of universal newborn hearing screening has decreased the age at which hearing loss is typically identified in many developed countries. However, even with early identification, deaf children who are born to hearing parents are first exposed to sign language at ages ranging from birth to adolescence (and some deaf individuals are never exposed to sign language). For these children, and specifically the ones who have insufficient access to spoken language to acquire it as a functional language, sign language becomes, *prima facie*, their first language. In this sense the population of deaf individuals offers researchers a unique opportunity to study the effects of delayed first-language acquisition, the relationship between age of acquisition (AoA) and language ability across domains, and the relationship between language proficiency and specific cognitive abilities – including theory of mind, executive function, working memory, and brain–language processing.

The impact of delayed first-language acquisition on later language ability and cognitive skills cannot be investigated through studies of spoken language acquisition because, except in extreme cases of neglect or abuse, hearing children are universally exposed to at least one language from the time they are born. In contrast, through studies of deaf individuals who acquired their first language in early or late childhood or even in adolescence, researchers have learned that, if a first language is not acquired during the critical or sensitive period, there are lasting differences in both receptive language processing and productive language proficiency (Mayberry and Eichen, 1991; Newport, 1990). In these studies acquisition is studied retrospectively, by observing deaf adults who vary on the basis of their age of first-language exposure. For example, in an experiment involving sentence repetition, native signers tended to make more errors at the semantic level, while late learners tended to make more phonologically based errors, which suggests that late learners expend more cognitive resources on the perceptual and word recognition stages of language processing than native or early learners (Mayberry and Eichen, 1991). These differences between native learners and late learners persist even after years of experience with sign language, indicating that it is the age of first-language exposure, not the amount of language experience, that leads to these deficiencies. Further, these differences do *not* appear in deaf or hearing individuals who learn sign language as a second language, confirming that it is the age of first-language exposure that leads to these critical differences (Cormier, Schembri, Vinson, and Orfanidou, 2012; Mayberry, 1993; Mayberry, Lock, and Kazmi, 2002). In ongoing research we are now using both a developmental and retrospective paradigm to investigate the neural correlates of these effects of delayed first-language learning (Mayberry, Chen, Witcher, and Klein, 2011; Ferjan Ramirez, Leonard, et al., 2013; Leonard et al., 2012).

A third branch of inquiry in sign language acquisition has grown from the fact that many deaf children learn sign language from a range of models other than their parents, and some are not exposed to sign language at all. This atypical situation has led to research on the nature of language acquisition in the absence of typical input. Work by Goldin-Meadow and colleagues, using analyses of naturalistic samples of child and mother communication elicited under controlled conditions (for instance, when the same set of toys and books has been provided for each participant), has shown that deaf children without adult sign language input develop a system for communication that contains linguistic structure at multiple levels; this system is often referred to as *homesign* (Goldin-Meadow and Mylander, 1998). A growing body of work on an emerging sign language among several school-based generations of deaf individuals in Nicaragua has revealed additional insights. In this population, important differences have been identified in the grammatical structure and cognitive sophistication of the language of children according to whether they were in the first, second, or subsequent cohorts of individuals exposed to a new sign language, with each cohort's language use becoming more linguistically structured (Senghas and Coppola, 2001). Data from homesigners continue to provide insights into the features of gestural communication in the absence of sign language input, particularly in countries in which there is not widespread access to formal education for deaf individuals (Coppola and Newport, 2005).

Finally, partially due to the increasing tendency for deaf children to receive cochlear implants from an early age, research has led to important findings about the potential benefits of early sign language exposure on spoken language acquisition (Hassanzadeh, 2012). Despite increasing pressure placed on families with deaf children to use an oral-only approach following cochlear implantation, research has found no conclusive evidence that the oral-only approach is correlated with improved spoken language outcomes. Given the widely established importance of early language exposure, which holds equally for signed and for spoken language, it is imperative that continued scientific research establish the potential benefits of early sign language exposure for all deaf children, regardless of the amount and type of assistive technology from which they can benefit (Davidson, Lillo-Martin, and Chen Pichler, 2014). This issue, which continues to arouse heated debate among the medical, social, and educational communities, is a prime example of the importance of methodologically sound sign language acquisition research and its practical application to the lives of deaf children and their families.

Although many methodological issues involved in sign language are similar to those involved in spoken language acquisition research and many approaches to sign language acquisition parallel those in spoken language acquisition, there are unique methodological challenges in studying sign language (Baker, van den Bogaerde, and Woll, 2005). As we describe below, such challenges are largely due to low incidence, the heterogeneity of the population, the need for highly skilled and proficient signers to carry out the research, and the scarcity of existing assessment tools and instruments for reliably and reasonably investigating the sign language skills of deaf individuals.

Identifying and Describing the Population

It is estimated that approximately one in every 1,000 infants is born with significant hearing loss (Kemper and Downs, 2000). The population of deaf individuals is small and highly heterogeneous. As a result, identifying a group of individuals in whom to study sign language acquisition requires careful consideration. Here we describe some of the key issues that arise in this line of work and we give examples of how researchers have addressed them.

Collecting background information

In studying language acquisition with cross-sectional or experimental designs, participants are typically observed at a single point in time. Thus the question arises as to how to accurately assess their language background, including the age of onset of hearing loss, the degree of hearing loss, and the amount and type of language the participant has been exposed to throughout his or her life. All of these variables can contribute significantly to performance on the outcome measure(s) being studied. Deaf individuals are often exposed to spoken and/or signed languages in varying proportions at different ages, and the amount and type of input they receive varies widely. It is common for deaf children to be exposed to mixed input (a combination of signs and speech) from an early age. Thus it is insufficient to simply ask at what age the individual was exposed to sign language, as the *amount* and *quality* of language exposure can vary as widely as the age of exposure. Deaf children born to hearing parents may be exposed to sign language only a few hours a week, as part of an intervention program; they may be immersed in a signing environment as their parents and others around them learn to sign; or they may receive nearly all their sign input from school interpreters.

To address these questions, participants in any study should be given an extensive language background questionnaire. Researchers can develop a customized questionnaire suited to their research interests. In our laboratory we ask participants to describe the type of language they were exposed to at every stage of their lives, asking about educational placement as well as language in the home environment. In order to assess whether sign language is their first language, we also ask questions about the degree to which they acquired and used spoken language, particularly if they were raised either partially or fully in an oral environment. We further ask participants to do a self-rating of their receptive and productive language skills using a 10-point Likert-type scale, which includes self-ratings on comprehension and production of sign language, fingerspelling, spoken language, and written language. The goal of this extensive profile is to understand to what degree participants have been exposed to and acquired both spoken and signed language. This information can help us understand sign language usage that is puzzling or unpredicted; we also find that these self-ratings correlate with performance on psycholinguistic tasks (Chamberlain and Mayberry, 2008). If the participants are children, then we ask a parent, a guardian, or another adult who knows the child's background well to fill out the questionnaire. The data from a background questionnaire provide a basis from which to compare participants on direct assessments of language ability.

Selecting and recruiting participants

In any research with a small and heterogeneous population, it can be a challenge to recruit sufficient numbers of participants per experimental group to conduct traditional statistical analyses. Thus in recruiting participants it is important to think about which variables are most important to control. When studying the effects of AoA on language proficiency, one must consider the age of language exposure, the amount of language experience, as well as chronological age (and level of hearing loss). One possible approach is to compare deaf adult participants who were exposed to sign language at birth, in early childhood, or in later childhood. Here, however, it is also important to consider total language experience (which is partially confounded with age of exposure). This can be addressed by limiting inclusion to participants who have been using the language for a minimum number of years, for example 10 years. It is also sometimes desirable to compare deaf participants to a control group of hearing participants. In this case, hearing and deaf participants can be matched on variables such as age, non-verbal IQ, or length of experience with sign language.

Regardless of the variables along which participants are matched, in working with the deaf population it is a challenge to obtain a sample of sufficient size for a statistical analysis of the data. Larger sample sizes are often attainable when it is possible for the researchers to travel to various sites – for instance to residential schools for the deaf or to large metropolitan areas with a sizeable deaf population – and collect data at those sites. In contrast, when the research must take place at a specific location, which is the case in most studies involving neuroimaging techniques or complex equipment, participants must be obtained from a specific geographical area. In these cases, providing additional incentives for participation, such as travel reimbursement, may help. For studies collecting natural language samples, it is often necessary to travel to the child's home or to bring the child and the caregivers into a semi-naturalistic lab setting.

Gathering Data: When and How to Measure Sign Language Acquisition

Longitudinal versus cross-sectional research

As with any population, research on sign language acquisition can be approached either through cross-sectional approaches or through longitudinal study, with accompanying advantages and disadvantages to each design. Longitudinal research on this population can be particularly informative, given the high amount of variability in deaf children's background experience. For example, important studies by Petitto and colleagues (see Petitto and Marentette, 1991) established the existence of a manual form of babbling through a longitudinal study of American Sign Language (ASL) production in two deaf children at 10, 12, and 14 months. They found an increase over time in the proportion of each infant's gestures that met the criteria of manual babbling. Longitudinal studies of children of deaf parents have also been conducted to track the developmental time course of early vocabulary (Orlansky and Bonvillian, 1985). Having a child serve as his or her own control can reduce some of the impact of external factors such as family characteristics, degree of hearing loss, and educational placement. If the data consist of observations of naturalistic behavior, it is ideal to obtain as much footage as possible – at least 30 minutes of time – from which a representative sample can be extracted.

Cross-sectional designs provide a faster snapshot than longitudinal ones, in that participants of varying ages are only assessed in a single session, although obtaining a sizeable group within a particular age range without introducing too much in-group variability is a potential concern. One large-scale study of background and educational characteristics of deaf children with cochlear implants included over 180 participants, but involved four years of data collection (Geers and Brenner, 2003). In studies of signed vocabulary development in deaf children that use adapted versions of the MacArthur–Bates CDI parent checklist, researchers have collected data using longitudinal sampling (Woolfe, Herman, Roy, and Woll, 2010 for British Sign Language, BSL) and a combination (i.e. cross-sectional and partially longitudinal) design (Anderson and Reilly, 2002 for ASL) that yielded multiple data points over time and documented children's development.

As a third option, case studies have also been a highly informative source of sign language acquisition patterns in individuals in specific circumstances. Case studies can yield rich information from a very small number of participants (Brown, 1973). In particular, studies of children learning homesign systems without formal exposure to a full sign language have revealed the contributions of the child's mind to language development (Goldin-Meadow and Mylander, 1998). Additionally, longitudinal case studies of several deaf individuals who were not exposed to any first language until adolescence have shown how language is acquired in these circumstances (Morford, 2003; Ferjan Ramirez, Lieberman, and Mayberry, 2013). In these very late learners, or linguistic isolates, it is highly informative to track language acquisition over time.

Comprehension vs. production

The particular aspect of acquisition being studied necessarily guides the choice of method or approach to assessment. At the broadest level, researchers must determine whether to study language comprehension, language production, or both. It has long been established that, in most areas of language, comprehension precedes production (Nelson, 1973). Thus, if a child produces a particular form, (s)he is naturally assumed to comprehend it as well. The extent to which this also characterizes sign language development has not been investigated thus far. Studies of language comprehension use a variety of approaches. A common approach is picture–sign matching, in which a child is shown a sign and then asked to pick the matching picture (by pointing or clicking on it) from an array of two or more pictures. This can be extended to dynamic stimuli, such that the child sees a video clip of a sign or phrase and then is asked to pick the matching scene. Participants can also be asked to carry out an action depicted by a single sign or phrase (Newport, 1988). Such tasks have the advantage of being easy to score (e.g. a simple yes/no score for whether or not the child points to the correct picture is sufficient). More complex studies of comprehension may include asking the child to respond to a series of questions in order to assess comprehension of a signed sentence or story. In any comprehension study, task design is an important issue. As is discussed further below, one cannot simply administer a task developed for spoken language when collecting sign language data without considering modality-specific features of sign language, for example its degree of iconicity, its ability to produce multiple structures simultaneously, or the extent to which the spoken language test material is representative of the lexical and morphosyntactic structure of sign language.

Studies of language production, in contrast, rely on techniques such as picture-naming, language-sampling, and elicited responses, for example sentences or short stories. Coding language production is significantly more time consuming and potentially more subjective than measuring comprehension, as the coder must determine the accuracy of the response. This issue highlights the importance of having highly proficient coders and/or consultants involved in research to evaluate the signs and structures being studied.

In analyzing children's language production, one important source of information is the overall developmental pattern observed for a particular linguistic structure. For example, foundational studies by Newport (1981) and Supalla (1982) on the acquisition of verbs of motion in ASL involved showing children short video clips depicting an animated character engaged in some action, and asking children to describe in sign what had happened. Through analyses of children's sign expression at various ages, a developmental pattern was observed in which children first acquire individual morphological components and only later combine them to produce complex forms.

A second important source of evidence gleaned from studies of language production is the analysis of error patterns, which can provide a window into children's understanding of generalizable principles of language and emerging knowledge of syntax. For example, longitudinal studies of handshape errors in young children's early sign productions have led to models of phonological development in the manual mode (Boyes-Braem, 1990; Siedlecki and Bonvillian, 1997; Conlin, Mirus, Mauk, and Meier, 2000; Marentette and Mayberry, 2000). At the level of syntax, analysis of children's error patterns in production has revealed that children produce unanalyzed forms at a young age and then gradually use some morphemes while omitting others, or use morphemes sequentially before combining them into more complex forms (Newport, 1988). A study of children's error patterns in a picture description task revealed a protracted acquisition of complex verb constructions in children acquiring BSL (Morgan, Herman and Woll, 2002).

Language production samples are also used to assess children's development of language beyond the word or sentence level. For example, studies of narrative development typically involve showing children a story – either through pictures, video, cartoons or in live action – and asking them to retell the story through sign language (Rathmann, Mann, and Morgan, 2007). To reduce memory demands, children are often given a picture book or a set of pictures to refer to while retelling a story (Morford, 2003). Using this approach, researchers can observe children's developing use of narrative devices such as connected discourse, sequencing of events, and anaphora.

Approaches to Measuring Language Acquisition in Deaf Individuals

Assessment instruments

Pervasive among child language researchers is the search for the "perfect" assessment tool – one that is easy to administer, adequately captures and describes language ability at a point in time, has an established validity, has been normed on a large group of children, and is fast and easy to score. Performance on such an idealized test can then serve as a means by which the language development of study participants can be sorted and/or controlled. In spoken language research, particularly with regard to English, there is an abundance of published assessments from which to choose, along with normed data from thousands of individuals. Unfortunately, for signed languages no such tools exist, and researchers have turned instead to an array of existing tools, or have developed their own for their unique research purposes. Several sign language assessment instruments have been developed in recent years and new instruments are currently in development (Haug, 2005; Haug and Mann, 2008; an extensive inventory of available sign language assessment tools is maintained at www.signlang-assessment.info). Because this line of research is relatively new, sign language researchers need to validate and supplement the results of such assessments through their own analyses of sign language development.

Many sign language assessment instruments are adaptations of tools designed for spoken language. One of the most widely used examples of this is the MacArthur–Bates Communicative Development Inventory (CDI) (Anderson and Reilly, 2002; Woolfe et al., 2010). The CDI is a powerful tool used in thousands of studies of spoken language acquisition, has been adapted for over 50 languages, and continues to be normed in additional languages (Fenson et al., 1993; current information is available online at http://www.sci.sdsu.edu/cdi). The CDI is a parent report measure in which the parent checks from a large list of vocabulary items those words that the child either understands or understands and says. The ASL adaptation of the CDI was normed on 69 deaf children between the ages of 8 and 36 months, while the BSL adaptation was normed on 29 deaf children in the same age range. The CDI targets vocabulary knowledge specifically. One major challenge in using the CDI with deaf children is the issue of who should complete the parent report. In many cases, hearing parents of deaf children are new learners of sign language themselves. These parents may not be familiar with all of the items on the list and may not be fully able to assess their child's vocabulary. In some cases, the child's teacher or other early intervention specialist may be asked to fill out the checklist, provided that that person spends enough time with the child to have a detailed knowledge of his or her vocabulary skills. An advantage in using the CDI with deaf individuals is that, although it is normed for children up to the age of 36 months, it can often be a useful assessment tool for older children, and even for adolescents who are newly acquiring sign language (Ferjan Ramirez, Lieberman, et al., 2013).

Other spoken language assessments have been adapted for use in specific research studies. For example, Schick and colleagues (Schick, de Villiers, de Villiers, and Hoffmeister, 2007) created an ASL version of the Peabody Picture Vocabulary test (PPVT; Dunn and Dunn, 1997), a widely used measure of English vocabulary comprehension in which the tester produces a single word and the child points to the correct picture from four possible choices. In adapting the test for ASL it was necessary to take into account unique features of sign language, such as iconicity and phonological relationships among signs, which are not present in the spoken English version of the task. Another adapted assessment is the ASL Sentence Reproduction test (ASL-SRT; Hauser, Paludnevičienė, Supalla, and Bavalier, 2008), for use with older children and adults, which is adapted from the Speaking Grammar Subtest of the Test of Adolescent and Adult Language (TOALT3; Hammill, Brown, Larsen, and Wiederholt, 1994). In this production test, participants view prerecorded sentences and are asked to reproduce them. Sentences vary in length and complexity. This test was designed to take approximately 30 minutes to administer and the same amount of time to score. It is currently being piloted for use with children and adults who are native and non-native signers. Finally, an adaptation of the semantic fluency test for BSL users (Marshall, Rowley, Mason, Herman, and Morgan, 2013) assesses participants' ability to name exemplars from specific semantic categories; this measure is very straightforward to score, as one simply counts the number of named items.

Occasionally, deaf children's language is measured using spoken language assessments that have *not* specifically been adapted for sign language. For example, children's language skills may be assessed using the PPVT or the Preschool Language Assessment Instrument (Blank, Rose, and Berlin, 1978). In such instances, children's global language may be the target of assessment (e.g., English vocabulary); however, the test itself may be administered in a variety of modes, such as spoken language or signed English (Moeller, 2000). The advantage of such instruments is that large-scale norms typically exist and the instruments are readily available for use. However, children's ability to perceive the instructions is often confounded with performance, and incorrect responses may be due to task demands rather than global language ability. Thus caution must be taken in interpreting results for sign language against norms for spoken language learners.

As an alternative to adaptations of spoken language assessments, efforts have been made to develop unique assessment instruments for sign language, either for use in a specific research study (Boudreault and Mayberry, 2006) or for widespread use among researchers and educators. An obvious advantage of such tools is that they are designed around the unique features of sign language, such as spatial grammar, classifiers, and fingerspelling. However, given the complexity of sign language, it is a challenge to develop an instrument that captures all of these aspects and has enough items to adequately sample knowledge of each structure, while still being relatively easy to administer and score. Examples of this class of assessment instruments are the BSL Receptive Skills test (RST) (Herman and Roy, 2006), the ASL Assessment Instrument (Hoffmeister et al., 2013) and the Assessment Instrument for Sign Language of the Netherlands (SLN) (Hermans, Knoors, and Verhoeven, 2010). In the BSL-RST, which has now been adapted for ASL (Enns, Zimmer, Boudreault, Rabu, and Broszeit, 2013), children see a short sign or phrase and then are presented with four pictures and asked to point to the matching one. In this way the task is similar to the widely used Test for Reception of Grammar (TROG) (Bishop, 2003). The BSL-RST has been normed for 135 children and is currently in the process of being renormed on a large number of deaf children. The ASL Assessment Instrument includes several measures of receptive and productive skills and was designed for use in educational settings in order to determine the relationship between ASL skills and English literacy in deaf students. Similarly, the Assessment Instrument for SLN is also comprised of several computerized tasks and is designed to measure a range of receptive and productive language skills. The last two instruments are more comprehensive than some in that they aim to provide a more complete picture of an individual's language ability. It is likely that additional assessment instruments will continue to be developed so as to meet the needs of researchers who look to target specific proficiencies and of educators who seek a metric by which to evaluate their students. Importantly, as new assessments are developed, there is a corresponding need for recruitment of fluent-signing researchers, and for specified training for researchers and others in order to ensure that tests are administered and scored appropriately.

Language samples and naturalistic data

At the other end of the spectrum from structured language assessments are naturalistic language samples. To obtain this type of data, researchers either bring participants to a lab or travel to the participants' home, school, or other setting and record them on video while engaging in communicative interaction with one or more partners. It is possible to obtain spontaneous language samples without any structure, by videotaping the participants as they engage in typical activities such as playing, eating, or reading with a parent. While this does typically yield a rich data sample, one disadvantage is the diversity of types and the amount of language that may be obtained from different individuals, which makes group comparison more difficult. It is also possible that the particular sample yielded in a spontaneous sample will not be representative of the individual's typical language, due to such factors as self-consciousness in the presence of the researcher or the specificity of the communicative topic. For this reason it is advisable to collect data on more than one occasion. Also, the researcher must decide whether to record the individual interacting with an experimenter, a peer, or a larger group. For individuals with limited language ability, it is often desirable to record group interactions in which the participants carry out a typical conversation in a routine setting, such as over dinner (Ferjan Ramirez, Lieberman, et al., 2013). Once the language sample is obtained, an additional challenge is to determine how much language constitutes a reasonable sample. Possible approaches include sampling a specific length of time (e.g., 30 minutes of interaction) or a specific number of sentences (e.g., 100 utterances) (Brown, 1973). Using some constant amount of utterances or a fixed time sample enables comparison across individuals and across points in time.

Another way to obtain a language sample is through a structured or semi-structured elicitation task. Foundational studies on children's early acquisition of facial grammar and affective facial expressions (Reilly, McIntire, and Bellugi, 1990) were obtained through a structured imitation task. Examples of tasks include semi-structured interviews, story retellings, or personal narratives. Researchers have also used standardized pictures as a basis for language elicitation, or have asked participants to describe a cartoon or movie sequence (Senghas and Coppola, 2001). For young children, one approach that we and others have used is to record a deaf child interacting with his or her parents with the same set of toys and/or books provided by the researchers (Lieberman, Hatrak, et al., 2014). This approach has the advantage of taking place in the child's home, which is a familiar and comfortable environment for the child, while keeping the objects constant and thus somewhat constraining the content of the accompanying language. Other researchers have recorded deaf children in a school setting (Lieberman, 2014; Singleton and Crume, 2010) in order to understand how children interact in a signing-rich environment and (often) to compare children with deaf parents to those with hearing parents.

Data collection, analysis, and sharing

Regardless of the type of language sample obtained, an important methodological consideration is how to capture these data for later analysis. In particular, one must consider the placement and the number of video cameras. In analyzing any type of interaction it is crucial to have at least two cameras, in order to obtain a direct view of each interlocutor. If the environment is a classroom or one that involves young children, it is sometimes necessary to have more than two cameras, to account for frequent movement and/or a large number of individuals participating in the interaction.

Once a language sample is obtained, there are countless additional issues to consider, including the type of transcription, coding, and linguistic analysis to pursue. Each of these decisions will be largely dependent on the specific research question, and particular approaches to transcription and coding are addressed elsewhere in this volume. Specific to acquisition research, however, is the decision about how to measure a child's language. Typical measures used in spoken language acquisition, such as mean length of utterance (MLU), can be a useful metric for the assessment of syntactic development. However, MLU is not a straightforward measure, due to the lack of widespread consensus regarding what constitutes a morpheme in sign language. In addition, there are no large-scale studies investigating how MLU increases over sign language development. Thus researchers must first invest time in defining units of analysis in order to analyze a large body of language data in a systematic way. Possible alternatives to MLU include a count of total signs used in a given time period, type-token ratio, or number of signs per utterance.

Of particular interest to child acquisition work is the issue of data-sharing. Due to the difficulty of obtaining a large sample of data, it is often advantageous for researchers to share data with one another, so that multiple studies can be conducted on a single, comprehensive data set. In spoken language work, language corpora exist for many aspects of acquisition, and many of these corpora are transcribed, coded, and made available to interested researchers through a data exchange system, CHILDES (MacWhinney, 2000). With sign language data, an obvious challenge to creating a large corpus for data-sharing is the lack of anonymity necessitated by the fact that participants' faces and bodies must be visible in order for their language to be seen. With current widespread access to data on the web, it is difficult to maintain privacy. For children, this becomes a problem as children may be too young to give consent to have their image shared, and, even if their parents consent to data-sharing when their children are young, when those children become of majority age they may no longer wish to have their image widely available. This issue is relevant to research ethics, which is discussed in detail elsewhere in this volume. The unique concerns raised in acquisition data involve the use of children as participants and obtaining consent.

Other approaches: Computerized testing, neuroimaging, eye tracking

As the field of language acquisition has evolved, sign language acquisition research has advanced in parallel. In particular, new approaches to measuring language ability have been developed through technology that allows researchers to measure participants' responses to stimuli with a high degree of spatial and temporal resolution. Such techniques include the use of computers, brain-imaging techniques, and automated eye-tracking technology, which enable researchers to capture neural and behavioral responses that are not possible to obtain through simple human observation. Sign language researchers have kept apace with these new technologies through innovative and carefully designed adaptations. For example, tests that were originally developed using paper-and-pencil data collection have been adapted to be used online, enabling wide distribution and automatic scoring. Automated eye-tracking techniques, which are used to study both language processing (Lieberman, Borovsky, Hatrak, and Mayberry, in press; Thompson, Vinson, Fox, and Vigliocco, 2013) and reading (Bélanger, Slatterly, Mayberry, and Rayner, 2012) in deaf individuals show exactly where the participant's gaze is focused during a computer-based reading or receptive task. Neuroimaging techniques including elecroencephalography (EEG), functional magnetic resonance imaging (fMRI), and magnetoencephalography (MEG) reveal insights into neural correlates of language processing and, depending on the particular technique, can give exceptionally detailed spatial and/or temporal information about when and how sign language is activated in the brain and how early experience affects neural processing (MacSweeney, Water, Brammer, Woll, and Goswami, 2008; Mayberry et al., 2011). The combination of these newly developed and highly sensitive measures with established metrics of individual differences and language performance has allowed new links to be established between various indices of language and cognitive functioning.

Conclusion

The study of sign language acquisition can address fundamental questions about the nature of language, the impact of early experience on later performance, the impact of modality on learning, and the relationship between language and cognition. Regardless of whether the participants are deaf children with deaf parents, deaf children with hearing parents, or deaf adults, in studies of sign language acquisition careful consideration must be given to the characteristics of the population and the range of possible factors affecting performance. Sign language assessment is in a period of dynamic development and increased data-sharing opportunities are emerging. As new technologies continue to be developed for the study of language acquisition and linguistic processing, sign language researchers have pioneered exciting new methodologies, which have enabled detailed analyses of language acquisition and processing.

Acknowledgments

This work was supported in part by NIH grants R03DC011615 (AL) and R01DC01 2797 (RM).

Note

1   We only use the spelling *deaf* in this chapter: we use it, as is common convention, to refer to individuals with hearing loss, without specific reference to the social or cultural identity of those individuals, and we remain neutral on its definition.

Keywords

Acquisition; assessment; methodology; sign language

See Also

Chapter 1; Chapter 4; Chapter 5; Chapter 17

Suggested Readings

Baker, A. E., and Woll, B. (Eds.) (2009). *Sign language acquisition* (Benjamins Current Topics, 14). Amsterdam: John Benjamins.

Chamberlain, C., Morford, J. P., and Mayberry, R. I. (Eds.) (2000). *Language acquisition by eye*. Mahwah, NJ: Lawrence Erlbaum Associates.

Goldin-Meadow, S. (2003). *The resilience of language: What gesture creation in deaf children can tell us about how all children learn language*. New York: Psychology Press.

Lillo-Martin, D. (2009). Sign language acquisition studies. In Edith L. Bavin (Ed.), *The Cambridge handbook of child language*. New York: Cambridge University Press, pp. 399–415.

Morgan, G., and Woll, B. (Eds.) (2002). *Directions in sign language acquisition* (vol. 2). Amsterdam: John Benjamins.

References

Anderson, D., and Reilly, J. (2002). The MacArthur communicative development inventory: Normative data for American Sign Language. *Journal of Deaf Studies and Deaf Education* 7(2), 83–106.

Baker, A., van den Bogaerde, B., and Woll, B. (2005). Methods and procedures in sign language acquisition studies. *Sign Language & Linguistics* 8(1/2), 7–59.

Bélanger, N. N., Slattery, T. J., Mayberry, R. I., and Rayner, K. (2012). Skilled deaf readers have an enhanced perceptual span in reading. *Psychological Science* 23(7), 817–823.

Bishop, D. V. (2003). *Test for reception of grammar: TROG-2 version 2*. London: Pearson Assessment.

Blank, M., Rose, S. A., and Berlin, L. J. (1978). *preschool language assessment instrument: The language of learning in practice*. New York: Grune and Stratton.

Bloom, L. (1970). *Language development: Form and function in emerging grammars*. Cambridge, MA: MIT press.

Boudreault, P., and Mayberry, R. I. (2006). Grammatical processing in American Sign Language: Age of first-language acquisition effects in relation to syntactic structure. *Language and Cognitive Processes* 21(5), 608–635.

Boyes-Braem, P. (1990). Acquisition of the handshape in American Sign Language: A preliminary analysis. In V. Volterra and C. J. Erting (Eds.), *From gesture to language in hearing and deaf children*. Berlin: Springer, pp. 107–127.

Brown, R. (1973). *A first language: The early stages*. Oxford: Harvard University Press.

Chamberlain, C., and Mayberry, R. I. (2008). ASL syntactic and narrative comprehension in skilled and less skilled adult readers: Bilingual–bimodal evidence for the linguistic basis of reading. *Applied Psycholinguistics* 29, 368–388.

Conlin, K. E., Mirus, G. R., Mauk, C., and Meier, R. P. (2000). The acquisition of first signs: Place, handshape, and movement. In C. Chamberlain, J. P. Morford, and R. I. Mayberry (Eds.), *Language acquisition by eye*. Mahwah, NJ: Lawrence Erlbaum, pp. 51–69.

Coppola, M., and Newport, E. L. (2005). Grammatical subjects in home sign: Abstract linguistic structure in adult primary gesture systems without linguistic input. *Proceedings of the National Academy of Sciences of the United States of America* 102(52), 19249–19253.

Cormier, K., Schembri, A., Vinson, D., and Orfanidou, E. (2012). First language acquisition differs from second language acquisition in prelingually deaf signers: Evidence from sensitivity to grammaticality judgement in British Sign Language. *Cognition* 124(1), 50–65.

Davidson, K., Lillo-Martin, D., and Pichler, D. C. (2014). Spoken English language development in native signing children with cochlear implants. *Journal of Deaf Studies and Deaf Education* 19, 238–250. doi: 10.1093/deafed/ent045

Dunn, L., and Dunn L. (1997). *Peabody Picture Vocabulary test* (3rd ed.). Circle Pines, MN: American Guidance Service.

Enns, C. J., Zimmer, K., Boudreault, P., Rabu, S., and Broszeit, C. (2013). *American Sign Language: Receptive Skills test*. Winnipeg, MB: Northern Signs Research.

Erting, C. J., Prezioso, C., and O'Grady Hynes, M. (1990). The interactional content of deaf mother–infant communication. In V. Volterra and C. Erting (Eds.), *From gesture to language in hearing and deaf children*. Berlin: Springer, pp. 97–106.

Fenson, L., Dale, P. S., Reznick, J. S., Thal, D., Bates, E., Hartung, J. P., and Reilly, J. S. (1993). *MacArthur communicative development inventories: User's guide and technical manual*. San Diego, CA: Singular Publishing Group.

Ferjan Ramirez, N., Leonard, M. K., Torres, C., Hatrak, M., Halgren, E., and Mayberry, R. I. (2013). Neural language processing in adolescent first-language learners. *Cerebral Cortex*. doi: 10.1093/cercor/bht137

Ferjan Ramirez, N., Lieberman, A. M., and Mayberry, R. I. (2013). The initial stages of language acquisition begun in adolescence: When late looks early. *Journal of Child Language* 40(2), 391–414.

Geers, A., and Brenner, C. (2003). Background and educational characteristics of prelingually deaf children implanted by five years of age. *Ear and Hearing* 24(1), 2S–14S.

Goldin-Meadow, S., and Mylander, C. (1998). Spontaneous sign systems created by deaf children in two cultures. *Nature* 391(6664), 279–281.

Hammill, D. D., Brown, V. L., Larsen, S. C., and Wiederholt, J. L. (1994). *Test of Adolescent and Adult Language*. Austin, TX: Pro-Ed.

Harris, M., Clibbens, J., Chasin, J., and Tibbitts, R. (1989). The social context of early sign language development. *First Language* 9(25), 81–97.

Hassanzadeh, S. (2012). Outcomes of cochlear implantation in deaf children of deaf parents: Comparative study. *The Journal of Laryngology & Otology* 126(10), 989–994.

Haug, T. (2005). Review of sign language assessment instruments. *Sign Language & Linguistics* 8(1/2), 61–98.

Haug, T., and Mann, W. (2008). Adapting tests of sign language assessment for other sign languages: A review of linguistic, cultural, and psychometric problems. *Journal of Deaf Studies and Deaf Education* 13(1), 138–147.

Hauser, P., Paludnevičienė, R., Supalla, T., and Bavalier, D. (2008). American Sign Language-Sentence Reproduction test: Development and implications. In R. M. de Quadros (Ed.), *Proceedings of the 9th theoretical issues in sign language conference*. Florianópolis, Brazil: Editora Arara Azul, pp. 160–172.

Herman, R., and Roy, P. (2006). Evidence from the wider use of the BSL Receptive Skills test. *Deafness and Education International* 8, 33–47.

Hermans, D., Knoors, H., and Verhoeven, L. (2010). Assessment of sign language development: The case of deaf children in the Netherlands. *Journal of Deaf Studies and Deaf Education* 15(2), 107–119.

Hoffmeister, R., Fisher, J., Fish, S., Henner, J., Benedict, R., Rosenburg, P., and McIntyre, K. (2013). The American Sign Language Assessment Instrument (ASLAI). Boston, MA: Boston University, Center for the Study of Communication and the Deaf.

Holzrichter, A. S., and Meier, R. P. (2000). Child-directed signing in American Sign Language. In C. Chamberlain, J. P. Morford, and R. I. Mayberry (Eds.), *Language acquisition by eye*. Mahwah, NJ: Lawrence Erlbaum, pp. 25–40.

Kemper, A. R., and Downs, S. M. (2000). A cost-effectiveness analysis of newborn hearing screening strategies. *Archives of Pediatric and Adolescent Medicine* 154(5), 484–488.

Leonard, M. K., Ferjan Ramirez, N., Torres, C., Travis, K. E., Hatrak, M., Mayberry, R. I., and Halgren, E. (2012). Signed words in the congenitally deaf evoke typical late lexicosemantic responses with no early visual responses in left superior temporal cortex. *The Journal of Neuroscience* 32(28), 9700–9705.

Lieberman, A. M. (2014). Attention-getting skills of deaf children using American Sign Language in a preschool classroom. *Applied Psycholinguistics*, 1–19. doi: 10.1017/S0142716413000532

Lieberman, A. M., Borovsky, A., Hatrak, M., and Mayberry, R. I. (in press). Real-time processing of ASL signs: Delayed first language acquisition affects organization of the mental lexicon. *Journal of Experimental Psychology: Learning, Memory, and Cognition*.

Lieberman, A. M., Hatrak, M., and Mayberry, R. I. (2014). Learning to look for language: Development of joint attention in young deaf children. *Language Learning and Development* 10, 19–35.

MacSweeney, M., Waters, D., Brammer, M. J., Woll, B., and Goswami, U. (2008). Phonological processing in deaf signers and the impact of age of first language acquisition. *Neuroimage* 40(3), 1369–1379.

MacWhinney, B. (2000). *The CHILDES project: Tools for analyzing talk* (3rd ed.). Mahwah, NJ: Lawrence Erlbaum.

Marentette, P., and Mayberry R. I. (2000). Principles for an emerging phonological system: A case study of acquisition of ASL. In C. Chamberlain, J. P. Morford, and R. I. Mayberry (Eds.), *Language acquisition by eye*. Mahwah, NJ: Lawrence Erlbaum, pp. 71–90.

Marshall, C. R., Rowley, K., Mason, K., Herman, R., and Morgan, G. (2013). Lexical organization in deaf children who use British Sign Language: Evidence from a semantic fluency task. *Journal of child language* 40(01), 193–220.

Masataka, N. (1992). Motherese in a signed language. *Infant Behavior and Development* 15, 453–460.

Masataka, N. (2000). The role of modality and input in the earliest stages of language acquisition: Studies of Japanese Sign Language. In C. Chamberlain, J. P. Morford, and R. I. Mayberry (Eds.), *Language acquisition by eye*. Mahwah, NJ: Lawrence Erlbaum, pp. 3–24.

Mayberry, R. I. (1993). First-language acquisition after childhood differs from second-language acquisition: The case of American Sign Language. *Journal of Speech and Hearing Research* 36, 1258–1270.

Mayberry, R. I., and Eichen, E. (1991). The long-lasting advantage of learning sign language in childhood: Another look at the critical period for language acquisition. *Journal of Memory and Language* 30, 486–512.

Mayberry, R. I., and Squires, B. (2006). Sign language acquisition. In K. Brown K (Ed.), *Encyclopedia of language & linguistics* (2nd ed.). Oxford: Elsevier, pp. 291–296.

Mayberry, R. I., Lock, E., and Kazmi, H. (2002). Linguistic ability and early language exposure. *Nature* 417, 38.

Mayberry, R. I., Chen, J. K., Witcher, P., and Klein, D. (2011). Age of acquisition effects on the functional organization of language in the adult brain. *Brain and Language* 119(1), 16–29.

Meier, R. P., and Newport, E. L. (1990). Out of the hands of babes: On a possible sign advantage in language acquisition. *Language* 66, 1–23.

Mitchell, R. E., and Karchmer, M. A. (2004). Chasing the mythical ten percent: Parental hearing status of deaf and hard of hearing students in the United States. *Sign Language Studies* 4, 128–163.

Moeller, M. P. (2000). Early intervention and language development in children who are deaf and hard of hearing. *Pediatrics* 106, E43.

Morford, J. P. (2003). Grammatical development in adolescent first-language learners. *Linguistics* 41(4), 681–722.

Morgan, G., Herman, R., and Woll, B. (2002). The development of complex verb constructions in BSL. *Journal of Child Language* 29, 23–66.

Nelson, K. (1973). *Structure and strategy in learning to talk.* Monographs of the Society for Research in Child Development, 38 (1/2, Serial No. 149).

Newport, E. (1981). Constraints on structure: Evidence from American Sign Language and language learning. In W. A. Collins (Ed.), *Aspects of the development of competence: Minnesota symposium on child psychology* (vol. 14). Hillsdale, NJ: Erlbaum, pp. 93–124.

Newport, E. (1988). Constraints on learning and their role in language acquisition: Studies of the acquisition of American Sign Language. *Language Sciences* 10(1), 147–172.

Newport, E. L. (1990). Maturational constraints on language learning. *Cognitive Science* 14, 11–28.

Orlansky, M. D., and Bonvillian, J. D. (1985). Sign language acquisition: Language development in children of deaf parents and implications for other populations. *Merrill-Palmer Quarterly* 31, 127–143.

Petitto, L. A., and Marentette, P. (1991). Babbling in the manual mode: Evidence for the ontogeny of language. *Science* 251, 1483–1496.

Preyer, W. T. (1889). *The mind of the child: The development of the intellect* (vol. 2). New York: Appleton.

Rathmann, C., Mann, W., and Morgan, G. (2007). Narrative structure and narrative development in deaf children. *Deafness & Education International* 9(4), 187–196.

Reilly, J. S., McIntire, M., and Bellugi, U. (1990). The acquisition of conditionals in American Sign Language: Grammaticized facial expressions. *Applied Psycholinguistics* 11(4), 369–392.

Schick, B. (1990). The effects of morphosyntactic structure on the acquisition of classifier predicates in ASL. In C. Lucas (Ed.), *Sign language research: Theoretical issues.* Washington, DC: Gallaudet University Press, pp. 358–374.

Schick, B., de Villiers, P., de Villiers, J., and Hoffmeister, R. (2007). Language and theory of mind: A study of deaf children. *Child development* 78(2), 376–396.

Senghas, A., and Coppola, M. (2001). Children creating language: How Nicaraguan Sign Language acquired a spatial grammar. *Psychological Science* 12(4), 323–328.

Siedlecki, T., and Bonvillian, J. D. (1997). Young children's acquisition of the handshape aspect of American Sign Language signs: Parental report findings. *Applied Psycholinguistics* 18(1), 17–39.

Singleton, J. L., and Crume, P. K. (2010). Socializing visual engagement in early childhood deaf education. Poster presented at the 21st international congress on the education of the deaf, Vancouver, Canada.

Slobin, D. I., Hoiting, N., Kuntze, M., Lindert, R., Weinberg, A., Pyers, J., Anthony M., Biederman, Y., and Thumann, H. (2003). A cognitive/functional perspective on the acquisition of "classifiers." In K. Emmorey (Ed.), *Perspectives on classifier constructions in sign languages.* Mahwah, NJ: Lawrence Erlbaum, pp. 271–296.

Spencer, P. E., Bodner-Johnson, B. A., and Gutfreund, M. K. (1992). Interacting with infants with a hearing loss: What can we learn from mothers who are deaf? *Journal of Early Intervention* 16(1), 64–78.

Supalla, T. R. (1982). Structure and acquisition of verbs of motion and location in American Sign Language. PhD dissertation, University of California, San Diego, ProQuest Information & Learning.

Templin, M. C. (1957). *Certain language skills in children.* Minneapolis: University of Minneapolis Press.

Thompson, R., Vinson, D., Fox, N., and Vigliocco, G. (2013). Is lexical access driven by temporal order or perceptual salience? Evidence from British Sign Language. In M. Knauff, M. Pauen, N. Sebanz, and I. Wachsmuth (Eds.), *Proceedings of the 35th annual meeting of the Cognitive Science Society.* Austin, TX: Cognitive Science Society, pp. 1450–1455.

Thompson, R. L., Vinson, D. P., Woll, B., and Vigliocco, G. (2012). The road to language learning is iconic: Evidence from British Sign Language. *Psychological science* 23(12), 1443–1448.

Tomasello, M. (1992). *First verbs: A case study of early grammatical development.* Cambridge: Cambridge University Press.

Woolfe, T., Herman, R., Roy, P., and Woll, B. (2010). Early vocabulary development in deaf native signers: A British Sign Language adaptation of the communicative development inventories. *Journal of Child Psychology and Psychiatry* 51(3), 322–331.

16 Research Methods in Studying Reading and Literacy Development in Deaf Children Who Sign

Fiona E. Kyle

Chapter Overview

This chapter discusses research concerning deaf[1] individuals' reading and spelling development, with a focus on collecting literacy data from deaf children and adolescents. I will begin by presenting an overview of what we know about reading development in deaf individuals, covering topics such as: What are the reading achievements of deaf children? How do deaf children learn to read? Do they learn to read in a similar way to hearing children? This will be followed by a more detailed discussion of the different types of methodologies that have been used to conduct literacy research with deaf children, highlighting important findings. Lastly I will describe some of the issues involved in researching literacy development in deaf children who sign and potential ways of dealing with these issues.

Research Methods in Sign Language Studies: A Practical Guide, First Edition.
Edited by Eleni Orfanidou, Bencie Woll, and Gary Morgan.
© 2015 John Wiley & Sons, Inc. Published 2015 by John Wiley & Sons, Inc.

Introduction to Key Topics in Reading and Literacy

Literacy achievements in deaf children

Becoming literate is one of the biggest challenges a deaf child or adolescent is likely to face at school. Most deaf children experience difficulties with learning to read and exhibit significant delays in comparison with their hearing peers. Because deaf children only make approximately a third of the progress that one would expect a hearing child to make each year (Allen, 1986; Kyle and Harris, 2010, 2011), their reading delay cumulatively increases as they progress through school. This results in the average deaf school leaver having a reading age equivalent to that of a 9-year-old (Allen, 1986; Conrad, 1979; Qi and Mitchell, 2011; Wauters, van Bon, and Tellings, 2006). Deaf children typically exhibit delays in most reading components, which suggests that they find reading difficult because deficits in bottom-up skills such as phonological processing and syntactical knowledge are compounded by top-down deficits in vocabulary, world knowledge, and inferencing skills. Nevertheless, it is important to note that not all deaf children find reading difficult and some do become skilled and fluent readers (Gravenstede and Roy, 2009; Harris and Moreno, 2006).

Deaf children come from diverse language and communication backgrounds, which range from native sign language users with Deaf parents through to the vast majority of the population of deaf children who communicate through speech and have hearing parents. In addition, a large proportion of deaf children have English as a second spoken language at home and, although this is beyond the scope of the current chapter, it is an important issue to bear in mind. Given this variety, an obvious question is: What effect do differences in language preference and background have on literacy skills? Higher levels of reading achievement have been reported in orally educated deaf children (Daneman, Nemeth, Stainton, and Huelsmann, 1995; Geers and Moog, 1989). For example, Daneman and colleagues (1995) described a group of orally educated deaf children who were reading at levels above their chronological age. Similarly, deaf children with cochlear implants, who typically use speech to communicate, are more likely to have reading levels commensurate with those of their hearing peers during the primary school years (Archbold et al., 2008; Geers, 2003), although these early high levels of reading achievements are not necessarily maintained in the teenage years (Geers, Tobey, Moog, and Brenner, 2008; Harris and Terlektsi, 2011). On the other hand, better reading skills have also been reported in Deaf children with Deaf parents, who generally use sign language to communicate (Vernon and Koh, 1970), and in Deaf children who are native signers (Strong and Prinz, 2000). On the face of it, these findings seem contradictory; however, the language preferences of the good deaf readers in Kyle and Harris (2010) help shed light on this issue. Although the good readers were predominantly those who used speech to communicate, four of the seven best readers had also been exposed to British Sign Language (BSL) from an early age and one was a native BSL user with Deaf parents. A plausible interpretation of these findings is that early exposure to language is essential for reading ability in deaf children, regardless of the modality of that language (see also Marschark and Harris, 1996).

Deaf Children's Use of Phonology during Reading

Despite decades of research, there is still no definitive answer to the question of *how* deaf children learn to read, and whether they do so in the *same* way as hearing children. Hearing individuals tend to utilize their knowledge of the relationships between letters and sounds when reading and spelling – that is, they use a phonological code. Indeed, one of the strongest predictors of reading development in typically developing children is their performance on tasks measuring phonological awareness (see Goswami and Bryant, 1990; Castles and Coltheart, 2004). Phonological awareness refers to the ability to detect and manipulate the constituent sounds of words. As deaf individuals typically have incomplete access to spoken language, it is interesting to consider if they also use phonology when reading. Furthermore, do signing deaf children learn to read in the same way as deaf children who communicate through speech? There is some evidence that deaf individuals use phonological coding strategies during reading and spelling, albeit to a lesser extent than hearing individuals (Dodd, 1987; Leybaert and Alegria, 1993; Hanson, Shankweiler, and Fischer, 1983), but equally, other studies find little evidence of phonological coding (Aaron et al., 1998; Beech and Harris, 1997; Ormel, Hermans, Knoors, Hendriks, and Verhoeven, 2010). Collating the findings suggests that deaf individuals *can* make use of phonological skills, but whether they *do* seems to be dependent upon experimental factors such as type of research paradigm used, task demands, and task stimuli and upon participant characteristics such as age, reading ability, educational level, and speech intelligibility.

Surprisingly few studies have actually measured whether the use of a phonological code is associated with reading achievements in deaf children; out of those that have, only a small number observed a positive relationship between the ability to use phonological coding and reading (Hanson, Liberman, and Shankweiler, 1984; Harris and Moreno, 2006; Leybaert and Alegria, 1993). Likewise, while some studies find a relationship between performance on a phonological awareness task and reading in deaf individuals (Colin, Magnan, Ecalle, and Leybaert, 2007; Dyer, MacSweeney, Szczerbinski, Green, and Campbell, 2003; Harris and Beech, 1998), most do not (Hanson and Fowler, 1987; Kyle and Harris, 2006; Leybaert and Alegria, 1993). Kyle and Harris (2010) reported a strong relationship between phonological awareness and reading in deaf children; however, it is important to note that the direction of this relationship was in fact from reading to phonological awareness. This finding is important, as it suggests that deaf children's phonological awareness skills develop as a consequence of learning to read rather than being a precursor of reading ability, as is typically found in hearing children (see also Musselman, 2000; Goldin-Meadow and Mayberry, 2001). Moreover, a very recent meta-analysis of the relationship between phonological skills and reading (Mayberry, del Giudice, and Lieberman, 2011) concluded there is little consistent evidence of the role of phonology in deaf individuals' reading.

The role of other cognitive and linguistic skills in reading

Given the inconsistencies in the findings concerning the role of phonological skills in deaf children's reading, it is not surprising that researchers have looked at the contribution of other cognitive and linguistic skills. Language skills, including vocabulary knowledge, are the strongest and most consistent correlate (Kyle and Harris, 2006; Moores and Sweet, 1990; Waters and Doehring, 1990) and longitudinal predictor (Easterbrooks, Lederberg, Miller, Bergeron, and Connor, 2008; Harris and Beech, 1998; Kyle and Harris, 2010, 2011) of reading skills in deaf children. Indeed, Mayberry et al. (2011) reported that language skills accounted for 35 percent of the variance in deaf reading ability in their meta-analysis. This is unsurprising, given the close relationship between reading and language in hearing children and the severe vocabulary delays exhibited by most deaf children (see Geers and Moog, 1989; Moores and Sweet, 1990; Kyle and Harris, 2006). Language delay has in fact been described as a hallmark of deafness (Musselman, 2000). In two longitudinal studies of reading development in deaf children from mixed language backgrounds (Kyle and Harris, 2010, 2011), we found that vocabulary and speech-reading were the strongest predictors of later reading ability. Other researchers have also found speech-reading to be a strong correlate of reading in deaf children (Arnold and Kopsel, 1996; Campbell and Wright, 1988; Harris and Moreno, 2006) and in deaf adults (Mohammed, Campbell, MacSweeney, Barry, and Coleman, 2006). Although it is plausible to assume that deaf children who use speech would rely more upon speech-reading than signing deaf children, the relationship between speech-reading and reading has in fact been observed in deaf children from a range of language backgrounds (Harris and Moreno, 2006; Kyle and Harris, 2010, 2011).

There is also evidence that good signing skills can facilitate reading in deaf children and adolescents, as positive relationships have been found between signing skill and reading ability (Hermans, Knoors, Ormel, and Verhoeven, 2008a; Padden and Hanson, 2000; Strong and Prinz, 2000). Strong and Prinz (2000) reported a medium correlation between American Sign Language (ASL) proficiency and English literacy skills whereby those with higher levels of ASL had better English literacy skills. The pertinent question remains as to exactly how the relationship between these two skills works. Goldin-Meadow and Mayberry (2001) argue that, although good signing skills result in deaf individuals having good language skills, which could provide a base for reading, these on their own are not sufficient, as children still need some way to connect the signs to the written words. Padden and Ramsey (2000) suggest that it is not general ASL skills that relate to reading, but specific skills that mediate the relationship between reading and ASL.

Theories of how deaf children learn to read

How can we assimilate the findings presented in this overview into a theory of reading development in deaf children? It is reasonable to assume that deaf children who use speech learn to read in essentially the same way as hearing children, namely through the use of a phonological code (see Perfetti and Sandak, 2000). However, it is possible that signing deaf children also learn to read in broadly the same manner, because research suggests that similar skills are important for their reading development. Let us consider what a deaf phonological code might look like: as deaf individuals typically do not have full access to spoken language, it is likely that any phonological code would be based upon phonological representations derived from speechread input (see Hanson et al., 1983; Kyle and Harris, 2010, 2011). It has been argued that a phonological code is abstract and not modality specific, which means that it could equally be derived from auditory or from visual speech (Alegria, 1996; Campbell, 1997). Evidence supporting this argument has been found in speechread errors observed in deaf children's spelling (Dodd, 1980) and phonological judgments (Leybaert and Charlier, 1996) and in the fact that speech-reading is a strong, longitudinal predictor of both reading development and phonological awareness in deaf children (Kyle and Harris, 2010, 2011).

The longitudinal results from Kyle and Harris (2010, 2011) suggest that reading development in deaf children is underpinned by both vocabulary knowledge and speech-reading. This argument can be conceptualized using the simple view of reading (SVR: Gough and Tunmer, 1986), which posits that reading has two components: a linguistic component (vocabulary knowledge and language) and a decoding component (phonological skills). Using this framework, I propose a model of reading development in deaf children (see Figure 16.1) in which the linguistic component of the SVR is captured by vocabulary knowledge and the decoding component encompasses the relationship between speech-reading and phonological awareness. The role of vocabulary is depicted in the model at (1) because it was the strongest and most consistent predictor of reading ability in deaf children. The complex relationship between speech-reading, phonological awareness, and reading depicted in Figure 16.1 originates in Kyle and Harris (2010). Speech-reading provides the input for deaf children's phonological representations and is a strong initial predictor of reading progress (entered in the model at (2)), because it directly taps the input for the phonological representations that are being used to support reading. For similar reasons, speech-reading predicts phonological awareness (3). Phonological awareness is not initially predictive of reading ability; however, as reading develops, deaf children's underlying representations become more specified (thereby enabling these children to make phonological judgments), and therefore reading ability predicts the development of phonological awareness (4). Phonological awareness and reading ability gradually develop a reciprocal relationship, and thus tasks measuring phonological awareness rather than speech-reading become associated with reading (5). This neatly fits in with the argument that deaf children develop their phonological skills through reading (Musselman, 2000; Goldin-Meadow and Mayberry, 2001). As this model is based upon research findings with deaf children from mixed language backgrounds, its applicability for separate language subgroups of deaf children is not yet fully tested.

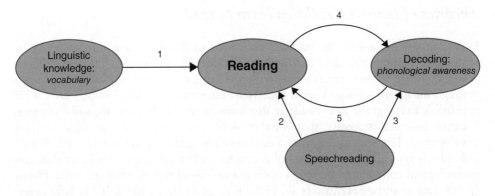

Figure 16.1 Proposed model of reading development in deaf children.

Alternatively, it is possible that deaf children who predominantly use sign language learn to read in a different way from that of deaf children who use speech. Deaf signers might somehow bypass the direct correspondence between letters and sounds. Hermans, Knoors, Ormel and Verhoeven (2008b) proposed that deaf children assimilate new written vocabulary into their existing sign language system and understand new words by creating associations between printed words and their sign equivalents. Other authors have suggested that fingerspelling could work as a bridge between sign language and reading (e.g. Emmorey and Petrich, 2012; Haptonstall-Nykaza and Schick, 2007; Padden and Ramsey, 2000). Padden and Ramsey (2000) observed that teachers were explicitly "chaining" fingerspelling, signs, and written words together when teaching deaf children to read. These arguments tend to be interpreted within a bilingual framework, whereby signing deaf children learn to read English as a second language once they are proficient in their first language (e.g. BSL or ASL). This is a contentious issue, the debating of which is beyond the scope of this chapter (for a full discussion, see Mason and Ewoldt, 1996; Mayer and Wells, 1996).

Spelling ability

Literacy is not just about reading; spelling is an equally important component. This chapter has focused on reading ability because, by comparison to the body of research on deaf children's reading development, there has been far less attention to the impact of deafness on spelling development. In general, although deaf children typically exhibit delays in their spelling ability, the delays are not as severe as those observed for reading (Harris and Moreno, 2004; Moores and Sweet, 1990). For example, Moores and Sweet (1990) found that a group of deaf 16–17-year-olds exhibited an average reading delay of five years, but a spelling delay of only three years. Broadly similar skills are known to be predictive of reading and spelling ability in hearing children (Juel, Griffith, and Gough, 1986) but recent research has suggested that this may not be the case for deaf children. In Kyle and Harris (2006, 2011) we found that, although the reading and the spelling ability were highly related in deaf children, different skills predicted each ability: speech-reading and vocabulary predicted reading development, but only letter knowledge was predictive of beginning spelling ability.

Summary of research into deaf children's literacy

Research suggests that the majority of deaf children are likely to read in the same way as hearing children in terms of requiring phonological skills, and that those with better phonological skills tend to be better readers (see Musselman, 2000 for a review); however, their phonological skills may differ in that they are mainly derived from visual rather than auditory speech. Recent evidence suggests that broadly the same skills are predictive of deaf children's reading as of hearing children's reading: language knowledge and phonological skills. Good signing skills have been found to be associated with higher reading levels in signing deaf children, but the mechanism for this relationship is not yet known or understood.

What Methodologies Have Researchers Employed to Investigate Literacy in Deaf Individuals?

This section will examine how researchers have investigated reading development and the different methodologies used. The relevant strengths and weaknesses of different methodological designs will be discussed along with suggestions for future research.

Large-scale nationwide surveys of reading achievements

The most representative method of investigating reading achievements in deaf individuals is through large-scale, nationwide studies that use standardized reading tests (see Allen, 1986; Conrad, 1979; Trybus and Karchmer, 1977). Researchers in the USA have tended to use the reading comprehension subtest from the Stanford Achievement Test (SAT), which is administered by schools. For example, Trybus and Karchmer (1977) examined the SAT scores for almost 7,000 deaf students in the USA and found that the average 18-year-old had a reading age of between 9 and 10 years. Furthermore, they found that only the top 10 percent were reading at, or above, the level expected for a 13-year-old hearing student. Conrad (1979) conducted an empirical investigation of the reading achievements of deaf school leavers in England and Wales using the individually administered Widespan Reading Test. He reported strikingly similar findings, as the mean reading age was equivalent to that of a 9-year-old hearing child. These large-scale studies are very useful for portraying the reading levels of average deaf children; however, the disadvantage is that they tend to conceal individual differences and successes, as some deaf children learn to read fluently and with comparative ease. They also tend to be cross-sectional in design, and therefore they demonstrate the end point of reading achievement rather than providing insight into how reading develops.

Longitudinal studies of reading ability

Longitudinal studies, in which the same cohort of children is followed over time, are essential in order to understand how reading develops in deaf children and adolescents and how their large reading delays occur. In a recent longitudinal study (Kyle and Harris, 2010), we followed a group of 29 severely and profoundly deaf children over a period of three years. At the beginning of the study, the deaf children, who came from a range of language backgrounds, were all between 7 and 8 years old and had a mean reading delay of 12 months. By the end of the study, three years later, the children had a mean age of 10 years 11 months and their reading delay had increased to almost 3 years. Longitudinal studies are important, as they show us not only the end point but also how that end point was reached. Kyle and Harris (2010) found that the deaf children, as a group, made slow but steady reading development equating to 0.3 grades each year, the same rate as reported 25 years earlier by Allen (1986). As demonstrated in Figure 16.2, the longitudinal design of Kyle and Harris (2010) reveals the huge

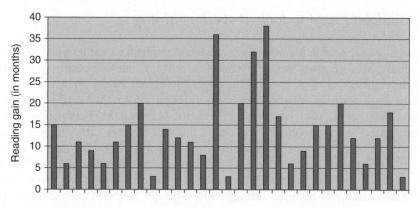

Figure 16.2 Graph showing the huge individual variation in reading progress (in months) over a 3-year period. Created from data reported in Kyle and Harris, 2010.

individual variation in reading progress: although a few deaf children made a full 36-month progress in reading over a 3-year period, the majority made far less.

Longitudinal studies tend to be a less common design, as they are very costly in terms of time and resources. As a result, the sample sizes tend to be relatively small, which can make interpretation and generalizability of results difficult. One of the main challenges of longitudinal designs is participant retention for the duration of the study, as these designs often suffer from high participant drop-out rates. In addition, the assessment battery needs to be appropriate for repeated use. Some tests have alternative versions that can be used at different time points or, depending upon the time interval between data points, it is usually acceptable for most standardized tests to be used again after approximately 12 months.

Selection of reading tests

Reading is not a simple unitary skill; it consists of many different components that are all necessary in order to achieve fluent and effortless reading. Collating the results from existing separate studies suggests that deaf children experience difficulties in almost all reading components: word recognition and identification (Waters and Doehring, 1990); single-word reading (James, Rajput, Brinton, and Goswami, 2008; Kyle and Harris, 2006, 2010); grammatical and syntactic knowledge (Lillo-Martin, Hanson, and Smith, 1991); and text comprehension (Allen, 1986; Kyle and Harris, 2011). There are many different reading tests that can be used to assess the various reading components. This makes it essential to know exactly which aspect of reading is being measured by the selected reading test, particularly as deaf children typically exhibit more severe reading delays on tests of comprehension than on word-reading tests, and different skills are known to be important for different reading components (see Kyle and Harris, 2006, 2010). Some standardized reading tests can be suitable for use with deaf children (with appropriate adjustments to the administration procedures). However, when interpreting the results, it is important to remember that the norms have been derived from hearing children. There are no reading tests designed especially for use with deaf children in the UK.

Methodologies used to look at spelling ability

It is not always possible for researchers to use standardized spelling tasks with deaf individuals, because most assessments use an oral spelling to dictation method. For example, if the target word is "car," the experimenter might say the word "car," then use it in a sentence, to ensure there is no ambiguity over the word (e.g. "my dad drives a blue car"), and then repeat the word "car" again. This method of oral administration is inappropriate for deaf children, as it is difficult to determine whether spelling errors occur because the child does not know how to spell the word or simply because of a misunderstanding about the target word. Researchers have resolved this issue by developing experimental picture-based spelling tasks in which individuals are shown pictures and asked to write the label (Burden and Campbell, 1994; Harris and Moreno, 2004; Kyle and Harris, 2006, 2011). Although this disambiguates the target word, it limits the test stimuli to words such as concrete nouns, which can be easily represented pictorially, and makes the inclusion of verbs and plural nouns difficult. However, it is possible to assess deaf children's knowledge of particular aspects of spelling, such as plural forms, through specially designed experimental tasks. For example, Breadmore, Olson, and Krott (2012) designed a picture-based test of children's plural noun-spelling in which children were shown a picture of a singular noun "person" along with the printed word "person" and then a picture of "people" and asked to write the corresponding plural noun.

Methodologies used to investigate the use of a phonological code

Researchers have used a range of different experimental paradigms to investigate whether deaf children and adolescents use a phonological code. Although evidence for phonological coding can be investigated in reading, spelling, and memory, this section will focus on methodologies used to look for evidence of phonological coding in reading and spelling. Lexical decision tasks, in which participants are shown letter strings and have to judge whether these strings are real words, are the main paradigm used to explore whether deaf adolescents use a phonological code. The hallmark of a phonological code is that individuals are faster and more accurate at judging a real word when it has a regular spelling pattern (e.g. "book" vs. "pint"). Little evidence of regularity effects has been found with deaf participants (e.g. Burden and Campbell, 1994; Waters and Doehring, 1990), although phonological manipulations in terms of rhyming (Hanson and Fowler, 1987) and homophony (Beech and Harris, 1997) have indicated the use of a phonological code. For example, Hanson and Fowler (1987) presented pairs of letter strings and asked deaf participants to indicate whether the pair consisted of two real words. Participants were faster in making a decision when the word pairs were both orthographically and phonologically similar (*SAVE–WAVE*) than when the pairs were only orthographically similar (*HAVE–CAVE*), indicating that they were accessing the phonological properties of the words.

Another paradigm used to investigate the type of strategy employed by deaf readers during silent reading is a letter cancellation task. Letter cancellation tasks require participants to read a passage for comprehension and cross out a target letter. If readers miss target letters that are either silent (e.g. the letter "e" in 'spade') or pronounced in an unusual way, this suggests that they are using a phonological strategy when reading (Dodd, 1987; Gibbs, 1989). For example, Dodd (1987) found that deaf adolescents missed significantly more silent "e"s than pronounced ones. Lexical decision and letter cancellation tasks are fairly unnatural and ecologically invalid paradigms, as they do not match the task demands of reading. Using a reading aloud task, which is closer to the actual reading process, Leybaert and Alegria (1993) found that orally educated deaf adolescents accessed phonological representations during reading as they read aloud pseudo-homophones as accurately as hearing children – a process that necessitates phonological coding.

The sheer number of studies with different cohorts employing a range of methodologies and designs to assess the use of reading strategies by deaf children clearly demonstrates that there is no best method to do so. Much of the discrepancy in results can be explained by experimental factors such as participants' age; levels of reading ability; levels of speech intelligibility; and specific task design. Therefore it is essential to control for these factors. Few studies have directly looked at deaf children's use of coding strategies during reading, and there is an opportunity for further research using eye-tracking paradigms.

There is more consistency in the methods used to study phonological coding in deaf children's spelling. The most common method is to examine their spelling errors to see whether the errors are phonetically acceptable, which suggests the use of a phonological code (Hanson et al., 1983; Harris and Moreno, 2004; Leybaert and Alegria, 1995). For example, Harris and Moreno (2004) found that less than 20 percent of deaf children's spelling errors were phonetically acceptable errors such as *baterre* or *battary* for the target word *battery*, by comparison with at least 60 percent of hearing children's errors.

Methodologies used to investigate reading-related skills

Another way of looking at how deaf children read is to examine which linguistic and cognitive skills are associated with, or predict, reading development. There are many different experimental tasks that have been used to measure phonological awareness, most of which require a judgment of rhyme similarity (Campbell and Wright, 1988; Colin et al., 2007; Harris and Beech, 1998). It is important to use picture-based tasks when assessing phonological awareness in deaf individuals, especially those who sign, as the usual oral testing format is inappropriate. For example, Campbell and Wright (1988) created a picture-based rhyme judgment task in which deaf adolescents were shown pairs of pictures (*VASE–CASE* or *DOG–FROG*) and asked to judge whether they rhymed. A disadvantage of using picture-based phonological awareness tasks is that it limits the complexity of the phonological manipulation that can be assessed. For example, it is very difficult to unambiguously, pictorially represent the stimuli for a spoonerisms test, in which children would typically be orally presented with two words "KING JOHN" and asked to swap the onsets of each word to form two new words "JING KOHN."

In contrast to phonological awareness, other reading-related skills, such as language skills and vocabulary knowledge, are often measured by using a range of standardized assessments. The only way to really gain an understanding of the relative predictive power of different reading-related skills is to assess several of them in the same group of deaf children; however, few studies have compared the relative predictive power of these cognitive skills in the same cohorts. In two longitudinal studies of reading development in deaf children from mixed language backgrounds (Kyle and Harris, 2010, 2011), children were assessed for vocabulary knowledge, speech-reading (silent lip-reading), phonological awareness, and short-term memory. The results were virtually identical in both cohorts: vocabulary and speech-reading were the strongest predictors of later reading ability, whereas neither short-term memory nor phonological awareness was predictive (once the effects of earlier reading ability were controlled). In addition to exploring the relative predictive power of reading related skills, there is also a need for more research directly comparing and contrasting predictors of reading development for deaf children from different language backgrounds. The best method of exploring the importance of reading-related skills for reading is through longitudinal studies (Colin et al., 2007; Harris and Beech, 1998; Kyle and Harris, 2010, 2011). These are superior to cross-sectional correlational studies, as they show the direction of the relationship between skills and can determine whether the predictors of reading ability change with increasing levels of proficiency.

Another way to examine the relationship between reading and reading-related skills is to conduct a meta-analysis of the existing research. To date, there has been only one such meta-analysis (Mayberry et al., 2011). Mayberry and colleagues computed effect sizes for 25 studies (out of an initial 230 publications) that investigated the relationship between phonological skills and reading ability. They calculated that phonological skills only had a small to medium effect (0.35) and accounted for 11 percent of the variance in reading ability.

Alternately, deaf children's reading development can be investigated by identifying good and poor deaf readers and by comparing their performance on reading-related skills. Because some deaf children learn to read comparatively easily, it is important to gain an understanding of what skills enable them to become good readers. Harris and Moreno (2006) compared two groups of deaf children who were either reading within 10 months of their chronological age (good readers) or at least 15 months behind chronological age (poor readers). The good readers were more accurate on tasks that measured orthographic awareness and speech-reading, and they showed more evidence of phonological coding during spelling. Another study of good and poor readers (Kyle and Harris, 2010), highlighted the importance of language exposure, as deaf children with small reading delays tended to have better levels of hearing, earlier diagnoses, and were more likely to use speech and to have deaf parents than children with large reading delays.

What Are the Issues When Conducting Literacy Research with Signing Deaf Children and How Can We Resolve Them?

This section will examine potential issues that can arise when conducting reading research with Deaf signing children and will discuss possible ways to address or resolve these issues. Some of them cannot necessarily be resolved, but rather are factors that must be taken into consideration.

Assessing literacy skills in a second language

One of the most important issues that researchers need to be aware of when investigating literacy with signing Deaf individuals is that they are assessing reading skills in a language (e.g. English) that is not the participant's first language (e.g. BSL). While this is unavoidable, as there is no written component for sign languages, it must be acknowledged that the situation is different from measuring reading skills in hearing individuals or in deaf individuals who use speech, where one usually assesses written and spoken knowledge of the same language. This issue introduces a bilingual element into the assessment of reading skills for signing Deaf children.

Reading tests have different task demands for signing Deaf children

Reading tests have different task demands for deaf children from diverse language backgrounds. Standardized tests of word-reading or reading accuracy are typically productive tasks; to understand the impact of this fact, it is helpful to consider how a hearing child completes a word-reading task. A hearing child can decode unfamiliar words by applying grapheme to phoneme correspondence rules; the child does not have to know the word or the meaning of it in order to produce it. A hearing child can attempt to decode the word into its parts, retrieve the associated sounds, assemble and synthesize them, and produce an answer. It is likely that deaf children who rely upon speech, however inefficiently, use the same route to reading as hearing children. In contrast, the demands on a signing child are different: that child has to recognize the word and access semantic properties in order to produce the correct sign; (s)he has no way of producing a correct response without knowing the meaning of the word. Therefore reading accuracy is a different task for Deaf children who sign from what it is for children who use speech, and researchers need to be aware of this issue when exploring deaf children's reading skills at the word level. This does not affect reading comprehension to the same extent, because both groups of deaf children can use context to infer the meaning of unfamiliar words.

Ensuring that test items are suitable for use with Deaf signing children

Few tasks are standardized on deaf children, and therefore most assessments of reading and reading-related skills were originally designed for use with hearing children. These tests cannot always be easily used with signing Deaf children without some modification. For example, there are often items on a word reading test for which there is no sign equivalent. These can include items for which there is no specific sign (for example there is no BSL sign for the English form "was"), or instances of plural nouns like "children" (the BSL sign for the singular "child" and the plural "children" is the same), or different forms or tenses of a verb (for example the BSL sign for "sing" and "sang" is the same). The challenge is therefore how to score answers on these types of items. Some researchers specify what they have done, but many do not. James and colleagues (2008) clearly detail their administration and scoring method for a word-reading test. They give an example of a test item "babies" and state that, for the item to be marked as correct, the child must indicate plurality. This is an interesting case: if researchers accept the sign "baby" for the word "babies" from Deaf signing children but will only accept the spoken form "babies" from non-signing children, then the signing deaf children could have an advantage that might result in overinflated scores. There is no definitive way to score these answers, so it is essential to be consistent and transparent about the scoring procedure; validity can be increased by conducting reliability checking on the scoring procedure. Another way to address the issue could be to devise a reading test especially designed for use with deaf individuals, so that it assesses reading for words that do have equivalent signs. However, any such test would need extensive verification in order to ensure that the content is valid and not oversimplified or too narrow.

Devising picture based tasks

Most of the tasks measuring reading-related skills in hearing children are delivered in an oral format. This is obviously not appropriate for deaf children, as researchers cannot be certain that the participants have unambiguously understood the target item. Instead researchers frequently devise picture-based assessments, especially when measuring phonological awareness (Harris and Beech, 1998; Kyle and Harris, 2006; James et al., 2008) and memory (Harris and Moreno, 2004; Kyle and Harris, 2006). Figure 16.3 presents an example of an item from a picture-based phonological awareness task from Kyle and

Figure 16.3 An item from the picture-based phonological awareness task that requires a judgment of rhyme similarity. From Kyle and Harris, 2006.

Harris (2006). Children were shown the top picture *train* and then the bottom two pictures *rain* and *star* and asked to point to the one that sounded the same at the end as the top picture. When designing picture-based tests, it is essential that all items are represented unambiguously, which does limit the choice of items (see the discussion under the section about spelling methodologies).

Tasks must contain appropriate language/vocabulary levels for Deaf signing children

Deaf children typically have language delays, and indeed reading is itself often a language-learning task for deaf children. If the language level of a test that measures reading or reading-related skills is not appropriate, deaf children's performance on that task might simply reflect their language level rather than the reading skill that is purported to be measured. For example, when assessing reading comprehension, if the comprehension questions contain complex grammatical structures, then a deaf child might perform poorly not because (s)he could not understand the text itself, but because (s)he could not understand the question about the text. Similarly, when designing tasks to measure reading-related skills – such as speech-reading – the lexical content of test items needs to be appropriate, to ensure that the task is an assessment of speech-reading ability rather than of vocabulary (see Kyle, Campbell, Mohammed, Coleman, and MacSweeney, 2013). Otherwise, for example, a deaf child may be able to speechread the item but be unable to select the correct picture from an array simply because (s)he does not know what the item is. Likewise, it is essential for children to know the vocabulary involved in a phonological awareness task in order to be able to make phonological judgments about the items. Researchers often address this issue by pretesting children on the items or pictures to ensure that the items are familiar and that children have the correct label for each item (see James et al., 2008; Harris and Moreno, 2004; Kyle and Harris, 2006).

Appropriate response method

Many tests of reading and reading-related skills require verbal responses, which is obviously not an appropriate format for many deaf children. For example, historically, most speech-reading tests required the participants to repeat aloud or to write down what they saw (Conrad, 1979). This makes it difficult to determine whether errors are due to poor speech-reading or to poor speech intelligibility. A more deaf-friendly method for assessing speech-reading and other reading-related tasks would be to devise picture-matching tasks or tasks in which children can point to the answer (see Kyle et al., 2013).

Heterogeneity of the deaf population

A final issue to consider when conducting literacy research with deaf children is the huge heterogeneity in their language skills, language backgrounds, and audiological factors. Although people talk about "oral" or "signing" deaf children, it is often difficult to categorize their language skills into these discrete categories. Deaf children's language preferences tend to be on a continuum ranging from signing through to speech, but most children are somewhere in the middle, combining sign and speech to a greater or lesser extent. It is important to note that, although this issue of language heterogeneity is not unique to reading research, it is of great consequence because of the close relationship between language and reading. There are many factors that contribute to heterogeneity within the deaf population and these can affect reading skills. Therefore researchers need to collect a range of background data about deaf participants in order to interpret findings in light of group characteristics. These include age of diagnosis; type of amplification aids and age fitted; family history of deafness; preferred language; exposure to sign and spoken language; and competency in sign and spoken language among other factors.

In conclusion, research suggests that deaf and hearing children show both similarities and differences in their reading development and in the skills that are important for literacy. Language skills play a key role, and deaf children with good phonological skills tend to be better readers. Evidence suggests that speech-reading provides the input for deaf children's phonological codes; and, on the basis of recent findings, I have proposed a model of deaf reading development. Many different experimental tasks have been devised to assess reading and reading-related skills through a range of methodologies. Further longitudinal and relatively large-scale and representative studies are needed to clarify some of the outstanding issues. There are many factors that need to be considered when conducting literacy research with signing deaf children – some of which can be resolved by adapting tasks to make them suitable and by collecting sufficient background data through which findings can be interpreted.

Note

1   In this chapter I focus on methods for investigating reading and literacy and use lowercase *deaf* to refer to the audiological meaning of deafness. I do not go a lot into the cultural meanings of uppercase *Deaf*, but I use it to refer to native signers.

Keywords

deafness; literacy; longitudinal; phonological awareness; reading; speechreading; spelling

See Also

Chapter 13; Chapter 15

Suggested Readings

Chamberlain, C., and Mayberry, R. I. (2008). American Sign Language syntactic and narrative comprehension in skilled and less skilled readers: Bilingual and bimodal evidence for the linguistic basis of reading. *Applied Psycholinguistics* 29(3), 367–388.

Chamberlain, C., Morford, J. P., and Mayberry, R. I. (Eds.) (2000). *Language acquisition by eye*. Mahwah, NJ: Lawrence Erlbaum.

LaSasso, C. J., Crain, K., and Leybaert, J. (2003). Rhyme generation in deaf students: The effect of exposure to cued speech. *Journal of Deaf Studies and Deaf Education* 8(3), 250–270.

Marschark, M., Rhoten, C., and Fabich, M. (2007). Effects of cochlear implants on children's reading and academic achievement. *Journal of Deaf Studies and Deaf Education* 12, 269–282.

Strong, M., and Prinz, P. M. (1997). A study of the relationship between American Sign Language and English literacy. *Journal of Deaf Studies and Deaf Education* 2(1), 37–46.

References

Aaron, P. G., Keetay, V., Boyd, M., Palmatier, S., and Wacks, J. (1998). Spelling without phonology: A study of deaf and hearing children. *Reading and Writing: An Interdisciplinary Journal* 10, 1–22.

Alegria, J. (1996). On the origin of phonological representations in deaf people. In M. Carreiras, J. E. Garcia-Albea, and N. Sebastian-Galles (Eds.), *Language processing in Spanish*. Mahwah, NJ: Lawrence Erlbaum, pp. 119–143.

Allen, T. E. (1986). Patterns of academic achievement among hearing impaired students: 1974 and 1983. In A. N. Schildroth and M. A. Karchmer (Eds.), *Deaf children in America*. San Diego, CA: College-Hill Press, pp. 161–206.

Archbold, S. M., Harris, M., O'Donoghue, G., Nikolopoulos, T., White, A., and Lloyd Richmond, H. (2008). Reading abilities after cochlear implantation: The effect of age at implantation on outcomes at five and seven years after implantation. *International Journal of Pediatric Otorhinolaryngology* 72, 1471–1478.

Arnold, P., and Kopsel, A. (1996). Lipreading, reading and memory of hearing and hearing-impaired children. *Scandinavian Journal of Audiology* 25(1), 13–20.

Beech, J. R., and Harris, M. (1997). The prelingually deaf young reader: A case of reliance on direct lexical access? *Journal of Research in Reading* 20(2), 105–121.

Breadmore, H. L., Olson, A. C., and Krott, A. (2012). Deaf and hearing children's plural noun spelling. *The Quarterly Journal of Experimental Psychology* 65(11), 2169–2192.

Burden, V., and Campbell, R. (1994). The development of word-coding skills in the born deaf: An experimental study of deaf school leavers. *British Journal of Developmental Psychology* 12, 331–349.

Campbell, R. (1997). Read the lips: Speculations on the nature and role of lipreading in cognitive development of deaf children. In M. Marschark, P. Siple, D. Lillo-Martin, R. Campbell, and V. S. Everhart (Eds.), *Relations of language and thought: The view from sign language and deaf children*. Oxford: Oxford University Press, pp. 110–146.

Campbell, R., and Wright, H. (1988). Deafness, spelling and rhyme: How spelling supports written word and picture rhyming skills in deaf subjects. *The Quarterly Journal of Experimental Psychology* 40A(4), 771–788.

Castles, A., and Coltheart, M. (2004). Is there a causal link from phonological awareness to success in learning to read? *Cognition* 91(1), 77–111.

Colin, S., Magnan, A., Ecalle, J., and Leybaert, J. (2007). Relation between deaf children's phonological skills in kindergarten and word recognition performance in first grade. *Journal of Child Psychology and Psychiatry*, 48(2), 139–146.

Conrad, R. (1979). *The deaf school child: Language and cognitive function*. London: Harper & Row.

Daneman, M., Nemeth, S., Stainton, M., and Huelsmann, K. (1995). Working memory as a predictor of reading achievement in orally educated hearing-impaired children. *The Volta Review* 97, 225–241.

Dodd, B. (1980). The spelling abilities of profoundly pre-lingually deaf children. In U. Frith (Ed.), *Cognitive processes in spelling*. London: Academic Press, pp. 423–440.

Dodd, B. (1987). Lip-reading, phonological coding and deafness. In B. Dodd and R. Campbell (Eds.), *Hearing by eye: The psychology of lip-reading*. London: Lawrence Erlbaum, pp. 177–189.

Dyer, A., MacSweeney, M., Szczerbinski, M., Green, L., and Campbell, R. (2003). Predictors of reading delay in deaf adolescents: The relative contributions of rapid automatized naming speed and phonological awareness and decoding. *Journal of Deaf Studies and Deaf Education* 8(3), 215–229.

Easterbrooks, S. R., Lederberg, A. R., Miller, E. M., Bergeron, J. P., and Connor, C. M. (2008). Emergent literacy skills during early childhood in children with hearing loss: Strengths and weaknesses. *The Volta Review* 108(2), 91–114.

Emmorey, K., and Petrich, J. A. F. (2012). Processing orthographic structure: Associations between print and fingerspelling. *Journal of Deaf Studies and Deaf Education* 17(2), 194–204.

Geers, A. E. (2003). Predictors of reading skill development in children with early cochlear implantation. *Ear & Hearing* 24(1S), 59S–68S.

Geers, A. E., and Moog, J. (1989). Factors predictive of the development of literacy in profoundly hearing-impaired adolescents. *The Volta Review*, 91, 69–86.

Geers, A. E., Tobey, E. A., Moog, J., and Brenner, C. (2008). Long-term outcomes of cochlear implantation in the preschool years: From elementary grades to high school. *International Journal of Audiology* 27(S2), 21–30.

Gibbs, K. W. (1989). Individual differences in cognitive skills related to reading ability in the deaf. *American Annals of the Deaf* 134(3), 214–218.

Goldin-Meadow, S., and Mayberry, R. I. (2001). How do profoundly deaf children learn to read? *Learning Disabilities Research & Practice* 16(4), 222–229.

Goswami, U., and Bryant, P. (1990). *Phonological skills and learning to read*. Hove, UK: Lawrence Erlbaum.

Gough, P. B., and Tunmer, W. E. (1986). Decoding, reading, and reading disability. *Remedial and Special Education* 7(1), 6–10.

Gravenstede, L., and Roy, P. (2009). Phonological awareness and decoding skills in deaf adolescents. *Deafness & Education International* 11(4), 171–190.

Hanson, V. L., and Fowler, C. A. (1987). Phonological coding in word reading: Evidence from hearing and deaf readers. *Memory and Cognition* 15(3), 199–207.

Hanson, V. L., Liberman, I. Y., and Shankweiler, D. (1984). Linguistic coding by deaf children in relation to beginning reading success. *Journal of Experimental Child Psychology* 37, 378–393.

Hanson, V. L., Shankweiler, D., and Fischer, F. W. (1983). Determinants of spelling ability in deaf and hearing adults: Access to linguistic structure. *Cognition* 14, 323–344.

Haptonstall-Nykaza, T. S., and Schick, B. (2007). The transition from fingerspelling to English print: Facilitating English decoding. *Journal of Deaf Studies and Deaf Education* 12(2), 172–183.

Harris, M., and Beech, J. R. (1998). Implicit phonological awareness and early reading development in prelingually deaf children. *Journal of Deaf Studies and Deaf Education* 3(3), 205–216.

Harris, M., and Moreno, C. (2004). Deaf children's use of phonological coding: Evidence from reading, spelling and working memory. *Journal of Deaf Studies and Deaf Education* 9(3), 253–268.

Harris, M., and Moreno, C. (2006). Speech reading and learning to read: A comparison of 8-year-old profoundly deaf children with good and poor reading ability. *Journal of Deaf Studies and Deaf Education*, 11(2), 189–201.

Harris, M., and Terlektsi, E. (2011). Reading and spelling abilities of deaf adolescents with cochlear implants and hearing aids. *Journal of Deaf Studies and Deaf Education* 16(1), 24–34.

Hermans, D., Knoors, H., Ormel, E., and Verhoeven, L. (2008a). The relationship between the reading and signing skills of deaf children in bilingual education programs. *Journal of Deaf Studies and Deaf Education* 13(4), 518–530.

Hermans, D., Knoors, H., Ormel, E., and Verhoeven, L. (2008b). Modeling reading vocabulary learning in deaf children in bilingual education programs. *Journal of Deaf Studies and Deaf Education* 13(2), 155–174.

James, D., Rajput, K., Brinton, J., and Goswami, U. (2008). Phonological awareness, vocabulary, and word reading in children who use cochlear implants: Does age of implantation explain individual variability in performance outcomes and growth? *Journal of Deaf Studies and Deaf Education* 13(1), 117–137.

Juel, C., Griffith, P., and Gough, P. (1986). Acquisition of literacy: A longitudinal study of children in first and second grade. *Journal of Educational Psychology* 78(4), 243–255.

Kyle, F. E., and Harris, M. (2006). Concurrent correlates and predictors of reading and spelling achievement in deaf and hearing school children. *Journal of Deaf Studies and Deaf Education* 11(3), 273–288.

Kyle, F. E., and Harris, M. (2010). Predictors of reading development in deaf children: A 3-year longitudinal study. *Journal of Experimental Child Psychology* 107(3), 229–243.

Kyle, F. E., and Harris, M. (2011). Longitudinal patterns of emerging literacy in beginning deaf and hearing readers. *Journal of Deaf Studies and Deaf Education* 16(3), 289–304.

Kyle, F. E., Campbell, R., Mohammed, T., Coleman, M., and MacSweeney, M. (2013). Speechreading development in deaf and hearing children: Introducing the Test of Child Speechreading. *Journal of Speech, Language and Hearing Research* 56(2), 416–426.

Leybaert, J., and Alegria, J. (1993). Is word processing involuntary in deaf children? *British Journal of Developmental Psychology* 11, 1–29.

Leybaert, J., and Alegria, J. (1995). Spelling development in deaf and hearing children: Evidence for use of morpho-phonological regularities in French. *Reading and Writing: An Interdisciplinary Journal* 7, 89–109.

Leybaert, J., and Charlier, B. L. (1996). Visual speech in the head: The effect of cued speech on rhyming, remembering and spelling. *Journal of Deaf Studies and Deaf Education* 1(4), 234–248.

Lillo-Martin, D. C., Hanson, V. L., and Smith, S. T. (1991). Deaf readers' comprehension of complex syntactic structure. In D. S. Martin (Ed.), *Advances in cognition, education, and deafness*. Washington, DC: Gallaudet University Press, pp. 146–151.

Marschark, M., and Harris, M. (1996). Success and failure in learning to read: The special case (?) of deaf children. In C. Cornoldi and J. Oakhill (Eds.), *Reading comprehension difficulties: Process and intervention*. Hillsdale, NJ: Lawrence Erlbaum, pp. 279–300.

Mason, D., and Ewoldt, C. (1996). Whole language and deaf bilingual–bicultural education: Naturally! *American Annals of the Deaf*, 141, 293–298.

Mayberry, R. I., del Giudice, A. A., and Lieberman, A. M. (2011). Reading achievement in relation to phonological coding and awareness in deaf readers: A meta-analysis. *Journal of Deaf Studies and Deaf Education* 16(2), 164–188.

Mayer, C., and Wells, G. (1996). Can the linguistic interdependence theory support a bilingual–bicultural model of literacy education for deaf students? *Journal of Deaf Studies and Deaf Education* 1(2), 93–107.

Mohammed, T., Campbell, R., MacSweeney, M., Barry, F., and Coleman, M. (2006). Speechreading and its association with reading among deaf, hearing and dyslexic individuals. *Clinical Linguistics & Phonetics* 20(7/8), 621–630.

Moores, D. F., and Sweet, C. (1990). Factors predictive of school achievement. In D. F. Moores and K. P. Meadow-Orlans (Eds.), *Educational and developmental aspects of deafness*. Washington, DC: Gallaudet University Press, pp. 154–201.

Musselman, C. (2000). How do children who can't hear learn to read an alphabetic script? A review of the literature on reading and deafness. *Journal of Deaf Studies and Deaf Education* 5(1), 9–31.

Ormel, E., Hermans, D., Knoors, H., Hendriks, A., and Verhoeven, L. (2010). Phonological activation during visual word recognition in deaf and hearing children. *Journal of Speech, Language and Hearing Research* 53(4), 801–820.

Padden, C. A., and Hanson, V. L. (2000). Search for the missing link: The development of skilled reading in deaf children. In K. Emmorey and H. Lane (Eds.), *The signs of language revisited: An anthology to honor Ursula Bellugi and Edward Klima*. Mahwah, NJ: Lawrence Erlbaum, pp. 435–447.

Padden, C. A., and Ramsey, C. (2000). American Sign Language and reading ability in deaf children. In C. Chamberlain, J. P. Morford, and R. I. Mayberry (Eds.), *Language acquisition by eye*. Mahwah, NJ: Lawrence Erlbaum, pp. 165–189.

Perfetti, C. A., and Sandak, R. (2000). Reading optimally builds on spoken language: Implications for deaf readers. *Journal of Deaf Studies and Deaf Education* 5(1), 32–50.

Qi, S., and Mitchell, R. E. (2011). Large-scale academic achievement testing of deaf and hard-of-hearing students: Past, present, and future. *Journal of Deaf Studies and Deaf Education* 17(1), 1–18.

Strong, M., and Prinz, P. M. (2000). Is American Sign Language skill related to English literacy? In C. Chamberlain, J. P. Morford, and R. I. Mayberry (Eds.), *Language acquisition by eye*. Mahwah, NJ: Erlbaum, pp. 131–141.

Trybus, R. J., and Karchmer, M. A. (1977). School achievement scores of hearing impaired children: National data on achievement status and growth patterns. *American Annals of the Deaf* 122(2), 62–69.

Vernon, M., and Koh, S. D. (1970). Early manual communication and deaf children's achievement. *American Annals of the Deaf* 115(5), 527–536.

Waters, G. S., and Doehring, D. G. (1990). Reading acquisition in congenitally deaf children who communicate orally: Insights from an analysis of component reading, language, and memory skills. In T. H. Carr and B. A. Levy (Eds.), *Reading and its development: Component skills approaches*. San Diego, CA: Academic Press, pp. 323–373.

Wauters, L., van Bon, W., and Tellings, A. (2006).Reading comprehension of Dutch deaf children. *Reading and Writing* 19(1), 49–76.

Part V   Collecting Brain Data on Sign Languages

17 Studying Sign Language Processing Using Functional Neuroimaging Techniques: FMRI, ERP, MEG and TMS

Cheryl M. Capek and Helen J. Neville

Chapter Overview

This chapter focuses on four main techniques for investigating the neural organization of cognitive functions, placing an emphasis on their use of studies of sign language processing. These techniques are: functional magnetic resonance imaging, event-related potential, magnetoencephalography, and transcranial magnetic stimulation. For each technique, a brief description of the methodology is followed by particular considerations for sign language research – experimental manipulation, selection of participant groups, and particular communication issues for testing deaf[1] participants.

Research Methods in Sign Language Studies: A Practical Guide, First Edition.
Edited by Eleni Orfanidou, Bencie Woll, and Gary Morgan.
© 2015 John Wiley & Sons, Inc. Published 2015 by John Wiley & Sons, Inc.

Over the last 15 years research into the neurobiology of sign language has flourished. Overall, these studies show that remarkably similar, but not identical, brain systems support signed and spoken language processing (for a review, see MacSweeney, Capek, Campbell, and Woll, 2008). This chapter focuses on four main techniques for investigating the neural organization of cognitive functions: functional magnetic resonance imaging (fMRI), event-related potential (ERP), magnetoencephalography (MEG), and transcranial magnetic stimulation (TMS).

FMRI

The magnetic resonance imaging (MRI) technique produces highly detailed pictures of the structure of both hard and soft tissue of the body, including the brain. It uses radio frequency (RF) pulses to briefly perturb the orientation of hydrogen nuclei in tissue, which are aligned either in a parallel or in an anti-parallel direction due to the presence of a strong magnetic field. Receiver coils, then measure the precessing (or rotation) of these nuclei as they return to their original state. The time taken to return to the original state varies as a function of tissue density; thus MRI produces exceptionally clear delineation of different tissue types, such as grey and white matter. Similarly, with functional MRI (fMRI), oxy-hemoglobin, the type of protein that carries oxygen in the blood, and deoxy-hemaglobin, its oxygen-depleted form, have different signal intensities. Neurons that are active in a particular task, such as processing meaningful sign or speech, will require more oxygen than when involved in a control task, such as processing pseudo-sign or pseudo-speech. The subtraction design aims to isolate activity in brain regions involved in a particular cognitive process by subtracting the signal elicited by a control task from the signal elicited by an experimental task. Comparing conditions using a factorial design may be advantageous over a simple subtractive method, as it can be used to isolate brain regions that are involved in specific interactions as well as regions specific to particular cognitive processes (Friston et al., 1996).

FMRI measures relative blood oxygenation-level-dependent (or BOLD) states across time and is an indirect measure of neural activity. The hemodynamic response is relatively sluggish, peaking at 6–10 s after the onset of a stimulus or task. However, despite its poor temporal resolution, it provides an exquisite spatial resolution, of the order of millimeters.

As the BOLD response signal change between conditions is typically about 4 percent in primary sensory cortices and only 2 percent in higher cortical regions, the main challenge of fMRI is to detect a small, experimentally induced response embedded in noise, or extraneous effects in the signal. Sources of noise are vast; they include system noise from the imaging equipment – for instance the magnetic field drifting over an experimental run – and noise from the participant – for instance head movement and changes in oxygen utilization over time. While suggestions for optimizing experimental design in fMRI experiments are discussed elsewhere (see Huettel, Song, and McCarthy, 2009; Wager and Nichols 2003; Jezzard, Matthews, and Smith, 2008), the following sections here focus on conducting efficient studies of sign language processing.

Experimental manipulations

As stated above, since fMRI measures the relative BOLD effect, characterizing active brain areas must always be described in comparison to the control condition. Whereas studies investigating the neural organization of speech processing use control conditions in which acoustic properties such as loudness and pitch can be closely matched to those in the experimental condition (for example, see Scott, Blank, Rosen, and Wise, 2000), selecting appropriate control conditions for sign language can be particularly challenging. First, since sign language is conveyed by using multiple articulators such as the head, face, and torso as well as the hands and arms (Boyes Braem and Sutton-Spence, 2001), selecting stimuli across conditions that are matched on movement complexity across all articulators may involve resorting to stimuli that are biologically implausible, such as distorted movements produced by an avatar. Second, while speech played backward is unintelligible, native signers can often understand even entire signed sentences played in reverse. Alternative control conditions include pseudo-signs (Neville et al., 1998; Newman, Bavelier, Corina, Jezzard, and Neville, 2002), manual gestures (MacSweeney et al., 2004; Emmorey, Xu, and Braun, 2011), or non-cognates from another sign language (Cardin et al., 2013). In order to ensure that patterns of activation are attributable to linguistic processing and not to differences in perceptual complexity across sign and non-sign conditions, non-signing participants should not show differential activation across conditions in regions involved in visual motion processing such as the medial temporal / medial superior temporal cortex (MT/MST).

Testing a group of non-signing controls can also be employed to help circumvent the need for a fully matched non-linguistic control condition (Capek et al., 2010; Campbell et al., 2011; Neville et al., 1998). For example, presenting meaningful sign language versus a still image of the signer will elicit activation for language processing as well as for biological motion in signers. However, if activation from a group of signers is compared to activation from a group of non-signers who are viewing the same material, biological motion processes may be subtracted, as the non-signers would be processing the sign material for motion but not for linguistic information. Thus brain areas showing greater activation for sign language viewing in signers than non-signers can be attributed to meaningful language processing. However, since only one parameter should vary in fMRI contrasts, comparing activation across groups requires the same stimuli and tasks across groups. Thus using non-signers as a control group may only be appropriate for examining language processes that are not explicitly linked to the accompanying behavioral task. In contrast to isolating effects due to language knowledge, effects of deafness can be examined by comparing groups that differ in audiological status, such as deaf and hearing individuals.

Attention should be paid to limiting extraneous processes that may differ across groups, such as eye movements. Differences in eye gaze between native and non-native signers have been observed. In particular, while both native and non-native signers fixate primarily on the face of the person who is signing, non-native signers show more gaze shifts to the hands than native signers (Emmorey, Thompson, and Colvin, 2009). Thus, to minimize differences in eye movement across testing groups, participants should be instructed to maintain fixation on the same location that native signers use. Ideally, compliance should be verified with eye-tracking data collected during the scan.

Homogeneity of participant groups

Given the relatively small BOLD response, heterogeneous participant groups will make finding significant differences across conditions or groups unlikely. In addition to the inclusion criteria for any fMRI study, such as not suffering from claustrophobia and being free from ferrous metal implants, participants in fMRI studies of language processing should be right-handed and have a similar age of language acquisition. Individuals born to deaf parents who sign are considered native signers, since they would have begun learning the signed language from birth from their parents, just like individuals learning a spoken language. Individuals who learned a sign language in early or late childhood or as adults should be organized into separate groups, as the brain organization for language processing varies as a function of the age of acquisition (Mayberry, Chen, Witcher, and Klein, 2011). The etiology of deafness should also be considered. Including participants whose deafness is likely due to genetic causes is preferable to including participants who became deaf due to illness or trauma, as illness or trauma may also result in a reorganized central nervous system. In addition, since there are differences in the neural organization of language as a function of hearing status (Capek, MacSweeney, et al., 2008), deaf and hearing signers should be grouped separately.

As analyses conducted between participant groups present more variability than analyses performed within participant groups, selecting homogeneous groups of participants will be particularly important if a non-signing group is employed as a control. Hence groups should be matched on participant characteristics such as age, gender, and non-verbal IQ.

Communication

Since more than a few millimeters of head movement will introduce inhomogeneity into the magnetic field, thereby markedly impairing the quality of the images, communication during the scan is not recommended for any fMRI study. However, between scans, communication between the hearing participant and the hearing experimenter is achievable via microphone and headset or speakers. For deaf participants or experimenters, alternative arrangements are necessary to enable communication. In the scanner room, MR-compatible cameras positioned on the participant's face and free hand (i.e., the hand not used for making button-press responses during the experiment) allow the participant's signing to be fed to monitors located inside the console room. As movement, even between scans, should be kept to a minimum in order to allow the participant to maintain a static head position, the participant should be asked to limit the size of her or his articulation to a "whisper" of the hand. In the console room, a camera focused on the experimenter can deliver the signed message to the participant.

ERP

Electroencephalography (EEG) measures the summation of postsynaptic potentials, or the voltage change caused when neurotransmitters bind to the membrane of postsynaptic cells, typically on the dendrites and cell bodies of pyramidal cells. The voltage of hundreds of thousands of neurons will summate when the neurons fire simultaneously and their dipoles – that is, the electrical charges of opposite polarity separated by a small distance – are spatially aligned. This summed voltage change can then be measured at the scalp by an array of electrodes. To extend this method to event-related potential (ERP), continuous EEG is separated into discrete time-locked epochs, marked by the onset of a particular stimulus or task. These individual epochs are then averaged over several trials and compared across experimental conditions to index various ERP components, or characteristic waveforms that are denoted by their polarity and latency.

Unlike fMRI, ERP provides a direct measure of neural processing and exquisite temporal resolution, of the order of milliseconds (msec). However, as the voltages are measured at the scalp, variable distances away from the neural generators, an ERP's spatial resolution is poor. Moreover, the skull acts as a volume conductor, spreading the distribution of the ERP across the scalp. Localizing the underlying neural generators is a considerable challenge and such findings should be interpreted with caution. While electrode placement is guided by the international 10–20 system, the exact location of underlying gyri and sulci will vary across individuals due to idiosyncratic folds of the cortex. While a magnetic resonance (MR) anatomical image can be used to guide localization in individual participants, definitively localizing the neural source is considered an ill-posed problem. In particular, a given voltage distribution can be produced by multiple configurations of dipoles (Luck, 2005). As guides for conducting ERP research are described in detail elsewhere (see Luck, 2005; Kappenman and Luck, 2012), this section will focus on common issues of using this technique in studies of sign language processing in particular.

ERP components first found for written and spoken language include the N400, which indexes semantic processing (e.g., Kutas and Hillyard, 1980) and the anterior negativity and P600, which index syntactic processing (e.g., Neville, Nicol, Barss, Forster, and Garrett, 1991). These classic ERP components for language processing have also been found for signed semantic and signed syntactic processing (Capek et al., 2009).

Experimental manipulations

Since EEG must be partitioned into epochs of the same type, it is crucial that the onset of each event is specified correctly in advance. Just like studies of spoken language, where the true onset of a word can be obscured by extraneous acoustic information, studies of sign language must define with precision the start point of the sign amid epenthetic movements and co-articulation cues from the preceding sign. For sign languages, these extraneous cues may have even greater temporal overlap with the true lexical onset, since independent articulators can express different linguistic cues. For example, coding the onset for grammatical constructions such as violations to subcategorization can be challenging, since transitive versus intransitive markers include a body shift as well as the handshape, movement and location cues of the manual verb. Coding any and all potentially relevant linguistic cues may help guard against missing the true onset. Coding onsets should be performed by linguists who specialize in the sign language of interest and by native users.

Since signers often communicate with people who have variable signing ability, it is worth highlighting in the experiment instructions for participants the need to use a strict standard of good signing for their behavioral judgments. This may be particularly relevant in violation paradigms, where participants may judge anomalous sentences to be acceptable if they are too lenient on the quality of the signed utterance.

Finally, long testing sessions may be necessary for ERP studies of sign language if many conditions are included. The number of trials needed per condition will depend on the size of the component of interest and on the amount of noise in the data. To capture large components in healthy adults, 30–60 trials are generally sufficient (Luck, 2004). To reduce effects due to participant fatigue, multiple testing sessions might be advisable.

Homogeneity of participant groups

Like fMRI studies of sign language, ERP studies of sign language should group their participants according to hearing status and age of language acquisition, as these are likely to introduce considerable between-participant variability. In addition, matching groups on other participant characteristics such as age, gender, and non-verbal IQ is advisable.

The published plots of the ERP waveforms are typically grand averages that represent the waveforms averaged across trials of a given condition in the group of participants, and these will mask individual differences. Hence examining the plots from each participant may help with data interpretation. To illustrate: in an ERP study we published, deaf native signers viewed American Sign Language (ASL) sentences that were either correct or contained a semantic or syntactic error (Capek et al., 2009). In one condition, sentences contained a particular verb agreement violation. In signed languages, agreement between the verb and object can be achieved by first establishing referents at particular locations in signing space (e.g., by signing CAR and then "placing" the car to the right of the signer); subsequent motion of the verb from one location to another indicates the subject and object, respectively. For example, "I wash the car" would involve movement of the verb WASH from the signer's body toward the location on the right where the car has been established. Reversed verb agreement violations were formed by reversing the direction of the verb such that the verb moved toward the subject instead of the object. Thus, while in signed languages verb agreement is considered a syntactic process, just as in spoken languages, one could hypothesize that these violations would elicit an N400 rather than an anterior negativity and P600, since the sentence meaning may be interpreted as anomalous (e.g., "I car washes me"). The grand average showed that, for the group of participants, these reversed verb agreement violations, compared to correct sentences, elicited a left anterior negativity followed by a P600. However, it could have been the case that these violations elicited an N400 in some participants. Inspection of the individual waveforms also showed that this was not borne out in the data, as the anterior negativity and P600 pattern was observed in each participant.

Communication

ERP studies of sign language processing that test deaf participants will require an additional person during the set-up, situated in front of the participant, who can communicate the information about electrode placement and testing procedure.

Likewise, during the testing, a set-up similar to the fMRI testing set-up can be implemented in which communication is made possible via a two-way camera system. Alternatively, an experimenter can remain inside the ERP booth during the testing session. Since the EEG signal will contain electrical signals from muscles and skin in addition to neuronal activity, communication (or any other movement) should be avoided when the stimuli are being presented. An experimenter viewing the waveforms online can indicate to the tester inside the booth when the participant's movement has contaminated the waveforms. The tester inside the booth can then request that the participant wait until the waves have settled before proceeding with the experiment.

Particular care must be taken to avoid movements that might contaminate the signal or the electrode placement. Thus participants should be asked to avoid actions such as producing signs where the hand touches the head or the electrodes on the face. In addition, securing the electrode cap with a chin strap rather than with a chest belt will allow participants to produce a greater variety of signs, such as those involving body movements, without displacing the electrodes.

MEG

Like ERP, magnetoencephalography (MEG) measures postsynaptic potentials on the dendrites and cell bodies of pyramidal cells. In addition to summed electrical currents, postsynaptic potentials induce small magnetic fields. However, while MEG measures the same underlying activity measured by ERP, the magnetic fields are orthogonally oriented to the electrical currents, due to the right-hand rule; that is, the magnetic field flows around the axis of the electric dipole. Tens of thousands of synchronously active neurons are necessary to produce a measureable MEG signal (Carter and Shieh, 2009). The signal is measured by a magnetometer typically comprising an array of superconducting quantum interference devices (SQUIDs), which is placed at the scalp. Thus MEG provides limited spatial detail of the underlying neural source. However, unlike in ERP, the magnetic signal is not further displaced by the skull, which may provide marginally better spatial resolution. As with ERP, high-resolution MR images of participants' brain structure can be used to constrain the MEG source localization to underlying cortical grey matter (Dale et al., 2000). Gross and colleagues (2013) provide a useful guide to conducting MEG research in general.

Experimental manipulations

As in ERP, coding the onsets of each event of interest correctly in advance is crucial to partitioning the MEG signal. Otherwise averaging the responses across trials will obscure any MEG differences across conditions, as the response to some of the stimuli may contaminate the preceding baseline interval. The majority of MEG studies with deaf individuals have presented non-linguistic sensory stimuli in order to characterize cortical plasticity effects due to auditory deprivation

(Hickok et al., 1997; Finney, Clementz, Hickok, and Dobkins, 2003; Levänen, Jousmaki, and Hari, 1998). For example, Levänen and colleagues (1998) presented vibrotactile stimulation to the fingers and palms of a deaf signer of Finnish Sign Language and to a group of hearing non-signing controls. Infrequent stimuli (180 Hz) were randomly interspersed among 85 percent of the standard stimuli (250 Hz). In the deaf participant the deviant stimuli elicited a greater MEG signal than the standard stimuli over the superior temporal cortices (200 msec after stimulation onset), whereas no discrimination differences were observed in the hearing controls. Similarly, Finney and colleagues (2003) found that viewing non-linguistic visual stimuli (sinusoidal luminance gratings) elicited greater MEG signal (100–400 msec after stimulus onset) over the right auditory cortex in deaf signers than in hearing non-signers. These studies suggest that the auditory cortex activation observed in deaf signers using fMRI may be due to initial stimulus processing rather than to back-projections from higher, multimodal cortex (Finney et al., 2003). Crucially, precise coding of the onset of these sensory stimuli is unambiguous, since the stimuli are categorically either present or not.

In MEG studies of sign processing (see Leonard et al., 2012; Leonard et al., 2013; Ferjan Ramirez et al., 2013), signers were presented with words (Leonard et al., 2013) or signs (Leonard et al., 2012) that were either congruent or incongruent with the meaning of a preceding picture. Sign onsets were coded as the first frame of each sign video when all phonological parameters were present, allowing for early sensory effects to be characterized within 80–120 msec from sign onset. At the time of writing, no MEG studies of signed sentence processing have been published. Correctly coding the sign onsets would involve the same considerations outlined for ERP studies. That is, sign onsets should be determined by sign language linguists and by native users, who can determine all likely onsets of the signs of interest.

Just like ERP studies, MEG studies may require relatively long testing sessions, depending on the number of conditions included. Multiple testing sessions might help reduce participant fatigue. Alternatively, depending on the effect of interest, a larger number of trials may be presented in quick succession and resultant data that include artifacts can be excluded offline. In addition, as in ERP studies, the duration of MEG testing sessions may be further lengthened so as to include a task involving a button-press, in order to allow for a neural response uncontaminated by motor planning and response. At a minimum, button press responses should be delayed until the time windows of the effects of interest have been completed. Thus, if mean-ingful reaction time information is important – to match across conditions, for example – it may be best to measure it offline.

Homogeneity of participant groups

As in other neuroimaging methods, the MEG effects are slight (of the order of a few femtotesla: 10^{-15} tesla) in relation to the substantial noise present, which makes it paramount to minimize potential sources of variance in the experimental design. Participants should be grouped according to hearing status and age of language acquisition as well as according to age, gender, and handedness. Even MEG effects elicited by late lexico-semantic processing can be affected by hearing status and age of language acquisition (Ferjan Ramirez et al., 2013). To illustrate: Ferjan Ramirez and colleagues (2013) found a weaker semantic congruency effect (300–350 msec after onset) in left fronto-temporal regions in hearing late learners of ASL than in deaf native signers. Similarly, Leonard and colleagues (2013) found that hearing late learners of ASL showed a stronger semantic effect (300–400 msec after onset) when processing their native language (English) than when processing ASL. This finding suggests that these group differences may be particularly due to age of language acquisition.

As in ERP studies, defining time windows for MEG effects should be guided by the grand average and verified in each participant. Defining each region of interest (ROI) for source localization can be difficult, as it is somewhat subjective. Typically, ROI selection is guided by the identification of candidate regions from fMRI studies; however, given that there are fewer studies of sign language processing than of spoken language processing, this selection can be particularly challenging. In addition, estimated sources are usually larger than neural sources and, as fMRI and MEG record different measures of brain activity, they yield non-identical localization even in early sensory regions (Sharon, Hamalainen, Tootell, Halgren, and Belliveau, 2007). Since some fMRI studies of sign language processing show additional activation in regions of the right hemisphere (Neville et al., 1998; Newman et al., 2002) by comparison to studies of spoken language (e.g., Capek et al., 2004), it is advisable to include homologous regions in both hemispheres as ROIs in MEG studies of sign language.

Communication

During the actual scan, participants should minimize all movement in order to reduce the likelihood of motion artifact contaminating the magnetic signal. As in fMRI, communication between scans can be achieved via a two-way microphone speaker set that connects the hearing participant and the hearing experimenter located outside the magnetically shielded testing booth. For deaf participants or deaf experimenters, a camera positioned inside the booth can relay the participant's signing. As with communicating between fMRI scans, the participant should be asked to limit her or his signing to the hand and to use only small articulations, in order to minimize the chance of head movement and the possible disruption of connections between the magnetic field sensors and the scanner. The experimenter can sign to the participant via a camera that feeds into the monitor used to show the experimental stimuli. Communicating to the participant via a camera would be preferable to having the experimenter sign to the participant in the testing booth, as the latter would involve moving the visual display in order to sign in the participant's field of view, which may result in slight displacements of the experimental display between scans.

TMS

The transcranial magnetic stimulation (TMS) technique applies localized magnetic field pulses to the part of the cortex located under a coil placed on the scalp. This magnetic pulse generates electrical activity that causes a depolarization and hyperpolarization of a large group of neurons. Thus, depending on the pulse strength and duration and the state of the stimulated area, the resulting behavior can be either a temporary loss or a temporary gain of function of the stimulated brain region. Unlike the methods described above, which are based on co-variation of neurological effects with particular cognitive tasks, TMS allows for the causal characterization of specific cortical regions that are necessary for performing particular cognitive tasks. It has proved a fruitful technique in understanding the cortical basis of language processing. As the TMS effect is brief, lasting approximately one millisecond per pulse, the resultant effects are not influenced by cortical reorganization, thus offering a key advantage over lesions evidence. An alternative TMS application is the motor-evoked potential (MEP), in which stimulation to portions of the motor cortex results in activity that is measured from the affected muscle such as the hand, foot, or tongue. MEPs can reveal functional associations between particular tasks and the brain region that supports a given process, such as perceiving speech and increased MEPs recorded from the listener's tongue (Fadiga, Craighero, Buccino, and Rizzolatti, 2002).

There are various TMS protocols, depending on the cognitive process of interest. These include online TMS, where the behavioral change follows magnetic stimulation immediately, and offline TMS, where task performance is measured before and after sustained stimulation over several minutes (approximately 10–20 minutes or twice the duration of the post-testing phase). Sandrini, Umilta, and Rusconi (2011) provide a comprehensive guide of methodological issues and technological considerations for TMS studies. The discussion below focuses on considerations particularly relevant for studies of sign language and testing deaf individuals.

Experimental manipulations

Specifying a task that is thought to be subserved by the stimulated brain area of interest is one of the fundamental requirements of TMS experimental design. This means that, if one is interested in identifying brain regions that are necessary for a particular linguistic process, it is best to choose a task that explicitly tests that process. For example, to examine the role of the inferior frontal cortex in signed semantic processing, the task would require some aspect of semantic processing – for example, animacy/inanimacy, or some other semantic categorization task. Thus, unlike in fMRI studies, where one might compare groups of signers and non-signers performing a non-semantic task (such as identifying the movement of a target sign (Capek, Waters, et al., 2008)), such incidental tasks will not be appropriate for TMS studies. However, incidental tasks may be appropriate if the experiment's aim is to identify the role of sensory cortices in these tasks. For example, Möttönen, Farmer, and Watkins (2010) used MEPs measured on the hand muscles to examine motor excitability in primary motor cortex (M1) when hearing participants viewed single British Sign Language (BSL) signs before and after learning the meanings of some of the signs. For the signed stimuli in Experiment 1, participants performed a visuospatial task – namely to judge the type of movement (single or repeated) – before learning the meanings of some of the signs and a semantic task – namely to state the meaning or to say "no" for untaught signs – after learning them. After they learned the meanings of some signs, a left-lateralized increase in M1 excitability was observed, for both known and unknown signs, in relation to viewing a still video. This finding was replicated in the second experiment, in which the post-learning phase task was either the visuospatial task or the semantic task. The replication demonstrated that the effect of sign learning observed in the first experiment was not due to the change of task (Möttönen et al., 2010).

Experimenters who use video stimuli, including sign language, in TMS studies must determine the precise point at which the TMS pulse should be delivered. This can be specified as a set point after the onset of all the stimuli (Möttönen et al., 2010; Pobric and Hamilton, 2006) or specified separately for each video (Beauchamp, Nath, and Pasalar, 2010). Determining the optimal pulse onset can be guided by findings of intracranial recordings (if such are available) and verified through piloting.

Homogeneity of participant groups

Large between-participant variability is a common issue in TMS studies. In order to increase the chance of finding any meaningful effect that survives statistical thresholding, participants should be organized into groups that are as similar as possible. The stimulation level necessary to obtain an effect varies by age and gender (Pitcher, Ogston, and Miles, 2003). In addition to matching for these characteristics, participants should be grouped by hearing status and age of sign acquisition, as well as by other potential sources of cognitive differences, such as non-verbal IQ.

Online navigation using a participant's high-resolution structural MR image can improve stimulation site localization; however, it is important to note that the magnetic pulses will also stimulate adjacent brain regions. Depending on the anatomical and functional characteristics of the stimulated regions, TMS may suppress the neural signals, add random neuronal activity or noise, or produce a combination of the two (Sandrini et al., 2011).

Communication

Using mechanical coil holders can free the experimenter to sit in front of the participant for signed communication. However, the experimenter may prefer to hold the coil and the participant's head in order to achieve greater consistency in the pulse delivery location. In this case an additional tester will be required to sit in front of the participant, in order to sign to the deaf participant and/or experimenter.

Finally, participants should be permitted to respond to the behavioral task in a manner sensitive to their communication preferences. For example, when measuring MEPs from the hand muscles, participants must keep these articulators fully relaxed. Therefore signed responses would be inappropriate. The behavioral response would have to be expressed using different articulators, which rely on cortically distinct regions from those that subserve hand motion. If the study only includes hearing participants, the response can be spoken (Möttönen et al., 2010). However, if the study includes deaf participants, the response might be delivered via mouth actions or foot taps; either response would likely necessitate presenting a forced-choice option (e.g., sign vs. non-sign).

Conclusion

This chapter focused on a number of popular techniques used to investigate the functional organization of cognitive processes, with an emphasis on their use in studies of sign language processing. Discussion of each technique included a brief description of the measurement and of the experimental areas for which it would be most appropriate. The pertinent considerations for sign language research that use each of these techniques focused on experimental manipulations, participant selection, and communication issues for testing deaf signers.

Most techniques covered are more appropriate for studying sign comprehension than sign production, owing to contamination of fMRI, ERP, MEG and MEP signals with motion artifact. The exception was TMS investigations of sign disruption. Similarly, motion between tasks introduced communication issues that typically require additional equipment, designed to enable signing between the experimenter and the participant. Due to relatively weak signals in the case of fMRI, ERP, and MEG and to variable behavioral effects in the case of TMS, suggestions were offered for inclusion criteria that would ensure that participants are as homogeneous as possible.

Investigating the functional neural organization of sign language provides unique insight into natural language processing in general and into brain reorganization as a consequence of unimodal sensory deprivation and altered language experience. Investigations using the techniques discussed promise to further our knowledge in these areas, thereby addressing fundamental issues in cognitive neuroscience.

Note

1   For the purpose of this chapter we do not distinguish between *deaf* and *Deaf*, since no points refer to either group exclusively. For simplicity, the spelling *deaf* is used throughout.

Keywords

brain imaging; cortical plasticity; cortical stimulation; deaf; electrophysiology; evoked potentials; methodology; neurophysiology; sign language

See Also

Chapter 15

References

Beauchamp, M. S., Nath, A. R., and Pasalar, S. (2010). fMRI-guided transcranial magnetic stimulation reveals that the superior temporal sulcus is a cortical locus of the McGurk effect. *Journal of Neuroscience* 30(7), 2414–2417.

Boyes Braem, P., and Sutton-Spence, R. (2001). *The hands are the head of the mouth: The mouth as articulator in sign language.* Hamburg: Signum.

Campbell, R., Capek, C. M., Gazarian, K., MacSweeney, M., Woll, B., David, A. S., McGuire, P. K., and Brammer, M. J. (2011). The signer and the sign: Cortical correlates of person identity and language processing from point-light displays. *Neuropsychologia* 49(11), 3018–3026.

Capek, C. M., Bavelier, D., Corina, D., Newman, A. J., Jezzard, P., and Neville, H. J. (2004). The cortical organization of audio-visual sentence comprehension: An fMRI study at 4 Tesla. *Brain Research: Cognitive Brain Research* 20(2), 111–119.

Capek, C. M., Grossi, G., Newman, A. J., McBurney, S. L., Corina, D., Roeder, B., and Neville, H. J. (2009). Brain systems mediating semantic and syntactic processing in deaf native signers: Biological invariance and modality specificity. *Proceedings of the National Academy of Sciences of the United States of America* 106(21), 8784–8789.

Capek, C. M., MacSweeney, M., Woll, B., Waters, D., McGuire, P. K., David, A. S., Brammer, M. J., and Campbell, R. (2008). Cortical circuits for silent speechreading in deaf and hearing people. *Neuropsychologia* 46 (5), 1233–1241.

Capek, C. M., Waters, D., Woll, B., MacSweeney, M., Brammer, M. J., McGuire, P. K., David, A. S., and Campbell, R. (2008). Hand and mouth: Cortical correlates of lexical processing in British Sign Language and speechreading English. *Journal of Cognitive Neuroscience* 20(7), 1220–1234.

Capek, C. M., Woll, B., MacSweeney, M., Waters, D., McGuire, P. K., David, A. S., Brammer, M. J., and Campbell, R. (2010). Superior temporal activation as a function of linguistic knowledge: Insights from deaf native signers who speechread. *Brain and Language* 112(2), 129–134.

Cardin, V., Orfanidou, E., Ronnberg, J., Capek, C. M., Rudner, M., and Woll, B. (2013). Dissociating cognitive and sensory neural plasticity in human superior temporal cortex. *Nature Communications* 4(1473), 1–5.

Carter, M., and Shieh, J. (2009). *Guide to research techniques in neuroscience.* Burlington, MA: Academic Press.

Dale, A. M., Liu, A. K., Fischl, B. R., Buckner, R. L., Belliveau, J. W., Lewine, J. D., and Halgren, E. (2000). Dynamic statistical parametric mapping: Combining fMRI and MEG for high-resolution imaging of cortical activity. *Neuron* 26(1), 55-67.

Emmorey, K., Thompson, R., and Colvin, R. (2009). Eye gaze during comprehension of American Sign Language by native and beginning signers. *Journal of Deaf Studies and Deaf Education* 14(2), 237–243.

Emmorey, K., Xu, J., and Braun, A. (2011). Neural responses to meaningless pseudosigns: Evidence for sign-based phonetic processing in superior temporal cortex. *Brain and Language* 117(1), 34–38.

Fadiga, L., Craighero, L., Buccino, G., and Rizzolatti, G. (2002). Speech listening specifically modulates the excitability of tongue muscles: A TMS study. *European Journal of Neuroscience* 15(2), 399–402.

Ferjan Ramirez, N., Leonard, M. K., Torres, C., Hatrak, M., Halgren, E., and Mayberry, R. I. (2013). Neural language processing in adolescent first-language learners. *Cerebral Cortex.*

Finney, E. M., Clementz, B. A., Hickok, G., and Dobkins, K. R. (2003). Visual stimuli activate auditory cortex in deaf subjects: Evidence from MEG. *NeuroReport* 14(11), 1425–1427.

Friston, K. J., Price, C. J., Fletcher, P., Moore, C., Frackowiak, R. S. J., and Dolan, R. J. (1996). The trouble with cognitive subtraction. *NeuroImage* 4(2), 97–104.

Gross, J., Baillet, S., Barnes, G. R., Henson, R. N., Hillebrand, A., Jensen, O., Jerbi, K., Litvak, V., Maess, B., Oostenveld, R., Parkkonen, L., Taylor, J. R., van Wassenhove, V., Wibral, M., and Schoffelen, J. M. (2013). Good practice for conducting and reporting MEG research. *Neuroimage* 65, 349–363.

Hickok, G., Poeppel, D., Clark, K., Buxton, R. B., Rowley, H. A., and Roberts, T. P. (1997). Sensory mapping in a congenitally deaf subject: MEG and fRMI studies of cross-modal non-plasticity. *Human Brain Mapping* 5(6), 437–444.

Huettel, S. A., Song, A. W., and McCarthy, G. (2009). *Functional magnetic resonance imaging* (2nd ed.). Sunderland, MA: Sinauer Associates.

Jezzard, P., Matthews, P. M., and Smith, S. M. (2008). *Functional MRI: An introduction to methods*. New York: Oxford University Press.

Kappenman, E. S., and Luck, S. J. (2012). ERP components: The ups and downs of brainwave recordings. In S. Luck and E. S. Kappenman (Eds.). *The Oxford handbook of event-related potential components*. New York: Oxford University Press, pp. 3–30.

Kutas, M., and Hillyard, S. A. (1980). Reading senseless sentences: Brain potentials reflect semantic incongruity. *Science* 207(4427), 203–205.

Leonard, M. K., Ferjan Ramirez, N., Torres, C., Hatrak, M., Mayberry, R. I., and Halgren, E. (2013). Neural stages of spoken, written, and signed word processing in beginning second language learners. *Frontiers in Human Neuroscience* 7, 322.

Leonard, M. K., Ferjan Ramirez, N., Torres, C., Travis, K. E., Hatrak, M., Mayberry, R. I., and Halgren, E. (2012). Signed words in the congenitally deaf evoke typical late lexicosemantic responses with no early visual responses in left superior temporal cortex. *Journal of Neuroscience:* 32(28), 9700–9705.

Levänen, S., Jousmaki, V., and Hari, R. (1998). Vibration-induced auditory-cortex activation in a congenitally deaf adult. *Current Biology* 8(15), 869–872.

Luck,S. (2004). Ten simple rules for designing and interpreting ERP experiments. In T. C. Handy (Ed.), *Event-related potentials: A methods handbook*. Cambridge, MA: MIT Press, pp. 17–32.

Luck, S. (2005). *An introduction to the event-related potential technique*. Cambridge, MA: MIT Press.

MacSweeney, M., Capek, C. M., Campbell, R., and Woll, B. (2008). The signing brain: The neurobiology of sign language. *Trends in Cognitive Sciences* 12(11), 432–440.

MacSweeney, M., Campbell, R., Woll, B., Giampietro, V., David, A. S., McGuire, P. K., Calvert, G. A., and Brammer, M. J. (2004). Dissociating linguistic and nonlinguistic gestural communication in the brain. *NeuroImage* 22(4), 1605–1618.

Mayberry, R. I., Chen, J. K., Witcher, P., and Klein, D. (2011). Age of acquisition effects on the functional organization of language in the adult brain. *Brain and Language* 119(1), 16–29.

Möttönen, R., Farmer, H., and Watkins, K. E. (2010). Lateralization of motor excitability during observation of bimanual signs. *Neuropsychologia* 48(10), 3173–3177.

Neville, H. J., Nicol, J. L., Barss, A., Forster, K. I., and Garrett, M. F. (1991). Syntactically based sentence processing classes: Evidence from event-related brain potentials. *Journal of Cognitive Neuroscience* 3(2), 151–165.

Neville, H. J., Bavelier, D., Corina, D., Rauschecker, J., Karni, A., Lalwani, A., Braun, A., Clark, V., Jezzard, P., and Turner, R. (1998). Cerebral organization for language in deaf and hearing subjects: Biological constraints and effects of experience. *Proceedings of the National Academy of Sciences of the United States of America* 95(3), 922–929.

Newman, A. J., Bavelier, D., Corina, D., Jezzard, P., and Neville, H. J. (2002). A critical period for right hemisphere recruitment in American Sign Language processing. *Nature Neuroscience* 5(1), 76–80.

Pitcher, J. B., Ogston, K. M., and Miles, T. S. (2003). Age and sex differences in human motor cortex input-output characteristics. *Journal of Physiology* 546(2), 605–613.

Pobric, G., and Hamilton, A. F. (2006). Action understanding requires the left inferior frontal cortex. *Current Biology* 16(5), 524–529.

Sandrini, M., Umilta, C., and Rusconi, E. (2011). The use of transcranial magnetic stimulation in cognitive neuroscience: A new synthesis of methodological issues. *Neuroscience and Biobehavioral Reviews* 35(3), 516–536.

Scott, S. K., Blank, C. C., Rosen, S., and Wise, R. J. (2000). Identification of a pathway for intelligible speech in the left temporal lobe. *Brain* 123(12), 2400–2406.

Sharon, D., Hamalainen, M. S., Tootell, R. B., Halgren, E., and Belliveau, J. W. (2007). The advantage of combining MEG and EEG: Comparison to fMRI in focally stimulated visual cortex. *Neuroimage* 36(4), 1225–1235.

Wager, T. D., and Nichols, T. E. (2003). Optimization of experimental design in fMRI: A general framework using a genetic algorithm. *Neuroimage* 18(2), 293–309.

18   Studying Sign Language Disorders: Considering Neuropsychological Data

Peter C. Hauser, David Quinto-Pozos, and Jenny L. Singleton

Chapter Overview

This chapter provides a clinical neuropsychological assessment approach for assisting with the identification of language disorders in signers. The areas covered include documenting the signers' history and background and testing their general cognitive ability, receptive and expressive language skills, facial processing abilities, vision, visual spatial processing, motor skills of the hands and fingers (including psychomotor skills), executive functioning, visual learning and memory, and social–emotional functioning. The assessment of these domains helps one to rule out a primary language disorder when the language symptoms may be secondary to a different primary disorder. This assessment approach also aids the researcher in determining the possible contributing cognitive factors and in describing the symptomology. This chapter is written for researchers who desire to study signed language disorders and is relevant for clinicians working with an individual with a

Research Methods in Sign Language Studies: A Practical Guide, First Edition.
Edited by Eleni Orfanidou, Bencie Woll, and Gary Morgan.
© 2015 John Wiley & Sons, Inc. Published 2015 by John Wiley & Sons, Inc.

suspected signed language disorder. While its focus is mainly on how to assess developmental language disorders in children, the same neuropsychological assessment approach can be used with adults who may have experienced a disruption to language functioning secondary to a stroke, a tumor, dementia, or a head injury.

Previous research has described the sign language characteristics of adults with Parkinson's disease (e.g., Brentari, Poizner, and Kegl, 1995) and other forms of dementia (e.g., Spanjer, Fieret, and Baker, 2014), as well as with strokes and head injuries (see Corina, 1998 for a review of older studies). Only recently has it become evident that developmental signed language disorders appear within the population of Deaf[1] children (Morgan, 2005; Morgan, Herman, and Woll, 2007; Mason et al., 2010; Quinto-Pozos, Forber-Pratt, and Singleton, 2011; Quinto-Pozos et al., 2013). An important question for researchers and clinical professionals who work with Deaf children is how to determine if a suspected case of signed language disorder is accompanied by non-linguistic deficits or if the impairment lies primarily with the comprehension and/or production of language. An approach that incorporates clinical neuropsychological practices allows examiners to rule out other deficits that might be interfering with typical language processing, such as deficits in attention, learning, or emotional difficulties. Deficits in any of these areas could presumably result in poor language development (also see Quinto-Pozos, Singleton, Hauser, and Levine, 2014). Such an approach provides the researcher with information about aspects of cognition that could be particularly important for the signed language modality, such as visual–spatial processing and visual memory. Additionally, the approach yields tools to identify non-cognitive factors that might offer information about the primary etiology of the sign language symptomology. This chapter outlines some of the diagnostic criteria and neuropsychological tools that will help researchers and practitioners evaluate a child with a suspected signed language disorder.

The Clinical Neuropsychology Approach

Clinical neuropsychologists in the United States and in various other countries assign diagnoses on the basis of criteria outlined in the *Diagnostic Statistic Manual of Mental Disorders*, 5th edition (DSM-V; American Psychiatric Association, 2013). The DSM-V diagnostic criteria for "language disorder" (DSM-V Code: 315.39) involve:

A   Persistent difficulties in the acquisition and use of language across modalities (i.e., spoken, written, sign language, or other) due to deficits in comprehension or production that include the following:

   1   Reduced vocabulary (word knowledge and use).
   2   Limited sentence structure (ability to put words and word endings together to form sentences based on the rules of grammar and morphology).

3   Impairments in discourse (ability to use vocabulary and connect sentences to explain or describe a topic or series of events or have a conversation).

B   Language abilities are substantially and quantifiably below those expected for age, result in functional limitations in effective communication, social participation, academic achievement, or occupational performance, individually or in any combination.

C   Onset of symptoms in the early development period.

D   The difficulties are not attributable to hearing or other sensory impairment, motor dysfunction, or another medical or neurological condition and are not better explained by intellectual disability (intellectual developmental disorder) or global developmental delay. (American Psychiatric Association, 2013, pp. 42–43)

The clinical neuropsychologist has to use quantitative and qualitative methods to determine whether a patient meets the diagnostic criteria. For the qualitative component of the evaluation, the neuropsychologist should (1) gain access to records of the participant's language development and other cognitive, academic, social, and emotional functions; (2) interview family, friends, and professionals; and (3) observe the participant's language and neurocognitive behaviors (also see Quinto-Pozos et al., 2014). For the quantitative component of the evaluation, the neuropsychologist must use standardized psychological tests with recognized psychometric validity and reliability. These tests have norms based on comparative data from children of a similar age. The norms allow the assessment expert to determine a participant's current level of functioning – in comparison to that of other children – in the area that the test measures.

Evaluating the neurocognitive functioning of Deaf individuals is complicated by test standardization concerns. The three primary limitations are administration and scoring issues, construct irrelevance (related to language confounds), and lack of normative comparisons (for discussion, see Harper, Allen, and Morere, 2012). The standardized administration procedures found in test manuals often cannot be implemented when testing Deaf participants. One of the most obvious test modifications is translating spoken English test directions into a sign language. Signs that are influenced by visual images may actually give Deaf individuals' clues to test answers that are not found in the spoken English instructions. If a test administrator were to translate the Peabody Picture Vocabulary test (PPVT-4: Dunn and Dunn, 2007) by signing vocabulary words, the test would no longer be an English test, and that would make the normative sample invalid. In essence, English to ASL translations are not de facto valid signed language tests. In addition, many of the PPVT vocabulary items do not have single sign equivalents; thus the evaluator would have to fingerspell these words. This modification creates, in part, a spelling test, whereas in the standard PPVT administration to a hearing individual the assessment itself is not considered a spelling test (i.e., a child who cannot spell could still perform well on this test).

The validity of a test depends on whether the test actually measures the construct it intends to measure. Constructs are the theoretical underpinnings that are measured by tests. Assessment instruments with good construct validity are usually those that have good psychometric properties. Cognitive assessment measures, for example, are designed to assess a specific cognitive construct through the administration of test items that elicit abilities related to the intended construct. In her evaluation of measures of non-verbal intelligence, Maller (2003) found that some individual test items could function differently with Deaf individuals, thus hindering measurement of the desired construct. The dilemma for an examiner is whether the intended construct is in fact measured when the test is administered to a Deaf participant.

The traditional assessment approach used by many clinical and school psychologists is a method that emphasizes the importance of administering a standard battery of tests following accepted practices for providing instructions to the test-taker and for interpreting the test results with the help of a test manual. This approach does not allow for deviation from the instructions even for Deaf individuals (e.g., by signing the instructions, by requiring eye contact during instructions, and by requiring signed responses), because any non-standard administration would invalidate the test results. In contrast, the process approach (also called the hypothesis, qualitative, or flexible approach) bypasses many of the limitations of standardized tests (for discussion, see Milberg, Hebben, and Kaplan, 2009) and is well suited for assessing Deaf participants. The process approach requires neuropsychologists to customize the assessment process in order to provide the most accurate evaluation. Performance tasks are selected on the basis of hypotheses rather than through administration of the whole test battery, and modifications are made in order to appropriately test the participant's functioning. A greater reliance is placed upon qualitative data obtained through interviews (parent, teacher, participant), observations (classroom, parent-child, and participant), and test responses. Contextual variables are all taken into account in order to develop a hypothesis that can be tested by gathering data, which will ultimately lead to the final case conceptualization. Hypothesis testing is the foundation of the process approach, where the examiner uses assessment tools to confirm or rule out specific options.

Using the process approach, a clinical neuropsychologist needs to first select tests to determine an individual's overall cognitive abilities; and this is often achieved by selecting the non-verbal items of a standardized intellectual test. Non-verbal measures are often appropriate to administer to Deaf individuals as long as the standardized instructions are minimal (Vernon, 2005; but also see Maller, 2003). Omitting verbal items usually means omitting at least half of the tests that are typically administered to a hearing individual. As a result, it is best to supplement the assessment plan with additional non-verbal tests. As the team formulates hypotheses on the basis of the individual's history and preliminary test results, specific language-based tests can be administered with caution for further information. There are research-based tests (for examples, see Quinto-Pozos et al., 2013), and these assess specific cognitive functions that are a part of sign language processing. Further information is provided below, in the discussion of the different cognitive domains that should be assessed.

In the context of evaluating a suspected signed language disorder, the neuropsychologist would have to be fluent in a sign language and be knowledgeable about sociocultural, educational, psycholinguistic, and cognitive factors related to being deaf and being a signer. This knowledge helps the examiner to appropriately formulate and test hypotheses related to the existence of a sign language disorder. The neuropsychologist needs to understand test and measurement principles and the population in order to be cognizant of the impact that modifications may have on the interpretation of test scores. Qualitative analyses of the participant's signing skills will uncover deficits, and the participant will likely perform poorly (in many research and clinical studies, the criterion for impairment is more than 1.5 standard deviation below Deaf peers) on quantitative measures of sign language competency. The participant's general cognitive ability needs to be measured taking into consideration assessment issues with this population. In order to appropriately diagnose a suspected sign language disorder, other possible explanatory factors must be ruled out – for example, general cognitive limitations, vision or motor difficulties, pervasive developmental disorder, or an impoverished language environment. If one uses the process approach and culturally appropriate test modifications, the results of the assessment of other neuropsychological domains should provide insight into the specific cognitive deficits that may underlie the sign language development impairment.

It is important for the research team to ensure that at least some, if not all, of the personnel consists of fluent signers. Ideally, there should be one or more native signers on the team. If the team is not fluent in signing, then at a minimum the team could have a certified Deaf interpreter (CDI) helping the team during data collection-planning, data collection, data analyses, and the interpretation of results. Ideally, there should also be a sign language linguist and a researcher familiar with theories and profiles of children with language impairment. Such an interdisciplinary team is necessary because the investigation of sign language disorders in children is new. It would be best if the CDI or a Deaf member of the team conducted the interview and served as the psychometrician (see Sweet, Moberg, and Westergaard, 1996), administering the neuropsychological assessment protocol under the supervision of a clinical neuropsychologist. This would maximize the internal validity of the testing process. Also, to further maximize internal validity, it is better to have multiple 1–2-hour testing sessions rather than one longer session, in order to avoid fatigue, which may have a confounding effect on test results.

Neuropsychological Domains and Assessment Tools

History and background

Background history of the child with a suspected sign language disorder is obtained through interviews with parents, teachers, educational interpreters, and other school professionals. Further information is obtained through the review of medical and educational records. It is important to know participants' early development and medical history in order to rule out other factors that may be interfering with language development. Quinto-Pozos and colleagues (2014) provide detailed descriptions of the type of information that should be collected for cases of sign language disorder and a list of questions that examiners can ask families in order to get an appropriate description of the participant's language environment. It will be important to know the family's signing skills, the age at which the participant was first exposed to sign language, and the quantity and quality of daily sign exposure at home and at school. The examiner would need to get adequate descriptions from school and professionals about the characteristics of the participant's suspected sign language disorder. The neuropsychologist would also want to know familial factors that can influence language development, for instance family attitudes toward their Deaf child, family mental health history, sibling relationships, and parental coping strategies. History on the participant's social development and peer relations should also be collected. The participant's background history might be adequate to determine the plausibility of developing a hypothesis about the presence of a sign language disorder.

General cognitive ability

It is necessary for the neuropsychologist to first evaluate the participants' intellectual capacity as a reflection of their current general cognitive ability. The participants' raw score is compared to the raw score of a large sample of others in the same age group. The results of these tests usually provide standardized scores (mean = 100, SD = 15), subtest scores (mean = 10, SD = 3), or t-scores (mean = 50, SD = 10). A person with average cognitive functioning would have a standard score or intelligence quotient (IQ) of 100. If that person obtained standard scores lower than 75 on language measures, then it would be likely that the person meets the criteria for a language disorder. However, an individual with language standard scores of 75 but an IQ of 75 would not meet the criteria for a language disorder. In addition to IQ and language testing, the neuropsychologist also administers tests of attention, executive functioning, memory, and visual–perceptual, motor, and socioemotional functioning. When weaknesses are identified and compared to the individual's IQ and strengths, a profile of the individual's functioning is formed. The profile illustrates whether or not a language disorder exists. The profile also and captures the specific neurocognitive functions that contribute to the language deficits. This kind of profile provides the basis for determining whether the child's symptomology reflects a sign language disorder that is domain-specific or domain-general.

Receptive and expressive language skills

Data on participants' language skills will be the focus of any evaluation of a suspected signed language disorder. Quinto-Pozos and his colleagues (2014) describe in depth the qualitative data to be collected and analyzed in cases of signed language disorders. The research team will want to observe the participant communicating in different settings. Informal conversations with the participant should be recorded. It would be ideal to also collect old videos of the participant's expressive signed language skills, as these can provide insight into the participant's language development over time. The linguistic analyses of naturalistic signing data should be supplemented with formal tests of signed language skills. The challenge is that there are few commercially available signed language assessment tools, and only in some sign languages. Ongoing international work on the development of signed language tests in research laboratories have resulted in working prototype tests (for review, see Haug, 2008; Singleton and Supalla, 2011). One of the challenges of developing a signed language test is that there are many sign variations within the same sign language – including regional, age, cultural, ethnic and gender variations (e.g., Haug and Mann, 2008). In the United Kingdom, as a response to the challenge of language variation, two different versions of the British Sign Language (BSL) Receptive Skills test were developed (Herman, Holmes, and Woll, 1999). Test development is beyond the scope of this chapter, but Paludnevičienė, Hauser, Daggett, and Kurz (2012) offer discussion on current issues and trends in sign language assessment.

Some current assessment tools are described here to illustrate how signed languages are measured formally. The Assessing British Sign Language Development Receptive Skills test (BSL-RST: Herman et al., 1999) was the first commercially available test, and it measures syntactic and morphological aspects of BSL through a video-based comprehension test. This test has been used as a template for the German Sign Language Receptive Skills test (Haug, 2011) and for the American Sign Language Receptive Skills test (ASL-RST: Enns and Herman, 2011). The VL2 Fingerspelling Reproduction test (Morere and Roberts, 2012) is an example of a fingerspelling test that involves raters. This test makes the participant watch video clips of fingerspelled items, and after each clip the participant is required to repeat (i.e., fingerspell) the item (s)he has just seen. The American Sign Language Sentence Reproduction test (ASL-SRT: Hauser, Paludnevičienė, Supalla, and Bavelier, 2008) is a global measure of ASL receptive and expressive skills that can be used with children and adults. The ASL-SRT contains sentences of increasing complexity and is an example of a test with a specific number of items that elicits a controlled set of responses. Test takers are asked to view an ASL sentence on a video and then reproduce the sentence from memory. The ASL-SRT also requires a knowledgeable rater but takes less than 10 minutes to score. German Sign Language (DGS) and BSL versions of the ASL-SRT are currently in development. The ASL Proficiency Assessment (ASL-PA: Maller, Singleton, Supalla, and Wix, 1999) focuses on expressive language skills. Raters view three short language samples collected from the individual and scores for 23 target linguistic features.

Processing of facial cues

The face plays an important role in the production of phonological, morphological, lexical, syntactic, and prosodic features of signed language utterances. To appropriately interpret linguistic information displayed on the signer's face, a perceiver must be able to rapidly identify and comprehend various facial features and expressions produced by the signer. A participant's observed or previously documented ability to comprehend and express linguistic features on the face needs to be recorded. The participant could be administered the Benton Facial Recognition test (Benton, Hamsher, Varney, and Spreen, 1983) as part of the screening for a signed language disorder. Signers have been found to perform on this test better than deaf and hearing non-signers (Bellugi et al., 1990; Bettger, 1992; Bettger, Emmorey, McCullough, and Bellugi, 1997). Emmorey (2002) explains that this test is not a recognition test or a memory test, but a test of the ability to discriminate faces. McCullough and Emmorey (1997) demonstrated that Deaf signers are better than hearing non-signers at discriminating local changes in eye and mouth features of the face. Signers are also better at producing facial expressions that are appropriately understood by others (Goldstein, Sexton, and Feldman, 2000). If a participant has difficulty producing facial expressions, or a history of misunderstanding or failing to attend to non-verbal cues and facial expressions in the absence of a pervasive developmental disorder, then it would be necessary to evaluate this skill, as well as to follow up with visual–perceptual testing in order to eliminate the possibility of a global visual–perceptual deficit.

Vision and visual–spatial processing

In screening an individual for a suspected signed language disorder, it is important to evaluate that individual's vision and visual–perceptual abilities. If visual–perceptual difficulties are present, it is possible that the person has a domain-general deficit that impacts his or her signed language, for example difficulties with spatial perception and the spatial syntax of the sign language. Examples of appropriate tests include the Visual–Perceptual Skills test (Martin, 2006), which evaluates a variety of visual–perceptual skills such as visual discrimination, visual–spatial relationships, form constancy, visual figure-ground, and visual closure. In a multiple-choice format, black and white designs are presented to the individual in a developmental progression of increasing complexity. The test requires minimal instructions, and the participant points to the correct answer. Performance weaknesses found with this test should be followed up with other visual–perceptual tests, such as the Judgment of Line Orientation test (Benton et al., 1983), and the Woodcock–Johnson Tests of Cognitive Abilities, Spatial Relations subtest (Woodcock, McGrew, and Mather, 2001). General visual–spatial difficulties might have an impact on a signer's ability to perceive small changes in visual phonology, to appropriately use classifier constructions, or to perceive spatial relations, for example. There are some assessment measures developed in laboratories to measure specific visual–perceptual abilities related to sign language processing. The ASL Perspective Taking Spatial Orientation test (ASL-PTSO) and the ASL Perspective Taking Comprehension test (ASL-PTCT) are examples of such tests (for descriptions, see Quinto-Pozos et al., 2013).

Hands, fingers, and psychomotor skills

An individual's hands, fingers, and motor abilities can be evaluated to determine whether physical or psychomotor challenges could explain observed signed language difficulties. A Deaf individual with cerebral palsy who has difficulty with expressive signed language skills because of motor challenges would not be considered to have a signed language disorder. A common neuropsychological test to measure gross motor strength is the hand dynamometer test or the grip strength test (see Spreen and Strauss, 1998). It requires the participant to hold the upper part of the dynamometer in the palm of the hand and to squeeze the stirrup with the fingers as hard as possible. Fine motor skills can be tested using the fingertapping test or the finger oscillation test, where the participant is instructed to tap a "tapper" as rapidly as possible using the index finger (Spreen and Strauss, 1998). It is used to assess subtle motor and other cognitive impairment and is sensitive to the presence and laterality of brain lesions. To test visual–motor coordination, the grooved pegboard test could be used (Baser and Ruff, 1987). Pegs with a key on one side must be rotated to match the hole before they can be inserted. The time it takes to insert all 25 pegs in the holes is documented. Individuals who exhibit difficulties on gross or fine motor tests might also have difficulty appropriately producing signs, for example signed utterance reproduction (visual–motor coordination) or fingerspelling tasks (rapid sequential movement). Motor problems could also affect overall speed of processing and fluency. Any difficulties with the fingers, hands, arms, or upper body might have an impact on non-verbal timed tests. Slow motor performance could have a negative impact on timed performance tests of cognitive abilities.

Executive functioning

The executive functions are responsible for higher order cognitive functions such as the behavioral regulation and metacognition that are necessary for learning, decision-making, and social behavior (for a review, see Diamond, 2013). Executive function difficulties can interfere with an individual's language development, and hearing children with language disorders often perform poorly on executive functioning measures (e.g., Marton, 2008). There are many cultural and linguistic factors that can contribute to Deaf children's development of executive functions (for discussion, see Hauser, Lukomski, and Hillman, 2008). The Behavior Rating Inventory of Executive Function (BRIEF: Gioia, Isquith, Guy, and Kenworth, 2000) could be used with Deaf children; for this tool parents and teachers complete the inventory. It also provides a global score and two indices, behavior regulation and metacognition. Oberg and Lukomski (2011) found that Deaf children with Deaf family members obtain better ratings on the BRIEF than Deaf children who are the only Deaf member of the family. There is an adult self-report version of the BRIEF (BRIEF-A: Roth, Isquith, and Gioia, 2005) reported to be a reliable, largely unbiased executive function assessment tool for Deaf college students (Hauser, Lukomski, and Samar, 2012). In addition to behavioral inventories, it is necessary to also administer performance tests of executive function. An example of a performance test of executive function that requires the ability to inhibit, shift attention, and employ cognitive flexibility is the Children's Color Trails test (CCTT: D'Elia, Satz, Uchiyama, and White, 1994). In the first trial the participant is asked to connect circles, 1 to 15, in the correct numerical order (1–25 in adult version). The second trial is the same task, except that each number alternates between pink and yellow. Both of these trials are timed. Oberg and Lukomski (2011) and Hauser, Contreras, and Israel (2013) found that Deaf native signers perform better on this task than individuals who learned to sign later in life. Hauser et al. (2013) found the same effect on the Color Trails test (D'Elia, 1996), the adult version of the CCTT. There are other formal executive function tests that are appropriate for Deaf individuals (see Morere, Goodman, Hanumantha, and Allen, 2012), and each test assesses a different component of the executive functions. Executive dysfunctions can have a negative impact on the test scores of other cognitive domains, including memory and general cognitive functioning, hence making it more difficult to tease apart the specific cognitive functions that may contribute to a signed language disorder. Further research in this area is indeed warranted.

Visual learning and memory

Sometimes symptoms of a language disorder are actually secondary to a general learning disorder or to memory difficulties. Memory is sensitive to many other cognitive factors such as attention, executive functions, and socioemotional factors.

There exist non-verbal tests of learning, short-term memory (STM), and long-term memory (LTM) that are appropriate for Deaf individuals. An example is the Brief Visuospatial Memory test, revised (Benedict, Schretlen, Groninger, Dobraski, and Shpritz, 1996), which involves being presented with six geometric figures to recall immediately through three trials and to recall again after a 20-minute delay; it provides scores on the participants' learning curve, STM, and LTM. The Rey–Osterrieth Complex Figure test (Meyers and Meyers, 1995) is a measure of visual STM and LTM, as it involves participants copying a complex figure, reproducing it from memory immediately afterwards, and reproducing it again after a 20-minute delay. Deaf native signers have been found to perform as well as hearing non-signers on this test (Hauser, Cohen, Dye, and Bavelier, 2007). Morere (2012) developed a list-learning test in ASL, the Morere Signed Verbal Learning test (M-SVLT), which requires learning a list of signs over repeated trials, under both immediate and delayed recall conditions. Further information can be drawn from signers by testing their visual working memory and spatial memory abilities.

Visual working memory

Using visual working memory (WM), an individual holds visual information in his or her STM and manipulates the images through mental representations (e.g., moves them around or decomposes them). WM is strongly connected with an individual's attention span, STM capacity, and executive function skills. Hearing children with language disorders often possess WM difficulties (Archibald and Gathercole, 2006). The mental rotation test (see Peters, Lehmann, Takahira, Takeuchi, and Jordan, 2006) is an example of a visual working memory test. A complex three-dimensional shape is shown to the test taker, and the same shape is rotated into a different position and shown along with a few other shapes that do not match the original shape. The test taker has to mentally rotate the original shape in his/her head so as to figure out which choice matches the original shape – the target choice is oriented differently from the original shape. Signers perform better on this test than deaf and hearing non-signers (e.g., Chamberlain and Mayberry, 2000). In addition, Hauser and his colleagues (2007) found no differences between Deaf native signers and hearing non-signers on the Stanford–Binet Intelligence Scale paper folding and cutting subtest (Thorndike, Hagen, and Sattler, 1986), a measure of visual working memory. If an individual with symptoms of language disorder performs well on visual working memory tasks and poorly on language comprehension or production tasks, it may be the case that he or she exhibits a domain-specific language disorder. Comparing an individual's relative performance across all of these neurocognitive functions thus enables the evaluator to narrow down the possible contributing factors to development language deficits.

Spatial memory

Spatial memory is a specific type of visual STM that is used when one holds spatial locations or images in his/her memory. Spatial images are a simple representation of how objects are arranged in space, while visual images carry information regarding how objects appear. An example of a spatial image would be imagining the layout of one's bedroom in one's head, for instance where each piece of furniture is set in relation to the others (regardless of what the furniture looks like). The Corsi Blocks test (Milner, 1971) is a measure of spatial memory, and signers have been shown to perform well on this test. The task involves a board with blocks glued on in a random order. The experimenter taps a sequence of blocks and the participant has to repeat the tapping sequence. The number of blocks involved in the tapping sequence increases through the test. The number of blocks a participant can remember before failing is considered their spatial span. Hearing children who learn to sign as a part of their regular curriculum show greater spatial gains than peers who do not have sign classes, which suggests that sign language skills enhance spatial memory abilities (Capirci, Cattani, Rossini, and Volterra, 1998). Spatial images are depicted frequently in signed language utterances for morphological and syntactic purposes. An individual, who shows difficulties comprehending spatial components of signed utterances and makes space errors in sign productions would thus be expected to perform poorly on the Corsi Blocks test. This observed weakness would be an example of a domain-general cause of a sign language disorder.

Social–emotional functioning

If a child with a suspected language disorder appears to be cognitively intact, there might be socioemotional factors that are influencing the child's learning. Even when cognitive weaknesses are present, such socioemotional factors could exacerbate the child's learning difficulties. While Deaf individuals have been found to have a higher incidence of depressive symptoms and anxiety and a greater tendency toward experiencing boredom (Watt and Davies, 1991; van Eldik, 2005), we also know that, for Deaf adolescents, isolation from other deaf peers can contribute to feelings of loneliness and to communication difficulties with parents and peers (Jambor and Elliott, 2005). To assess social, emotional, and behavioral domains, traditional methods include a clinical interview, projective testing, self-report rating scales, and informant rating scales. An example is the Behavior Assessment System for Children (BASC: Reynolds, 2004), which includes a comprehensive set of rating scales and forms for the teacher, the parent, and the participant. Examples of the BASC scales include ratings for adaptability, aggression, anxiety, conduct problems, depression, functional communication, and social skills. Even if a child has rich and consistent sign language input, there may still be underlying social–emotional issues that impede his or her opportunities for typical peer and adult language interaction experiences (Hauser, Wills, and Isquith, 2006). Again, in the context of a suspected signed language disorder, it is important to evaluate the child's overall socioemotional functioning to determine whether that might be a contributing factor to the child's challenges.

Further Considerations

This chapter provides an overall clinical neuropsychological approach to evaluating an individual with a suspected sign language disorder. The process approach is strongly recommended for test selection and administration. An interdisciplinary research team is best suited to properly consider the different cognitive domains discussed here. Still, there remains a great need for more signed language assessment tests, as these are necessary for warranting the diagnosis of a language disorder. It would be ideal to have a full battery of tests that measure different domain-specific and domain-general aspects of signed language processing. There is a need for more collaboration between sign language linguists and neuropsychologists who are trained to work with Deaf individuals. The results of neuropsychological evaluations provide linguists with valuable information on how to conceptualize sign language disorders. While empirical studies of sign language disorders typically involve native signers, there is a great need for research on the nature of signed language disorders among Deaf non-native signers who, due to linguistic isolation or impoverished first-language environments, can be characterized as language-delayed. Such studies would help both researchers and clinicians understand the role that language isolation plays in language development.

Note

1   We adopt the common convention in this literature of capitalizing the term *Deaf* to refer to the community of individuals who identify with Deaf culture and consider themselves a part of a linguistic and cultural minority group.

Keywords

assessment; deaf; language impairment; motor abilities; neuropsychological assessment; signed language disorders; specific language impairment; visual processing; visual–spatial

See Also

Chapter 13; Chater 19

Suggested Readings

Quinto-Pozos, D. (Ed.) (2014). *Multilingual aspects of signed language communication and disorder*. Bristol: Multilingual Matters.

Woll, B., and Morgan, G. (2011). Language impairments in the development of sign: Do they reside in a specific modality or are they modality-independent deficits? *Bilingualism: Language and Cognition* 15, 75–87.

References

American Psychiatric Association (2013). *Diagnostic and statistic manual of mental disorders* (5th ed.). Washington, DC: Author.

Archibald, L. M. D., and Gathercole, S. E. (2006). Short-term and working memory in specific language impairment. *International Journal of Language and Communication Disorders* 41, 675–693.

Baser, C. A., and Ruff, R. M. (1987). Construct validity of the San Diego neuropsycholgocial test battery. *Achieves of Clinical Neuropsychology* 2, 13–32.

Bellugi, U., O'Grady, L., Lillo-Martin, D., O'Grady, M., van Hoek, U., and Corina, D. (1990). Enhancement of spatial cognition in deaf children. In V. Volterra and C. Erting (Eds.), *From gesture to language in hearing and deaf children*. New York: Springer, 1990, pp. 278–298.

Benedict, R. H., Schretlen, D., Groninger, L., Dobraski, M., and Shpritz, B. (1996). Revision of the Brief Visuospatial Memory test: Studies of normal performance, reliability, and validity. *Psychological Assessment* 8, 145–160.

Benton, A. L., Hamsher, K., Varney, N. R., and Spreen, O. (1983). *Contributions to neuropsychological assessment: A clinical manual*. New York: Oxford University Press.

Bettger, J. (1992). The effects of experience on spatial cognition: Deafness and knowledge of ASL. Unpublished PhD dissertation, University of Illinois, Urbana-Champaign.

Bettger, J., Emmorey, K., McCullough, S., and Bellugi, U. (1997). Enhanced facial discrimination: Effects of experience with American Sign Language. *Journal of Deaf Studies and Deaf Education* 2, 223–233.

Brentari, D., Poizner, H., and Kegl, J. (1995). Aphasic and Parkinsonian signing: Differences in phonological disruption. *Brain and Language* 48, 69–105.

Capirci, O., Cattani, A., Rossini, P., and Volterra, V. (1998). Teaching sign language to hearing children as a possible factor in cognitive enhancement. *Journal of Deaf Studies and Deaf Education* 3, 135–142.

Chamberlain, C., and Mayberry, R. I. (2000). Theorizing about the relationship between ASL and reading. In C. Chamberlain, J. Morford, and R. I. Mayberry (Eds.), *Language acquisition by eye*. Mahwah, NJ: Lawrence Erlbaum, pp. 221–260.

Corina, D. (1998). Aphasia in users of signed languages. In P. Coppens, Y. Lebrun, and A. Basso (Eds.), *Aphasia in atypical populations*. Mahwah, NJ: Lawrence Erlbaum, pp. 261–309.

D'Elia, L. F. (1996). *Color Trails test*. Lutz, FL: Psychological Assessment Resources.

D'Elia, L. F., Satz, P., Uchiyama, C. L., and White, T. (1994). *Children's Color Trails Test*. Lutz, FL: Psychological Assessment Resources.

Diamond, A. (2013). Executive functions. *Annual Review of Psychology* 64, 135–168.

Dunn, L. M., and Dunn, D. M. (2007). *Peabody Picture Vocabulary test* (4th ed.). Minneapolis, MN: Pearson Assessments.

van Eldik, T. (2005). Mental health problems of Dutch youth with hearing loss as shown on the Youth Self-Report. *American Annals of the Deaf* 150, 11–16.

Emmorey, K. (2002). *Language, cognition, and the brain: Insights from sign language research*. Mahwah, NJ: Lawrence Erlbaum.

Enns, C. J., and Herman, R. C. (2011). Adapting the Assessing British Sign Language Development Receptive Skills test into American Sign Language. *Journal of Deaf Studies and Deaf Education* 16, 362–374.

Gioia, G. A., Isquith, P. K., Guy, S. C., and Kenworth, L. (2000). *Behavior Rating Inventory of Executive Function*. Odessa, FL: Psychological Assessment Resources.

Goldstein, N. E., Sexton, J., and Feldman, R. S. (2000). Encoding of facial expressions of emotion and knowledge of American Sign Language. *Journal of Applied School Psychology*, 30, 67–76.

Harper, E., Allen, T., and Morere, D. (2012). The "Toolkit Project": Introduction. In D. Morere and T. Allen (Eds.), *Assessing literacy in deaf adults: Neurocognitive measures and predictors*. New York: Springer, pp. 3–19.

Haug, T. (2008). Review of signed language assessment instruments. In A. E. Baker and B. Woll (Eds.), *Sign language acquisition* (pp. 51–86). Philadelphia, PA: John Benjamins.

Haug, T. (2011). Approaching sign language test construction: Adaptation of the German Sign Language Receptive Skills test. *Journal of Deaf Studies and Deaf Education* 16, 343–361.

Haug, T., and Mann, W. (2008). Adapting tests of sign language assessment for other sign languages: A review of linguistic, cultural, and psychometric problems. *Journal of Deaf Studies and Deaf Education* 13, 138–147.

Hauser, P. C., Contreras, J., and Israel, E. (2013). *Deaf individuals' performance on the Color Trails test: Effect of early sign acquisition.* Poster presented at the conference "Theoretical issues in sign language research," University College London, London.

Hauser, P. C., Lukomski, J., and Hillman, T. (2008). Development of deaf and hard of hearing students' executive function. In M. Marschark and P. C. Hauser (Eds.), *Deaf cognition: Foundations and outcomes.* New York: Oxford University Press, pp. 286–308.

Hauser, P. C., Lukomski, J., and Samar, V. (2012). Reliability and validity of the BRIEF-A for assessing deaf college students' executive function. *Journal of Psychoeducational Assessment* 31, 363–374.

Hauser, P. C., Wills, K., and Isquith, P. K. (2006). Hard of hearing, deafness, and being deaf. In J. E. Farmer, J. Donders, and S. Warschausky (Eds.), *Neurodevelopmental disabilities: Clinical research and practice.* New York: Guilford Publications, pp. 119–131.

Hauser, P. C., Cohen, J., Dye, M. W. G., and Bavelier, D. (2007). Visual constructive and visual–motor skills in Deaf native signers. *Journal of Deaf Studies and Deaf Education* 12, 148–157.

Hauser, P. C., Paludnevičienė, R., Supalla, T., and Bavelier, D. (2008). American Sign Language–Sentence Reproduction test: Development and implications. In R. M. de Quadros (Ed.), *Sign language: Spinning and unraveling the past, present and future.* Petropolis, Brazil: Editora Arara Azul, pp. 160–172.

Herman, R., Holmes, S., and Woll, B. (1999). *Assessing BSL development: Receptive Skills test.* Coleford, UK: Forest Bookshop.

Jambor, E., and Elliott, M. (2005). Self-esteem and coping strategies among deaf students. *Journal of deaf Studies and Deaf Education* 10, 63–81.

Maller, S. J. (2003). Intellectual assessment of deaf people. In M. Marschark and P. E. Spencer (Eds.), *Oxford handbook of deaf studies, language, and education.* New York: Oxford University Press, pp. 451–496.

Maller, S., Singleton, J. L., Supalla, S. J., and Wix, T. (1999). The development and psychometric properties of the American Sign Language Proficiency Assessment (ASL-PA). *Journal of Deaf Studies and Deaf Education* 4, 249–269.

Martin, N. A. (2006). *Test of visual perceptual skills* (3rd ed.). Novato, CA: American Therapy Publications.

Marton, K. (2008). Visuo-spatial processing and executive functions in children with specific language impairment. *International Journal of Language and Communication Disorders* 43, 181–200.

Mason, K., Rowley, K., Marshall, C. R., Atkinson, J., Herman, R., Woll, B., and Morgan, G. (2010). Identifying specific language impairment in deaf children acquiring British Sign Language: Implications for theory and practice. *British Journal of Developmental Psychology* 28, 33–49.

McCullough, S., and Emmorey, K. (1997). Face processing by deaf ASL signers: Evidence for expertise in distinguishing local features. *Journal of Deaf Studies and Deaf Education* 2, 212–222.

Meyers, J., and Meyers, K. (1995). *Rey Complex Figure test and recognition trial.* Odessa, FL: Psychological Assessment Resources.

Milberg, W. P., Hebben, N., and Kaplan, E. (2009). The Boston process approach to neuropsychological assessment. In I. Grant and K. Adams (Eds.), *Neuropsychological assessment of neuropsychiatric and neuromedical disorders* (3rd ed.). New York: Oxford University Press, pp. 42–65.

Milner, B. (1971). Interhemispheric differences in the localization of psychological processes in man. *British Medical Bulletin* 27, 272–277.

Morere, D. (2012). Memory. In D. Morere and T. Allen (Eds.), *Assessing literacy in deaf adults: Neurocognitive measures and predictors.* New York: Springer, pp. 75–104.

Morere, D. A., and Roberts, R. (2012). Fingerspelling. In D. Morere and T. Allen (Eds.), *Assessing literacy in deaf adults: Neurocognitive measures and predictors.* New York: Springer, pp. 179–190.

Morere, D. A., Goodman, E., Hanumantha, S., and Allen, T. (2012). Measures of general cognitive functioning. In D. Morere and T. Allen (Eds.), *Assessing literacy in deaf adults: Neurocognitive measures and predictors.* New York: Springer, pp. 39–57.

Morgan, G. (2005). Biology and behavior: Insights from the acquisition of sign language. In A. Cutler (Ed.), *Twenty-first century psycholinguistics: Four cornerstones.* Mahwah, NJ: Lawrence Erlbaum, pp. 191–208.

Morgan, G., Herman, R., and Woll, B. (2007). Language impairments in sign language: Breakthroughs and puzzles. *International Journal of Language and Communication Disorders* 42, 97–105.

Oberg, E., and Lukomski, J. (2011). Executive functioning and the impact of a hearing loss: Performance-based measures and the Behavior Rating Inventory of Executive Function (BRIEF). *Child Neuropsychology* 17, 521–545.

Paludnevičienė, R., Hauser, P. C., Daggett, D., and Kurz, K. B. (2012). Issues and trends in sign language assessment. In D. Morere and T. Allen (Eds.), *Measuring literacy and its neurocognitive predictors among deaf individuals.* New York: Springer, pp. 191–207.

Peters, M., Lehmann, W., Takahira, S., Takeuchi, Y., and Jordan, K. (2006). Mental rotation performance in four cross-cultural samples: Overall sex differences and the role of academic program in performance. *Cortex* 42, 1005–1014.

Quinto-Pozos, D., Forber-Pratt, A., and Singleton, J. (2011). Do developmental signed language disorders exist? Perspectives from professionals. *Language, Speech, and Hearing Services in Schools* 42, 1–21.

Quinto-Pozos, D., Singleton, J., Hauser, P., and Levine, S. (2014). A case-study approach to investigating developmental signed language disorders. In D. Quinto-Pozos (ed.), *Multilingual aspects of signed language communication and disorder.* Bristol: Multilingual Matters, pp. 70–89.

Quinto-Pozos, D., Singleton, J. L., Hauser, P. C., Levine, S. L., Garberoglio, C. L., and Hou, L. (2013). Atypical sign language development: A case study of challenges with visual–spatial processing. *Cognitive Neuropsychology* 30, 332–359.

Reynolds, C. (2004). *Behavior Assessment System for Children* (2nd ed.). Circle Pines, MN: American Guidance Service.

Roth, R. M., Isquith, P. K., and Gioia, G. A. (2005). *BRIEF-A: Behavior Rating Inventory of Executive Function, adult version.* Lutz, FL: Psychological Assessment Resources.

Singleton, J., and Supalla, S., (2011). Assessing children's proficiency in natural signed languages. In M. Marschark and P. E. Spencer (Eds.), *Oxford handbook of deaf studies, language and education* (2nd ed.). New York: Oxford University Press, pp. 306–319.

Spanjer, P., Fieret, M., and Baker, A. (2014). The influence of dementia on language in a signing population. In D. Quinto-Pozos (Ed.), *Multilingual aspects of signed language communication and disorder.* Bristol: Multilingual Matters, pp. 186–208.

Spreen, O., and Strauss, E. (1998). *A compendium of neuropsychological tests: Administration, norms, and commentary.* New York: Oxford University Press.

Sweet, J. J., Moberg, P. J., and Westergaard, C. K. (1996). Five-year follow up survey of practices and beliefs of clinical psychologists. *The Clinical Neuropsychologist* 10, 202–221.

Thorndike, R. L., Hagen, E., and Sattler, M. (1986). *Stanford–Binet Intelligence Scale* (4th ed.). Chicago, IL: Riverside.

Vernon, M. (2005). Fifty years of research on the intelligence of deaf and hard-of-hearing children: A review of literature and discussion of implications. *Journal of Deaf Studies and Deaf Education* 10, 225–231.

Watt, J. D., and Davis, F. E. (1991). The prevalence of boredom proneness and depression among profoundly deaf residential school adolescents. *American Annals of the Deaf* 136, 409–413.

Woodcock, R. W., McGrew, K. S., and Mather, N. (2001). *Woodcock–Johnson III Test of Cognitive Abilities*. Rolling Meadows, IL: Riverside Publishing.

19 Using and Developing Language and Cognitive Assessments with Deaf Signers

Tanya Denmark and Joanna Atkinson

Chapter Overview

In this chapter we highlight that researchers interested in assessments need separate, specifically designed tests of language and cognition for deaf[1] sign language users rather than relying on tests designed for users of spoken languages. Tests that are developed specifically for deaf signers and that produce deaf norms are an invaluable tool in both sign language research and clinical practice. When deaf signers are given spoken language-based tests designed to be suitable for hearing populations, there is a potential for linguistic and cultural biases to occur, which can lead to an unreliable assessment. In this chapter we review language and cognitive assessments that have been developed for deaf children and adults to date, demonstrating examples of good practice. We use this review to present a range of important points to consider when conducting assessments with deaf signers. We conclude with considerations for developing future assessments.

Research Methods in Sign Language Studies: A Practical Guide, First Edition.
Edited by Eleni Orfanidou, Bencie Woll, and Gary Morgan.
© 2015 John Wiley & Sons, Inc. Published 2015 by John Wiley & Sons, Inc.

Introduction

Before we talk about specific guidelines for conducting language and cognitive assessments, we will discuss some general principles that are important to keep in mind. Deafness is not a cognitive disability and, where there is timely access to language through exposure to sign language in deaf families, deaf children mirror hearing children in their achievement of language and cognitive milestones (e.g. Morgan and Woll, 2002). However, where there is no early exposure to accessible language and communication, there may be developmental consequences for language and cognition (e.g. Cormier, Schembri, Vinson, and Orfanidou, 2012). Ninety-six percent of deaf children are born to hearing parents, and many of them experience such language delay (Mitchell and Karchmer, 2004). Sign language assessments are needed to measure language ability in a population where language delay is prevalent, in order to distinguish delay from deviant language and to identify typical patterns of language acquisition. Assessment test results can inform research and add to what we know to date about deaf signers' language and cognitive skills; this will lead to more research and better intervention and services. There are several implications associated with the inappropriate use of spoken language assessments with deaf signers. The most important one is the possibility of missed or incorrect diagnosis, which leads to a lack of intervention and specialist support (Wisniewski, DeMatteo, Lee, and Orr, 1989).

There has been an increase in the number of assessments that have been developed and used to identify normative language acquisition, language-learning impairments, and acquired language and cognitive impairments in deaf sign language users. However, the development of such tests is not straightforward. Many factors have to be considered, such as the participants' delayed language acquisition, lower levels of literacy, language and cultural differences.

The first point we highlight is how written language should not be used during an assessment test of a deaf signer. Much research has demonstrated that delayed exposure to language leads to problems of literacy (Mayer, 2007). In the United Kingdom deaf school leavers have low literacy levels; the average reading age is 9, regardless of intellectual function (Conrad, 1979; Powers, Gregory, and Thoutenhoofd, 1999). Therefore it is inappropriate to use English-based written assessments or instructions when testing deaf adults. When designing an assessment, researchers should be mindful that English is often a second (or weaker) language for deaf individuals.

In general the development of any assessment tests should take into consideration that Deaf signers differ in many ways from hearing speakers, language differences being just one element. Some research has shown that a combination of the absence of early auditory stimulation and the use of a visual–spatial language has led to differences in the cognitive profiles of deaf signers (Fellinger, Holzinger, and Pollard, 2012). For example, when designing a memory test, researchers should be aware that some deaf signers have shorter serial memory spans for verbal material, for example numbers and fingerspelled letters (Boutla, Supalla, Newport, and Bavelier, 2004), but superior performance for spatially organized material (Wilson, Bettger, Niculae, and Klima, 1997). In addition, signers are less affected by backward recall on digit span tasks and have greater attention to peripheral stimuli (Bavelier et al.,

2000). When designing assessments for deaf signers, researchers should familiarize themselves with the existing literature relating to this population, as findings of differences may guide design and intervention work. Researchers might therefore design an assessment test utilizing spatial rather than serial processing in memory tasks, or accounting for greater awareness of visual peripheral stimuli in test design. There should be a reciprocal relationship between research and assessment. Research findings are used to feed into test development, and test results influence future research and lead to a better understanding of sign language development, processing, and cognition. A crucial issue in any assessment of a deaf person is that deaf populations are heterogeneous (e.g. Mann, Roy, and Marshall, 2013). When assessing deaf signers, researchers need to gather as much background information as they can about the individual, as different aetiologies associated with deafness can have neurological concomitants, for example those individuals who were deafened due to meningitis may display a range of difficulties with language and cognitive skills (Woods and Dockrell, 2010). Therefore it is important to know from the outset the full developmental history of an individual prior to assessment or inclusion in a research sample.

The different backgrounds of deaf and hearing individuals reinforce the need for assessments to be created for deaf individuals with the help of representative samples, since comparison with hearing norms overlooks these differences in background between deaf and hearing individuals and prevents accurate conclusions about whether or not impairment is present (Reynolds and Suzuki, 2013). With these background issues covered, we now move to identify specific examples from research we have been involved in, in order to describe how assessment tests were developed.

Translated, Adapted, and Novel Tests Developed for Signed Languages

With the aim of putting forward pointers of good practice and recommendations for researchers interested in test development, we review assessments that have been developed with deaf people in mind. We will discuss both tests of sign language ability and cognitive assessments. These range from whole-scale translations of tests to slight adaptation of existing spoken language assessments. We also review completely new assessments that have been created by focusing on the needs of deaf signers. There are relatively few sign language tests available in this field, and most of those developed to date relate to British Sign Language (BSL) or American Sign Language (ASL). For brevity, this chapter focuses on assessments for these languages; but it should be born in mind that there are tests available for other signed languages as well. We recommend Tobias Haug's webpage for a comprehensive list of the different sign language assessments that are currently available across the world (www.signlang-assessment.info).

Many of the issues relating to test development are transferable to other signed languages; some may translate relatively easily, others will require careful adaptation from sign language to sign language.

Examples of translated tests

The aim of a direct translation from spoken test to a signed language is to maintain test integrity and to attempt to demonstrate a similar pattern of results in deaf signers to that of the equivalent tests for hearing people. Tests that translate well tend to have relatively simple content and instructions to participants on tasks that aim to tap developmental processes that are similar in both deaf and hearing children.

The Macarthur Communicative Development Inventory (MCDI)

This is a language measure that looks at early vocabulary development, from 8 to 36 months. Parents complete a paper-based checklist of words that are used and understood by their child. The English CDI (Fenson et al., 1993) was translated into ASL (Anderson and Reilly, 2002) and later into a BSL version (Woolfe, Herman, Roy, and Woll, 2010). Anderson and Reilly (2002) collected CDI data from 69 deaf native infants, 34 of whom were followed longitudinally. For the BSL CDI percentiles are given for an expressive and receptive vocabulary based on 29 deaf native infants who were followed longitudinally from 8 to 36 months. Both the ASL and the BSL CDIs were used to compare deaf children's vocabulary development against that of other deaf children in the population, to determine whether their vocabulary range was age-appropriate and, to some extent, to compare deaf individuals with hearing children. Findings from both versions of the CDI demonstrate that deaf native signers learn vocabulary in a way similar to that of hearing children learning spoken language. Administration of the ASL and BSL CDIs is straightforward; the forms are applicable to very young children and both tests have good reliability and validity. One caveat of the CDI is that it is limited by parental knowledge of signs, as many hearing parents learn sign language in parallel with their children and may not comprehend signs that their children produce as readily as deaf parents do. Therefore a number of signs could be missed, with the result that deaf children from hearing parents seem to have even smaller vocabularies than deaf children from deaf families.

During the development of the BSL CDI, a deaf researcher visited the homes of some of the children in the sample and filmed the child and the parent interacting with a number of toys and books, in order to validate whether some of the signs that were reported as being present in the child's vocabulary were in fact understood and produced by the child. This was an effective way to strengthen the reliability of the parental report data. Another issue with the CDI is making sure that parents are aware that they are rating their children's signs rather than their gestures. With the BSL CDI, the researcher collecting the forms had to do some work with parents about what is a sign and what is a communicative gesture. There was also a website where video examples of the signs from the forms could be viewed. This was very useful for hearing parents. In general, development of a CDI in sign languages requires this close quasi-training of parents in order to ensure that the forms are filled in correctly. This normally is not required for spoken language CDIs. However, because deaf children samples for these assessments are significantly smaller, this should be achievable.

Semantic fluency tasks

Fluency tasks tap both language and cognitive abilities. They measure the efficiency of lexical search strategies, which are highly dependent on executive function and working memory. Marshall, Rowley, Mason, Herman, and Morgan (2013) translated instructions for an English semantic fluency task into BSL and asked 22 deaf children aged 4–15 years to produce their responses in BSL using the semantic categories "food" and "animals." Children were asked to name as many different food items (in Task 1) and animals (in Task 2) as they could think of in one minute. This task tests participants' semantic organization. Results showed that the pattern of responses was very similar to that found for hearing children in terms of mean number of responses, production of prototypical category members, semantic clustering, and tailing off of responses over the one-minute period. Further investigations need to be conducted to compare directly deaf and hearing children on semantic fluency tasks and to allow for normative data to be collected. This test requires good instructions and video recording.

Marshall, Rowley, and Atkinson (2013) investigated how deaf adults fare with semantic and phonological fluency tasks. Deaf adults completed two semantic fluency tasks (naming animals and food items) and six phonological fluency tasks. For hearing individuals, phonological fluency tasks require participants to name different words that begin with a certain sound, for example "S" – as many as they can in one minute. In the adaptation of these tests for deaf adults, participants can be asked to produce items that feature a certain handshape, location, or movement in BSL, for example an index finger point – as many as they can in one minute. The phonological fluency task used in the Marshall, Rowley, and Atkinson (2013) test, unlike the semantic fluency task in Marshall, Rowley, Mason et al. (2013) test, involved more than just a translation in its development, as it uses phonological parameters in BSL rather than single letters in English. The handshapes consisted of "I," "G," and "Claw 5"; the locations were above the shoulders and on the palm of the non-dominant hand; and the movements were two hands and both hands moving (for further details, see Marshall, Rowley, and Atkinson, 2013). In developing this kind of task, one aim is to find similarities between patterns of responses for deaf and hearing adults across these same tasks in different modalities. For example Marshall, Rowley, and Atkinson (2013) found that participants produced more items for the semantic fluency tasks than for the phonological fluency tasks; that there was a decline in responses across time, which is observed with hearing participants on comparable tasks; and that clusters were generated for both semantic and phonological tasks. Differences between deaf and hearing adults also emerged, which stemmed from differences in modality: for deaf signers there was a high level of semantic clustering on the phonological fluency tasks, clusters of sign homonyms were produced, and there was greater clustering for handshape and location than movement. Performance on the phonological fluency tasks varied according to the individual task, deaf signers producing an average of 19 signs per minute for above-the-shoulder task, but only 7 for the "I" handshape task.

The authors propose that differences in performance across phonological fluency tasks may be related to the frequency of signs across these categories, with more signs being documented above the shoulders than with an "I" handshape in the BSL dictionary. Many signers were reported to have found the phonological fluency tasks much more difficult than the semantic fluency tasks. This is not reported for spoken language versions of this test. This finding may be linked to the fact that deaf signers are typically given less opportunity to explore phonological parameters in BSL. However, future work investigating phonological awareness alongside phonological fluency tasks is necessary if we are to understand more about deaf signers' metaphonological skills. The authors recommend the use of semantic fluency tasks for deaf clinical populations, provided that norms are collected for a large sample of deaf adults beforehand. They argue that phonological fluency tasks are less appropriate for clinical use, due to their difficulty and variation in performance across tasks. This final point highlights that translation of tests is not always straightforward. Differences between language modalities may favor or disfavor specific linguistic assessments in different ways. Consequently any comparison between spoken and signed language skills as assessed by translated tests needs to be done with great care.

Further issues with translation of tests

Problems with translation can make a test invalid and inaccurate for deaf signers. For example, the Mini Mental State Examination (MMSE) (Folstein, Folstein, and McHugh, 1975) was translated into ASL by Dean, Feldman, Morere, and Morton (2009), to be made to measure cognitive function in 117 older deaf adults aged 55–89. Minimal changes were made to lexical items, just to eliminate regional signed variants. The mean score for the sample was below the cutoff for normal function. The authors concluded that cultural and linguistic factors rather than cognitive impairment accounted for decreased scores in healthy deaf people. For this type of assessment, test constructs that are relevant to deaf culture rather than to mainstream hearing culture may have been more appropriate; for example, in the MMSE the item, spell WORLD backwards would be problematic for some deaf signers, as it requires good literacy skills. This study demonstrates that it is imperative to carefully consider what constructs may not be transferable for deaf signers when translating a test. Issues with incorrectly translating items are that deaf individuals may be misdiagnosed with cognitive impairment or dementia on the basis of an inappropriate assessment, which is used instead of one that may be representative of their true ability.

Tests that have been adapted

Adapted tests adopt their format from existing spoken language tests, but test items are revised to maximize validity, and (ideally) new normative data for deaf signers are collected. As an illustration, the Nonsense Sign Repetition test (NSRT: Mann, Marshall, Mason, and Morgan, 2010) is a language measure that looks at the development of sign language phonological skills in deaf children. The NSRT also functions in a battery of other tools, as a diagnostic test for language impairments in BSL. It is normed on a sample of 91 deaf children aged 3–11 and was adapted from non-word repetition tests that are used in spoken language, with items that are phonotactically possible but carry no meaning in the target language (Gathercole and Baddeley, 1996). The complexity of nonsense signs was manipulated along two phonological parameters: handshape and movement. For each parameter, items are either phonetically "simple" or "complex." Phonetically complex items consist of handshapes that are more difficult to articulate and movements that include both path and internal motion. There are 40 nonsense signs, which are viewed as video clips for immediate repetition by the child being tested. Responses are recorded on video and accuracy scores are calculated for handshape, internal movement, and path movements. Some work is needed in this test to discount nonsense signs that are similar to real signs or in fact are regional variants of standard signs. It is also necessary to have a sign linguistics background, to ensure that the test is phonologically sound and appropriate. For example, the BSL test has several items that use hand-internal movements. It was important to have both a good understanding of how these elements are used in real BSL signs and some idea about the developmental trajectory of these elements in native signing children. This was in order to make sure that the items used as nonsense signs are neither too complex nor too simple for the age range of the participants.

The results of Mann et al.'s (2010) study indicated that repetition accuracy improved with age and was lowest for signs that were phonetically complex. Advantages of this measure are that it is child-friendly, engaging, and simple to administer in a video-based format; and hearing children can also complete this assessment, as no prior knowledge of sign language is needed. Great care was taken for the signed instructions for this test. They were simple and very explicit. The signer who gives the video instructions also uses a child-addressed register. It is crucial that the piloting of instructions is done, because in any kind of test a child can infer the wrong meaning in instructions if they are not clear. The NSRT was found to show some construct validity, as it correlated with scores on the BSL receptive skills task (Mann et al., 2010). However there is a distinct lack of information about other psychometric properties such as reliability measures. Marshall, Mann and Morgan (2011) noted that the NSRT was more difficult than non-word repetition tasks for hearing English-speaking children of equivalent ages. Therefore it may not be appropriate to compare deaf and hearing children directly across the two different signed and spoken language measures; rather only the BSL version of the NSRT should be used as a measure for comparing deaf children with other deaf children or deaf children with hearing children.

The ASL-Sentence Reproduction test (ASL-SRT, Hauser, Paludnevičienė, Supalla, and Bavelier, 2008) measures sign language proficiency; it is an adaptation of the Test of Adult and Adolescent Language (Hammill, Brown, Larsen, and Wiederholt, 1994). Participants are given one sentence at a time and are instructed to repeat each sentence exactly as they see it. The sentences start with fewer signs and simpler grammatical structure and gradually increase in difficulty. The ASL-SRT aims to distinguish ASL competence in both native and non-native children and adults. All levels of grammar – that is, phonology, morphology, and syntax – are scored. Data were collected from 120 deaf and hearing native and non-native signing children (aged 10–17) and adults (aged 18–60) (Hauser et al., 2008). Deaf signers had better performance than hearing signers on the ASL-SRT. Within the deaf group, performance on the ASL-SRT was sensitive to differences in ASL fluency between native and non-native signers; the ASL-SRT also effectively distinguished between children and adults. These findings suggest that the ASL-SRT can be effectively used as a baseline to differentiate between levels of fluency, depending on the native versus non-native background of children and adults.

The ASL-SRT was adapted into a BSL version: the BSL Sentence Reproduction test (BSL-SRT; see Cormier, Adam, Rowley, Woll, and Atkinson, 2012). Initial results from the BSL-SRT indicate that adult native signers are significantly better at accurately reproducing sentences than adult non-native signers. The BSL-SRT has not yet been administered to deaf children. For both tests, wider normative data and standardization is needed. Weaknesses with the sentence repetition tests are that scorers need training and that each video can be time-consuming to score.

The Signed Paired Associates test (SPAT; see Pollard, Rediess, and DeMatteo, 2005) assesses verbal memory for deaf adults in ASL. It is based on the paired associates subtest of the Wechsler Memory Scale (Wechsler, 1987). The original English lexical items were replaced by new ASL lexical pairs. The SPAT has 14 sign pairs, half of which are semantically related and easier pairs, while half are semantically unrelated, harder pairs. All sign pairs are presented to participants over 4 learning trials, and after a 20-minute delay a free recall and a cued recall trial are given. Six recall scores are generated in total: free recall from easy pairs, free recall from hard pairs, total free recall, free recall plus cued recall easy, free recall plus cued recall hard and free recall plus cued recall total. DeMatteo, Pollard, and Lentz (1987) gave 45 healthy deaf adults the SPAT, and results showed clear learning curves where participants retained more pairs over the 4 learning trials. They also showed better retention of semantically related pairs than of semantically unrelated pairs. The same outcome is found for hearing individuals on the spoken paired associates subtests. Rediess, Pollard, and Veyberman (1997) compared a small group of deaf healthy adults aged 18–34 (N = 38) and a clinical group of deaf individuals aged 18–57 (N = 37) who had been referred for clinical evaluation on the SPAT. They found that the clinical group was significantly poorer than the healthy group on a number of outcomes on the SPAT. Therefore provisional findings suggest that the SPAT is effective at identifying learning and memory deficits in deaf adults. A larger sample size study would be needed to validate this conclusion and to further develop the clinical properties of the test. Work to finalize this test is still in progress, so it can be made available with the development of a manual and a guide to administration.

The BSL Verbal Learning and Memory test (BSL-VLMT; see Denmark, Atkinson, Marshall, and Woll, 2014) is an example of a verbal memory test for older deaf signers that retains the format of the Hopkins Verbal Learning test, revised (HVLT-R: Brandt, 1991; Benedict, Schretlen, Groninger, and Brandt, 1998). It was not possible to simply translate items from the HVLT-R, as many of the semantic categories did not effectively transfer into BSL – for example precious gemstones. Therefore completely novel stimuli were used with careful consideration. Twelve items were chosen from a list of 300 signs used in a BSL lexical norming study (Vinson, Cormier, Denmark, Schembri, and Vigliocco, 2008), which provided ratings for familiarity, iconicity, and age of acquisition. Semantic categories were matched to ensure they were equivalent with low iconicity and regional variation. Standardized instructions and test stimuli were administered on video by a deaf native signer. The same list of 12 signs was presented three times, to allow learning with immediate recall of all signs, in any order, after each trial. Delayed recall was tested after a further 20 minutes during which other tasks were completed. This was followed by a recognition trial featuring 24 items: half were original test items and half were distracter items. The distracter items were either from the same semantic categories as the original items (relevant-6/12) or from different semantic categories (irrelevant-6/12). Participants identified which of the items they had seen before and which were novel by responding after each item was shown on the video. Normative data were collected from 222 cognitively healthy deaf participants aged 50–89 years. Findings demonstrated that the test was sensitive to ageing. Response patterns by signers were similar to those found for hearing people on the HVLT-R, with clear evidence of learning over trials and lower responses in older participants. There was some evidence of slightly lower recall scores in deaf signers, which is likely to be an effect of modality, as signs take longer to articulate than spoken words (Boutla et al., 2004). These similarities in results suggest that both tests may be tapping similar psychological constructs of memory for "verbal" material. Only one form is available on the BSL-VLMT – unlike on the HVLT-R, which has six forms that can be used for repeated testing. The BSL-VLMT is the only verbal learning measure with normative data for older deaf adults to date. The BSL-VLMT is not yet available for general use; clinical data need to be collected so that it may be further validated with clinical populations.

Novel tests developed for signed language

The BSL Receptive Skills test (BSL-RST; see Herman, Holmes, and Woll, 1998) measures comprehension of BSL grammar in children aged 3–13 years. The BSL assessment was developed as part of a collaboration between three individuals: a speech and language therapist who is a specialist within the field of deafness, an expert in BSL and sign linguistics, and a deaf researcher with considerable experience of working with deaf children. This collaboration emphasizes the importance of having a good team of experts involved in a test development from the outset. The BSL-RST focuses on selected aspects of morphology and syntax in BSL. The assessment includes a vocabulary check and a video-based receptive skills test. There are no clear-cut norms for native and non-native signers, as mixed normative samples were collected. The test was originally standardized on 135 deaf children who were either native signers or carefully selected non-native signers exposed to BSL before the age of 5. This population was chosen due to the difficulty of creating a standardized population of non-native signers, who have such diverse experiences of language input.

Herman and Roy (2006) collected follow-up data on an additional 181 BSL users aged between 3 and 14. This sample consisted of 35 native signers and 113 non-native signers; the remaining individuals did not have information available regarding parental hearing status. The original sample of 135 children, over half of whom were native signers, was compared to the new sample, where participants had varying ages of exposure and only a fifth were native signers. Overall, children in the original sample achieved significantly better BSL-RST scores, although no difference was observed in the scores of native signers across samples. Herman and Roy (2006) concluded that deaf children in hearing families are less likely to achieve age-appropriate BSL skills than those from deaf families, adding construct validity to the test as a measure of normative sign language development. Herman is currently collaborating with researchers across different sign languages – ASL, German Sign Language (DGS), Australian Sign Language (Auslan), and Spanish Sign Language (LSE) – in order to adapt both the receptive and the productive skills tests to these different languages. A computer version of the BSL-RST has been developed in DGS. The BSL-RST has good psychometric properties with inter-rater reliability and test–retest reliability. The BSL-RST functions as a useful screen of morphology and syntax but lacks more detailed resolution, which would allow impairments with specific constructions to emerge in signers with developmental or acquired language impairments. A weakness of the assessment is that it lacks a measure of general communicative competence.

The BSL Production test (Narrative Skills) (BSL-PT: Herman et al., 2004) measures the ability of deaf children to produce a signed narrative. The team of researchers was expanded to include two experts in narrative development in deaf children. The child is asked to render a story sequence on video into BSL. The actors in the video use no language, but retelling their interactions accurately requires narrative skills. The test is standardized for children between the ages of 4 and 11 years and produces percentile scores for narrative content, structure, and grammar. Strengths of the BSL-RST and BSL-PT are that intervention can be offered where individuals fall below the norm on these assessments. A disadvantage of the BSL-PT is that scoring can be time-consuming and requires specialist training. More recently the test has been used for oral deaf children who prefer spoken English, as well as for hearing children. This required adapting one aspect of the test (grammar) from BSL to English. In making this adaptation the researchers chose a range of grammatical features that typically developing English-speaking children aged 6–11 produce in response to this stimulus. Early results suggest that the oral version of the test is reliable.

The British Sign Language Vocabulary test (BSL-VT: Mann and Marshall, 2012; Mann, Roy, and Marshall, 2013) assesses deaf children's lexical sign development from the age of 4 to the age of 16. The BSL-VT consists of two comprehension tasks and two production tasks. Comprehension is measured by (1) a meaning recognition task (a lexical sign is displayed together with four pictures and participants choose the picture that corresponds to the meaning of the sign) and (2) a form recognition task (a picture and four signs are shown and participants pick the sign that matches the picture). Production is measured by (1) a form recall task (a picture is shown and participants are asked to produce the corresponding sign) and (2) a meaning recall task (a sign is shown and participants are asked to give its meaning). These tasks were given to 24 deaf BSL users aged 5–15 (7 native, 17 non-native). It was hypothesized that the tasks would be progressively more difficult and that acquisition across the four tasks would increase with age. Results showed that the meaning recognition task was produced with the greatest accuracy and the meaning recall was the most difficult. This study contributes to a better understanding of the nature of vocabulary acquisition in deaf signing children. The findings indicate that knowledge of form–meaning mappings improves with age; however, this relationship is conflated with non-verbal ability. A benefit of the BSL-VT is that it has a wide scope, covering as it does both comprehension and production of vocabulary. The BSL-VT is also advantageous as it can be administered using the Internet, which allows online testing access, administration, and scoring. The accessibility of this test removes some of the difficulty with recruitment of deaf children, as it is important to always be mindful of timetables when arranging research visits to schools with deaf children. If teachers can access test materials online, there is more flexibility about when the research can be carried out. More data need to be collected to create a bigger normative sample; Wolfgang Mann is currently adapting this test into ASL.

The BSL Cognitive Screening test (BSL-CST; see Atkinson, Denmark, Marshall, and Woll, 2014) screens for orientation, memory, executive function, sign language, and visuospatial impairment in older deaf signers. It is designed to detect acquired cognitive impairment caused by neurodegenerative conditions such as dementia. The format was loosely based on the revised Addenbrookes Cognitive Examination (ACE-r: Mioshi, Dawson, Mitchell, Arnold, and Hodges, 2006) with additional novel and adapted items. The test was developed by a deaf-led team of psychologists and sign linguists. This is a test that has its origins entirely in signed language and has no English language requirements. It includes items that specifically assess integrity of language function in BSL. Standardized BSL test instructions and questions are signed in video format by an older deaf native signer. Participants view the video and respond using sign language. A trained investigator who is fluent in BSL records responses on the score sheet. Norms were collected from 226 cognitively healthy deaf adults aged 50–89 years. The BSL-CST is highly sensitive to age: scores decrease as participants get older. It is also sensitive to length of education and non-verbal intellectual ability. It is now used during routine clinical practice with deaf patients at the National Hospital for Neurology and Neurosurgery in London, within its Cognitive Disorders Clinic, to detect levels of change indicative of neurodegeneration and dementia in deaf BSL users (visit http://www.uclh.nhs.uk/HP/GPNEWS/Pages/CognitivedisordersclinicattheNHNN.aspx). The BSL-CST is an example of good test development for deaf signers, where the test has been developed with deaf signers in mind, with careful consideration for the psychological constructs of cognitive screens for hearing people and how to retain them while making the test appropriate for deaf individuals.

The assessments mentioned in this chapter are groundbreaking, because they provide the first linguistically appropriate tests of language and cognition for deaf signers. The best type of assessments are those that are carefully designed for their target population, are transferable, measure performance adequately – for example they are not at ceiling or floor (too easy or too difficult) – and are valid and reliable.

A common caveat with many of these tests is the small sample sizes and the lack of standardized normative data. However, it is important to be cautious with assessments that do provide deaf norms: comparisons are not straightforward, because deaf people are highly heterogeneous in terms of cognitive and language development (Fellinger, Holzinger, and Pollard, 2012). Results from assessments should be used alongside a complete developmental history and other measures, such as observation in different environments, in order to gain an understanding of whether deaf individuals are performing normally or at an impaired level by comparison to their deaf peers of the same age. An important issue to consider during the assessment of deaf populations is the representativeness of the sample: within the deaf population, approximately 30–40 percent of the children are identified as having additional needs. Often these individuals are not included in language and cognitive assessments on deaf populations, as only "typical deaf" individuals without any additional needs are recruited (Mann, Roy, and Marshall 2013). There is a need for more assessments to be done with deaf individuals with additional needs, so that we learn more about differences between the "typical" and the "atypical" deaf populations.

Future Directions

There are still very few tests that include large normative samples and that are available off the shelf, for free access and use. For some assessments, only trained clinicians such as psychologists can use them clinically (e.g. the BSL-CST). Other assessments require at least a training course to be undertaken before they can be used (e.g. the BSL-PT). There is a clear need for more work to be done in order to make the existing tests available or accessible through training courses, packaging, and online resources.

The majority of the language assessments that have been described in this chapter focus on the single-sign level (MCDI, fluency tasks, SPAT, NSRT, BSL-VLMT, etc.); there are fewer assessments focusing on the sentence level (ASL-SRT, BSL-SRT, BSL-RST) and on the narrative level (BSL-PT). This is possibly because assessments at the single-sign level are easier to develop and quicker to score. There is a need for more assessments that look beyond the single sign, at broader measures of sign proficiency.

Most sign language assessments use either a live fluent signer or standardized video administration with a deaf native signer in order to carry out the testing. However, for many of these video-based assessments, a competent signer still needs to be present during testing to record responses and ensure that instructions are understood. Currently there is a real shortage of clinicians who have knowledge of Deaf culture and are fluent in sign language, and this has implications for the quality of assessments that take place with deaf signers; as we know from research in the Hispanic community, direct testing in the same language is preferable (Acevedo, Reyes, Annett, and Lopez, 2003; Casas, 2010). Further research is required to establish whether tools derived in BSL can be administered by non-signing clinicians using the services of a sign language interpreter who is qualified and has specialized training in interpreting in psychological assessment, or whether such a paradigm introduces an additional cognitive load for respondents, with consequences for test accuracy. In future such tests may be accessible to clinicians via the Internet, and touch screen responding would eliminate the need for translation. The possibilities for remote assessments via telemedicine also warrant exploration.

Dynamic assessment investigates children's potential for learning rather than measuring their performance on a single test at a fixed point in time. It works by exploring the processes of why a child made an error rather than looking at test scores (Hasson and Joffe, 2007). Despite its potential value, it has never been adapted for deaf signers. Wolfgang Mann is currently working on a project that focuses on the use of dynamic assessment to measure deaf children's semantic skills in ASL and English. This methodology, which uses a combination of static (i.e., standardized test) and dynamic (intervention) assessments, draws from research on hearing children from non-mainstream language backgrounds (Peña, Iglesias, and Lidz, 2001; Peña et al., 2006). There could be great potential to use more dynamic assessment in the future with deaf signers.

While there is a growing number of assessment tools, there is a lack of validated tools for intervention and evaluation of treatment outcome. It is just as important to devise linguistically and culturally suitable measures in order to ensure that deaf signers, once diagnosed, have equitable access to healthcare treatments and psychological interventions (Lala, 1998). Training needs to be carried out with professionals in the health service and with sign language interpreters, in order to ensure that deaf service users experience appropriate treatment, which is given in signed language and not based on spoken language.

Overall Recommendations

Research and test development should be led by sign language users themselves, in order for cultural and linguistic validity to be maximized. Where adaptations are made to existing tests, it is imperative that they are conducted by native or near-native signers who are fully immersed in deaf culture and also have expertise in psychological and language assessment, as they will be more likely to be cognisant of psychometric conflicts that arise through the translation process. There needs to be cautious consideration of test validity, particularly in terms of whether the test still measures the construct that the original test set out to measure in spoken language.

It is vital that individuals who want to create assessments for deaf signers work on acquiring a number of skills in order to ensure that assessments are appropriately developed and used. Desirable qualities that researchers should aim to achieve are a high level of BSL fluency, knowledge of sign linguistics and language development in BSL, and an understanding of Deaf culture, Deaf history, and deaf education. Researchers should aim to meet and work with different groups of deaf people, for example children, adults, older adults, signers, and oral deaf individuals from non-signing backgrounds, so as to be well aware of the heterogeneity of the deaf population. They need to be committed to ensuring that tests incorporate robust psychometric properties and cultural acceptability to the Deaf community. A good starting point recommended by the authors is to work with individuals who have expertise in test development and in-depth knowledge of both sign linguistics and Deaf culture. This skill set is something that, we are aware, takes a long time to achieve; where it is not possible for researchers to meet these requirements, they should consult with specialists for advice when designing new measures or carrying out testing (Lane, 2005). DCAL currently offers short-term internships for individuals who want to learn more about undertaking research on deafness and sign language (visit http://www.ucl.ac.uk/dcal/getting-involved/Vacancies/extras/intern).

Conclusion

This chapter has provided an overview of the different language and cognitive tests available for deaf signers. Tests that are developed from scratch and standardized with suitable norms are invaluable for completing appropriate and accurate assessments with deaf individuals. There is a lot to consider when developing assessments; it is imperative that deaf signers with knowledge of psychometric testing are involved in the design, in test procedure, and in analysis, to ensure that testing is conducted with minimal bias.

Note

1   For the purposes of this chapter we will use lower case *deaf* to refer to deaf people.

Keywords

adaptation; assessment; cognition; culture; language; literacy; neurocognitive; signing; testing; translation

See Also

Chapter 1; Chapter 15; Chapter 18

Suggested Readings

Wood and Dockrell (2010) outline general assessment considerations for psychologists who work with deaf children. Hambleton (2005) covers broader issues related to adapting tests into other languages and across different cultures, and Reynolds and Suzuki (2013) provide a good overview of different types of bias in psychological assessment. Tobias Haug's website (http://www.signlang-assessment.info) covers sign language assessments from language acquisition to second-language learning, linguistic research studies, and tests of cognitive development. We recommend reading Tobias Haug's doctoral dissertation, which has been published as a book (Haug, 2011).

References

Acevedo, M. C., Reyes, C. J., Annett, R. D., and Lopez, E. M. (2003). Assessing language competence: Guidelines for assisting persons with limited English proficiency in research and clinical settings. *Journal of Multicultural Counselling and Development* 31, 192–204.

Anderson, D., and Reilly, J. (2002). The MacArthur Communicative Development Inventory: Normative data for American Sign Language. *Journal of Deaf Studies and Deaf Education* 7(2), 83–119.

Atkinson, J., Denmark, T., Marshall, J., and Woll, B. (2014). The British Sign Language Cognitive Screening test. Manuscript in preparation.

Bavelier, D., Tomann, A., Hutton, C., Mitchell, T. V., Corina, D. P., Liu, G., and Neville, H. J. (2000). Visual attention to the periphery is enhanced in congenitally deaf individuals. *Journal of Neuroscience* 20, 1–6.

Benedict, R. H. B., Schretlen, D., Groninger, L., and Brandt, J. (1998). Hopkins Verbal Learning test–revised: Normative data and analysis of inter-form and test–retest reliability. *The Clinical Neuropsychologist* 12(1), 43–55.

Boutla, M., Supalla, T., Newport, E. L., and Bavelier, D. (2004). Short-term memory span: Insights from sign language. *Nature Neuroscience* 7(9), 997–1002.

Brandt, J. (1991). The Hopkins Verbal Learning test: Development of a new memory test with six equivalent forms. *The Clinical Neuropsychologist* 5(2), 125–142.

Casas, R. N. (2010). Interpreter-mediated neuropsychological testing of monolingual Spanish speakers: Does it have an effect on test scores? PhD dissertation, University of Iowa, Iowa.

Conrad, R. (1979). *The deaf school child*. London: Harper & Row.

Cormier, K., Schembri, A., Vinson, D., and Orfanidou, E. (2012). First language acquisition differs from second language acquisition in prelingually deaf signers: Evidence from sensitivity to grammaticality judgement in British Sign Language. *Cognition* 124 (1), 50–65.

Cormier, K., Adam, R., Rowley, K., Woll, B., and Atkinson, J. (2012) The British Sign Language sentence reproduction test: Exploring age-of-acquisition effects in British deaf adults. Paper presented at the sign language workshop "Experimental studies in sign language research," at the annual meeting of the German Linguistics Society.

Dean, P. M., Feldman, D. M., Morere, D., and Morton, D. (2009). Clinical evaluation of the mini-mental state exam with culturally deaf senior citizens. *Archives of Clinical Neuropsychology* 24(8), 753–760.

Denmark, T., Atkinson, J., Marshall, J., and Woll, B. (2014). A new test of verbal learning and memory in British Sign Language. Manuscript submitted for publication.

Fellinger, J., Holzinger, D., and Pollard, R. (2012). Mental health of deaf people. *Lancet*, 379, 1037–1044.

Fenson, L., Dale, P. S., Reznick, J. S., Thal, D., Bates, E., Hartung, J. P., Pethick, S., and Reilly, J. S. (1993). The MacArthur Communicative Development Inventories: User's Guide and Technical Manual. Baltimore, MD: Paul H. Brokes Publishing.

Folstein, M. F., Folstein, S. E., and McHugh, P. R. (1975). "Mini-mental state": A practical method for grading the cognitive state of patients for the clinician. *Journal of Psychiatric Research* 12(3), 189–198.

Gathercole, S., and Baddeley, A. (1996). *Children's test of non-word repetition*. London: The psychological corporation.

Hambleton, R. K. (2005). Issues, designs, and technical guidelines for adapting tests into multiple languages and cultures. In R. K. Hambleton, P. F. Merenda and C. D. Spielberger (Eds), *Adapting educational and psychological tests for cross-cultural assessment*. Mahwah, NJ: Lawrence Erlbaum, pp. 3–38.

Hammill, D. D., Brown, V. L., Larsen, S. C., and Wiederholt, J. L. (1994). *Test of adolescent and adult language* (3rd ed.). Austin, TX: PRO-ED, Inc.

Hasson, N., and Joffe, V. (2007). The case for dynamic assessment in speech and language therapy. *Child Language Teaching and Therapy* 23(1), 9–25.

Haug, T. (2011). *Adaptation and evaluation of a German Sign Language test: A computer-based receptive skills test for deaf children ages 4–8 years old*. Hamburg: Hamburg University Press

Hauser, P. C., Paludnevičienė, R., Supalla, T., and Bavelier, D. (2008). American Sign Language–Sentence Reproduction test. In R. M. De Quadros (Ed.), *Sign languages: Spinning and unraveling the past, present and future*. Petrópolis, Brazil: Editora Arara Azul, pp. 160–172.

Herman, R., and Roy, P. (2006). Evidence from the wider use of the BSL Receptive Skills test. *Deafness and Education International* 8(1), 33–47.

Herman, R., Holmes, S., and Woll, B. (1999). Assessing British Sign Language development: Receptive Skills test. Gloucester: Forest Bookshop.

Herman, R., Grove, N., Holmes, S., Morgan, G., Sutherland, H., and Woll, B. (2004). Assessing BSL development: Production test (Narrative Skills). London: City University Publication.

Lala, F. J. J. (1998). Is there room in the DSM for consideration of Deaf people? *American Annals of the Deaf* 143(4), 314–317.

Lane, H. (2005). Ethnicity, ethics, and the deaf world. *Journal of Deaf Studies and Deaf Education* 10(3), 291–310.

Mann, W., and Marshall, C. (2012). Investigating deaf children's vocabulary knowledge in British Sign Language. *Language Learning* 62, 1024–1051.

Mann, W., Roy, P., and Marshall, C. (2013). A look at the other 90 per cent: Investigating British Sign Language vocabulary knowledge in deaf children from different language learning backgrounds. *Deafness & Education International* 15(2), 91–116.

Mann, W., Marshall, C., Mason, K., and Morgan, G. (2010). The acquisition of sign language: The impact of phonetic complexity on phonology. *Language Learning and Development* 6, 60–86.

Marshall, C., Mann, W., and Morgan, G. (2011). Short term memory in signed languages: Not just a disadvantage for serial recall. *Frontiers in Psychology* 2(102). doi: 10.3389/fpsyg.2011.00102

Marshall, C., Rowley, K., and Atkinson, J. (2013). Modality-dependent and independent factors in the organisation of the signed language lexicon: Insights from semantic and phonological fluency tasks in BSL. *Journal of Psycholinguistic Research*. Accessed September 17, 2014. http://link.springer.com/article/10.1007%2Fs10936-013-9271-5

Marshall, C., Rowley, K., Mason, K., Herman, R., and Morgan, G. (2013). Lexical organization in deaf children who use British Sign Language: Evidence from a semantic fluency task. *Journal of Child Language* 40, 193–220.

deMatteo, A. J., Pollard, R. Q., and Lentz, E. M. (1987). Assessment of linguistic functions in brain impaired and brain intact prelingually deaf users of American Sign Language: A preliminary report. Paper presented at the biennial meeting of the American Deafness and Rehabilitation Association, Minneapolis, Minnesota.

Mayer, C. (2007). What really matters in the early literacy development of deaf children. *Journal of Deaf Studies and Deaf Education* 12(4), 411–431.

Mioshi, E., Dawson, K., Mitchell, J., Arnold, R., and Hodges, J. R. (2006). The Addenbrooke's Cognitive Examination revised (ACE-R): A brief cognitive test battery for dementia screening. *International Journal of Geriatric Psychiatry* 21, 1078–1085.

Mitchell, R. E., and Karchmer, M. A. (2004). Chasing the mythical ten percent: Parental hearing status of deaf and hard of hearing students in the United States. *Sign Language Studies* 4(2), 138–161.

Morgan, G., and Woll, B. (2002). Directions in sign language acquisition. Amsterdam: John Benjamins.

Peña, E., Gillam, R.B., Malek, M., Ruiz-Felter, R., Resediz, M., Fiestas, C., Sabel T. (2006). Dynamic assessment of school-age children's narrative ability: An investigation of reliability and validity. *Journal of Speech, Language, and Hearing Research* 49, 1037–1057.

Peña, E., Iglesias, A., Lidz, C. (2001). Reducing test bias through dynamic assessment of children's word learning ability. *American Journal of Speech–Language Pathology* 10, 138–154.

Pollard, R. Q., Rediess, S., and DeMatteo, A. (2005). Development and validation of the Signed Paired Associates test. *Rehabilitation Psychology* 50(3), 258–265.

Powers, S., Gregory, S., and Thoutenhoofd, E. D. (1999). The educational achievements of deaf children: A literature review executive summary. *Deafness and Education International* 1(1), 1–9.

Rediess, S., Pollard, R. Q., and Veyberman, B. (1997). Assessment of verbal (ASL-based) memory in deaf adults: Clinical utility of the Signed Paired Associates test. Paper presented at the annual meeting of the International Neuropsychological Society, Orlando, Forida.

Reynolds, C. R., and Suzuki, L. A. (2013). Bias in psychological assessment: An empirical review and recommendations. In J. R. Graham, J. A. Naglieri, and I. B. Weiner (Eds.), *Handbook of psychology: Assessment psychology* (vol. 10, (2nd ed.). Hoboken, NJ: John Wiley & Sons, 67–94.

Vinson, D. P., Cormier, K., Denmark, T., Schembri, A., and Vigliocco, G. (2008). The British Sign Language (BSL) norms for age of acquisition, familiarity and iconicity. *Behavior Research Methods* 40(4), 1079–1087.

Wechsler, D. (1987). *Wechsler Memory Scale, revised* (WMS-R). San Antonio, TX: Psychological Corporation.

Wilson, M., Bettger, J. G., Niculae, I., and Klima, E. S. (1997). Modality of language shapes working memory: Evidence from digit span and spatial span in ASL signers. *Journal of Deaf Studies and Deaf Education* 2(3), 150–160.

Wisniewski, A., DeMatteo, A., Lee, M., and Orr, F. (1989). Neuropsychological assessment. In L. G. Stewart (Ed.), *Clinical rehabilitation assessment and hearing impairment: A guide to quality assurance*. Silver Spring, MD: National Association of the Deaf, pp. 49–69.

Wood, N., and Dockrell, J. (2010). Psychological assessment procedures for assessing deaf or hard of hearing children. *Educational & Child Psychology* 27(2), 11–22.

Woolfe, T., Herman, R., Roy, P., and Woll, B. (2010). Early vocabulary development in deaf native signers: A British Sign Language adaptation of the communicative development inventories. *Journal of Child Psychology and Psychiatry* 51(3), 322–331.

Index

Note: Page numbers in *italics* refer to Figures; those in **bold** to Tables.

Research Methods in Sign Language Studies: A Practical Guide, First Edition.
Edited by Eleni Orfanidou, Bencie Woll, and Gary Morgan.
© 2015 John Wiley & Sons, Inc. Published 2015 by John Wiley & Sons, Inc.

Index of Sign Languages

Note: Page numbers in *italics* refer to Figures; those in **bold** to Tables.

Research Methods in Sign Language Studies: A Practical Guide, First Edition.
Edited by Eleni Orfanidou, Bencie Woll, and Gary Morgan.
© 2015 John Wiley & Sons, Inc. Published 2015 by John Wiley & Sons, Inc.